Music in Childhood

Music in Childhood

 From Preschool through the Elementary Grades

PATRICIA SHEHAN CAMPBELL
CAROL SCOTT-KASSNER

*Technology for Music Instruction (Chapter 12)
by Kirk Kassner*

Photographs by Jerry Gay

SCHIRMER BOOKS
Simon & Schuster Macmillan
NEW YORK

Prentice Hall International
LONDON   MEXICO CITY   NEW DELHI   SINGAPORE   SYDNEY   TORONTO

Schirmer Books
Simon & Schuster Macmillan
866 Third Avenue
New York, NY 10022

Library of Congress Catalog Card Number: 94–30663

Printed in the United States of America

printing number
  2 3 4 5 6 7 8 9 10

Library of Congress Cataloging-in-Publication Data

Campbell, Patricia Shehan.
    Music in childhood : from preschool through the elementary grades
 / Patricia Shehan Campbell, Carol Scott-Kassner : photographs by
Jerry Gay.
      p. cm.
    Includes bibliographical references and index.
    ISBN 0–02–870552–1
    1. Music—Instruction and study—Juvenile. 2. School music-
-Instruction and study. I. Scott-Kassner, Carol. II. Title.
MT1.C226   1994
372.87′044—dc20   94–30663
                                                          CIP
                                                          MN

The paper used in this publication meets the minimum requirements of American National Standard for Information Services—Permanence of Paper for Printed Library Materials. ANSI Z39.48–1984.⊗™

To our families,
especially Andrew and Courtnay,
who have expanded our joy and understanding
of music making with children

Contents

4 Rhythm and the Child   73

5 Pitch and the Child   106

6 The Singing Child   126

7 The Listening Child   158

13 Music, Multiculturalism, and Children 310

14 Music for Exceptional Children 331

15 Music in an Integrated Curriculum 356

Photographs

Preface

Of all the beautiful things in this world, there are few that surpass the images of music in childhood. Our own earliest memories are rich with music: soft lullabies on a parent's lap; patty-cake rhymes in the nursery; parade music played by brass bands that marched in time; seasonal songs at the dinner table, at the piano, or around the campfire; chants for jumping rope and clapping hands; and the music played with friends on homemade instruments. Music played a prominent role in our childhoods then, as it still does for children today.

Music emerges magically from children, as they search for and find ways to represent their world. Intuitively and naturally, young children respond to music as they communicate through it. Music is part of their process of enculturation. They develop as members of their family, their neighborhood community, and religious and ethnic groups through music. Parents are the first music teachers, transmitting to children the songs they remember, and filling their ears with the music they love. Children learn a musical system—its tuning, timbres, predominant pitch and rhythmic patterns, textures, and formal structures—as surely as they learn other aspects of their family and then their community cultures. They are socialized into these groups through music and are deeply rooted in this first musical system early in childhood.

As children begin their formal schooling, in preschool or in kindergarten, they are ready to begin their formal musical education as well. With their intuitive learning in tow, children can develop musical literacy and the conceptual understanding of music as one among many disciplines featured within a school curriculum. The musical competence to sing in tune and step in time, to listen perceptively, to perform from notation, and to create a personal music that is as musically logical as it is expressive are all skills taught in a music curriculum. Unlike intuitive musical responses, however, these competences do not appear magically: they are the outcomes of a musical education, with an expert musician–teacher as guide. If children are to become competent and even masterful musicians, a formal musical education is necessary.

Music teachers continue the musical development that began with children's early enculturation. They are the principal players in the spiraling development of children's listening, performance, literacy, and creative-expressive skills. Music teachers are the catalysts that stimulate children's musical intelligence, and the guides to the pathways through which children can channel their ideas. Music teachers tap the beauty that is within children, awaiting a way out.

The benefits of a musical education are many. Musically trained children are able to add layer upon layer of musical knowledge to their earliest experiences. This early training can inspire children to continue musical activities into their adult years: singing a Bach chorale after supper; reading recorder music with friends on a Sunday afternoon; becoming wholly engaged while listening to the sounds of a Beethoven sonata or a jazz session; folk dancing in time and in a musical way to the tunes of a string band; creating spontaneous harmonies vocally, or on an instrument; and writing music for personal expression or to share with others. These are the sophisticated behaviors of musically educated people who were brought beyond the playful musical experiences of their childhoods by teachers who taught them repertoire and notational literacy, and developed in them the skills for performing, responding to, and creating music. When people mature musically, and maintain musical interactions that remain meaningful to them in their adult lives, the benefits of a musical education are apparent. The beauty of music in childhood becomes more than mere memory: it is the seed that takes root and is nourished through training.

A commitment to raising more musical children requires information. We trust that the information we have provided within these pages can be translated from words to actions both by teachers who are musicians and by musicians who are teachers. With an accumulated forty-five years of teaching music to children, teachers, and teachers-to-be between us, we offer ideas garnered from our experiences that have been evaluated, revised, and tested again, in many settings, with many students. The commitment we have to a substantive and meaningful musical education for all children is both the impetus and the desired outcome of the volume.

The following chapters delineate music and instructional approaches suited to the perceptual–cognitive, physical, and affective development of children in early and middle childhood. The various ways in which children manifest their musicality form the basis of a number of chapters: Rhythm and the Child; Pitch and the Child; The Singing Child; The Listening Child; The Moving Child; The Playing Child; and The Creating Child. Natural and incipient musical behaviors associated with child development are noted, and become the backdrop to recommendations for teacher-directed musical experiences and educational sequences.

We have attempted to present music as a developmental process in the intellectual and affective lives of children, one that is accelerated, enriched, and deepened through the guidance of the expert musician–teacher. We offer a sampling of musical experiences that can be presented by teachers to children in graduated fashion and in increasingly complex matrices that continue to challenge preschool and school-age children, through the sixth grade. We will discuss how to: (1) structure a classroom for maximum learning; (2) preserve children's natural motivation for experiencing and knowing music; (3) plan lessons and long-term goals; and (4) measure, grade, and report musical competences of children to them, their parents, and administrators. We present models, samples, and graphs to illustrate techniques and systematic methods for teaching musical concepts, and for developing musical skills in children. Questions, Activities, and References are found at the conclusion of each chapter, for purposes of reviewing, extending, and putting into practice the information given.

In addition to practical information, we provide the conceptual frameworks that initiate and stimulate thinking on issues of music, teaching, and children. We have not intended this as a collection of recipe-like lessons, although examples of partial and complete lessons can be found scattered throughout the book. Instead, we present a broad array of concept-associated musical experiences in each chapter as the best way for teachers to develop lessons for children. We believe that the most successful lessons spring from the selection of a concept, embedded in a song or musical piece, which is then reinforced and expanded on through a variety of instructional strategies. The full flowering of a lesson is best left to the insightful teacher, who can match the musical concept, repertoire, and teaching and learning strategies to the classroom context with a thorough knowledge of what children need to know.

Chapter 3 addresses method: the classic techniques and systems of Dalcroze, Kodály, and Orff; the recently emerging pedagogies; and the personal methods that evolve through experience. We believe that teachers will combine techniques from various philosophies to develop a personal pedagogy that suits them, their students, and the instructional content.

Chapters on music technology, world music/multicultural music education, and the special learner address contemporary issues that greatly impact on the teaching and learning of music. We are grateful for the expert contributions of Dr. Kirk Kassner, author of Chapter 12, whose wealth of knowledge of technology spans the continuum from the highly theoretical issues relevant to instruction to the details of technological systems, and the most feasible and user-friendly classroom applications. Regarding world music and its place in a multicultural curriculum, we have attempted to thread its themes throughout the book, while concentrating on curricular trends and issues in Chapter 13. Likewise, while we believe that each child is individual and special in his or her approach to the musical experience, and have maintained this position as central to the volume, Chapter 14 presents perspectives relevant to children who are variously challenged in learning music and who require a teacher's sensitivity to meet special needs.

Along with the developmental approach and contemporary issues we have emphasized, we hope that the reader senses the joy, the musical stimulation, and the intellectual challenge that comes from teaching music to children. We have known these sensations often, and we are restored and invigorated by them. *Music in Childhood* provides a channel for teachers to develop musically and pedagogically in ways relevant to children's growth from musical intuition to musical mastery. The ultimate result of its reading—and application—may be a more musical world, through the bonding of children, music, and teachers.

P. S. C., C. S.-K.

Acknowledgments

We wish to thank Jerry Gay for his photographs as well as Jo Daly and the teachers at the B.F. Day School in Seattle and Ann Palmason and the teachers at the Bush School in Seattle—and their children, for helping us to fill our book with so many images of joyous music making. In addition, we thank Kirk Kassner for writing Chapter 12 on Music Technology. His contributions to our book, including his editing, have been invaluable. Thanks to Peter Webster for reviewing the chapter on Creativity, Annette Robinson for helping with the chapter on Exceptional Children, and to reviewers Shirley McRae, Jean Sinor, and Sandra Stauffer for their insightful comments along the way. Finally, but certainly not least, we thank the many mentors and colleagues who have stimulated our thinking and encouraged our growth as musicians and teachers. This book would not be possible without their inspiration and nurturance.

1

The Multiple Meanings of Music for Children

"I like music. I can't explain it: Sometimes it makes me happy, sometimes sad, but all the times it's there like a friend, and I need it."

—First-grade child

"I want my child to know what I never was privileged to learn, and that includes learning how to sing, dance, and draw artistically."

—Parent of second-grade child

"I've found enjoyable ways to achieve the curricular goals of literacy and numeracy through music, from chanting rhymes and singing songs to counting rhythms and moving in geometric patterns across the floor."

—Third-grade teacher

"I enjoyed the winter concert, and am especially impressed with how, as they sang and played, music seemed to bring a coalescence to a crowd of what I know to be some pretty ornery and unsettled kids."

—Parent of fourth-grade child

"You should see what's happened to kids' interests since we added music to our classes on American history and culture. Overnight success!"

—Fifth-grade teacher

"I think I might be making as important an impact in the musical world teaching kids to sing and play and read music, maybe as much as I might have as a world-class concert pianist. Who knows what musical minds I may tap?"

—Elementary school music teacher

"Schools are reconsidering earlier educational plans that underscored the basics: We now see that guiding children's holistic development, to include experiences in the expressive arts of language, music, and the visual arts, *is* basic to their more complete and evolving intellectual, emotional, and physical well-being."

—Elementary school principal

"I don't know everything about music yet, but I guess it just grabs me the right way."

—Sixth-grade child

Music is important to children. Some wish to listen to it, isolated and all alone through headphones, while others are inclined to sing it, or to hum, whistle, or chant it. Some want to play it on a musical instrument—solo, or with friends, while others enjoy dancing to it, and thus music gives rise to physical responses. Some wish to create "brand new music" and poems, plays, and dances to go with it. Whether listening, singing, playing, moving, or creating it, musical experiences are prominent in the lives of children: they themselves, as well as their spokespersons—parents and teachers—attest to this fact.

Music's Many Functions

Music is one of life's essential ingredients. For children, it is often the substance of their playful exploration of and experimentation in the world around them, the core of their socialization and expressive communication with one another, and the refuge where they find peace, joy, and fulfillment away from the worries of their young lives. For the adults they will become, music is an avenue for expressing what cannot be verbally expressed, a source of profound enjoyment, lighthearted amusement, a critical component of customs, traditions, and rituals, and the release valve for excess energy and emotions through physical response via movement and dance.

Music's powerful role offers compelling reasons for its inclusion in the schools. The numerous ways in which children engage in music underscore its appeal for them, as well as highlighting the many dimensions of their beings that can be met by the musical experiences they have. Given that music is embraced by people everywhere for its unique qualities, to deny it a solid place in curricular studies would be a terrible mistake. Music is too powerful to be excluded from children's lives, whether in school or out.

The uses of music by children (and adults) of all ages and cultures are evidence of its staying power; music has maintained its prominence among people over time and distance. Anthropologist Alan P. Merriam (1964) has outlined music's many functions, along with their relevance to children's own musical involvement:

1. *Emotional expression:* the releasing of emotions and the expression of feelings. Children may "release" sadness in a song they sing, or joy in their dancing.

2. *Aesthetic enjoyment:* the use of music for deep emotional and intellectual enjoyment, for experiencing artistic and nonverbal expressions of life's beauty. The music that children listen to or perform touches them in profound ways that are not easily expressed through the words they know.

3. *Entertainment:* the use of music as diversion and amusement. Children enjoy the musical diversions presented by the media, from the current pop genres to the background music for videos, films, and television shows; media music is effortless "easy listening" for them, and greatly entertaining.

4. *Communication:* the conveying of feelings and emotions that are understood by people within a particular culture. Children receive and can be led to the musical expression of ideas and feelings in styles that are meaningful to them within their family, community, and societal cultures.

5. *Symbolic representation:* the expression of symbols exists in the texts of songs and in the cultural meaning of the musical sounds. Overlapping the communication function, children find the sounds of certain musical modes and meters more meaningful than others, through their conditioning within the musical cultures of their families, communities, and society at large.

6. *Physical response:* the use of music for dancing and other physical activity. Children are greatly affected in physical ways by the music they hear or perform, and may be drawn to dance, to hop, to skip, or to sway to the sounds; they may also be soothed to sleep by the qualities of sedative music.

7. *Enforcement of conformity to social norms:* the use of music to provide instructions or warnings. Children, especially young children, are often taught the rules of social etiquette by adults (say "please" and "thank you," wash your hands before meals) through chanted rhymes and songs.

8. *Validation of social institutions and religious rituals:* the use of music in religious services and state occasions. Children frequently build

music into the rituals of their play, including chants and songs to accompany games or to select team members ("eeny meeny miney mo"). They also validate their civic and religious affiliations through the patriotic, sacred, and/or seasonal songs they sing.

9. *Contribution to the continuity and stability of culture:* music as an expression of cultural values. Few other cultural elements are such complete vehicles for the transmission of history, literature, and social mores as is music, offering children an understanding of the long life and stability of their culture.

10. *Contribution to the integration of society:* the use of music to bring people together. Children are socialized through music, and recognize their membership within a group through music that is shared among its members; singing games increase their integration within a group, just as a school song offers children a common bond with other children.

Music is a human phenomenon, with its uses by children as widespread as they are for adults. Music is much more than an addendum in the lives of children: It is part and parcel of their development as individuals and as members of social groups of family, neighbors, and friends. While it exists "for its own sake" (as in the aesthetic principle of "art for art's sake"), music also functions as a vehicle for teaching children ways of living their lives according to the fundamental values of a culture. Countless communities of people hold music in high esteem for its functional life-guiding and life-giving properties. If music is thus understood to be at the core of human thought and behavior in so many communities, then it logically follows that it must be placed at the core of learning provided for children in the schools. Musical training can supply components critical to children's holistic development, including their intellectual, emotional, physical, and spiritual selves.

Music at the Curricular Core

Because children are drawn quite naturally to singing, moving, and other playful musical experiences, it is difficult for some educators to view music as a discipline as worthy of study as other academic subjects in the humanities, the sciences, and the social sciences. Is music truly basic to a rock-solid education, or more a marginal nicety, a pleasurable pastime for the privileged classes, a channel for the talented few, to be sampled through passive watching and listening by the "undertalented" multitudes?

In recent years, considerable attention has been given to identifying subjects as part of an "elite core" of "basic knowledge" to be mastered by all children. Music and the arts have been marginalized by many in American schools and society, and viewed as less central for development than linguistic and mathematical knowledge and skills. As defined by Ernest L. Boyer (1983), however, the "basics" would seem to encompass a musical education: "Broadly defined, [a basic curriculum] is a study of those consequential ideas, experiences, and traditions common to all of us by virtue of our membership in the human family at a particular moment in history" (p. 95). Music is basic because it is a critical component of American and international societies, and a repository of historical traditions and contemporary ideas.

Music deserves a rightful place at the core of a preschool through elementary school curriculum. All children have equal rights to: knowledge of their cultural heritage, including music; the development of their aural, artistic-expressive, and musical sensibilities; and to familiarity with music beyond the commercially available and currently popular. The National Standards for Arts Education (1994) stipulates that children should know and be able through training to communicate through the arts, develop and present basic analyses of works of art, and have an informed acquaintance with exemplary works of art from a variety of cultures and historical periods. In considering what a curriculum should contain, Elliot Eisner (1982) warned that denying children access to music as an avenue of expression is equivalent to depriving them of "the meanings that the making of music makes possible" (p. 55). Schools that seek to enrich children's lives through knowledge and skill development cannot afford to relegate music to the curricular periphery, but should instead place music alongside language arts, mathematics, and other basic subjects.

Music is its own discipline, while it also informs children of their world in interdisciplinary ways. It is critical that teachers understand the many dimensions of the musical experience for children, and the significance of instruction to accomplish goals that run broad and deep, from the culturally general to the musically specific. The making of music is a discipline, in the training and rehearsal vital to the development of singing and instrumental performance skills, as well as the growth of critical and creative musical thinking skills. Children are stimulated intellectually, physically, and even spiritually in their recognition of music for its own sake as well as its integration with their knowledge of the humanities, the sciences, and the social studies.

Children's Musical Capacities

What does it mean to be musical? Some might say that a child who plays an instrumental piece accurately and with attention to the nuances of dynamics and tempo is more musical than one who moves easily to the rhythm of a

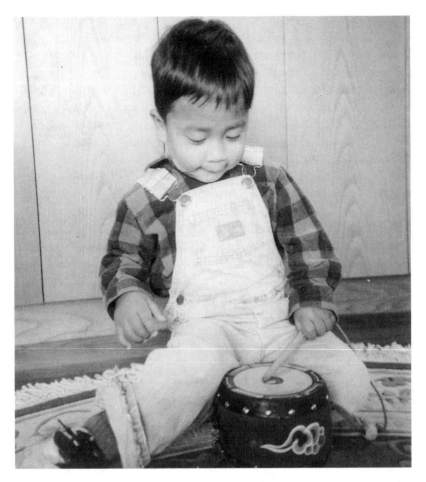

Young child playing drum. *Photo by Patricia Shehan Campbell.*

musical beat. Or that the child with the sweet and melodious voice is more musically talented than the one who can quickly identify timbres, textures, or modes and meters in the music he or she hears. Or that the child who can create music is the most musical of all. Is there a hierarchy of qualities that make some children musical, or more musical than others? Should musical training be reserved for musically talented children who will reap the greatest benefits?

All children are musical. Anthropologist John Blacking (1977) observed the musical nature of children of the Venda people of South Africa, and then developed his position on the musical capacities of all children. Cognitive psychologist Howard Gardner (1983) suggested in his theory of multiple intelligences that, while children may demonstrate greater strength in one rather than all seven intelligences, all children possess musical abilities that can be nurtured through instruction.

In various forms and degrees, children possess the capacity to become more musical than they may currently demonstrate. Children quite naturally listen, sing, dance, play, and express themselves musically, with little or no previous training. When learning experiences are tailored to develop their musical abilities, then the complete musicians inside them begin to emerge. Certainly, because there are differences in children's individual interests and aptitudes, there is some variance among children regarding the extent to which a particular musical intelligence, or specific musical talent, can be developed. Some may prefer to sing rather than to play, and some may be driven toward creating original musical expressions.

Children are capable of careful and attentive listening, so they are able to perceive and understand the musical language they will create or recreate. Some children will need greater help in focusing their listening and may require the removal of aural and visual distractors so that they might tune in to the components of a song or musical work. Through directed listening, children will learn a vocabulary of recurring melodic and rhythmic phrases that represent a given musical style or culture, and that may reappear in music they perform or in their original improvisations and compositions. Because most children possess the physical capability to hear sounds, they can then be led to listening intelligently to the manner in which these sounds are organized as music.

Nearly all children possess the ability to sing accurately in tune, although vocal qualities may vary slightly from lighter to darker, whispery-soft to fuller in tone, and with minor differences in range. Good singers develop through frequent listening and then by replicating the sound of the singing model. Even the more powerful and resonant young singers are likely to have developed their abilities through practice, singing regularly because they enjoy it. Adults who sing regularly, in tune, for and with children, make ideal models for emulation. The capacity to sing "sweetly" in tune is well within the reach of children, awaiting discovery and development.

Children can respond to music through movement in controlled and expressive ways. The following of the musical pulse is just one of the initial milestones in movement development; this skill is directly related to attentive listening. Movement can demonstrate the extent to which children are focused on rhythmic durations and patterns, the rising and falling contours of melodies, or the different phrases in a musical composition. While children may need to be taught gestures, steps, and sequences, nothing can replace their careful listening so that the movement—or the dance—will be musically rendered.

Musical performance on an instrument is viewed by some as a more sophisticated musical activity than other modes of musical skills, and thus may be deemed to suit only those who show great musical "talent." However, all children who are good listeners, and who have the interest and discipline to take the daily time for building both the physical and the musical skills, will make good players. Children may begin with musical toys in their earliest years, progress to nonpitched percussion instruments, and then to xylophones, recorders, and keyboards. Strings, wind, and brass instruments of the orchestral and band variety are likely to be introduced to children in the intermediate grades. Given strong musical experiences in their early years, all children are thus capable of further musical growth through instrumental study.

Children are refreshingly creative when given the chance. With guidance, they can project both logic and expressiveness in their musical inventions, improvisations, and compositions. Their musical expressions are influenced by the music they know, and the choices they make as musical creators are greatly expanded through their listening experiences. Given opportunities to create, some children may require frameworks: pitch, rhythm, and even the length of the work are some of the "game rules" they may need to guide their musical inventions. Children may also look to adults for inspiration, as well as to stories, poems, photographs, or illustrations. However, children primarily come to realize their musical creativity through an understanding of musical structure, and how the components of music have been manipulated by other composers or performers before them. This understanding is attained best through instruction.

Clearly, if all children are inherently musical, then musical training should not be reserved for the hypothetical "talented" few. The myth that few children are musically endowed is a dangerous one that threatens the right of all to a musical education, and may even endanger a musical culture.

Music's Historical Role in the Curriculum

Since the earliest conceptions of schools and schooling in the Western world, music has been considered a "basic" subject. The ancient Greek philosophers, and later the Romans, claimed music and the arts to be key to children's moral development. Through the centuries, Europeans regarded the study of music as part science, in its theoretical analysis, and part art, in its performance practice. Musical training was considered one of the high marks of refinement in the Middle Ages, from the twelfth through the fifteenth centuries. A musical education was central to those seeking to fulfill humanistic goals or striving to become "Renaissance men" (and women). Journal accounts document the significance of vocal and instrumental instruction for children not only of the nobility, but also of the rising middle class. By the time of the Enlightenment in the eighteenth century, the artistic–expressive needs of children were as likely to be addressed through schooling as their intellectual–logical needs were. Music instruction was more than "window-dressing" in European schools: It was viewed as "basic" to the education of all children.

Formalized musical training in the United States began with the establishment of singing schools in the late seventeenth and eighteenth centuries. People in towns and rural or frontier settlements were visited for a week or two at a time by singing masters who offered instruction in singing and note-reading. At the close of the day's labors, adults and their children would gather to be instructed on the use of tunebooks, which featured notational exercises and hymns. Communities were well-served by singing schools, and the congregational singing at church services greatly improved as a result.

Music was included in the curricular programs of private academies in colonial America, and music of the Baroque (ca. 1600–1750) and then of the Viennese Classical (ca. 1750–1820) periods was spread through the efforts of European-trained masters. While European arts and culture were a class privilege for the Southern gentry, New England progressively looked toward providing all children with cultural knowledge through education in "common schools" (Keene, 1982). Growing support for public education, along with the expansion of cultural societies dedicated to choral (and less frequently, instrumental) music, set the scene for the introduction of music into the curriculum of the elementary school by Lowell Mason in Boston in 1838.

The Boston schools, persuaded by Mason to test the inclusion of music in the curriculum, stipulated that children be given vocal training and music-reading lessons twice weekly. Soon, children presented public concerts that demonstrated their considerable musical progress, much to the delight (and surprise) of school officials, parents, and community members. Mason's method of instruction emphasized pragmatic learning-by-doing techniques, beginning with focused listening and rote repetition of vocal music that advanced children toward music literacy. Swiss educator Heinrich Pestalozzi (1746–1827) was undeniably influential in Mason's approach, particularly as evidenced by the application of the principles of "anschauung" (literally, "sense intuition"), or learning through the senses. The earliest methods used in public school music instruction thus were based on the logic of "sound before sight" and "practice before theory"; listening and singing experiences led to an understanding of notation and theory.

The emergence of music as a curricular subject in the elementary schools unfolded gradually through the nineteenth and twentieth centuries. Vocal music was praised for its contribution to children's "moral culture," and for its functional means of cultivating the speaking voice, of developing correct expression and diction, and of providing concentration at the start and close of the day. Music listening and note-reading developed in tandem, as children were directed by the music masters to attend to the intervals between pitches, to associate solfège syllables with the melodies they sang, and to sight-read songs and exercises.

Not until schools had access to recordings and radio, however, did a more global form of music listening begin to occur; music-appreciation classes for children were developed as early as the 1920s. The infusion of rhythmic movement and dance into children's music classes began to flourish in the opening decades of the twentieth century, when movement was recognized as offering an avenue for musical expression as well as for physical, social, and cultural growth. The eurhythmics of Émile Jaques-Dalcroze (1865–1950) first intrigued and then guided teachers toward the development of children's greater musical sensitivity through whole-body movement. John Dewey's (1859–1952) advocacy for music, movement, and the arts in a child-centered curriculum helped to stabilize music as a part of the curriculum, even through the troubled economic and political times of the Depression and World War II.

Music for children was sparked by numerous innovations in the second half of the twentieth century. From Hungary came the philosophy and practices of Zoltán Kodály (1882–1967) and his associates, with their emphasis on music literacy through rigorous ear-training and vocal exercises. The early experiments in music for children by German composer Carl Orff (1895–1982), first with dancer Dorothee Günther and then with colleague Gunild Keetman, evolved into practices that merge music with children's play and with dance and the dramatic arts. Over several decades, both Kodály's and Orff's approaches have been embraced by music educators and given American perspectives.

Various professional gatherings of teachers at conferences and in projects have further impacted on music instruction for children. In the 1960s, the Yale Seminar, the Manhattanville Music Curriculum Project, and the Tanglewood Symposium made recommendations for: (1) a broader and more representative music repertoire for listening and performance, including music of all Western historical periods, world cultures, popular, "avant-garde," and American styles; (2) greater opportunities for musical expression and creativity, through composition and improvisation experiences; and, (3) more extensive use of technology and the media to aid instruction. The challenges have continued through the end of the century, as teachers confront ways to balance experiences in European art music with the musical interests of an increasingly diverse population of children, and as they consider computers, laser discs, and interactive videos as user-friendly enhancements—rather than threats—to children's musical education.

Music takes its rightful place in the school curriculum today, resting on the long history of its acceptance in children's education. Through the ages, music instruction has provided children with skills for their musical expressions and knowledge of their cultural heritage(s). Despite societal changes, the need for a musical education continues. Children still learn to sing beautifully through instruction, and produce sounds that please them and their listeners. They become independent musicians as they learn to read musical notation, and as they become more analytical of musical sounds and structure. Through a musical education, children may learn the many facets of the uniquely aural art that allows them an opening through which to channel their many personal expressions.

Music for Children in a Changing Society

How quickly the world has changed and is changing still! Could our grandparents have envisioned a world of palm-sized videocameras, MTV, MIDI, and CDs? Could our parents have imagined the rise of rock music from its cult-like appeal to teenagers (only), to its pervasive presence on AM and FM stations, in films and on television, and even, occasionally, embedded in the music of "serious" composers? Could we ourselves have guessed when we were children that a "global village" would emerge, and that the world's peoples and their cultural expressions would arrive to the shores and doors of America's society and its schools? The changes are riveting, their pace rapid and relentless, and their impact on American musical culture profound.

Children at the brink of the twenty-first century face challenges very differ-

Children gathered in schoolyard, singing and clapping hands.

ent from those just a generation ago. They grow up within family units of various sorts, including single-parent families, working-parent families, and extended families of aunts, uncles, and cousins. They know about substance abuse and sexual abuse, some from first-hand experience. They are bombarded with media images offering examples of deviant behavior, and hear dialogue on television and radio that was once considered inappropriate for previous generations. They worry about the environment, about people living in poverty both at home and abroad, about wars, and about the spread of diseases that threaten lives with no certain remedies in sight. Today's world can overwhelm children with challenges.

Enter music into this world of changes and challenges. Music is, for children, a port in the storm, a resting spot, a retreat from the madding crowd and their hectic lives. It is their safety valve, an appropriate release of energy at those times when no other channel seems possible. As music is transformed by technology and by the blending of cultural traditions from near and far, children are offered a wide array of expressions from which to choose for listening and performing. Their out-of-school musical experiences are greatly enriched by in-school instruction, so that the meaning of multiple musical expressions is deepened for them.

A Musical Future

With an understanding of the functions and meanings of music, along with a sensitivity to children's musical capacities and modes of musical experiences, teachers can develop their own personal method for stimulating the musical development of their students. Children will be guaranteed a musical future when the design of a curriculum takes into account the comprehensive goals of a musical education, and the sequence for its attainment. Children have their first musical experiences in the home, under the tutelage of their mothers and fathers, but teachers are entrusted with the responsibility for building upon these experiences. The transmission of musical culture is in our hands.

Music transmission cannot be haphazard if it is to be especially meaningful. Throughout their schooling, children need musical nurturing by trained music specialists, so that the experiences they know are musical as well as thoughtfully presented. The music teacher possesses the knowledge and skills honed through many years of solo and ensemble performance experience, and the study of music history, theory, and cultures. The music teacher also brings a sense of sequence, and a delivery style that appeals to children, based on an understanding of child development and pedagogical methods. Through a long and specialized training, the music teacher can ensure that quality music instruction is provided.

The musical future of children rests on careful selection of music and instructional techniques to maximize the sometimes minimal curricular time explicitly assigned to music. It rests on the imaginative ways in which creative teachers infuse music into the school days, weaving music into lessons in the language arts, social studies, mathematics, and the sciences. It rests on the belief that the tremendous cultural diversity and technological advances will enhance, embellish, enlighten, and expand the musical experiences of children.

Most importantly, the musical future of children rests on the teacher's confidence that he or she is first and foremost a musician, one with a lifetime of music to share. Live music-making led by the teacher's own performance, along with opportunities for guided listening to performances and recordings of other professional musicians, makes music meaningful to children. While there are many effective instructional techniques, there is probably no certain method for teaching music to children, anymore than there is just one way to climb a mountain or to fall in love. The comprehensive and most effective method through which children become musically educated is to be found within the teacher's own training and interests. The possession of musical knowledge and skills, coupled with a love and understanding of children, will pave the way for a combination of techniques from various philosophical approaches into a personal pedagogy that suits the teacher, the children, and the music.

Questions

1. List the ten functions and uses of music. Are some more prominent in your life, and in the lives of children, than others?

2. How do children demonstrate their musical capacities?

3. How has music been placed historically within the curriculum?

4. What recommendations for changes in the music curriculum emerged from various events of the 1960s? Have those recommendations been heeded?

Activities

1. Conduct a series of interviews to determine the meaning of music to people, both currently and from their memories. Ask open-ended questions not only of children, but of friends, family members, colleagues, and teachers. Analyze the responses according to the Merriam chart of musi-

cal uses and functions. Compare the current musical involvement of adults with their childhood memories of musical experiences.

2. Prepare a three-minute speech to be given to the board of education to support the benefits of music instruction for children. Present it to the class, and be prepared to respond to questions regarding your position.

3. Stage a scenario: a music teacher's consultation with a concerned parent who wonders whether her child is "musical" or "musically talented."

4. How can in-school instruction in music expand on the musical interests and experiences that children have "on the outside"? Suggest three "outside" musical experiences that merit deeper exploration through the guidance of the music teacher.

References

BLACKING, J. (1977). *How musical is man?* Seattle: University of Washington.

BOYER, E. L. (1983). *High school: A report on secondary education in America.* New York: Harper & Row.

EISNER, E. W. (1982). *Cognition and curriculum: A basis for deciding what to teach.* New York: Longman.

GARDNER, H. (1983). *Frames of mind: A theory of multiple intelligences.* New York: Basic Books.

KEENE, J. A. (1982). *A history of music education in the United States.* Hanover, NH: University of New Hampshire.

MERRIAM, A. P. (1964). *The anthropology of music.* Evanston, IL: Northwestern University.

Music Educators National Conference (MENC). (1994). *National standards for arts education.* Reston, VA: MENC.

2

From Theory to Practice in Teaching Music to Children

There are theories of learning, teaching, and instruction embedded in nearly every musical experience. Jeremy and Bryan playfully explore the music-making possibilities of spoons, cups, pots, and pans; Bruner (1966) and Vygotsky (1978) have developed theories to explain this behavior. Annmarie works best alone at a listening station, while Rosa grows musically when in a socially interactive group; theories on field dependence and independence explain some of the differences. Inga follows the teacher's modeling of a musical phrase, and then imitates it a bit better with each successive trial; both Skinner (1953) and Bandura (1977) offer theoretical explanations. Rob acquires and retains music aurally, Tony through symbols, graphs, and notes on staffs, and Charissa through associated movements and gestures; these learning modalities are theorized, analyzed, and classified in the literature on learning styles. When Donny doesn't attend to a listening lesson, Ausubel (1968) suggests "advance organizers" (or building a foundation of familiar ideas for the new learning situation), Gagné (1977) recommends ways of gaining attention, and Skinner offers behavioral techniques for bringing him to task.

Theories about how children learn and how teachers can help maximize this learning are at the heart of every practical musical experience that teachers provide for children. Rather than being dull, dry, and remotely related to the real-life challenges of teaching music to children, theories can illuminate for the teacher how children gain musical knowledge, skills, and values. Theories of instruction are based on effective techniques used by teachers, and

15

from scientific observation of and experimentation in how children learn. By understanding theory as the fruit of multiple lifetimes spent explaining how children acquire, retain, and then rework musical knowledge into their personal expressions, teachers can become more efficient at guiding this musical development. Theory is wedded to practice, in that it emanates from practical teaching and learning experiences as it also informs these practices.

Teachers need theory as a thoughtful guide to what they do. Music instruction without theories is like a car without a driver, a bird with no wings, or a computer with no program. It is helter-skelter and scattered, without offering an explanation of how children learn the music that teachers present. Teachers who think about what they do, and are informed by theory, are deeply committed to leading children to their maximal musical development.

A theory of music instruction can describe factors related to the teacher, the children, their family, social, and cultural influences, and of course, the classroom environment. A theory of music instruction is comprised of three components: (1) instruction, a set of events provided by the teacher; (2) learning processes of the child/learner, including attention, perception, memory, rehearsal, and recognition and recall; and, (3) learning outcomes in the forms of a child's demonstration of verbal information, intellectual skills, motor skills, cognitive strategies, and attitudes. Thus, theory directs the teacher in providing sequential experiences for understanding a rhythmic pattern or for gaining techniques necessary for playing the xylophone. It describes the child's need for initial attention to the learning task and the progression through which the child learns and remembers it, and it suggests the means by which the child demonstrates such learning. Theory links the teacher to the child/learner, as it relates teaching events to learning processes and demonstrated learning outcomes.

Teachers—and parents—concerned with enhancing the musical development of children will be well served through a brief introduction to theories of instruction and learning. Selected research and recommendations by theorists in psychology, sociology, anthropology, and education are noted, followed by ways in which they can inform the practice of music instruction. Table 2.1 sketches selected theories that are relevant to teaching music to children.

Stage and Phase Theories

A number of theories refer to stages, phases, or levels through which children or adult learners proceed in gaining knowledge. Some of these multileveled theories stem from developmental psychology and are called "stage dependent," referring to the intellectual stages that children pass through as they mature. Others are not governed by maturation, but nonetheless feature earlier

Table 2.1   Summary of Selected Theories Informing Music Instruction

Theorist	Theory	Principal Features
Jean Piaget	Stage-Dependent Theory	Children progress through four stages of intellectual development: sensorimotor; preoperational; concrete operations; and formal operations
Jerome Bruner	Modes of Representation	Learners progress through three ways of representing meaning or understanding, related to, but not dependent on, maturation: enactive; iconic; and symbolic
Lauren Sosniak	Developmental Stages of the Pianist/Performer	Student musicians progress through three phases: tinkering; technical; and masterful music making
Gregory Bateson; Catherine Ellis	Learning I, II, III	Learners progress through three phases: enculturation; acquisition of skills/competence; and personal and aesthetic expression
G. Stanley Hall	Musical Play	Children train for adulthood through games; musical play leads to musical understanding
Lev Vygotsky	Socialization	Children are socialized through adult intervention and guidance; socialization leads to acquisition of cultural knowledge
B. F. Skinner; Robert Thorndike	Reinforcement	Learning can be shaped through the process of positive or negative reinforcement; appropriate behaviors are shaped through successive approximation techniques
Albert Bandura	Social Learning	Children observe and emulate their adult models
Richard Restak	Cerebral Dominance	Learners are dominated by left- (linear) or right- (holistic) hemispheric processing
Howard Gardner	Multiple Intelligences	Learners possess one or more types of intelligence, or ways of being intelligent

(continued)

Table 2.1 Continued

Theorist	Theory	Principal Features
Walter Barbe; Raymond Swassing	Learning Modalities	Learners process information through a preferred sensory channel: visual; auditory; kinesthetic
Rita and Kenneth Dunn	Learning Style Model	A variety of factors influence learning: environmental; emotional; social; and physical
Harold Witkin	Field Dependence/ Field Independence	Learners may be content-bound, experiencing concepts as embedded within their environment; or content-independent, experiencing concepts as discrete entities removed from their background
Isabel Meyers; Peter B. Briggs	Meyers–Briggs Type Indicator	Learners may demonstrate one or several of sixteen Briggs personality types that influence the way they approach the learning task: extroversion/introversion; sensing/intuitive; thinking/feeling; judging/perceiving
David Ausubel	Meaningful Reception	Students acquire information most effectively when teachers package lessons well and prepare students through "advance organizers"
Jerome Bruner	Discovery Learning; Spiral Curriculum	Students learn through exploration and problem solving; subject matter can be taught to children through age-appropriate experiences, and can be embellished through repeated exposure
Robert Gagné	Events of Instruction	Learners progress through eight instructional events, from awareness and attention through concept formation and transfer
Edwin Gordon	Music Learning Theory	Students progress through an eight-stage process that begins with aural/oral experiences with music, and ends with theoretical understanding; audiation is the goal

stages of learning that provide the foundation for later, more complex learning. Whatever the emphasis, multileveled theories establish that children do not learn "all at once" but bit-by-bit and in increasingly complex ways over time.

The stage-dependent theory of Swiss biologist Jean Piaget (1952) provides one model of cognitive development that combines the child's biological growth with an increasingly mature intellectual grasp of concepts. Through longitudinal observations of children from birth through late adolescence, Piaget evolved a theory that has greatly influenced views on child development. He observed that children progress through four stages of thinking: sensorimotor (ages 0–2), learning through direct sensory experience; preoperational (ages 2–7), learning through the manipulation of objects, noting the consequences, and internalizing them for the future, thus transforming stimuli to symbols; concrete operations (ages 7–11), viewing objects in concrete, tangible, and systematic ways but not abstractly; and formal operations (ages 11 through adulthood), learning abstractly using logic and deductive reasoning.

The stages suggest that younger children in particular be given many opportunities to listen, sing, play, and move to music. The introduction of staff notation should occur only after preliminary experiences; Piagetian theory implies that music instruction follow a sound-before-symbol approach. Other notable applications of Piaget's principles to music learning indicate that age eight is a "watershed" year in a child's cognitive development. At this time, children are quite capable of identifying timbres, discriminating among random melodies, and perceiving structure in simple melodies, although they are less successful in perceiving the sound of more than one simultaneous musical line (or harmony). As they progress into the stage of concrete operations, children also begin to conserve, or to realize the invariance of one musical element when another is altered. In other words, they begin to recognize a melody when it has been sung in a minor rather than a major modality, or in triple rather than duple time. By the time they complete fifth grade, many children are capable of thinking in the abstract about music, and are able to manipulate musical structures through improvisation and composition experiences.

In his modes of representation, Jerome Bruner (1966) suggests a type of stage progression that is somewhat dependent upon maturation, but can be applied to all ages and intellectual stages. He proposed three teaching and learning strategies: enactive, learning through a set of actions; iconic, learning through images and graphs; and symbolic, learning by going beyond what is immediately perceptible in the environment. For example, learning to read notation can be broken into three stages corresponding to Bruner's model. Instruction may begin with arm and body movement to represent melodic

Children's concentrated performance on instruments.

contours (enactive), followed by line graphs that trace these contours (iconic), and ending with the reading and writing of notation itself on the staff (symbolic). These modes of representation are useful in providing increasingly sophisticated instructional sequences for any concept.

In a longitudinal study of concert pianists, Lauren Sosniak (1985) developed a theory also involving three phases of learning. During the initial phase, the young musician "tinkers" at the piano in playful exploration, and is encouraged and supported by her or his parents to do so. The teacher is positive, gentle, and thus motivating for the learner. The second phase emphasizes a more systematic and technical approach to instruction. The development of playing technique brings a need for greater repetition, and more careful listening to and emulating of the model, the teacher. The playfulness of the first phase is replaced by a more concentrated and serious attention to detail. In the third phase, mastery emerges in the young pianist's performance of targeted pieces. Gone is the positive and playful instructional approach as the teacher becomes more critical of the smaller flaws in an attempt to develop a near-perfect performance. The instructional mission changes, as do the student's goals, over the three phases. While the theory is hardly one of cognitive development in the Piagetian sense, there is nonetheless progressive maturation that occurs over the time of five or ten years (or more) of lessons. A parallel can be drawn for children's study of any instrument or voice.

Anthropologist Gregory Bateson (1978) defined three broad dimensions of learning similar to Sosniak's three-phase model. These types were related to music learning by Catherine Ellis (1986). Learning I occurs without effort, as music within the environment is absorbed by the learner. Such informal encounters with music are part of the enculturation process by which children come to know the components of their society. In Learning II, thinking is combined with experience when the child/learner strives to become a competent performer through lessons or classroom instruction. This is the phase in which the child becomes more seriously interested in music, and engages in practice that develops coordination, strength, agility, and speed on a given instrument or voice. The final phase, which Ellis contends is attained only rarely, takes the performer past the technical skills to music as a personal expression of joy and even religious faith.

Children who study instruments may well make their way through the phases proposed by Sosniak, and by Bateson and Ellis (Figure 2.1). Certainly, children everywhere have an initial enculturation experience; musically, this may well be their development as perceivers and performers of simple songs and instrumental pieces in their musical "mother tongue." The second phase in both theories indicates a commitment to practice in order to develop technique and build a performance repertoire. The ultimate phase is reached when

Mature: Musical mastery
Refinement and
  perfection
Music as personal
  expression and
  aesthetic experience

Middle: Conscious attention
  to performance
  technique
Commitment to
  practice
Concentration for
  competence

Early: Musical
  enculturation
Playful exploration
  of music
Informal encounters with
  music in the environment

Figure 2.1. Three Phases of Musical Learning.

performance skills are refined and the goal of music as an aesthetic expression can be attained. Few children realize this goal, although many are well on their way. The greatest focus of music instruction for children through the sixth grade is on the second phase, the skill-building stage.

Theories of Musical Play and Socialization

When children play with other children and socialize with adults, they are learning as well. Contrary to the word's connotation, "play" can thus be serious business for children. Socialization, a type of play in which children engage in social interactions with adult guides, can be a weighty endeavor for children with serious implications for their cognitive development. Musical play and socialization through music (and for the sake of music learning) can be bona fide means for children to gain information about the world around them.

Various schools of child psychology have supported play as a natural process and a part of child development. G. Stanley Hall and Sigmund Freud were in agreement that young children are in training for adulthood through the games they play. Musical play should be nurtured in the nursery school and continued through the primary grades, according to the pedagogies of Zoltán Kodály, Emile Jaques-Dalcroze, and Carl Orff. Singing games, newly invented songs by children, musical improvisations, and compositions that are practiced, preserved, and performed repeatedly are examples of musical play at its best.

Musical play deserves a prominent place in the education of children—at least through the primary grades—with improvisation occurring throughout the elementary grades. The key to successful music learning may be at least partly linked to the songs children know, invent, and transmit to each other while at play, and to the music they create on instruments during free-play time. Certainly, a teacher's goals and well-planned lessons are necessary in the educational process, as is an open mind to the music that children themselves know and spontaneously create. Children's musical play can be the means by which a conceptual understanding of music is more fully developed in the classroom. The teacher's role as guide rather than solely as leader can foster learning and the development of favorable attitudes toward music that will long endure.

The Russian social psychologist Lev Vygotsky (1978) established that the adult, primarily the parent and teacher, is the primary influence on a child's socialization process. The adult not only transmits music to a child, but also participates in the child's discovery and manipulation of the music to be acquired. During musical play, the teacher or parent delivers to the child cultural "signs"—such as verbal comments, facial expressions, or indicatory gestures—that direct the child's attention to specific elements of an experience and that activate appropriate learning behaviors. According to Vygotsky, these signs provide the means for drawing children into knowing their culture (in this case, musical culture) while also shaping and coloring their perceptions and eventual understanding of the cultural object (the music). As the teacher interacts musically with children, for example, while singing, the children come to know that song and to progress toward singing it independently. They grow in ownership of the song, and become more familiar as well with elements of that musical tradition. Their musical interactions with the adult while singing, moving, listening, and playing musical instruments are vital not only to their musical independence, but also to their coming into the musical culture itself.

Social Learning and Reinforcement Theories

Two theories from the fields of sociology and psychology, both highly relevant to teaching and learning, are linked by their examination of environmental agents that promote and influence learning. Neither is technically an instructional theory, although they each target behaviors that frequently appear

Teacher-as-model singing with children.

in classrooms. Social learning theory explains the significance of environmental models for learning, while reinforcement theory describes the manner in which persons in the environment shape and increase learning behaviors.

Albert Bandura's (1977) social learning theory is a provocative view of the power of persons within an environment to serve as models of behavior that are later replicated by the observer. Children choose to watch and listen to their parents and teachers, whose behaviors they later emulate. Their observations of these models are mentally organized, memorized, and recalled when similar situations for thinking and acting arise in their lives. The process of environmental influences and social learning are played out as the student recalls the visual or aural codes of earlier observations and practices the behaviors first demonstrated by the models. Social learning theory is prominent in musical settings, because modeling is critical to the student's watching, listening, and then performing the music in the manner and style of the teacher. Children learn to sing and play instruments, as well as how to listen, by doing as their models do.

Table 2.2 shows how social learning theory can be adapted to a learning sequence that integrates the act of listening in the development of performance skills, in this case, singing. A song is learned in three stages: First, it is introduced by the teacher; secondly, an intermediate stage is reached several "run-throughs" or even weeks later; and third, a final stage of refinement is achieved some time after that. The teacher as model is central to the develop-

Table 2.2   Applications of Social Learning Theory to Music Instruction: Modeling, Imitation, and Evaluation in Teaching a Song

Early	The model (teacher) sings/children listen
	Can you sing the final tone?
	What is the meter?
	How many phrases are there?
	Are there any repeated patterns?
Middle	The model sings/children listen; children sing
	What pitches are to be accented?
	Have you lowered (raised) the pitch?
	Are you sustaining for the complete duration?
	Can you achieve the rhythmic "swing" or "flow"?
Late	Children sing; the model sings/children listen; children sing
	How closely can you approximate the model?
	How might you vary the model's rendering?
	Where are the "peak" expressive points?
	What are the overlaps and distinctions between you and the model?

ment of listening and performance skills. The children imitate the model and evaluate their attempts to recreate it, showing increasing ability to match the model's performance, even as they offer personal expression in their rendering of the song. Questions by the teacher direct children to careful listening in order to develop their ability to sing accurately and expressively. This sequence could be also contained within a single lesson; thus, it becomes a lesson plan for teaching a song.

The reinforcement theory of the behavioral school of psychology has been embraced by teachers and parents, having long provided suggestions for effective means of shaping children's behaviors toward those considered acceptable and appropriate. B. F. Skinner's (1953) classic theory of operant conditioning is at the heart of behavioral change, including learning. Operant conditioning is a three-part instructional "kernel," or process, comprised of a stimulus that is presented to the learner, a response that is elicited by the learner as a consequence of the stimulus, followed by the presentation of another stimulus that reinforces the response. Stimuli operating in the environment, including the verbal and nonverbal approval of a teacher, impact on children's learning behaviors. Skinner's reinforcement theory holds that when a child's behavior—singing in tune or playing rhythms accurately—is positively reinforced by the teacher's smile, nod, or positive comment, that behavior will be maintained or increased. As well, "punishers" can also decrease inappropriate behavior through the teacher's frown, finger snap, or shake of the head.

The Skinnerian technique of successive approximation, or the shaping of behavior by reinforcing each progressive step toward an ideal, is one of the most common ones used by teachers. Shaping requires teachers to break songs, pieces, or musical passages into small parts, to offer approving remarks for musical behaviors that are similar to, or that approximate, the desired performance behaviors ("Yes, now you've got the right rhythm!"), and to use punishers to state what needs to change in moving learners toward the ideal ("No, you need to sing it a half-step higher"). The teacher reinforces less perfect musical behaviors in the hopes of directing children to more perfect ones. The teacher's reinforcing comments are eventually diminished, as children begin to evaluate their own musical behaviors as approximating the model or ideal sound. Reinforcement theory is recognized by behaviorists as a premiere influence on learning, with the teacher acting as environmental agent, dispenser of feedback, and model of appropriate behavior.

Reinforcement theory is also the basis of the system of classroom management called behavior modification, in which children are given external reinforcement for appropriate social or academic behaviors. In its classic form, children receive rewards contingent on or following "good" behavior; these rewards have included M&M candies, tokens to be applied to prizes, "free time," and field trips. This system is well-known for keeping children "on task," or focused on goals of cooperative and nondisruptive behavior and on the completion of projects and assignments.

The work of Clifford K. Madsen and his associates (Madsen and Madsen, 1981; Madsen and Yarbrough, 1985) on the application of reinforcement theory to musical settings has inspired a host of research studies and teaching practices. He has developed four observational research principles: pinpointing a "trouble" behavior; observing and recording the frequency of the behavior; applying a teaching strategy to reduce the behavior; and evaluating the effect of the strategy by observing the frequency of the behavior. In countless studies, inappropriate behaviors are reduced while appropriate behaviors emerge; the key appears to be viewing the "trouble behaviors" one at a time, and to applying teaching strategies that work.

Another use of reinforcement theory as applied to music is the study of its power as a reinforcer for appropriate and nondisruptive social behaviors; this perspective underscores the function of music as a therapeutic agent.

Learning Style Theories

Several learning style theories have been developed from research on the functioning of the human brain and on the complexities of the human personality. While these are not instructional theories per se, they underscore the individual differences among children's learning styles for which an array of instructional strategies may be necessary.

Research has shed considerable light on the different but complementary tasks of the brain's right and left hemispheres. When the corpus callosum, or bundle of nerves connecting the two hemispheres, is severed, the left hemisphere responds better to verbal, sequential, and linear processing, while the right hemisphere is inclined toward nonverbal, spatial-visual, and simultaneous processing. This has led cognitive psychologists to develop a theory of cerebral dominance, which suggests that some individuals are "left-brain convergent" thinkers while others are "right-brain divergent" thinkers (Restak, 1979). More recent research suggests that, depending on the task and on the level of learning already attained, people use both sides of the brain with facility and that communication between both hemispheres is rapid and complex. Some educators have taken steps past the conceptual theory to the design of instructional strategies that reach both "brains."

Stemming partly from cerebral dominance research and from his observations of brain-damaged individuals who demonstrated specific types of intelligence even though they showed an intellectual deficiency, Howard Gardner (1983) proposed a theory of multiple intelligences. He suggested that there may be seven intelligences, one or several of which are dominant in the learner's processing of the world. Gardner was concerned that the definition of intelligence was too limited, and that a person may be intelligent in more than one domain, or especially strong in one area while only moderately so in another. The seven intelligences of Gardner's theory include linguistic, logical-mathematical, spatial, interpersonal, intrapersonal, musical, and bodily-kinesthetic.

Clearly, Gardner's theory stands on its own, but if each intelligence is more centered in one hemisphere or the other, then his theory can be related to research in cerebral dominance. Left hemisphere processes are emphasized in linguistic and logical–mathematical intelligences, while spatial intelligence reflects right-hemisphere excellence. Interpersonal and intrapersonal intelligences emanate from right-hemisphere functions. Musical intelligence is balanced by processes of both hemispheres, for it allows both sequential (left-brain) processing through its perception of durational and pitch patterns and phrases, and simultaneous (right-brain) processing through its perception of various polyphonic textures, including harmony. The bodily-kinesthetic intelligence is the only emphasis that appears to stem more from the motor and sensory parts of the cortex than from either hemisphere in particular. Each intelligence is like a learning style that calls for specific instructional strategies.

Along with its reference to cerebral dominance theory, Gardner's theory of multiple intelligence suggests that there is more than one intellect, and that nonverbal forms of learning merit greater attention than is currently given to them by educators. If it can be accepted that the two hemispheres have specialized yet complementary functions, then it would seem critical to pay greater attention to teaching to the somewhat neglected right hemisphere. The exercise of children's subjective, affective, and divergent qualities can be greatly served through lessons in music and the arts. While music can be analyzed linearly by the left hemisphere, it can also be nonverbally experienced and creatively expressed by the right hemisphere. The nature of music instruction allows children occasions for activating the best of both brains.

A theory of learning modalities proposed by Walter Barbe and Raymond S. Swassing (1979) submits that a learner processes information most efficiently through one of three sensory channels: visual; auditory; or tactile/kinesthetic. The visual learner absorbs information by seeing, reading, and observing demonstrations by others. The auditory learner benefits from verbal instructions and from oral examples presented by the teacher, another student, or recordings. The kinesthetic learner develops knowledge and skills by touching, moving, and physically acting on his or her environment. Learning modalities are thought to be relatively stable over time, but there is also evidence that very young children tend to be kinesthetically oriented, primary-grade

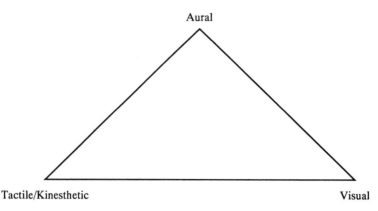

Aural

Tactile/Kinesthetic

Visual

Figure 2.2. Learning Modalities: Independent Yet Able to Be Integrated.

children more inclined toward auditory learning, with adolescents shifting towards the visual modality. Figure 2.2 illustrates the modalities; their configuration within a single closed shape suggests the three modalities should all be included in lessons.

Learning modalities can be applied to music instructional approaches. While music classroom environments must be rich in stimulation for all the senses, it is helpful to know the modality strengths of individual students. Visual learners acquire music by seeing, reading notation, and watching others make music; auditory learners from verbal instructions and musical examples; and kinesthetic learners by feeling, participating, and becoming involved with music in a physical way. The best teaching involves the stimulation of all modalities. This is particularly easy to do in music, which is multimodal by nature. Table 2.3 offers a sample lesson that utilizes the three modalities in developing an understanding of pitch and duration within the traditional song, "Charlie Over the Ocean."

Charlie Over the Ocean

Char - lie o - ver the   o - cean.   Char - lie o - ver the   sea.

Char - lie caught   a   black - bird   he   can't   catch   me.

Environmental, emotional, sociological, physical, and psychological issues affecting learning are addressed by Rita and Kenneth Dunns's (1984) Learning Style Model. The environmental set of factors is perhaps the most unique aspect of the model, because it includes sound, light, temperature, and classroom design—all of which can be adjusted by the teacher. Some children are negatively affected by loud and noisy environments, while others require some ambient sound in order to think. Some children's quality of thinking is diminished by learning spaces that are too bright or too dull (dim). If children are too hot or too cold, they may not attain their learning potential. A fourth environmental factor involves that the design of a room, which may appear too crowded, overstimulating, and distracting for some, but not stimulating

Table 2.3   Lesson Featuring Three Modalities

Grade Level	One–two
Focus	d-r-m, m-r-d, d-s$_1$ $\frac{6}{8}$ rhythms: ♩♪; ♫♫; ♩.
Objectives	Children will be able to: 1. Sing and chant pitch and rhythm patterns noted above, in isolation and in the context of the song, "Charlie Over the Ocean" (a).* 2. "Map" the pitch and rhythm patterns as they are sounded in the song, in the air, on paper, and on the blackboard (v, k).* 3. Identify pitch and rhythm patterns as they are sounded vocally or on instruments (a). 4. Walk the pulse while patting rhythm patterns (k). 5. Show pitch levels of patterns through gestures while singing (k, v). 6. Notate the song on music staff (v).
Sequence	1. Children pat the pulse, while teacher chants $\frac{6}{8}$ rhythms in various patterns: ♩♪ (ta-ti); ♫♫ (ti-ti-ti); ♩. (ta-i) (a). 2. Teacher chants $\frac{6}{8}$ rhythms of song in one- and two-measure phrases. Children pat the pulse while listening and then chanting in imitation (a). 3. Children pat the pulse, while teacher sings pitch patterns: d-r-m; m-r-d; d-s$_1$ (a). 4. Teacher sings song in one- and two-measure phrases, using tonic solfa (solfège) patterns. Children pat the pulse while listening and singing in imitation (a). 5. Teacher sings song with words: in full, and then in two-measure phrases, to be imitated by children (a). 6. Children sing the song, "mapping" in the air, on paper, and on the blackboard the pitch levels of the melody and their durations (v, k):

(*continued*)

Table 2.3 Continued

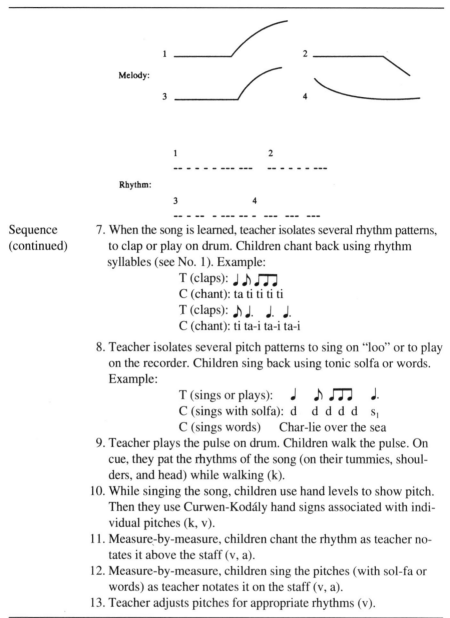

Sequence
(continued)

7. When the song is learned, teacher isolates several rhythm patterns, to clap or play on drum. Children chant back using rhythm syllables (see No. 1). Example:

      T (claps):
      C (chant): ta ti ti ti ti
      T (claps):
      C (chant): ti ta-i ta-i ta-i

8. Teacher isolates several pitch patterns to sing on "loo" or to play on the recorder. Children sing back using tonic solfa or words. Example:

      T (sings or plays):
      C (sings with solfa): d   d d d d s_1
      C (sings words)   Char-lie over the sea

9. Teacher plays the pulse on drum. Children walk the pulse. On cue, they pat the rhythms of the song (on their tummies, shoulders, and head) while walking (k).

10. While singing the song, children use hand levels to show pitch. Then they use Curwen-Kodály hand signs associated with individual pitches (k, v).

11. Measure-by-measure, children chant the rhythm as teacher notates it above the staff (v, a).

12. Measure-by-measure, children sing the pitches (with sol-fa or words) as teacher notates it on the staff (v, a).

13. Teacher adjusts pitches for appropriate rhythms (v).

*a, aural; v, visual; k, kinesthetic.

enough for others. Each learner may require a somewhat unique combination of these factors; their proper adjustment by teachers can enhance children's learning potential.

Two personality theories contribute to an understanding of learning style.

Field dependence/field independence is postulated by numerous psychologists including Harold Witkin (1977). Field dependence is defined as the content-bound, experiencing concepts as embedded within their environment, whereas field independence is content independent, experiencing concepts as discrete entities removed from their background. The field dependent learner learns best from other people in a social setting, and through class discussions and teacher-directed activities. The field independent learner prefers learning alone and in an autonomous manner, and is most comfortable setting his or her own goals and working at his or her own pace. In a musical setting, field dependent learners may thrive on singing games, group improvisation, and ensemble performance. Field independent learners may more easily gain knowledge through computer-assisted programs of instruction, solo practice, and individual composition. The astute observer, teacher, or parent soon distinguishes among these learners and makes allowances for them.

A related theory by Isabel Myers and Peter B. Briggs (1985) postulates that there are four types of personality factors that inform learning—(1) extroversion/introversion; (2) sensing/intuitive; (3) thinking/feeling; and (4) judging/perceiving—which they measure through the Myers-Briggs Type Indicator. Extroverted learners are more socially directed to the external world, thinking aloud to process ideas, while introverted learners require silent internal processing time to figure out what they have observed or experienced. Sensing learners rely heavily on their sensory channels to give them information, while intuitive types invent and reason new information from previous experiences. Thinking learners make decisions based on objective rational analysis, and feeling learners rely on subjective personal values as the basis of decisions. Finally, judging learners make decisions easily and promptly, while perceivers are tentative, choosing to delay decisions while gathering further information. These varied personalities challenge the teacher to carefully gauge the personalities of their students, and to creatively develop ways to enhance their learning.

Theories of Instruction

Over the past several decades, instructional psychologists have developed many theories about the effects of interactions between teachers and learners. Only a small selection of the more significant theories to music instruction for children are described here.

David Ausubel (1968) maintained that a person's existing cognitive structure is the foremost factor governing whether new material is potentially meaningful as well as how readily it can be acquired and retained. In his theory of meaningful reception, the role of the learner is to receive ideas and information, with the teacher playing the role of lecturer or explainer. Critical to the learner's meaningful reception of new information is the provision of "advance organizers" by the teacher, the structuring of a foundation of familiar ideas on which new information can be laid. The teacher who outlines the material to be covered and goals to be met is also organizing for children in advance the learning that will occur. Children must listen intently and seek actively to reorganize their existing knowledge in view of the teacher's ideas, so that they can then formulate new ways of looking at the world.

Jerome Bruner (1966) is the major proponent of the "discovery method." The discovery method is a type of learning that involves problem solving, requiring the learner to manipulate materials and to cope with incongruities from which information is derived. Discovery learning encourages taking risks, guessing, and exploring student-initiated hypotheses. Exploratory experiences and occasional nonconformity are indicators of creative thinking, which is the ultimate goal of all learning. Improvisation and composition experiences are the most obvious examples of musical exploration and experimentation, but any musical experience that challenges children to think while listening, performing, or creating can exemplify discovery learning. Musical concepts can be most effectively taught via the discovery method. By allowing children to experience a concept (such as pulse, meter, a three-pitch melody, or binary form) without initially labeling it, they can explore and be guided toward an understanding of that concept and then learn its official name.

Brunerian ideas have been influential in the development of curriculum and instruction in music, most notably on the Manhattanville Music Curriculum Project, or MMCP (1970). In addition to directing musical experiences for children to include musical exploration, improvisation, and composition, Bruner's concept of a spiral curriculum that allows children to learn music through age-appropriate experiences was also put to its test through MMCP. The spiral curriculum recommended that "any subject could be taught to any child at any age," so long as it is set in lessons suitable for the intellectual level of the child. Thus, the components of music, e.g., melody and rhythm, can be taught to preschool and secondary school students, just as the music of Mozart and Messiaen, and from Bali and Bulgaria, can be experienced earlier and later in a child's school career.

Robert Gagné's descriptive studies of cognitive processes in the 1960s led to his development (with his colleagues) of eight "events of instruction" or "conditions of learning" (1977). The events or conditions include a progression of sensory information from perception to concept formation. These events embrace the needs for preparing children for new information, for offering occasions for their responses to and practice of new information, and for supporting the transfer of information gained to the greater acquisition of knowledge. The teacher's role in engaging children's interest is an important first step for knowledge acquisition; that role becomes increasingly prominent later when he or she introduces the more complex process of problem solving. More than most theories, Gagné's events of instruction are clear-cut steps that can be readily applied to music. See Table 2.4 for an application of Gagné's eight events to music for children; these steps may apply to a complete lesson or to single activities within a lesson.

Edwin E. Gordon's (1984, 1993) music learning theory appears to be at least partially influenced by some of Gagné's early theoretical work. In fact, his earlier work (1971) was nearly a direct application of Gagné's events to music. Like the events of instruction, Gordon's theory is hierarchical in nature, progressing through eight levels that begin with aural/oral reception and transmission and lead to generalization, improvisation, and finally music theory—the whys and hows of musical pitch and rhythm functions. Gordon compares learning music to mastering a spoken language, as a progression from first simply perceiving and responding to sounds to the advanced levels of problem solving and conceptual understanding. Gordon also addresses the sequential nature of acquiring basic discrimination and music literacy skills, and the use and transfer of these skills to bring about more sophisticated possibilities for music learning possibilities.

Gordon's music learning theory is a comprehensive model of skill development; founded on the principle of audiation, or inner hearing: the ability to "hear" notation, and to notate what one hears. In a Pestalozzian manner, and related to the pedagogical approaches of Lowell Mason and, much later, Europeans Emile Jaques-Dalcroze, Zoltán Kodály, and Carl Orff, Gordon's recommendations for music instruction begin with the musical sound and vocalized patterns, proceeding gradually to the notational symbols of pitch and rhythm. His music learning sequence is a prescribed succession of music skills, or performance behaviors, music content, and tonal and rhythm patterns that is intended to develop musical audiation and understanding. See Chapter 3 for further explanation of the method that Gordon developed from his theory.

Relating Theory to Practice

The preceding explanation of theories of teaching and learning can be viewed as frameworks for instructional practice; this section presents guidelines based on these theories for the effective delivery of instruction by teachers to children in preschool and the elementary grades. Five components are described: the classroom environment; the child-centered curriculum; the teacher as transmitter; instructional strategies; and motivation and management.

Table 2.4   Gagné's Events of Instruction: Applications to Music for Children

1. Gaining/maintaining attention
   Ask a probing question to pique curiosity
   Present a startling statement
   Tell a short story
   Sing with children a favorite familiar song
   Clap a rhythm children can imitate
   Play a recording that encourages children's movement responses
   Engage children in immediate participation

2. Preparing learners for instruction
   Repeat #1, but with relevance to the new music to be learned
   Share with children the goals and expectations of lesson/activity
   Present fragments and phrases of the new music to be learned as "teasers"
      for children's imitation

3. Presenting the material
   Present the lesson's music in live or recorded form
   Present small sections or "chunks" of the new music that can be linked to-
      gether to form the whole

4. Prompting/guiding learning
   Illustrate problem melodic and rhythmic phrases through mnemonics
   Call attention to repeated patterns and unusual musical features
   Allow time to rehearse individually, in small or large groups

5. Providing conditions for response
   Offer occasions for active participation/performance by all
   Switch from playing to singing a piece; from singing to moving to its rhythm
      or pulse

6. Providing feedback for response
   Remind children of learning goals and expectation of lesson/activity
   Offer specific comments when possible
   Allow children opportunities to change and to perfect their performance

7. Promoting/measuring retention
   Critique children's performance
   Allow children to evaluate their performance
   Provide opportunities for children to develop the musical ideas of the piece
      through improvisation

8. Enhancing transfer of learning to new tasks/information
   Transfer concepts and skills to performance of unfamiliar piece
   Transfer concepts and skills to listening of unfamiliar piece

The Classroom Environment

What should the music classroom look like? Theories of child development, musical play, and learning styles inform the physical setting of the music classroom. Most importantly, furniture in the music room must be minimal so that a great variety of musical play and performance experiences can occur. A piano is always useful, preferably one with wheels for easy maneuvering. Various types of xylophones and percussion instruments can be laid on tables for easy access by children. Larger drums and bass xylophones can be laid across the floor, or kept in storage until needed. Computers for independent and small-group projects can be set up in one corner of the room, to which a MIDI station can be attached. Even in a medium-sized room, a small keyboard lab of four to six pianos can be placed at one end.

For seated activities, floor space is still preferable to desks. Children can pick up three-foot carpet squares (usually available as remnants from a carpet store) when they enter the classroom. Choral risers can make for useful seating or standing arrangements, especially for the upper grades; these should be located against a wall so that there is still open space in the center for movement activities.

Various audiovisual resources are vital for teaching and can be kept on wheel carts for greater portability. A high-quality sound system with the capacity to play CDs, cassette tapes, and records is basic to any successful music instruction. Overhead transparency projectors and VCR equipment are also critical. A table with chairs, on which cassette tape players with headphones can be set, can make for an ideal independent listening and ear-training lab. A teacher's desk, files, and storage cabinets complete the list of necessary furniture.

What should the music classroom feel like? Teachers need to be aware of factors that create an environment conducive to music listening, performing, and creating. The music room should be well-ventilated, with plenty of windows for fresh air and light. It should be low on ambient sound and moderate in temperature, ventilation, and light. Cafeterias, with the noise of cookware clanging together, are not ideal for use as music rooms. Gyms are built for sports and games, but are not appropriate for developing musical sensitivity, performance techniques, and aural skills due to their poor acoustics.

What other resources can enhance a music classroom's potential for effective instruction? Visual appeal can motivate children to want to come to music, and to learn. A chalkboard, preferably with staff lines, is the sine qua non of the music room, especially by the time notation is introduced. Felt and bulletin boards can be places for attractive posters and color photographs of performers, composers, dancers, instruments, maps, and timely announcements. Notational symbols make pleasant borders, and colorful lists of terms can be pinned to these boards. Instruments should be labeled in bold letters so that their names are known. Sheets of butcher paper (available from art supply or butcher's shops) are useful for writing and posting song words and key concepts of a lesson.

What print, audio, and video materials should a teacher have available for music instruction? A personal collection of recordings, videotapes, books, and basal series textbooks can stimulate the design of successful lessons. An annotated listing of the contents of such a collection can trigger the memory, and serve as a guide for lesson plans. Basal series textbooks often feature attractive recordings and sometimes other sources such as videotapes, posters, and computer-assisted instruction programs. Sources for beginning to build a personal library are listed at the end of each chapter. Collections of slides, color transparencies, and photographs complete a teacher's personal storehouse of instructional materials.

Whatever is not available within the music classroom itself may be found in a school's learning resource center, in the library, or even in the faculty lounge! When fundamental materials, such as a sound system and musical instruments, are not available, small educational grants or gifts can be obtained to provide for them.

A Child-Centered Curriculum

A child-centered curriculum offers instruction that is relevant to the child's experiences and abilities, needs, and interests. This curriculum is more playful, more integrated, and more likely to be led by the responses of children than by the whims of the teacher.

What are the realities of a child-centered curriculum in music? Several key issues merit consideration in the design of a music program.

1. Knowing the children. What musical skills and knowledge do they possess? What music interests and "moves" them? What are their learning styles? What subject strengths do they possess? Where are they developmentally? What are their cultural and familial backgrounds? What, if any, are the musical and educational expectations of their parents? Do they have musical goals and dreams they hope to attain? Generalizing about children leads to surefire foiled experiences that fail to reach them. By talking to teachers and parents, by reviewing school files, and by asking questions of the children themselves, teachers can offer far more relevant musical experiences and training.

2. Beginning where the children are. While there are many specific questions for which answers should be sought, there are also "universal" concepts to consider when designing music instruction for children. These include: (a) providing lessons that lead children from the familiar to the unfamiliar, e.g., teaching ♩♪♩ after they know ♪♪♪♪, and teaching $\frac{7}{8}$ after they understand two- and three-beat meters; (b) giving children many occasions for active rather than passive experiences (most children achieve their greatest learning when they have actively participated through manipulation of a concept or through performance); and, (c) offering children lessons with variety (various approaches to a concept, various musical examples, various musical pieces and styles).

3. Allow time for musical play and exploration. For young children, musical sound is a discovery of how loud and how soft, how choppy and how smooth, how long and how short, how fast and how slow, how high and how low a set of pots and pans, the teeth of a comb, or two pencils can sound. Given a drum, sandblocks, or a xylophone, how many different sounds can a young child play? For older children, the music curriculum can be linked to solving musical problems creatively through experimentation: Choose the pitches for a rhythmic pattern and create a new song; or write a poem and perform it rhythmically and with dynamic expression. Time must be allotted as well for experimentation and personal expression through music.

4. Integrate music into the other parts of a child's life. Songs blend with stories, music listening mixes with movement, and a study of musical instruments is also a lesson in the science of acoustics. Like the whole-language approach in other subject areas, music is not to be treated as a separate entity, but can be coupled with the learning of concepts in social studies, language arts, mathematics, and the sciences. A musical experience can be enhanced by experiences in the visual arts, stories, poetry, theater, and movement and dance.

The Teacher as Transmitter

Teachers are transmitters of culture; how they package and present information to children is critical to whether the transmission process is completed, i.e., whether the information is received and assimilated by children. Theories of instruction, reinforcement, socialization, and social learning underscore the powerful impact that a teacher can have on children's learning and development. Of the many qualities that good music teachers possess, several are more prominent.

1. Knowing and liking the subject matter. The effective music teacher knows well the music, concept, or technique to be taught. Knowing the music requires preparation; without it, the lesson will fail. A Russian folk song cannot be taught before the teacher has practiced the song's words, melody, and rhythm. Neither can a xylophone arrangement be masterfully taught if the teacher has not worked out the parts: by reading and rereading, chanting, patting, singing, or even playing them. The teacher should be able to sing, play, or move to the music selected for lessons with ease and refinement. As the teacher transmits the music, his or her enjoyment and love for it is also passed on to the children. Music concepts must be clearly understood in terms of their critical perceptual qualities so activities can be chosen to highlight those qualities.

2.   Modeling the musical behaviors. The effective music teacher serves as the live model for the music to be learned. Performance skills are learned by children who imitate or are otherwise influenced by the behavior and comments of their teacher. Verbal explanations are far less effective than demonstration; how can children be told in words alone how to sing staccato, to sustain a sound, or (initially) to play a bourdon (bass drone) or xylophone? As the adage goes, a teacher's "actions speak louder than words." Many children will know no other musicians who can sing well and perform proficiently on musical instruments; for them, the teacher who performs is critical to their musical well-being. While absolute mimicry by children is not the goal of a teacher's musical demonstrations, model musicianship can be observed, absorbed, and reinterpreted by children in their own performance.

3.   Presenting with energy and enthusiasm. The effective music teacher is enthusiastic about music and children, and presents lessons that are charged with energy. Enthusiasm is conveyed in many ways: a broad spectrum of vocal inflections and facial expressions; steady eye contact; varied gestures and demonstrative movements of the body; and descriptive vocabulary. The teaching pace needs to at least occasionally match that of television programs to which children are accustomed, with quick changes of experiences and approaches to a musical concept. High energy and vitality most successfully convey ideas. While it is natural for some teachers, it can also be learned by others who review their teaching behaviors via videotaped recordings, and who then make a conscientious effort to increase their eye contact or to vary their facial expressions. No doubt, a teacher's enthusiasm is also related to job satisfaction as well as his or her interest in the music selected for the lesson.

Instructional Strategies

What are some of the recent instructional strategies that promote learning, and develop strong and lasting interactions between teacher and children? There is no clearer way to understanding instructional theories than to apply them to

Children's choir in the setting of the music classroom.

your teaching. Some strategies are governed by children's age, stage, or phase of development, while others relate to their individual learning styles and personalities.

1. Starting the class. The manner in which a class begins can entice and motivate children to learn, or can turn their attentions away from the subject for the remainder of the period. Gaining children's attention may proceed in many ways. Play live or recorded music as children enter. Ask a question ("How might a composer portray the sound of a train?," leading to playing Honneger's *Pacific 231*). Tell a story ("Beauty and the Beast," leading to Ravel's piece of the same title). Make a bold and startling statement ("People in Mozambique don't sit still at concerts," leading to a lesson incorporating song, story, dance, and xylophone performance). Clap a rhythm to be imitated by children. Give a silent gesture that, over time, means to come to attention, a signal that something important is about to happen. As a musician-teacher, sing a song or play a piece. Perform with a class a familiar song. Show a photograph or illustration, in silence or with a leading question. Depending on the lesson, any number of these strategies will direct children's attention toward class.

2. Ending the class. The music and the learning will linger longer when the class ends in a memorable or stimulating fashion. There are many possibilities. Sing or play a familiar song. Play or snap/clap/pat/stamp a rhythmic piece or passage. Ask a question to be answered in the next music class ("What could we do to make this song more interesting texturally?"). Tease by previewing the next class ("And if you want to know how to play an Afro-Cuban rhythm on the conga drum, you'll have to come back next _____!"). Rapidly review the main points of the lesson. Play live or recorded music as children exit.

3. Supplying feedback: the TST. The interactive instructional "kernel" of the teaching and learning process is a three-step process that involves the (T)eacher's presentation of information, the (S)tudents' response to that information, and the (T)eacher's specific feedback to the response. Based on operant conditioning, the TST is the Skinnerian stimulus-response-stimulus sequence that makes for effective instruction. There are multiple TST kernals in a lesson, because the teacher's feedback in the third step progresses to the next TST. An example of three TSTs in a row is this interchange at the beginning of a recorder lesson:

T: Let's learn the playing position of the recorder. Hold the recorder in your left hand.
S: (Children hold the recorder in their left hand)
T: Good. Now relax. It should feel easy, almost natural.
T: Now, let's blow air out gently, as if into a straw.
S: (Children blow air)
T: Not too hard. Gently. Pretend you're blowing small bubbles.
T: Let's try this out on the recorder. Ready, blow.
S: (Children blow air into recorder)
T: Not bad. You're on your way.

Clearly, the lack of any of these three steps means that the instruction is not complete. There must be information from the teacher, followed by a response from the children, and concluding with the teacher's evaluation of their response. From one TST to the next, the teacher is interacting with students in information given and gained.

4. Stimulating aural learning. Understanding and skill-building in music require careful listening. Music literacy is advanced through aural learning, which includes the use of modeling, imitative devices, and strategies for strengthening the memory. The instructional approaches of Kodály, Dalcroze, and Orff suggest that melodic and rhythmic ideas, phrasing and form, expressive elements, and performance techniques initially can be taught aurally. The aural acquisition of music may even facilitate music literacy; it is a necessary phase toward that development. Recorded music for aural learning can be supplemented by live performances given by the teacher, older and more experienced students, visiting artists, and amateur musicians from the community. Musical patterns, fragments, phrases, and pieces can help to build in children a functional musical vocabulary for their later listening and performance. Learning by listening is a logical procedure, bringing children directly into the sound of the music.

5. Providing for repetition and rehearsal. The acquisition of performance and listening skills takes time and effort, and children can show considerable progress through repeated attempts to achieve them. Learning to sing four phrases of a traditional song like "Charlie Over the Ocean" is a complex endeavor for very young children: the words, rhythm, melodic patterns, and tonality may take many listenings and even more occasions for singing it, before the components begin to fall in place. Listening to Stravinsky's "Greeting Prelude" or to Bach's "Little Fugue in G Minor" is challenging to older children, when the object is to listen analytically for the formal organization of melodic and rhythmic ideas. Preference for, or at least tolerance of, a musical piece may require a bare minimum of ten listenings, and probably more. Fleeting experiences do not guarantee learning; repetition can.

Motivation and Management

What can the teacher do to assure an effective learning environment for children? Motivating children to want to learn and keeping their interest in the content of the lesson are two of the teacher's greatest challenges. The proactive teacher who knows children—their learning styles and interest levels—will be able to "read" them best before attention wanes, learning ceases, and disruptions begin. The effective teacher understands the importance of carefully selected music to meet the skills and interests of children and recognizes the power of positive interaction with children. Reinforcement and instruction theories suggest motivation techniques, as well as intervention techniques when children do become distracted or disruptive.

The interaction, or the verbal and nonverbal exchange that occurs between teachers and children, is critical in the greater learning and more positive attitudes that children develop for music and the music class. Four characteristics of the effective teacher nearly guarantee gains in both musical knowledge and enjoyment. The teacher: (1) moves easily between directed and didactic comments and comments that gently support children's own initiatives to learn; (2) is able to control spontaneous verbal and nonverbal responses, and reacts quickly to them; (3) recognizes the role and effectiveness of the verbal and nonverbal responses; and, (4) is a sensitive observer of classroom conditions and children's behaviors. Children who are fortunate to have positive interactions with their teacher are likely to grow musically, and be pleased and proud of their development.

The choice of music to be listened to, or to sing, play, or move to is one of the primary means of gaining and maintaining children's attention and interest. Children will become involved learners if they value the music and the musical activity. If the music is technically too easy or too difficult, motivation for learning will lag. If the music is appealing, then it has intrinsic value for children; if mastering it will lead them to personal goals, including building self-esteem, then it has utility value. Not only popular music, but other musical styles as well fulfill these maxims. A good teacher can take virtually any music and "sell" it to children through his or her own excellent musicianship and enthusiasm. However, the music needs to have musical merit to have lasting aesthetic appeal.

Various other elements motivate learning. Incentive motivation may be useful in rewarding the musical and social behaviors of younger children. These "activator" rewards include gold stars, medals, gifts, as well as punishment for negative behaviors. Older children may be drawn toward a more intrinsic motivation as they seek to master tasks of increasing difficulty through the teacher's guidance and feedback. Motivators take up where activators leave off. They include participative goal-setting, in which children work with the teacher in setting task goals and rules of the classroom, their fond memories of past successes, and the teacher's accurate and very explicit feedback of what may or may not be quite right in their performance. Activators reward simpler behaviors while motivators guide children to higher levels of learning and mastery.

What can be done when children act inappropriately, interfering with their own learning and the learning of others? Children's behavior in the music classroom can be the source of much fretting and frustration, particularly for the novice teacher. Proactive teachers understand that children will behave, that behavior is learned, and that by setting rules to be adhered to, children can learn to behave appropriately. Classroom rules can be established in the following ways: (1) democratically involving children in setting rules; (2) keeping the rules brief; (3) phrasing rules without negatives (Not "Do not talk" but "Sit quietly"; and (4) posting and reviewing rules on a regular basis.

Classroom rules vary. One teacher might use only one word to bring her primary-grade children to attention: "soft." Except for singing and playing that may need to be more musically energetic, the start and close of class and time between activities are to be quiet times, with talking limited to soft exchanges between neighbors. Another teacher might have three rules: "raise your hand when you wish to comment or participate in classes"; "remain in seats during class"; and, "use classroom instruments when directed to do so." The rules depend on the children, the teacher's philosophy, and the curricular goals.

Equally important to rule making is enforcement: The consequences of not following rules must be clear, and applied consistently. Minor infractions of the rules can be corrected immediately: sometimes eye contact alone will stop the misbehavior. At other times, a teacher's hand wave or a clap can signal to children to come to attention. The consequences of breaking the rules can also lead to a change of placement for the misbehaving child, or even temporarily taking away opportunities for participation in the most preferred musical experiences—whatever they may be. But more important than looking for ways of punishing the inappropriate behaviors is the need for recognizing good behaviors. Children need to be rewarded when they are paying attention, singing in tune, moving in time, and responding creatively to the music. These musically appropriate behaviors are learned through the teacher's recognition and reinforcement of them.

Some of the most effective techniques of classroom management derive from reinforcement theory. The Skinnerian theory was transformed into practice through the system of behavior modification, the practice of strengthening good behaviors and weakening inappropriate ones. A teacher's smile, handshake, pat on the back, and specific comments are effective types of approval, just as a frown, a stare, or the ignoring of inappropriate behavior function as disapproval. Table 2.5 offers further suggestions for making the music classroom more conducive to learning through behavior modification.

Without a doubt, the management of children's behaviors is closely connected to the motivational techniques that the teacher employs. When lessons are challenging, positive, and pleasant, children will be less likely to fidget, fuss, daydream, and become distracted. Music is a powerful motivator all its own; it is the task of the teacher to understand how to select music and musical experiences that are appropriate for children developmentally, to make music learning most meaningful to them.

Informed Teaching

All practices are guided by theory; music teaching and learning are no exception. Several disciplines offer theories for framing music instruction for children, from the developmental and stage/phase theories, to theories of musical play and socialization, social learning and reinforcement, and learning style theories, and the blossoming field of instructional psychology.

Teachers engaged in the design of curriculum and instruction in music for

Table 2.5   Making Way for Learning By Modifying Children's Behaviors

Strengthening Appropriate Behaviors

1. Ascertain that the selected reinforcement is truly perceived as positively reinforcing to the child
2. At first, give continuous and consistent reinforcement for every instance of appropriate behavior; then slowly fade to irregular and periodic reinforcement
3. At first, give reinforcement immediately following appropriate behavior
4. Move from extrinsic reinforcement (gold stars and grades) to intrinsic reinforcement (the child's own good feeling that he or she has done well)

Weakening Inappropriate Behaviors

1. Provide alternate behaviors to replace inappropriate ones ("We can't talk while we sing, but we will have several minutes of free time for talking at the close of class")
2. Ignore inappropriate behaviors (while also recognizing every appropriate behavior)
3. Punish rarely: immediately following behavior, give an explanation of the reason for punishment, and use the same words of explanation each time

children would do well to pursue additional reading of the sources cited, and then to compare these ideas to their own practical perspectives. A theory can be an academic endeavor, evolved by those who once taught and later thought. It can also be a personal effort, a marriage of ideas by insightful teachers who think as they do. By knowing the literature on instructional theory and connecting it to their own practice, teachers can have a significant impact on the music instruction that children receive.

Questions

1. Why do teachers need theory for teaching music to children?
2. How are "stage-dependent" and "phase" theories related?
3. What theories support the following statements: (1) Good teachers are models for children to emulate; (2) Children should be allowed to learn through their own experimentation; (3) The interaction of teachers with children leads to learning; and (4) Children may respond to one form of presentation more favorably than another.

4. What implications do brain and personality theories hold for instruction?

5. Are the theories of Ausubel and Bruner mutually exclusive? Why or why not?

6. What are some facets of a child-centered curriculum in music?

7. Which theories govern children's motivation to learn as well as the teacher's management of their behaviors?

Activities

1. In small groups, choose a theory, articulate its principal features, and prepare for demonstration a lesson segment that illustrates the theory in action. As an alternative activity, prepare a lesson to teach, and then discuss what theories are illustrated within it.

2. Observe a music class for children, and draw relationships between the instructional procedures and theories.

3. Observe the individual responses of children in music classes, and discuss learning style theories as they relate to these responses.

4. Design and teach a lesson based on Gagné's eight "events of instruction" (see Table 2.4).

5. Enumerate a set of behavioral rules that you will use as guidelines to ensure an effective learning environment for children.

References

AUSUBEL, D. P. (1968). *Educational psychology*. New York: Holt Rinehart & Winston.

BANDURA, A. (1977). *Social learning theory*. Englewood Cliffs, NJ: Prentice-Hall.

BARBE, W. B., & SWASSING, R. S. (1979). *Teaching through modality strengths: Concepts and practices*. Columbus, OH: Laner Bloser.

BATESON, G. (1978). *Steps to an ecology of mind*. New York: Ballantine Books.

BRUNER, J. (1966). *Toward a theory of instruction*. Cambridge, MA: Harvard University.

DUNN, R. (1984). Learning style: State of the science. *Theory into Practice*, *23*(1), 10–19.

ELLIS, C. J. (1985). *Aboriginal music, education for living: Cross-cultural experiences.* St. Lucia, Queensland: University of Queensland.

GAGNE, R. M. (1977). *The conditions of learning.* New York: Holt, Rinehart, & Winston.

GARDNER, H. (1983). *Frames of mind: A theory of multiple intelligences.* New York: Basic Books.

GORDON, E. E. (1971). *The psychology of music teaching.* Englewood Cliffs, NJ: Prentice-Hall.

———. (1994). *Learning sequences in music: Skill, content, and patterns.* Chicago: GIA Publications.

MADSEN, C. H., Jr., & MADSEN, C. K. (1981). *Teaching/discipline* (3rd ed.). Boston: Allyn and Bacon.

MADSEN, C. K., & YARBROUGH, C. (1985). *Competency-based music education.* Englewood Cliffs, NJ: Prentice-Hall.

MYERS, I., BRIGGS, P., MCCAULLEY, M. H., & MOST, R. (1985). *Manual: A guide to the development and use of the Myers-Briggs Type indicator.* Palo Alto, CA: Consulting Psychologists Press.

PIAGET, J. (1952). *The psychology of intelligence.* (Percy, M., & Berlyne, D. E., Trans.). London U.K.: Routledge & Kegan Paul.

RESTAK, R. M. (1979). *The brain: The last frontier.* Garden City, NY: Doubleday.

SKINNER, B. F. (1953). *Science and human behavior.* New York: Macmillan.

SOSNIAK, L. (1986). Three phases of learning. In B. S. Bloom (Ed.). *Developing talent in young people.* New York: Ballantine Books.

THOMAS, R. (1970). *Manhattanville music curriculum project.* Bardonia, NY: Media Materials.

VYGOTSKY, L. S. (1978). *Mind in society: The development of higher psychological process.* Cambridge, MA: Harvard University.

WITKIN, H. (1977). Field dependent and field independent cognitive styles and their educational implications. *Review of Educational Research, 47,* 1–64.

Methods of Teaching Music to Children

There may be as many methods of teaching music as there are teachers. Still, certain images conjure up some of the best known instructional approaches. Julia's bourdon-playing with felt-covered mallets on metallophones recalls the Orff-Schulwerk approach, as does the rhythmic chanting of the poem that Jimmie and George later set to temple blocks and kettle drums. Donna, Jeb, and Soo Mee add hand signals to the melodies of traditional singing games they know, putting the Kodály philosophy to practice. As José skips to a $\frac{6}{8}$ melody, changing directions at the change of phrases, two facets of Dalcroze Eurhythmics are clearly evident. Angela's free exploration of sounds on bottles, boxes, and plastic balls brings to mind the Manhattanville Music Curriculum Project (MMCP). Lisa and her classmates study a Mozart minuet in the multiple ways espoused by proponents of Comprehensive Musicianship. Denny's chanting of rhythms in imitation of his teacher's presentation underscores Gordon's initial aural/oral stage, while Clarice and Catherine learn folk dances through Weikert's sequence of saying-while-doing.

Of the numerous instructional approaches used in music classes for children, some are familiar and, couched in traditions, have stood the test of time and experience. Other approaches have been developed more recently through changes in societal values, patterns of living, and technology. Some teachers hold steadfastly to a single method, while others merge techniques from many methods to convey even a single aspect of music. In the end, every teacher finds his or her own pathway to a *personal teaching method* that works effectively in guiding children toward the development of musical skills and understanding. This personal teaching method depends on the teacher's training and experience, the instructional goals, the classroom set-

47

ting, and the musical (and extramusical) needs and interests of the children to be taught. The manner in which "musicality" is defined also provides for the variety of techniques used.

A selection of classic and contemporary methods of music instruction, many of them familiar to experienced teachers, are described according to their principal goals and techniques. Sample experiences are presented for three of the best-known pedagogies: Dalcroze, Kodály, and Orff. Their instructional techniques are also delineated throughout the book. A comparison of the methods and further discussion of the development of a personal method conclude the chapter.

Dalcroze

"Movement with a mission" is one description of the Dalcroze approach to music instruction. Dalcroze eurhythmics has been inaccurately described as dance; the stereotypical image of a Dalcroze lesson featuring young dancers in black leotards leaping to the rhythms of improvised piano music is not entirely accurate. The Dalcroze approach is three-pronged, including not only a unique form of rhythmic movement called Eurhythmics but also ear-training (solfège and solfège-rhythmique) and improvisation. The key qualities that link accomplishment in each of these elements are imagination, a keen listening sense, and an immediacy of response to the musical stimulus.

The founder of the Dalcroze approach was Émile Jaques-Dalcroze (1865–1950), a Swiss musician who served as professor of solfège, harmony, and composition at the Geneva Conservatory. His pedagogy originated at the turn of the century as he experimented with approaches to ear training. He astutely recognized that despite the advanced stages of technical proficiency that his students demonstrated through the playing of their instruments, there were notable gaps in their musical abilities. Simple rhythms were wrongly rendered, and flaws in pitch and intonation were frequent. Students were demonstrating mechanical rather than musical understanding.

Beginning with "rhythmic gymnastics" that activated the diaphragm, lungs, and articulatory functions of the mouth and tongue, the students of Professor Jaques-Dalcroze were soon singing scales in dichord (d-r, r-m, m-f, etc.) and trichord (d-r-m, r-m-f, m-f-s, etc.) arrangements, in canon with the teacher, at double and half the speed of the original statement, and alternating "silent" internal song and singing aloud on cue. As his eurhythmics approach evolved, students developed the muscular rhythms and nervous sensibilities that would allow them to discriminate among even the slight gradations of duration, time, intensity, and phrasing. Jaques-Dalcroze believed that people were musical when they came to possess "an ensemble of physical and spiritual resources and capacities" comprising the ear, brain, and body. Eurhythmics became the core of his approach, and the foundation for raising each person's musical sensitivity to its fullest potential.

For experienced performers and children alike, the Dalcroze techniques lay the foundation for a thorough musicianship. The achievement of proficient eurhythmic movement requires a repertory of complex kinesthetic reactions. Children's eurhythmic movement will include any number of possibilities in space and in place, locomotor and nonlocomotor movement, isolated gestures using the hands, arms, head, shoulders, or a combination of body parts. Their movement is a personal and immediate response to the music, played on the piano, on percussion instruments, performed vocally, or (more rarely) on recordings. Children become proficient as they follow the tempo, rhythm, and meter of music with their bodies, learning to react quickly to changes in any aspects of the music, e.g., changes in meter, rhythm patterns, dynamics, or phrase length.

Ear training, including solfège and solfège-rhythmique, is a second critical component in a Dalcroze education. Children are taught to understand tones and semitones and their relationships in scales, songs, and musical passages. The *fixed do* system is advocated by most Dalcroze teachers, in which C is the starting note of the scale regardless of the tonic. For example, when the fixed do system is used, a G Major scale begins on C and contains an F♯. Jaques-

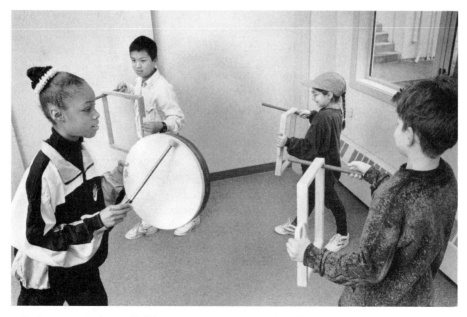

A Dalcroze technique: Children conducting while stepping the pulse.

Dalcroze reasoned that children develop absolute pitch as the sense of C is impressed on the ear, the muscles, and the mind. He believed that the inter-relationship of the scales would become clear, with children able to aurally determine the order of tones and semitones that constitute each scale. Singing via the Dalcroze approach is accompanied by hand gestures that show the position of the pitch in space or by movement of the fingers on the arm as an imaginary keyboard. Children are led to hearing and responding through movement to harmonic progressions: facing center for tonic, turning right for dominant, and left for subdominant chords.

The third Dalcroze component, improvisation, opens children to a freedom of expression through movement, in rhythmic speech, with instruments, or at the keyboard. Beginning with precise imitation of the teacher's or a partner's melodies, rhythms, and movements, children eventually acquire a repertory of movement and musical ideas from which they can draw for improvisation. Both eurhythmics and solfège offer a base of musical knowledge for im-provisation. See Table 3.1 for some sample experiences using Dalcroze's components.

Dalcroze techniques have permeated the teaching of music to children, even though few teachers in the U.S. are trained in the pedagogy. This may be due to the widespread recognition of movement as an important channel of musical response for children, as well as the method's long-time presence in the U.S., albeit in isolated instances, since the 1920s. The training for certifi-cation in the method is challenging due to its reliance on piano as the principal medium for providing music for eurhythmic response. The certification test calls for mastery of piano improvisation that demonstrates a variety of rhyth-

Table 3.1 Sampling Dalcroze

---

1. Eurhythmics: To teacher's improvised piano (or xylophone) music, children walk the pulse, clapping on beat one. On cue, change clap to beat two, three, or four. Clap on several beats: one and three, two and three. Bend the knees on beat one while clapping on others.

2. Solfège: While conducting a $\frac{4}{4}$ meter, chant the solfège syllables (do, re, mi, fa, sol, la, ti, do), one per beat; chant them backward, repeating the do. Sing the as-cending and descending scales on solfège syllables while conducting. On cue, sing them twice as fast or twice as slow.

3. Improvisation: In a frame of four or eight beats, partner 1 plays on piano (or on xylophone or drum, for example) an antecedent, to which partner 2 plays an im-provised consequent phrase of equal length. Eventually, musical questions should end on sol and answers on do, with no pauses between phrases that would break the rhythmic flow.

---

mic qualities for movement, in various keys, rendered in musically expressive ways. For further reading on the Dalcroze techniques, see the classic work by Jacques-Dalcroze (1921), and the writings of Findlay (1971) and Mead (1994) for practical applications of eurhythmics with children.

Kodály

If there is a single underlying philosophy of the Kodály approach to music instruction, it is that "music belongs to everyone." Zoltán Kodály and his Hungarian associates who first evolved the method maintained that music is the right of not only the talented few, but that all children can and should develop performance, listening, and literacy skills. With music instruction beginning in early childhood, children discover folk and art music through a sequence that begins with singing and leads to the development of musically independent individuals who can read and write with ease. Kodály proponents believe that the content and sequence of the curriculum should be derived from children's musical development and from their musical literature. While hand signs and rhythm syllables are closely associated with this approach, it is far more comprehensive than these techniques suggest, with systematic training that results in musical and musically literate children at an early age.

Zoltán Kodály (1882–1967) was a composer, ethnomusicologist, and advocate of music education for children. He and Béla Bartók collected songs in Hungary, Rumania, and in other parts of Southeastern Europe; his Ph.D. thesis was on the stanzaic structure of Hungarian folk song. He lectured on composition, harmony, counterpoint, and orchestration at the Academy of Music in Budapest from 1907 to 1940. His best-known works, including the *Háry Janós Suite, Dances of Marosszek, Dances of Galanta*, and *Summer Evening*, feature folk song and folk-like melodies for orchestral instruments. As a vocally oriented composer, his many choruses and eleven books of folk-song arrangements demonstrated the characteristic features of his cultural heritage to Hungarians and to the world.

By the early 1920s, he was writing singing and reading exercises and composing group vocal works that revived the Hungarian choral movement. Kodály started a singing movement for young people in the 1930s that soon brought about a radical change in the manner in which children were musically educated in elementary schools. Although he never taught in a primary or secondary school, Kodály's ideas on pedagogy challenged generations of musicians and teachers to raise the music potential of their students. His educational ideas on singing, solmization, reading, and folk song material crystallized in what has become known as the "Kodály method." The method was elaborated by students and colleagues, including Jenö Adám, Lajos Bárdos,

Katalin Forrai, György Kerényi, Benjamin Rajeczky, and Erzsébet Szönyi. Kodály traveled through Hungary, giving encouragement to group singing as the basis for a broad musical culture. In his later years, the Hungarian government was persuaded to give financial support to strong school music instruction.

The Kodály pedagogy in Hungary stipulated four to six weekly periods of music from kindergarten through secondary levels, and a sequence of musical experiences that progressed from rhythm training through singing to instrumental lessons. American-style Kodály retains the use of pentatonic folk songs, the Tonic Sol-fa approach to sight reading with its hand signs, a rhythmic system of mnemonic syllables, and an emphasis on unaccompanied song. As part of the focus on music reading and writing, a preparatory period of ear training emphasizes rhythmic and melodic patterns that are encountered in songs and later in visual form. The development of inner hearing—the capacity to "think" musical sounds without hearing or necessarily voicing them—is important to Kodály training.

Relative or *movable do* is used for solfège exercises, where the tonic of the scale moves: C is do in C Major and D is do in D Major, and so on. Such a system is seen as an efficient means of understanding the function of individual scale degrees in various keys, by allowing the tonic of the key to provide an aural anchor for dominant, subdominant, and other tonal functions. An adaptation of the French Cheve system of rhythmic mnemonics is also a critical

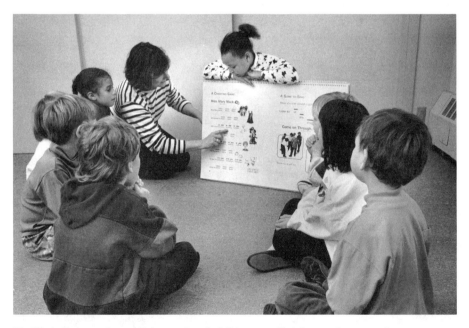

Kodály's literacy thrust: Primary-level children reading large-chart notation.

Table 3.2 Sampling Kodály

---

1. Inner hearing I: Recall the melody of an art-music selection or folk song, and sing it using solfège syllables. Later, sing with hand signs. In a similar way, chant the melodic rhythm of an art music or folk selection using rhythm syllables.

2. Inner hearing II: Sing a familiar song. On cue, continue to sing it silently. On another cue, sing it aloud.

3. Literacy I: Following study of isolated rhythmic and melodic patterns—their sounds and notational symbols—sight-read a new song that includes these patterns.

4. Literacy II: Take dictation on familiar, and later not-so-familiar, songs and musical selections. Allow the use of invented notation, then stick notation for rhythm, and finally staff notation for melodies.

---

technique, particularly for younger children, in learning rhythmic values and their relationships in a pattern. The chanting of "ta ti-ti's" is well-known as a technique to be used by students of every level for mastering difficult rhythms. The sequence by which rhythmic and melodic phrases and fragments are taught is also specified by the Kodály approach (see also Chapters 4–6).

The most basic of Kodály's ideas, that the use of good music is vital to the life of every person, is a challenging one for American teachers. Kodály recognized art music of the European tradition and its folk or traditional origins as "good." He especially favored the beautiful pentatonic melodies of the Hungarians, and greatly admired the a cappella vocal music of the Renaissance. For American teachers, not only Western European art music, but also the many coexisting musical cultures of American society present rich resources of "good" music for use with children. Some popular music is equally vibrant, with beautiful melodies, exciting rhythms, and resonant timbres. Table 3.2 presents some sample experiences in the Kodály method.

Works by Choksy (1981, 1988), Szönyi (1974–1979), and Forrai with Sinor (1988) provide information on materials and sequence espoused by Kodály. Kodály's philosophical position on music instruction, and a history of the early years of the "movement," are set down in his collected writings (1974).

Orff

The influence of the Orff approach on the teaching of music to children has been explosive since its introduction to North America in the 1960s. The natural behaviors of childhood—singing, saying, dancing, playing, along with improvisation and creative movement—form the basis of the Orff-Schulwerk (literally "school work"). Frequently referred to as "elemental" music making, the pedagogy is closely linked to the child's world of play and fantasy, of games, chants, and songs. In its original form, elemental music was pre-intellectual and exploratory, with music, movement, and speech interrelated and overlapping. While the prevalence of special-model "Orff xylophones" of wood and metal are testimony to its popularity, the Orff approach is far richer and more varied in its musical experiences than initial exposure to the pedagogy may suggest.

The Schulwerk grew from the ideas of German composer Carl Orff (1895–1982), whose experimentation with musicians and dancers in the 1920s planted the seeds for his method's association of music with dance and theater. Together with dancer Dorothee Günther, Carl Orff established an experimental school in Munich, the Güntherschule, for the integration of the performing arts. A Güntherschule ensemble of dancers, players, and singers, many of them preparing to be teachers, performed at educational conferences throughout Europe.

With the destruction of the Güntherschule during World War II, Orff set out with a young musician–teacher named Gunild Keetman to restore the spirit of integrated music and movement through radio broadcasts, focusing on children rather than adults. He believed children to be naturally musical, uninhibited in their expressive movement, and more receptive to his brand of musical training than adults. Their collaborative efforts resulted in the establishment of the Schulwerk method and the publication of five volumes of chants, songs, and instrumental pieces called *Musik für Kinder* (Music for Children). Canadian and then American adaptations of Orff's and Keetman's work in the 1960s helped to spread their pedagogy across the world.

Principal components of the Schulwerk as conceived and practiced in Europe are the imitation and exploration of music and its components, with opportunities to improvise original pieces available as learners become more musically skilled. As adapted in the United States, the process is extended to four stages: imitation; exploration; literacy; and improvisation. *Imitation* may be simultaneous, or it may be canonic—either echo-like in the form of an interrupted canon (leader claps, then the group) or overlapping in a continuous canon. Imitation may occur through song, movement, or through performance on pitched or nonpitched percussion instruments. *Exploration* challenges children's imaginations to find new ways to apply learned information, for example, "Now that we know the rhythm ♩ ♩. ♫♩ ♩., can you play it (faster/slower, louder/softer, on a different instrument, on two alternating pitches)?"

Literacy, or competence in reading and writing music, is a development of children's earlier musical experiences, and progresses toward the skillful use

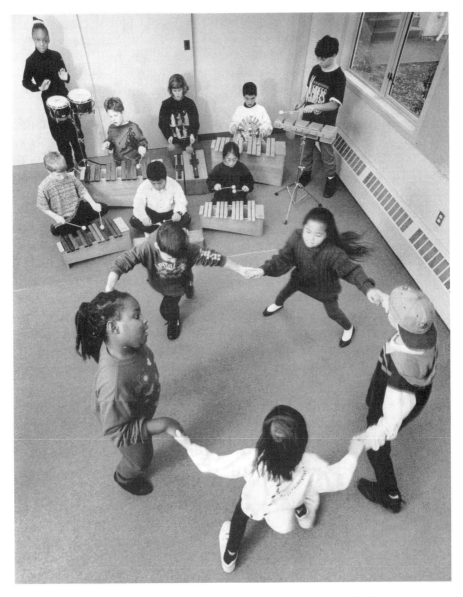

Integrating musical experiences via the Orff approach: Children singing, moving, and playing.

of both graphic and conventional staff notation. The Schulwerk advocates extensive musical experience before literacy can become a truly musical rather than a mechanical tool, and a means for children to preserve the music they create. Rhythmic notation for quarter notes and eighth notes may be introduced in kindergarten and first grade, with melodic notation beginning with limited pitches (sol-mi and mi-re-do) in the first grade, proceeding to the pentatonic scale by second and third grade, and extending to the reading and writing of the diatonic scale by the fifth grade.

Improvisation is the ultimate stage of the Orff process, allowing musical invention that emanates from earlier learning. It is conceivable for improvisation to occur in preliterate stages as well, but the abilities to read and write music provide children with greater knowledge of musical structures for the original works they create. In this sense, improvisation is the culminating experience that demonstrates extensive musical knowledge and creative expression. The earlier stage of growth (exploration) involves changing one component within a familiar rhythm, chant, song, movement, or instrumental piece, while improvisation is the combination of skills and understanding into new and original forms. In this way, improvisation becomes the ultimate aim of comprehensive musicianship for children through the American-style Orff approach.

The Orff process is complemented by the use of such musical features as folk and folk-like songs in the pentatonic mode, ostinato patterns that are spoken, sung, played, and moved, tonic drones or pedal tones, and static and moving bourdon accompaniments on xylophones and various other percussion instruments. These are the more prominent facets of the Schulwerk; the modes of music making in the four-step process are its pedagogy. Table 3.3 offers some suggestions for incorporating Orff approach into classes.

Among the most thorough accounts of the Orff-Schulwerk are the volumes by Frazee (1987), Steen (1992), and Warner (1991), while Keetman presents earlier perspectives on the Schulwerk (1970). The classic Schulwerk in its

Table 3.3 Sampling Orff

---

1. Imitation: Imitate a partner's eight-beat body percussion piece. Turn the piece into a movement piece, again with one partner following the movement immediately after its performance by the other partner.

2. Exploration: Experiment with different ways of rendering a familiar folk song, altering just one musical element at a time (for example, dynamics, tempo, mode, meter, accompaniment).

3. Literacy: Compose an eight-beat piece that can be graphically notated. Write it as closely as possible on staff notation. Pass the piece to a friend or a new group to perform.

4. Improvisation: Choose a poem. Chant it rhythmically, and then add a non-pitched percussion accompaniment. Turn it into a three-pitch song with pitched accompaniment and movement to express its form.

---

original but translated (1978) version, as well as Orff's and Keetman's *Musik für Kinder* (1950–1954) and the English-language version by Hall (1956) are particularly valuable to those wishing to pursue the historical foundations of the approach.

Other Approaches

Comprehensive Musicianship

The interdisciplinary study of music is the thrust of the approach called Comprehensive Musicianship, which advocates the integration of performance, theory, history and literature, and composition in the music curriculum—all in a single lesson. The Ford Foundation funded the Contemporary Music Project (CMP) in 1963 to reshape school music programs to give greater emphasis to creative composition and contemporary music, to bring composers into contact with children, and to reduce the compartmentalization of the music profession into separate subdisciplines.

The CMP sponsored a Seminar on Comprehensive Musicianship at Northwestern University in 1965. This seminar changed the direction of CMP from one of contemporary music in the schools to that of the broad-based teaching of all musical styles through the development of performance, listening and analysis, and compositional and improvisational competences. A series of regional institutes brought these ideas on curriculum revision to collegiate, secondary, and elementary teachers.

While Comprehensive Musicianship was intended to influence all levels of music instruction, it appears to have quite naturally found a home in music classes for children. One of its major thrusts is the common elements approach to music, such that music of any style can be studied through its sound properties of frequency (pitch), duration (rhythm), intensity (loudness), and timbre. These elements make for convenient organizers of listening lessons, suggesting questions on high and low pitches, short and long rhythmic values, loud and soft volumes, and the quality of instrumental, vocal, and other sounds. They are related to the six elements made popular by the basal music textbook series: melody, rhythm, texture, form, dynamics, and timbre.

Children who are taught with the goals of Comprehensive Musicianship in mind are actively involved in listening to and performing representative musics of many cultures and time periods. There are few lessons devoted completely to singing or playing of instruments without some opportunity to experience the "real thing" on recordings, as performed by trained musicians. Children are led to understand music by listening analytically to a piece, performing it when possible (or sampling fragments of it, such as a recurring rhythmic pattern or melody), and by taking what they know and transferring it creatively to new compositions and improvisations they invent. Fuller explanations of Comprehensive Musicianship can be found in Thomson (1974) and by Choksy et al. (1986).

Gordon

American music educator Edwin E. Gordon (b. 1928) began to develop a sequence for music instruction in the 1970s, culminating in the formulation of his music learning theory. He coined the term "audiation" to refer to the goal of music instruction: inner hearing (or hearing music in the mind when it is not physically present). Similar to the classic European pedagogies, Gordon supports the sound-before-symbol approach to music instruction. As in the development of language, children listen to tonal and rhythm patterns, imitate them, and then read and write them. Audiation occurs when children have had ample listening experiences, so that they can see a notated rhythm or melody and make musical sense of it, "hearing" it even if it is not sounded aloud.

Gordon's theory of music learning suggests a hierarchy of musical skill-building that begins with aural perception and discriminative listening, progresses through the development of music reading and writing, improvisation, and on to a theoretical understanding of music. The eight-step hierarchy of his learning sequence is:

Discrimination learning
    Aural/oral
    Verbal association
    Partial synthesis
    Symbolic association
    Composite synthesis
Inference learning
    Generalization
    Creativity/improvisation
    Theoretical understanding

Discrimination learning begins with listening and imitation of small patterns of sound, often on a neutral syllable. These tonal and rhythm patterns are then given *verbal associations* by way of solfège syllables and a set of mnemonic rhythm syllables [for example, ♩♫ = du du-de or ♩♫♫ = du du-ta-de-ta]. *Partial synthesis* is the testing of children to determine how well they are able to aurally recognize and discriminate tonal and rhythm patterns that have been taught. Their success in this stage prepares them for *symbolic association*, the introduction of the written symbols for the solfège and rhythmic mnemonic syllables students have listened to, imitated, and aurally identified. There is no discussion of "quarter notes and eighth notes" at this level, but rather the shift of what they hear to how it is symbolized—and vice versa. A *composite synthesis* is achieved when isolated notational patterns can be grouped in a series (in a song's notation), and read with ease. Likewise, children should be able to notate an aurally dictated melody or rhythm that uses familiar patterns that have been previously sounded and symbolized.

Inference learning is a higher-order learning, largely of unfamiliar stimuli. It begins with *generalization*, a test of whether children can transfer familiar tonal and rhythm patterns to new pieces, to be read or written. *Improvisation and composition* encourages the use of learned patterns in new and personally creative ways, with opportunities for children to notate what they have invented. The final stage, *theoretical understanding*, allows for the acquisition of knowledge about why music is what it is, as well as what meter and key signatures mean, how lines and spaces of a staff are "lettered," what relationships a series of pitches may have, and the mathematical values of rhythms. Theory is last in the sequence, following all opportunities to know music aurally, orally, and symbolically.

Gordon's sequence is further revealed in the textbook series he coauthored with David Woods, *Jump Right In! The Music Curriculum* (1990). Exercises and songs that reinforce tonal and rhythm patterns are included for children from kindergarten through middle school. The theoretical framework for the series is found in Gordon (1984, 1994).

Manhattanville Music Curriculum Project

During the review and redesign of music instruction programs in the 1960s, the Manhattanville Music Curriculum Project (MMCP) emerged as one of the most progressive and influential programs. Funded by the U.S. Office of Education and named for Manhattanville College where it originated, it was as intensive as it was extensive. The project resulted in a comprehensive curriculum for grades three to twelve that derived from children's rather than the teacher's perspective, providing a sequence of basic musical concepts to be learned through exploratory yet teacher-guided experiences. MMCP connected learning from one grade level to the next via a spiral of progressively more sophisticated aspects of the musical elements, in a variety of musical styles.

MMCP is strongly anchored in the tradition of perceiving by exploring, and of understanding by creating, improvising, and composing. Children are encouraged to experience music by sampling their own sound world, by making sounds with their bodies: snapping; clapping; patting; stamping; whistling; tapping; shuffling; moaning; and various vocalizations. They are stimulated to produce "found sounds" through objects they gather, and new instruments they can build. They develop concepts of pitch (melody and texture), rhythm, form, dynamics, and timbre by creating their own musical expressions, and eventually notating them. These concepts become increasingly more sophisticated as children mature (Figure 3.1).

As advocated by director Ronald B. Thomas (1970), MMCP includes seven types of experiences: MMCP strategies (composing, performing, evaluating, conducting, listening); student recitals; listening to recordings; research and oral reports; guest recitals; skill development; and group singing. Children's musical expressions are stimulated through new ideas in the music selections they hear. Composed pieces are approached holistically, so that children not only listen to them, but conduct them, perform them, invent variations, and then create entirely new compositions inspired by them. MMCP supports the development of aural, dexterous (performing and conducting), and translative (notational) skills—with emphasis on graphic forms invented by children.

MMCP has fostered an attitude that some of the most meaningful music learning occurs when the environment is informal and relaxed, and when the teacher's approach flexible enough to accommodate children's unique learning styles. Effective music instruction incorporates alternative sound sources for making music, the room and space for movement and for gathering in groups of performers and composers, and enough time to work through musical problems.

Music in Education

In the 1980s, technology-assisted music instruction entered the realm of the music classroom. The Yamaha Corporation developed a new interest in children's conceptual learning of music through the computer and computerized keyboard programs. Their Music in Education (MIE) approach suggests that children supplied with keyboards can build aural, performance, and notational skills in an integrative way.

The MIE goals are to develop intelligent listeners who can describe and discuss the music they hear, make, and create. The curriculum includes print materials, software, and hardware, each integrated with one another, and divided into 145 learning modules that focus on specific elemental areas and musical concepts—from beat and meter to tonality and atonality, and from ostinato accompaniments to chord progressions in major and minor keys. The curriculum offers a repertoire that includes folk songs ("New River Train"), patriotic songs ("America"), "pop" songs, songs from popular musicals ("My

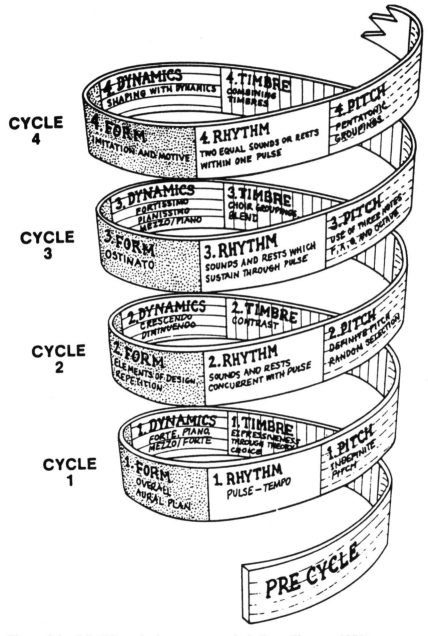

Figure 3.1. MMCP curriculum concept spiral. *From Thomas (1970).*

Favorite Things"), and classical selections ("Eine Kleine Nachtmusik"). Children progress at their own pace through exercises in melodic and rhythmic dictation, composition, and, of course, keyboard performance. Ensemble and independent performances, and class and independent study, are possible through MIE.

The computer is critical to the MIE program, allowing children access to instruction, rehearsal and review, and evaluation of their skill and knowledge attainment. It is central in providing children with performance experience on keyboards that utilize MIDI (Music Instrument Digital Interface) technology. Children thus learn concepts, performance skills, and repertoire through the synthesized MIDI sounds they make and create. Pilot programs have proven MIE to be a highly successful curriculum for attaining music literacy. The continuing evolution of MIE can be traced by reading the two manuals entitled *Program Components* and *Scope and Sequence*, both published in 1989.

Education through Music

As the sound of its title indicates, Education Through Music (ETM) is a holistic approach to music instruction. American music educator Mary Helen Richards was fascinated with ways in which the Kodály pedagogy could be adapted to the needs of children and teachers in the United States. Following extensive correspondence with Zoltán Kodály and observations in Hungarian schools, she began her adaptation of the Kodály principles to English-language songs and American curricular emphases. In the 1960s, Richards published her songs and instructional sequence in *Threshold to Music*, a series of books and charts that were a prelude to ETM. She used Kodály's suggestions in finding folk songs from the North American continent to introduce to children, and became fascinated with the relationship between the ways songs and language were acquired through pattern recognition.

The first- and second-level goals of ETM are to bring children comfort and self-esteem, as well as cooperation with others, within the context of group music making. These are followed and supported by the goals of aural skill acquisition and an understanding of the melodic and rhythmic patterns of the musical language. The ETM approach makes use of folk songs and singing games of the United States and British Isles. Many of the songs are selected because of their involvement of children in both singing and kinesthetic experiences ("actions," circle games, line and partner dances, and so forth). Movement is viewed as a necessary technique for leading children in their discovery of melodic and rhythmic patterns, and repeated words and word-phrases. The pattern recognition touted by ETM prepares children for sight-reading. With literacy accomplished, the relationship of ETM to the Hungarian approach is undeniable—and is certainly acknowledged by its founder. Bennett (1987) offers a more complete description of the ETM approach.

Weikert

The growth of interest in movement as a component of music instruction in the 1980s led to the acceptance of the work of Phyllis Weikert. In her work in physical education and recreational folk dance, Weikert observed that people struggle with basic movement because they cannot maintain a steady beat. She devised a sequence for teaching folk and choreographed dance that takes into account the relationship between language and movement, and that underscores the development of beat competence through movement and dance. That four-step process has been found to be effective by music teachers who incorporate structured movement in their music classes, particularly folk dance, and who view the development of the feeling for steady beat as a primary instructional objective. Weikert's process is as follows:

Step I	Say	"Step-hop, step-hop, side-close"
Step II	Say and do	"Step-hop, step-hop, side-close"
Step III	Whisper and do	"Step-hop, step-hop, side-close"
Step IV	Do (think and do)	"Step-hop, step-hop, side-close"

Weikert's sequence is straightforward, and can be used by classroom teachers and physical-education instructors with limited musical training. Its chief contribution in music education is as a technique for teaching steady beat, rather than as a comprehensive method. It may best be used in remedial ways, or as supplementary to more musical pedagogies such as Dalcroze eurhythmics or Orff-Schulwerk. Weikert (1982) has published several volumes of folk-dance instructions that are accompanied by recordings of arranged dance music.

A Comparison of Methods and Techniques

Table 3.4 offers a comparison of the various pedagogical approaches, focusing on several categories: goals; recommended musical material; principal experiences; aural skills/ear-training techniques; approaches to literacy/notation; and instructional structure. Because of the necessary brevity of the chart, prominent factors are highlighted rather than all aspects of the pedagogy.

For discussion and comparison of several of these pedagogies, readers may wish to consult Carder (1991), Choksy et al. (1986), and Shehan (1986).

Table 3.4 A Comparison of Methods for Teaching Music to Children

Method	Founder	Goal	Musical Material
Dalcroze, or Dalcroze Eurhythmics	Émile Jaques-Dalcroze, theorist and composer	Natural rhythmic movement of the body to improve aural skills	Improvised music on the piano
Kodály; the Hungarian method	Zoltán Kodály, composer and ethnomusicologist	Musical literacy and inner hearing	Traditional folk music, and art music (in Hungary, Hungarian music first)
Orff-Schulwerk	Carl Orff, composer	Musical experience, expression through music	Folk songs and children's melodies
Comprehensive musicianship	Norman Dello Joio, composer (Contemporary Music Project), Robert Werner, music educator, and others	Descriptive, performing, and creative competence	Composed music, including contemporary, and traditional/world

Principal Experiences	Aural Skills	Notation	Instructional Sequence
Eurhythmics, solfège, improvisation	Fixed do, dichords, trichords, solfège combined with conducting/ movement	Phrases are mapped; single- and double-line staves lead to full staff	Germinal, building from a rhythmic phrase to a complete piece
Singing (a cappella), directed listening, folk songs, singing games, folk dance	Movable do and rhythmic mnemonics	Song patterns are heard, then sung/ chanted, then notated	Sequential development of melodic/ rhythmic vocabulary
Speech chants, movement, singing, instrumental performance, improvisation	Imitation and exploration of rhythmic and melodic patterns	In its original form: No prescribed system; preliterate experiences. In its American adaptation: Experiences preceding notational symbols	From imitation to exploration (to notational literacy) to improvisation
Relating theory/history to performance and composition; "common elements"	Listening and performing large works and discrete patterns	Representational icons leading to conventional notation	Sequence stemming from working curriculum

(*continued*)

Table 3.4 Continued

Method	Founder	Goal	Musical Material
Gordon; Music Learning Theory	Edwin E. Gordon, music educator	Audiation (Hearing music in the mind)	Tonal and rhythm patterns; folk and composed songs in *Jump Right In*
Manhattanville Music Curriculum Project (MMCP)	Ronald Thomas, music educator, and others	Improvement of musicianship through experimentation and exploration	Contemporary and other composed music, children's sound pieces
Music in Education (MIE)	Yamaha Corporation	Keyboard, aural and notational skills	Keyboard arrangements of folk, patriotic, popular songs; classical works
Education through Music (ETM)	Mary Helen Richards, music educator	Musical literacy and inner hearing	Traditional folk music of the United States and British Isles
Weikert	Phyllis Weikert, physical education specialist	Development of feeling for steady beat	Recorded arrangements of folk-dance music

Principal Experiences	Aural Skills	Notation	Instructional Sequence
Listening, reading, writing discrete tonal and rhythm patterns	Aural/oral rote learning, to movable do and rhythmic mnemonics	Easy, moderate, and difficult patterns to hear, read, write	Eight-step process in two phases: discrimination and inference learning
Exploring, creating, performing	Listening to environmental sounds and composed pieces	Emphasis on invented icons and graphs	Stemming from children's needs and interests; seven guides
Keyboard experiences	Melodic and rhythmic dictation exercises at the keyboard	Staff notation and terminology through keyboard performance	Designated through 145 instructional modules
Singing, directed listening, games/dances	Movable do and rhythmic mnemonics	Song patterns are heard, sung/chanted, then notated	Sequential development of melodic/rhythmic vocabulary
Folk dancing	Not addressed	Not addressed	Four-step sequence for folk-dance instruction; books with recordings

A Personal Method

Despite the myriad of techniques intended to advance the musical development of children, each teacher in the end chooses to incorporate those pedagogical aspects that are harmonious with his or her personal goals and definitions of music education. Often, those goals are based upon the teacher's own
musical strengths and personal preferences in music and instruction. Singers
may be inclined to sing more than to move or to play, pianists may be more
prone to utilize a keyboard laboratory or to accompany songs and movement
on the piano, and kinesthetically oriented teachers may center their music instruction on assorted movement experiences. There is no one correct way to
teach musical understanding, skills, and values, nor is there only one of ten
standard ways to approach these goals.

"We teach as we have been taught" is an adage relevant to the philosophy
that guides instruction, and to the techniques selected and blended into each
teacher's personal pedagogy. Undergraduate programs leading to degrees and
teaching certification in music provide teachers with extensive preparation in
applied music, aural and keyboard skills, ensemble performance, conducting,
theory, and history/culture, with occasional courses in improvisation and
composition. This training, when coupled with methods courses that emphasize musical materials and techniques proven to be effective in teaching children, holds the potential for producing independent and successful musician–
educators. Instruction is further shaped through additional training in music.
A postgraduate course in conducting may direct a teacher's attention toward
potential movement and expressive gestures that children may learn to use as
they listen and perform a song. A clinic taken in improvisation may inspire
lessons in creative musical thinking and doing. A string of workshops in tech-
nology-oriented instruction or in the music of world cultures will provide a
teacher not only with new musical materials, but also with innovative instructional techniques. A graduate course in ear-training, theory, or analysis will
hone a teacher's listening skills, while also providing approaches for training
children's ears. The development of musicianship is an ongoing process. To
use colloquial expressions, when we don't (continue to) train, we don't gain,
and when we don't use it (the musical skills we may have earlier developed),
we lose it.

Training in the classic and contemporary methods of music instruction for
children can greatly enhance the development of a personal teaching method.
Summer courses in Kodály, Dalcroze, and Orff are provided at universities
throughout North America and abroad, with certification available following
extensive coursework and demonstration of selected proficiencies in music,
teaching, and planning. Also, there are summer courses on the approaches

espoused by Gordon, Weikert, Education through Music, and Music in Education. Training in these methods leads to the adaptation of aspects of their philosophies, goals, and techniques, for these all are logical pathways that have been "tested" with children. In the end, however, the teacher's interests, strengths, and classroom needs emerge again to bring about the blend of a newly acquired layer of skills with those that the teacher has used for some time.

A personal method of music instruction does not preclude the opportunity to find affinities with certain established methods. More than likely, the teacher who strives for greater musicianship will seek out the set of techniques that appeal to his or her personal interests. But does the provision of movement experiences classify her as a follower of Dalcroze? Does an emphasis on folk song and the great art music make him a Kodály teacher? Does the rhythmic chanting of poetry brand them followers of Orff? Or is there variation among the practices of teachers who have been influenced by the pedagogical emphases of Dalcroze, Kodály, or Orff? All teachers make choices in the techniques and musical materials they select for use with children, and most might conceivably be judged as showing an inclination toward one or another known method. Still, the personalization of these techniques and methods following training is the true test of the teacher's independent musicianship and ability to lead children in their own musical development.

Questions

1. What are the relationships among the three classic European methods (Dalcroze, Kodály, Orff) regarding the development of: (1) aural skills; (2) musical literacy; and (3) creative musical expression?

2. Which pedagogies stress the use of movement as an instructional technique? To what extent does movement advance musical understanding in these pedagogies?

3. What is the relationship of "inner hearing" to "audiation"? Which methods espouse these goals?

4. Which approaches are "American-made"? In what ways? Are the European methods suitable for adaptation in American settings? How?

5. What aspects of these notated pedagogies for children can be continued into the realm of music instruction for adolescents? Adults? In choral settings? Instrumental settings?

Activities

1. Identify and observe the teaching of those trained in the techniques of a specific pedagogy. Discuss with them their philosophy and goals, and note their use of specific techniques and media.

2. Experiment with the samples of the Dalcroze, Kodály, and Orff pedagogies. Design and implement original examples of the principles.

3. Select a musical concept: $\frac{3}{4}$ meter, m-r-d, ♫ ♩ ♫ ♩, binary form. Design three (or more) ways of teaching the concept, using the distinctive techniques and materials of three (or more) methods.

4. Interview teachers regarding their personal goals of music experience and instruction for children, their preferred techniques, and professional activity and advanced training/certification. Later, note any overlap of goals and techniques.

5. In a letter to the principal, describe your personal method of instruction. Include a statement of goals, principal experiences, musical materials and techniques you use.

References

BENNETT, P. (1987). The evolution of education through music. *Music Educators Journal, 74,* 1.

CARDER, P. (Ed.). (1991). *The eclectic curriculum in American music education.* Reston, VA: Music Educators National Conference.

CHOKSY, L. (1981). *The Kodály context.* Englewood Cliffs, NJ: Prentice-Hall.

———. (1988). *The Kodály method* (2nd ed.). Englewood Cliffs, NJ: Prentice-Hall.

CHOKSY, L., ABRAMSON, R. M., GILLESPIE, A. E., & WOODS, D. (1986). *Teaching music in the twentieth century.* Englewood Cliffs, NJ: Prentice-Hall.

FINDLAY, E. (1971). *Rhythm and movement: Applications of Dalcroze eurhythmics.* Evanston, IL: Summy-Birchard.

FORRAI, K., with SINOR, J. (1988). *Music in preschool.* Budapest, Hung.: Corvina Press.

FRAZEE, J. (1987). *Discovering Orff: A curriculum for music teachers.* New York: Schott.

GORDON, E. E. (1994). *Learning sequences in music: Skill, content and patterns.* Chicago: G.I.A. Publications.

GORDON, E. E., & WOODS, D. (1990). *Jump right in! The music curriculum.* Chicago: G.I.A. Publications.

HALL, D. (1956). *Music for children.* Mainz, Ger.: B. Schott's Sohne.

JAQUES-DALCROZE, ÉMILE (1921/1970). *Rhythm, music and education.* Rubenstein, H. F. (Trans.). London: The Dalcroze Society.

KEETMAN, G. (1970). *Elementaria: First acquaintance with Orff-Schulwerk.* London: Schott.

KODÁLY, ZOLTÁN (1974). *The selected writings of Zoltán Kodály,* F. Bonis, (Ed.), L. Halapy, & F. Macnicol, (Trans.). London: Boosey and Hawkes.

MEAD, V. (1994). *Dalcroze eurhythmics in today's music classrooms.* New York: Schott.

Music in Education. (1989). *Program components.* Buena Park, CA: Yamaha Corporation.

———. (1989). *Scope and sequence.* Buena Park, CA: Yamaha Corporation.

ORFF, C., & KEETMAN, G. (1950–54). *Musik für Kinder.* Mainz, Ger.: B. Schott's Sohne.

SHEHAN, P. K. (1986). Major approaches to music education. *Music Educators Journal, 72*(6), 26–31.

STEEN, A. (1992). *Exploring Orff.* New York: Schott.

SZÖNYI, E. (1974–79). *Musical reading and writing* (3 vols.). New York: Boosey and Hawkes.

THOMAS, R. B. (1970). *Manhattanville Music Curriculum Program: Final report.* Washington, DC: U.S. Office of Education, Bureau of Research. ERIC document ED 045 865.

THOMSON, W. (1974). *Comprehensive musicianship through classroom music.* Belmont, CA: Addison-Wesley.

WARNER, B. (1991). *Orff-Schulwerk: Applications for the classroom.* Englewood Cliffs, NJ: Prentice-Hall.

WEIKART, P. S. (1982). *Teaching movement and dance* (2 vols.). Ypsilanti, MI: High Scope.

Organizations

The Dalcroze Society of America. Julia Schnebly-Black, President. School of Music DN-10, University of Washington, Seattle, WA 98195.

Education through Music (Richards Institute of Music Education and Research). 149 Corte Madera, Portola Valley, CA 94028.

Institut Jaques-Dalcroze. M. Dominique Porte, Directeur, 44 Rue de la Ter-rassiere, Geneva, Switzerland 1206.

Organization of American Kodály Educators. Richard Merrill, Executive Di-rector, 823 Old Westtown Rd., West Chester, PA, 19382.

International Kodály Society. Budapest, P.O. Box 8, H-1502, Hungary.

American Orff-Schulwerk Association. P.O. Box 391089, Cleveland, OH 44139.

Music Learning Theory/Edwin E. Gordon. G. I. A. Publications, Inc. 7404 S. Mason Ave., Chicago, IL 60638.

Music in Education, Yamaha International, 6600 Orangethorpe Ave., Buena Park, CA 90622-6600.

4

Rhythm and the Child

Rhythm is everywhere in the life of children. When children speak, their words tumble and flow in regular streams of sounds, in starts and stops, with emphasis or not. When they move, they step regularly; they run, hop, jump, and skip in rhythms of their own. The rhythms they experience extend beyond speech and movement: Maria hears the rhythm of her mother's heartbeat, soft and steady, and is soothed by it. Ryan can feel the throbbing of his own pulse as he holds his wrist, feeling it gradually decrease in speed as he settles down after hopping around the playground. When Lamont recites a favorite poem, he gives accent and rhythm to the rhyming words, shaping them into units of loudness and softness, and faster and slower sounds. Jacqueline pours her very own rhythm into the teddy bear, dancing him in time to the tune she hums. When the grind of a homework assignment presses him, Robby raps as he rhythmically reads aloud his weekly list of spelling words. With surprising frequency, rhythm emerges in the things that children do.

Children at play or at work show their natural attraction to and fascination with rhythm. The word comes from the Greek verb "rhein" meaning "to flow." Children flow eagerly through rhythmic experiences that engage them in listening, speaking, or moving. They develop greater rhythmic facility naturally and easily while singing, and when rhythm is embedded in language and movement. The counting of beats can be experienced later as a higher level of musical knowing, but children's first experience with rhythms is through their daily speech and movement.

Children learn to understand concepts of rhythm in music through their teachers and musically sensitive parents. In school music classes as well as through private instrumental instruction, children learn by participating in the activity of a sequenced curriculum. Children chant, sing, listen, play, read, and write their way to a thorough knowledge of pulse (or beat), subdivisions and extensions of the pulse (for example ♫ and ♩), other durations and patterns of rhythm (and their related rests), accents, meter, syncopation, and polyrhythms. Children's natural affinity for rhythm is more fully realized through training, taking them from the experiences of listening and responding to rhythms to reading and writing the notes that symbolize them, or music literacy.

Rhythm and Child Development

The mother's heartbeat, initially experienced in the prenatal environment, may be the earliest rhythmic experience of all. In early infancy, children then add the rhythmicity of sounds in their environment—the rocking movements and rhythmic cooings made by their parents, the pulse of music emanating from televisions and stereos, and the often regular loud-soft and fast-slow gradations of speech in conversations that surround them. Well within their first year, children respond rhythmically to music as they sway, rock, and bounce. Toddlers may "show" their perception of rhythm through the rhythmic dance-like movements they perform, first with others and then by themselves. Indeed, young children experience rhythm by feeling, hearing, and moving to it. Table 4.1 summarizes aspects of children's developmental stages of rhythmic perception and understanding.

The spontaneous songs children sing become increasingly rhythmic with age. Beginning with musical babbling at one year to eighteen months, when their singing is often a string of pitches with occasional and often irregular pauses for breaths to occur, children at two years may already be framing their melodies around steady beats within and between phrases. By three years of age, children's songs may take on rhythmic structures that include strong metric tendencies and recurring patterns. With increasing exposure to standard nursery rhymes, chants, and songs, as well as to folk and popular songs, preschool children are often integrating rather sophisticated rhythmic patterns into their spontaneous songs. Their attempts to reproduce songs presented to them also become more accurate in both rhythmic and melodic elements as they approach school age.

Moorhead and Pond (1978) observed that preschool children's spontaneous sounds are first regular in pulse but unaccented. Keeping a steady pulse appears to be developmental; while few three-year-old children can tap, clap, or pat in time to a set regular pulse, most six-year-olds accomplish this task with great accuracy. "Beat competence" is widely evident by first grade, and yet some children still require training, or at least reinforcement of the skill, to maintain a steady beat. The accurate replication of short rhythmic patterns by young children reveals a similar developmental progression from toddler

Table 4.1 Children's Rhythmic Development

Age (years)	Developmental Skill
Less than one	Demonstrates rhythmic swaying, rocking, bouncing
One/two	Demonstrates babbling in irregular rhythmic patterns Performs dancelike rhythmic movements
Two	Sings spontaneous songs framed around regular rhythmic pulses and patterns
Three	Sings spontaneous songs with some feeling for meter, and with regularly recurring rhythmic patterns Imitates short rhythmic patterns
Four/five (Kindergarten)	Taps in time to a regular set pulse Begins to develop rhythmic clapping and patting Replicates short rhythmic patterns on instruments
Six/seven (Grades one/two)	Distinguishes fast and slow, long and short Can perform songs faster and slower Can PRW* quarter, eighth, and half note rhythms
Eight/nine (Grade three)	Can PRW dotted-quarter/eighth notes (♩. ♪), and syncopated quarter and eighth note rhythms (♪♩ ♪) Can recognize and conduct music in $\frac{2}{4}$, $\frac{4}{4}$, $\frac{6}{8}$, and $\frac{3}{4}$ meter
Nine/ten (Grade four)	Can PRW sixteenth note patterns (♬♬ ♫♬ ♬♩) Can recognize and conduct music in "cut time" and compound meters ($\frac{9}{8}$, $\frac{12}{8}$)
Ten/eleven/twelve (Grades five/six)	Can PRW dotted eighth and sixteenth note patterns (♪. ♪.) Can recognize and conduct music in asymmetric meters ($\frac{5}{8}$, $\frac{7}{8}$)

*PRW, perform, read, and write.

through kindergarten age. Not only does rhythmic perception develop quite early, but also the abilities to perform (or "produce") pulse and to reproduce patterns emerge even before most children begin formal schooling.

With increasing musical exposure, children in the elementary grades evolve a sophisticated understanding of how music is organized rhythmically. Primary-grade children demonstrate their readiness for learning about tempo, durations, and metric groupings through their rhythmic chants and through the rhythmic recitation of numbers, letters, words, and word-phrases. They learn to use the regular rhythmic pulses and patterns of spoken language, and how to use expressively the accents, flow, and shadings of language in ways that parallel musical expression.

In first grade, children typically can discern fast from slow, and long from short; this prepares them for experiences in performing songs faster and slower, and for recognizing the sounds of quarter notes and their eighth note subdivisions. By second grade, they usually are capable of reading and writing various rhythmic patterns based first on quarter and eighth notes, and then with the addition of half notes. Third-grade children (who have had sufficient practice with earlier durations) are ready for directed listening and the performance of music with dotted quarter notes and syncopated patterns that mix quarter- and eighth-notes (♪ ♩ ♪) and can develop the skills to read and write patterns with these durations. During this period, children become capable of discerning the metric grouping of pulses in simple duple ($\frac{2}{4}$ and $\frac{4}{4}$), compound duple ($\frac{6}{8}$), and triple ($\frac{3}{4}$) time, showing their knowledge through conducting patterns and various other movements.

With a solid foundation of rhythmic understanding, and the development of skills for performing, reading, and writing, children in the intermediate grades can progress easily into experiences with rhythms of greater complexity. Sixteenth notes, along with patterns combining sixteenth and eighth notes (♬ and ♬), can be introduced to fourth-grade children, dotted eighth and sixteenth note patterns (♪♪ and ♪♪.) to fifth-grade children, and triplets to children in the sixth grade. With an understanding of music in $\frac{2}{4}$, $\frac{4}{4}$, $\frac{6}{8}$, and $\frac{3}{4}$ underway, children can then explore other compound meters ($\frac{9}{8}$, $\frac{12}{8}$), "cut-time" or "alla breve" ($\frac{2}{2}$) as symbolized by ¢, as opposed to "common time" ($\frac{4}{4}$), and "irregular" or asymmetric meters ($\frac{5}{8}$ and $\frac{7}{8}$, for example). Many of the more sophisticated rhythmic concepts targeted for learning at the intermediate level are nonetheless inherent in popular music and children's listening preferences, and thus were experienced at younger ages.

The logic of a rhythm learning sequence must be set by teachers with a comprehensive knowledge of music and children's developmental levels. A large part of children's rhythmic perception develops without training, but the capacity to perform it, code it through notation, and decode it by reading the notation is dependent on instruction and a long experience in hearing these rhythms. A refined ability to discern the rhythmic nuances of music also is greatly enhanced through the directed listening that teachers provide. The rhythmic development and training of children is explored in a classic text by Hood and Schultz (1949), and more recently by others noted in this chapter.

Rhythm in Speech

The rhythm of spoken language is the natural gateway to musical rhythm. Words and word-phrases provide children with every component of rhythm—from the basic pulse to the multilayered complexity of polyrhythm.

Words become musical when: (1) they are spoken over the foundation of a set pulse; (2) their sounds are transformed into chants of longer and shorter musical durations; and, (3) some words in a group are emphasized over others. From the discovery of language in early childhood through the sophisticated wordplay of preadolescence, children develop musical understanding in their rhythmic chants.

Children can be made aware of musical rhythm through experiences that engage language as a tool for learning duration, accent, and temporal units. Because speech is oral, children learn its rhythmic patterns through enculturation, for example, by listening to their parents, older siblings, relatives, neighbors, and friends, as well as to speakers on the television, radio, and film. The media present "universal" patterns of the rhythmic flow and stress of language, a "homogenized" pronunciation of words and phrases. Children are not likely to intentionally distort or perform inaccurately the spoken language they have learned orally, and thus are readied for learning concepts of musical rhythm by the very nature of their extensive listening to language and speaking of it.

The Orff approach adheres to the development of rhythmic understanding through chant. Words of one, two, and three syllables form the building blocks of music, because they provide the substance for the recitation of longer and shorter durations equivalent to quarter, eighth, half, whole, and sixteenth notes, as well as triplets. Typically, children's names, or names of colors, fruits, or animals, provide occasions for chanting to a steady pulse. From single words, children can explore word-phrases, sentences, and paragraphs that equate to half-phrases of two measures, full phrases of four measures, and musical forms such as binary, ternary, and rondo. Greetings and farewells, colloquialisms, proverbs, rhymes, famous quotations, and poems are rich with potential for musical rhythm. As children recite these bits of speech and language, they come into contact with rhythmic values and nuances.

The pedagogy of Orff-Schulwerk provides not only experiences for rhythmic chanting, but also for the abstraction and accompaniment of speech rhythms by clapping, tapping, snapping, and stamping. While Carl Orff did not specify the transfer of rhythmic speech to the reading and writing of rhythmic notation, American proponents of the approach have successfully developed music literacy by following the extensive rhythmic experience with wordplay that they provide for their children. See Table 4.2 for examples of rhythm embedded in spoken phrases that can be incorporated within a lesson on pulse, durations, and durational patterns.

Because language is so fundamental to children's daily lives, they comfortably and easily express rhythmically its phonemes (sounds, including syllables) and phrases. While rhythmic chant is a musical realization of language,

Table 4.2 Rhythm in Speech

Rhythmic duration through name chants
Patting the pulse, chanting the words:

Rhythmic chants: Colors
Patting the pulse, clapping the off-beats, chanting the words:

Rhythmic chants: Animals
Patting the pulse, clapping the off-beats, chanting the words:

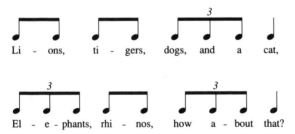

Table 4.2   Continued

Rhythmic chants: Fruits

Chanting with body rhythms:

Snap	pear.
	where.
Clap	peach - es
	fruits from
Pat	pine-ap-ple
	ev - 'ry
Stamp	Man - go,
	Tas - ty

A half-phrase of rhythm

Patting the pulse, chanting the words:
In a feeling of twos (2):

Birds   of   a   fea - ther

In a feeling of threes (3):

Birds   of   a   fea - ther

A full-phrase of rhythm

Patting the pulse, chanting the words:
In a feeling of twos (2):

Red   sky   at   morn - ing,

sail - ors   take   warn - ing.

In a feeling of threes (3):

Red   sky   at   morn - - ing,

sail - ors   take   warn - - ing.

(*continued*)

Table 4.2 Continued

A musical form: Rondo

Chanting the words, choosing the body rhythms:

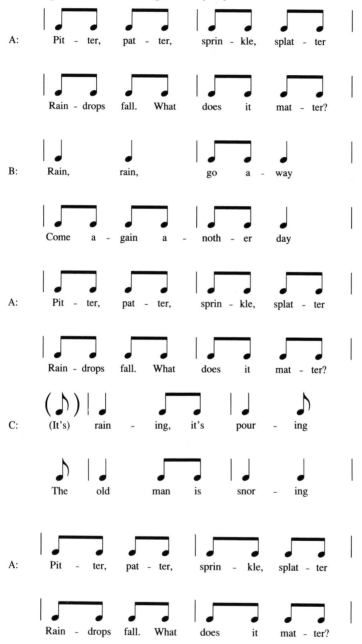

A: Pit – ter,   pat – ter,   sprin – kle,   splat – ter

      Rain – drops   fall.   What   does   it   mat – ter?

B: Rain,   rain,   go   a – way

      Come   a – gain   a – noth – er   day

A: Pit – ter,   pat – ter,   sprin – kle,   splat – ter

      Rain – drops   fall.   What   does   it   mat – ter?

C: (It's)   rain – ing,   it's   pour – ing

      The   old   man   is   snor – ing

A: Pit – ter,   pat – ter,   sprin – kle,   splat – ter

      Rain – drops   fall.   What   does   it   mat – ter?

Table 4.2 Continued

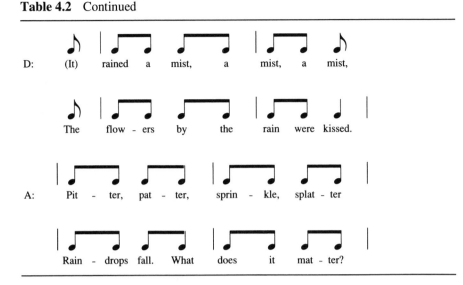

the challenge is to eventually "perform" the rhythms of the words while silencing the words themselves, to achieve a more complete musical understanding of the rhythmic components. After chanting, patting, clapping, tapping, stamping, and stepping the rhythm, can children fade away the words and maintain the integrity of the rhythm itself? After internalizing the rhythmic phrase, can they graph it—through dots, dashes, lines, and shapes? Can they notate it? Can they hear the rhythm of the word phrase in a new musical context—a song or recorded piece? Can they recognize the rhythm and read it when it occurs in notated music? These are sophisticated skills in the development of rhythmic understanding. It all begins with an awareness of the rhythm of speech. The work of Frazee (1987), Keetman (1974), Orff and Keetman (1956), Steen (1992), and Warner (1991) provide many examples of Orff practices of rhythmic speech.

Rhythm in Movement

Children of all ages enjoy physical activity. Together with speech, movement is a natural means by which children can develop an understanding of rhythm. Their movement to an underlying pulse, to subdivisions of the beat, and to rhythmic patterns almost guarantees their understanding of these musical elements. Once their ears receive and bodies respond to rhythm, children internalize the sound and feeling, leading to conceptualization. They come to know quarter notes, because they have walked them, and a pattern such as ♩♪ because they have skipped it. No mathematical analysis nor counting-out procedure is necessary. No notation is meaningful to children until they have sensed through movement its rhythmic essence.

When children are provided with occasions for moving rhythmically to music, they develop conceptual understanding relative to their natural developmental stage. Rhythmic movement may require their coordinated use of larger muscles in such locomotor activities as walking, running, skipping, galloping, hopping, jumping, or swaying, and in kinesthetic activities such as swinging the arms and conducting. Movement can also complement speech chants when children engage in patting, clapping, snapping, and stamping. Whether moving in place or across space, children grow in their understanding of rhythm when they can kinesthetically respond to what they hear.

The classic music pedagogies underscore the importance of movement as a tool for enhancing rhythmic development. The techniques of Dalcroze Eurhythmics are based on the belief that rhythm is the fundamental element of music, whose source is the natural locomotor rhythms of the human body. Dalcroze Eurhythmics includes exercises in conducting, stepping the beat, and changing movement qualities of speed, direction, and weight, all in an effort to reflect the rhythm of the music through movement. Carl Orff's elemental approach is based on the premise that rhythmic movement is inseparable from music itself, as it is also critical to the child's natural responses to his world. Rhythmic movement is not as central to the broader-based Schulwerk as it is to Dalcroze Eurhythmics, but it nonetheless is a very important avenue through which children can learn to sense rhythms more fully through basic body rhythms (patting, clapping, snapping, and stamping) and locomotor activities. The sequential teaching of proponents of the Kodály method maintains the use of folk dances as well as songs, and recommends the curricular infusion of dances that demonstrate rhythmic concepts such as pulse, pattern, and metric unit. The logic of teaching rhythm through movement is undeniable, and is woven throughout these and other pedagogies. See Chapter 8 for sample experiences in rhythmic movement for children.

The Pulse

Of the fundamental elements of rhythm, none is more basic in the Western world (and perhaps universally) than the pulse, or beat. Its presence is heard or felt in almost all music. It regulates music, because it is a recurring and steady stress underlying a variety of other rhythms, melodies, and textures. Regardless of whatever else is sounding within the music, "the beat (usually) goes on."

Children may demonstrate a sensitivity to the pulse as toddlers, rocking steadily to recorded music. Other children are still coming to terms with a feeling of pulse in the intermediate grades. While sensitivity varies, most children can maintain a steady pulse by clapping by the age of eight. For a comprehensive rhythmic development to occur, children must first be able to follow the pulse present in the music. The following list gives several experiences for establishing a sensitivity to musical pulse, which can be expanded to the length of a complete lesson.

1. Play a recording of a Sousa march, or a rock song. Ask children to clap the pulse. Model the clapping of the beat in correct time. Pat the beat on the shoulder of those who are having difficulty, or place your hands on theirs to direct their clapping.

2. Ask children to show the pulse by patting their knees. On the cue word "change," children show the pulse elsewhere (clapping hands, patting shoulders or head, snapping fingers).

3. Write the one-syllable names of children in the group horizontally across the board. Ask children to pat a steady pulse on their knees, and then to chant:

Juan   Anne   Jim   Jane   Pat   Tom   Mike   Lynn

4. Ask children to pat the pulse on their knees as they sing familiar songs such as "Knick Knack Paddy Whack," "Frère Jacques," or "Old Joe Clark."

5. Play a steady pulse on a drum, or a melody with a steady pulse on piano or xylophone. Ask children to sit facing a partner, and to roll balls or pass bean bags to each other on every pulse.

6. Ask children to form small groups, and to create a chant of one-syllable and two-syllable words in a single category: colors, animals, insects, flowers, and cars. Ask them to determine a way of sounding a steady beat as they prepare their chant pieces for performance.

Meter

In most music, the steady and regular pulse, or beat, is defined by accent, or emphasis that is given to some but not all pulses. The recurring pattern of stronger and weaker pulses is called meter. More than independent pulses, an understanding of meter enables the listener to perceive the flow of musical ideas.

Time signatures at the beginning of a notated piece are indications of

Older children conducting the meter.

meter, or the number of pulses in a musical unit or measure. Bar lines separate one measure from another. In general, the top number shows the number of pulses, while the bottom number signifies the value of the note that receives one pulse. For example, in $\frac{2}{4}$ meter, there are two pulses per measure, and the pulse is notated as a quarter note ($\quarternote$). In a compound meter such as $\frac{6}{8}$ or $\frac{7}{8}$, there are six or seven pulses per measure, and the pulse is notated as an eighth note ($\eighthnote$). An exception to this rule is when the tempo quickens: then the six eighth notes in $\frac{6}{8}$ are heard and felt in two groups of three rather than as six separate pulses ($\musicnote$ $\musicnote$). For children, the feeling of a quick $\frac{6}{8}$ in a song like "Oh Dear, What Can the Matter Be?" or "The Farmer in the Dell" is easily felt; it is only the explanation that appears complex.

Children come to understand meter through attentive listening, and through kinesthetic responses that follow the musical flow of stronger and weaker sounds. As early as age three or four, children listen and respond to music in two or four beats (or duple meter), three beats (or triple meter), and to a quick-paced compound meter. Some children respond naturally by rocking, swinging, swaying, chanting rhymes, and singing, but most require a model to lead them to sensing the appropriate loud-and-soft metrical pulses. Children in the intermediate grades who are skilled in identifying these basic meters can be challenged to combine 2 + 3 pulses or 3 + 2 + 2 pulses in asymmetric meters such as $\frac{5}{4}$, $\frac{5}{8}$, $\frac{7}{4}$, or $\frac{7}{8}$, or to alternate meters such as $\frac{4}{4}$ and $\frac{3}{4}$ in mixed meter.

There are various approaches that lead children to an understanding of meter, some requiring movement. Speech rhythms accompanied by rhythmic ostinatos involving body rhythms such as patting, clapping, snapping, and stamping reinforce the concept of meter. Conducting is another primary means of sensing the strong and weak pulses: the strong pulse of each measure is shown by a vertical downbeat, while all other pulses are indicated somewhat horizontally. Children are frequently quite adept at learning conducting patterns for some of the commonly found meters. The following list offers experiences in sensing and understanding meter; they are techniques and strategies to be used in lessons of various levels. Taken collectively, they are the substance of a lesson on meter.

1. Play a selection of recordings in various meters. Ask children to pat their knees on the strong beat, and to hold on the weak beats. Play the recordings again, asking children to continue to pat their knees on the strong beat, and to find another movement (clap, snap, or pat floor) for each of the weak beats.

2. Lead children in chanting the following phrases while patting the strong beats and clapping the weak beats (p = pat, c = clap).

3. Draw basic conducting patterns on the board. Lead children in drawing the conducting patterns in the air. Chant aloud the words "strong" for the first downbeat, and "weak" for all other pulses. As children learn the conducting patterns, sing or hum familiar songs in the appropriate meters.

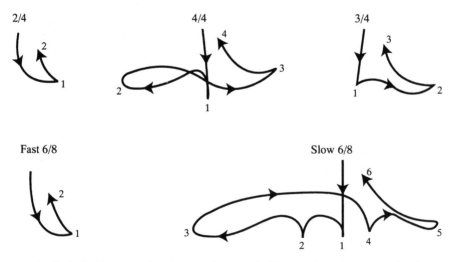

4. Ask children to play improvised melodies on the piano or xylophone. Other children can listen, step the pulse, and identify the meter by conducting.

5. Sing a familiar song such as "Row Your Boat" or "Yankee Doodle" in a different meter while patting and clapping, or conducting.

6. In a small groups, create a recurring movement pattern that can be repeatedly performed to a predetermined song or recording.

Durations and Their Patterns

As the fundamental pulse, or beat, and then the accented and unaccented pulses of meter are understood, children gradually become aware that chants, songs, and recorded musical works contain other rhythmic elements as well. While keeping the pulse, children may be rhythmically chanting two words or three syllables. They may be singing songs that appear to have "faster rhythms"; for example, with more rhythmic durations and pitches than they are conducting. In fact, the rhythms are more accurately viewed as shorter rather than faster (and also longer rather than slower) than the pulse. As they listen to a recording, children may be finding more rhythmic diversity than the meter beats they have been asked to identify. Rhythm is fundamental to music in its underlying pulse, but it also decorates and energizes music through its many durations that are longer and shorter, and faster and slower, than the pulse.

Durational values may be viewed as subdivisions or extensions, for example, elongations, of the basic pulse. If the pulse is symbolized by ♩, then its subdivision is ♫ or two eighth-notes. Twice the length of the quarter-note pulse is ♩, and four times the pulse is o . While these durational values can be analyzed mathematically, this is not the manner by which rhythm is perceived by children—or adults. Instead, music is commonly perceived as patterns of durations and pitches rather than as single isolated sounds. These patterns often occur more than once in a song or musical composition, offering coherence, tying musical ideas together, and giving the work a sense of a unified whole. Thus, children learn rhythmic durations with relative ease when sounds are linked together in patterns rather than when single sounds are treated mathematically.

When rhythmic patterns are associated with the chants and songs children have performed, their learning is accelerated. Once children have had opportunities to perform rhythmic patterns within the music, these patterns and even individual durations can be extracted, chanted, played on pitched and nonpitched percussion instruments, and used as a basis for improvisation. Further rhythmic development can occur as children are challenged to identify these patterns in new songs, to create chants and songs that incorporate them, and ultimately to read and write them.

Proponents of the Kodály method offer a sequence for the teaching of rhythmic patterns that derive logically from traditional songs that children sing. The sequence begins with quarter and eighth note patterns and is followed by the introduction of the half note, sixteenth notes, syncopated patterns, and patterns of compound meters such as $\frac{6}{8}$, $\frac{8}{9}$, $\frac{5}{8}$, and $\frac{7}{8}$. The first patterns of quarter and eighth notes are usually four pulses long, but those patterns with other durations may be briefer than that. Table 4.3 provides a logical order for the presentation of rhythmic patterns to children, along with familiar children's songs in which the patterns are found. Information on Kodály-inspired sequences for teaching rhythm may be found in works by Szabó (1969), Szönyi (1974–79), and Choksy (1981, 1988).

Many other permutations of single rhythmic durations are possible; in fact, the possible combinations of durations are nearly infinite. Likewise, most songs are likely to contain more than one pattern that can be highlighted and extracted for chanting, clapping, stepping, and playing experiences. The pedagogical mission is to lead children to a more complete and lasting understanding of rhythm when it is experienced in the songs that they sing.

Mnemonics

Because music is an aural phenomenon, it is logical to assume that rhythm can be learned by listening—at least at first. In many cultures, rhythms are transmitted by master musicians and teachers to their students without the assistance of notation, graphs, or other visual aids. While literacy is an important goal of school music instruction, it cannot be fully developed without children first internalizing the sound of the rhythm. As in many oral cultures, rhythm is thus effectively taught to children through rhythm syllables called mnemonics (pronounced, "neh-mon-iks"). These mnemonics have no semantic meaning, and are associated with specific rhythmic durations.

There are several mnemonics systems that have proven successful in introducing rhythms to children, that develop their inner hearing of these rhythms, and that lead to their reading and writing of rhythms. They include the word-chant system similar to the speech rhythms of Orff-Schulwerk, and Kodály and Gordon syllables. There are also notable historical systems, counting systems, culture-specific systems, and systems that combine duration and drum syllable strokes. Those systems most commonly and effectively used in teaching rhythm to children in American schools will now be described.

In that speech-rhythms are fundamental to the Orff-Schulwerk, the fixed word-chant system may have been derived from that approach. In the word-chant system, each rhythmic duration is assigned a specific word, often at the discretion of the teacher; these words may be chosen from one category or

Table 4.3 A Sequence of Rhythmic Patterns

Meter	Rhythm	Song
Duple Meter: 4/4	♩ ♩ ♩ ♩	Bounce High
	♩ ♩ ♫ ♩	Rain, Rain, Go Away
	♩ ♫ ♩ ♩	Hey, Betty Martin
	♫ ♫ ♩ ♩	Little Sally Walker
	♫ ♩ ♫ ♩	Knick Knack Paddy Whack
	𝅗𝅥 𝅗𝅥	Tinga Layo
	♩. ♪ ♩	Mighty Pretty Motion
	♪ ♩ ♪ ; also 𝅗𝅥 𝅗𝅥	I Got a Letter This Morning
	𝅘𝅥𝅰𝅘𝅥𝅰𝅘𝅥𝅰𝅘𝅥𝅰 ; also ♫♬	Kookaburra
	♫♬ ; also 𝅘𝅥𝅰𝅘𝅥𝅰𝅘𝅥𝅰𝅘𝅥𝅰	Zum Gali
	♬♫ ; also ♫♬	Skip to My Lou
Triple Meter: 3/4	𝅗𝅥 ♩ ; also ♩ ♫ ♫	Doraji
	♩. ♪ ♫	Did You Ever See a Lassie
Compound Meter: 6/8	♩. ♩. ; also ♫ ♫	Sing Together
	♩ ♪ ♩ ♪	Oh, How Lovely Is the Evening
Compound Meter: 5/8	♩. ♫	The Ship's Carpenteer
Compound Meter: 7/8	♩ ♪ ♩ ♩	Mountain Climbing

Kookaburra (Australia)

Kook-a-bur-ra sits on an old gum tree,__ Mer-ry, mer-ry king of the bush is he.__

Laugh, kook-a-bur-ra, laugh, Kook-a-bur-ra, Glad your life must be.

Zum Gali Gali (Israel)

Fine

Zum ga-li ga-li, ga-li, Zum ga-li ga-li, Zum ga-li ga-li, ga-li, Zum ga-li ga-li.

D.C. al Fine

1. Pi - o-neers work hard on the land;____ Men and wom-en work hand in hand.
2. As they la - bor all day__ long,____ They__ lift their voice in__ song.

Skip to My Lou (U.S.)

Fly's in the but-ter-milk, Shoo fly shoo, Fly's in the but-ter-milk, Shoo fly shoo,

Fly's in the but-ter-milk, Shoo fly shoo Skip to my Lou my dar - ling

Doraji (Korea)

Do - ra - ji, do - ra - ji, pek do ra ____ ji, sim - sim __

san - chuh oh pek do - ra - ji. Hahn __ du bu - ri-man keh - yuh -

do _____ Teh kwang-chu-ri su-ri sal __ sal __ dah - nuh - nun - da

Mountain Climbing (Bulgaria)

Climb-ing up the moun-tains see the pret - ty sights be - low.
Lead the way up to the moun-tain, sing - ing as we go.

See the vil - lage hous - es scat - tered by the riv - er - side.
At the top we'll dance to - geth - er cel - e - bra - ting time.

another. For example, if "fruit" is the selected category, then a quarter note may be chanted as "pear" whenever it occurs in a pattern, eighth notes as "ap-ple," sixteenth notes as "boy-sen-ber-ry," and so on. Any word combination is possible in a longer phrase, and because these words designate specific durations, they serve as mnemonics for internalizing the rhythms and patterns.

One well-known tool of the Kodály method is its rhythm duration syllables. The syllables are related to the French Chevé system of mnemonics that date to the early nineteenth century, and which were practiced in conservatories throughout Europe before the Hungarians popularized them in their musical education of children. The crisp dental "t" sound begins most syllables, and the more sustained syllables are sounded as "ah" for each pulse. Like the Orff-inspired word-chant, the Kodály syllables can be combined in as many ways as there are rhythmic patterns and phrases. The chanting of these syllables is known to lead successfully to the reading and writing of notation.

Edwin E. Gordon has proposed another mnemonics system, based on the rhythm syllables first suggested by McHose and Tibbs in the 1940s. Similar to the word-chant and Kodály systems, syllables are learned orally in order that audiation, or inner hearing, can be developed before the introduction of notation. Similar to the Kodály syllables, there is a crispness to the "d's" and "t's" that initiate them. In the Gordon system, certain syllables fall only on the downbeat, such as "du," and others like "ta" function only as an unaccented divider syllable in a pattern, such as in "du-ta-de-ta." Gordon's system may offer the listener an additional aid in identifying the meter based on the placement of the strong beat "du," always (and only) at the initial pulse of a measure. This differs from the Kodály system where, for example, "ta" or "ti-ti" may fall anywhere in a rhythmic pattern.

Table 4.4 offers a comparison of the word-chant, Kodály, and Gordon syllable systems, featuring rhythmic durations and patterns that can be offered intact or adapted to suit the musical needs of children. In all three systems,

Table 4.4   Rhythm Mnemonics

Duration	Word-Chant	Kodály	Gordon
♩	pear	ta	du
♫	ap - ple	ti - ti	du - de
♪	date	ti	du, de, or ta
(four sixteenths)	boy - sen - ber - ry	ti - ri - ti - ri	du - ta - de - ta
(triplet)	pine - ap - ple	tri - o - la	du - da - di
♩.	peach	ta - i	du —
(dotted eighth-sixteenth, quarter)	co - co - nut	tim - ri - ta	du - ta du
𝅗𝅥	plum	ta - ah	du - u

Phrase

pear   pear   ap - ple   pear
ta   ta   ti - ti   ta
du   du   du - de   du
1   2   3   +   4

boy - sen - ber - ry   pine - ap - ple   plum
ti - ri - ti - ri   tri - o - la   ta - ah
du - ta - de - ta   du - da - di   du - u
1   e   and   a   2   and   a   3 - 4

co - co - nut   ap - ple   pear
tim - ri - ta   ti - ti   ta
du   - ta du   du - de   du
1   - a 2   3   +   4

peach   date   co - co - nut
ta - i   ti   tim - ri - ta
du —   de   du   - ta du
1   +   2 +   3   - a 4

95

rests are taught as beats of silence. They may be chanted in hushed tones, or their durational words and syllables merely thought and felt rather than voiced.

The use of a mnemonics system is an important part of children's music learning, and it is most effective when used consistently and without overlap into other systems. Rhythm syllables allow children to build an extensive vocabulary of rhythmic patterns, and to discriminate between individual durations, their patterns, and the characteristic meters in which they are set. Children who have internalized rhythms through chant are thus prepared to read and write the notation that symbolizes their sounds.

Notation

All avenues of musical experience lead eventually to notational literacy, so that children may attain a comprehensive musicianship. While a sensitivity to music's rhythm—its pulse, meter, and durations—is developed through chants, songs, and movement, a child's musical education is more encompassing when he or she becomes musically literate. Music literacy is the ability: (1) to see symbols and to think or reproduce the sound; and (2) to hear the sound and to think or write the symbols. Just as the reading of words can be systematically learned by children following their experience in the spoken language, music notation can be learned when its teaching is systematically addressed.

The adage of "sounds before symbols" serves as a slogan for the teaching of rhythmic notation to children. A rhythmic pattern sounded by the teacher— played on piano, xylophone, or hand drum—often is understood by children through movement. When children coordinate their bodies to step, clap, or "realize" this pattern through a combination of body rhythms, they are then prepared for the Dalcrozian "dash-a-note" challenge. Children can draw horizontal dashes from left to right on a chalkboard to represent what they hear and feel: the longer the sound, the longer the dash. The dashes are eventually converted into notes, with vertical stems and noteheads drawn. "Dash-a-note" maps can be drawn in the air or on paper, but the rhythmic patterns require ample large-muscle movement experience before they can be accurately drawn. Before and after the advent of literacy, this technique can solidify the relationship of rhythmic sound to symbol.

One of the tools of the Kodály practice involves the initial use of note stems for rhythm reading. All stem notes (except half notes) are notated without the body of the note (e.g., | = ♩ and ⊓ = ♫). For children, this releases them from the time-consuming act of coloring in the noteheads, so that dictation can then envelop a greater number of rhythms per class period. Rhythmic

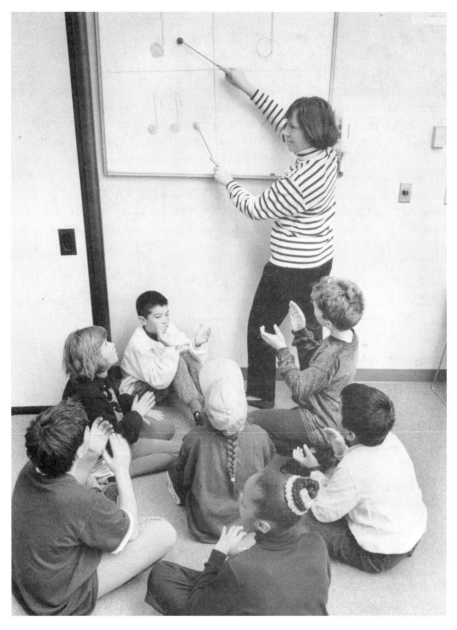

The whiteboard as an aid for teaching rhythm.

patterns can then be heard and quickly depicted by writing only the stems. Variations of this technique include the use by younger children of popsickle sticks, rhythm sticks, and dowels for representing patterns.

If children can learn to read and write letters, words, and sentences, they can also decipher, interpret, and write rhythmic notation. Through the kindergarten year, rhythmic learning should be experiential, while children are discovering the sounds of their environment, and playing with them. By first grade, children are ready to match rhythms to circles or discs, squares, diamonds, hearts, stick-people, or vertical lines; these images represent the rhythms of familiar songs children have previously sung. As children hear the various combinations of quarter notes and eighth notes, they can follow the images that represent the pulse and its subdivision, pointing to the sounds that are ordered from left to right on the blackboard, feltboard, or the floor. If children have sung "Knick Knack Paddy Whack," for example, and have chanted the syllables for some of its patterns, then they are ready to "read" the images that represent the rhythm and to "write" them out using selected shapes or sticks. Such a lesson follows, suitable for children in grades one and two:

1. Pat the pulse while singing "Knick Knack Paddy Whack."
2. Ask children to listen to the clapped pattern while they pat the pulse:

3. Identify the words for the pattern:

   "This old man, he played one"
4. Chant mnemonics for the pattern:

   ti - ti   ta   ti - ti   ta
5. Draw the pattern in the air, and on the blackboard:

   -- -- — -- -- —
6. Follow images on blackboard or feltboard while chanting and clapping:

   ap-ple   pear   ap-ple   pear
   ti-ti   ta   ti-ti   ta
   du-de   du   du-de   du
7. Construct the rhythmic pattern by laying sticks on the floor:

8. Point to sticks or blackboard images while singing "Knick Knack Paddy Whack."

9. At a later time, children can be evaluated for their ability to: (1) aurally identify the sounded pattern; (2) to read and perform its notation; and (3) to notate its aurally presented sound.

The process for learning to read and write other patterns continues similarly as the children mature, using rhythms that are increasingly complex. When they have developed their ability to print legibly (no later than second grade), children are also ready to take "rhythmic dictation" with paper and pencil. They no longer require the iconic visual images. Sticks and shapes are replaced by stem notation, and eventually children gain the facility to quickly attach noteheads to the stems; with practice, this can occur by the fourth grade. Central to the process of reading and writing, however, are singing, chanting, and movement experiences that must come first. The rhythm patterns presented above provide a logical progression for not only the "performance experience" in assorted rhythms, but also the development of notational literacy.

Syncopations

Some of the most exciting music that children can know consists of syncopation, rhythms that have "displaced accents," in which unaccented rhythms are given emphasis while normally-accented pulses are de-emphasized. Popular, rock 'n' roll, Sub-Saharan African, African-American, and Latin American music are replete with syncopated rhythms. While syncopation in its notated form is seldom introduced before the intermediate grades, children have listened to off-the-beat rhythms for many years. The concept of syncopation can be taught at an earlier stage through experience, analysis, and more experience. The following provides a sampling of these experiences that can be partly or fully incorporated into lessons appropriate for use in grades three and four:

1. Clap or pat even pulses, accenting the first of every two.

2. On the cue word "change," syncopate by accenting the second of every two pulses.

3. In two "on-beat" and "off-beat" groups, accent the first or second of every two pulses by patting the accent and clapping the unaccented pulse.

Group I: on-beat

4. Practice chanting rhythm syllables, and applying body rhythms for syncopated patterns.

date	pear	date	date	pear	date
ti	ta	ti	ti	ta	ti
du	de	de	du	de	de

5. Seek out the syncopated patterns in these songs, chanting and clapping them while tapping the steady pulse or conducting the meter.

Bucket of Water (Jamaica)

Draw me a buck-et of wa - ter for my old - est daugh - ter,

none in the bunch, no none in the bunch you go un - der sis-ter Sal - ly.

Sansa Kroma (Ghana)

San - sa kro - ma Ne nay woo ah chay chay ko - ko - ma.

San - sa kro - ma Ne nay woo ah chay chay ko - ko - ma.

Kye Kye (Ghana)

Kye kye ku - le
(Chay chay koo - lay)
Kye kye ku - le
Kye kye ko - fee - sah

Kye kye ko - fee - sah ko - fee - sah lang - a ka - ka shi - lang - a

Ka - ka - shi - lang - a ka - ka - shi - lang - a kum a - den - de (day)

kum a - den - de (day) kum a - den - de (day) Hey!

Polyrhythms

Rhythms can occur one after another—sequentially—or they can occur simultaneously. In the polyphonic music from the European Renaissance, and in much of the music of Sub-Saharan Africa, the Caribbean, and African-influenced music of both North and South America, two or more rhythmic layers that sound simultaneously provide the striking rhythmic feature known as polyrhythm. When children are capable of keeping a steady pulse, and of chanting, clapping, and playing rhythmic patterns that last eight or more pulses, then they have achieved the musicianship required to perform one rhythm as other rhythms are sounding. By the third grade, most children possess the rhythmic stability necessary for performing polyrhythmic pieces. It will take the teacher's careful sequencing of lessons, however, for children to perform them cleanly, steadily, and independently yet cooperatively, as is the nature of polyrhythm. The following are suggested lessons that develop an understanding of the intricacies of polyrhythm:

1. Learn to perform the eight-count polyrhythm.
   (a) Chant the two rhythmic patterns separately.
   (b) Clap and chant the patterns separately.
   (c) Clap and (silently) chant the patterns separately.
   (d) Divide into two groups; clap the patterns separately.
   (e) In two groups, clap the patterns together (four or more times).

(f) For greater rhythmic clarity, choose different body sounds on which each group "plays" its rhythm: hand-clap, lap-pat, foot-stamp, finger-snap, vocalizations.

(1)

1 — 3 4 — 6 7 —

(2)

1 2 — — 5 6 — 8

2. Follow the same sequence as above, but increase the groups in clapping this four-part polyrhythm. Transfer to different body rhythms, and instruments.

(1) (clap, woodblock)

1 — 3 4 — 6 7 — 9 10 — 12

(2) (snap, rattle)

1 2 3 4 5 6 7 8 9 10 — —

(3) (pat, iron bell; tone bell)

1 — — — 5 6 — 8 9 — 11 12

(4) (stamp, drum)

1 2 3 — 5 6 — 8 — 10 — 12

3. Challenge children to perform a personal polyrhythm in their bodies.

(a) Clap and chant the following rhythm:

1 — 3 — 5 6 7 —

(b) Step and chant the following rhythm:

— 2 — 4 — — — 8

(c) Combine the stepping and clapping patterns.

From Natural Rhythms to Rhythmic Training

Children demonstrate their natural rhythms in nearly all that they do, but primarily through speech and movement. The challenge for teachers is to chan-

Children playing polyrhythms on African/Latin instruments.

nel these natural rhythms into an understanding of one of music's most elemental parts. The challenge becomes greater when teachers recognize the need to season instruction with the playfulness with which children have perceived and explored rhythm from their earliest years. Some of the most powerful musical experiences children can know may be the discovery of how their own physical energy can be ordered, regularized, and combined with others in rhythmic chant, song, and movement. Rhythm may well be the magical dynamism that attracts and maintains the interest of children in music, both in school and out.

Teachers and parents can explore with children the rhythmic components of language, and the manner in which rhythmic movement can add to their enjoyment of singing a song or listening to music. Children's conceptual understanding of rhythm—its pulse, meter, and durations—can be developed further through experiences that associate listening with speech and movement, leading to inner hearing. There is a logical sequence in the introduction of rhythm patterns from pulses and their subdivisions, to sixteenth notes, to syncopations, and from rhythms in duple meter to those in triple and compound meters. There is a logical learning order as well in the progression from sound to symbol, as teachers guide children through listen-and-response experiences in rhythm, to chanting their mnemonic syllables, to reading the rhythms that are notated, and to notating the rhythms that are heard. This is the musical foundation that can be formed in the elementary grades, and from which more sophisticated musical understanding can proceed.

Questions

1. Differentiate between speech and "rhythmic speech." In what ways does language offer a means by which rhythmic understanding can be developed?

2. In what order should these rhythmic concepts be presented to children, and at what ages or grade levels: accents; duration and durational patterns; syncopation; pulse; meter; polyrhythms.

3. Why is $\frac{6}{8}$ called a "compound meter"? How does the definition apply to $\frac{5}{8}$ or $\frac{7}{8}$?

4. Discuss the function of mnemonics, and compare the "grammar" of the more frequently found systems. What other systems are in use?

5. How does the achievement of music literacy contribute to the comprehensiveness of children's musical sensitivity and understanding?

Activities

1. Listen to recordings of musical works of various styles. Compile a list of ten works that can be used in teaching concepts of rhythm to children. For each work, determine its (a) meter and (b) prominent rhythmic patterns.

2. Choose five colloquialisms, proverbs, or famous quotations. Recite them aloud, listening for accents and durations. Notate their rhythms in duple and triple meter.

3. Select a rhythmic pattern, and prepare a ten-minute lesson that incorporates rhythmic speech chant and body rhythms.

4. Analyze the rhythmic contents of ten traditional children's songs. Arrange them in order of complexity, noting the repeated rhythmic pattern(s) that might be highlighted in a lesson for children. Recommend the grade level at which the song's rhythms would be suitable for learning.

References

CHOKSY, L. (1981). *The Kodály context*. Englewood Cliffs, NJ: Prentice-Hall.

————. (1988). *The Kodály method* (2nd ed.). Englewood Cliffs, NJ: Prentice-Hall.

FRAZEE, J. (1987). *Discovering Orff: A curriculum for music teachers*. New York: Schott.

HOOD, M. V., & SCHULTZ, E. J. (1949). *Learning music through rhythm*. Boston: Ginn.

KEETMAN, G. (1974). *Elementaria: First acquaintance with Orff-Schulwerk*, M. Murray (Trans.). London: Schott.

MOOG, H. (1976). *The musical experience of the pre-school child*, Clarke, C. (Trans.). London: Schott.

MOORHEAD, G. E., & POND, D. (1978). *Music of young children*. Santa Barbara, CA: Pillsbury Foundation.

ORFF, C., & KEETMAN, G. (1956). *Orff-Schulwerk: Music for children* (5 vols.). English adaptation by Doreen Hall and Arnold Walter. Mainz, Ger.: B. Schott's Sohne.

SZÖNYI, E. (1974–79). *Musical reading and writing* (3 vols.). New York: Boosey and Hawkes.

STEEN, A. (1992). *Exploring Orff*. New York: Schott.

WARNER, B. (1991). *Orff-Schulwerk, Adaptations for the classroom*. Englewood Cliffs, NJ: Prentice-Hall.

CHAPTER **5**

Pitch and the Child

Jeffrey listens dreamily to the rise and fall of his parents' voices as he plays with his toys. Later, he is rocked to sleep by the soothing sounds of a lullaby. Mindy hums a self-made song to her doll as she dresses it. Tyler and Jared look forward to times on family vacations when they all sing together in the car. Katie laughs with the surprise of recognition as her music teacher introduces a song based on the melodies of some of her favorite television jingles. Melody, the linear use of pitch and rhythm, comes to children in many places and forms, sometimes through listening and sometimes through performing. These experiences create a foundation for building conscious understanding of melodic concepts.

Eventually, children also become aware of harmony, the simultaneous sounding of pitches. Ian's dad plays a guitar as they sing together. Esther hears people sing in harmony in her church and she eagerly joins in. Rashad's class is learning to play the autoharp to accompany some of their songs. Arianne sings second soprano in her fifth grade choir. As children experience different harmonies, feeling the tension and release that results from the various uses of consonance and dissonance, they build the concrete basis for understanding harmony's theoretical structures.

The word, *melody*, comes from the Greek words *melos* meaning "song" and *aeidein* meaning "to sing." In the Greek sense, melody is inextricably bound with the idea of song. For children, song is undoubtedly the most immediate experience they have of melody. The ability of children to master the production of melodies and, eventually, to sing in harmony, will be addressed in Chapter 6.

The focus here is on ways teachers and parents can enhance children's perception and understanding of different aspects of melody and harmony. Numerous techniques for developing sensitivity to pitch and pitch patterns will

106

be provided. These activities are important in helping children to: (1) think about music; (2) discuss what they notice happening in musical events, eventually using musical terms; and (3) use these ideas creatively. These techniques will help children focus on pitch, as a part of an entire lesson. Teachers can incorporate them in lessons as a part of ongoing work on pitch development.

Growth in Understanding of Linear Pitch Structures

Many challenges face children as they grow in their ability to perceive and understand the pitch-related aspects of melody. At the most basic level is the task of *discrimination*: Are two pitches, patterns, or melodies the same or different? At the next level is recognition of *shape* or *contour*. What is the overall curve of a melody? These abilities, along with the ability of children to form aural images of songs, result in *recognition:* Is the melody familiar?

Next comes a focus on more discrete aspects of melody including: *pitch register* (are pitches relatively high or low?); *pitch direction* (is the melody moving upward or downward?); *pitch motion* (are the pitches moving by steps, leaps, or repeats?); and *interval size* (are the leaps large, medium, or small)?

Later children become aware of: *tonality* (what is the focal point of the melody?); *melodic phrase* (what constitutes a complete idea melodically?); *scale* (what is the underlying pattern of tones for the melody?); and additional concepts such as *major* and *minor* modes, and *melodic sequence*.

At a remarkably early age, children develop a sense of their own culture's ways of constructing melodies, probably in the same way they develop a sense of the syntax of their native language. Such sensitivities emerge gradually and are retained through adulthood, regardless of training in music. A knowledge of when these perceptual sensitivities emerge can help the parent or teacher plan developmentally appropriate activities.

The teacher or parent can help children move from *percept*, or the ability to notice these various qualities of melody, to *concept*, or the ability to identify these qualities in a variety of settings and permutations. However, they need to be conscious of the readiness of children for a particular level of thinking. For example, a child may perceive that some pitches are high and some are low but may not be able to group the highest and the lowest ones in separate categories. In addition, the child may or may not be ready to explain his or her thinking in familiar terms such as high/low or upward/downward. Table 5.1 may help to guide planning an appropriate sequence for teaching these con-

Table 5.1   Children's Melodic Development

Age	Percept/Concept	Teacher Actions
Less than six months	Responds to differences in pitch Can match vocally sustained pitches and begins to imitate sounds	Sing with words or neutral syllables like "loo" Sustain pitches in middle register Imitate sounds Generate new ideas
Six months to 1½	Differentiates between pitch contours Sensitive to phrase endings and intervals	Continue vocal play Sing nursery songs and other simple songs from child's culture Play recorded music
1½ yrs. to four	Able to recognize familiar phrases and songs based on contour and rhythm Increased ability to replicate familiar material More attention to absolute value of pitches than to relative value Sensitivity to phrase, shown through movement	Sing many songs with children Engage in vocal play—extending the range upward and downward Add words, upward/downward and high/low to vocal play to match pitch patterns Experiment with keyboards and computer programs that reinforce contour and pattern discrimination skills Show contour and phrase with bodies
Four to eight (Kindergarten to Grade three)	Beginning to conceptualize aspects of pitch and melody such as high/low, upward/downward Able to demonstrate this knowledge first through showing (age four to five) and later through telling (age five to six) Sensitivity to intervals and to tonality emerges Continued development of phrase as unit	Provide many opportunities through singing, movement, use of bells, and use of computer programs to demonstrate pitch concepts and contours Have children vocally supply endings to familiar songs Help them add musical vocabulary to describe melodic events Respond to phrase endings

(continued)

Table 5.1 Continued

Age	Percept/Concept	Teacher Actions
Eight to twelve (Grades three to six)	Can identify discrete aspects of pitch motion such as steps, leaps, and repeated tones Easiest to perceive patterns moving downward—later moving upward Recognition of melodic sequence Can build concepts of scale and mode around age ten to eleven	Continue to build experience with melodies through singing, shaping through movement, and playing instruments Add reading of contours and patterns using precise notation

cepts. It shows that rapid growth in pitch perception occurs in the early childhood years, birth through age eight. Percepts and concepts stabilize and are refined after that. The development of individual children can vary. Some musically experienced children may have clear, foundational pitch concepts at the age of four. Most children seem to develop these concepts around the ages of six to eight, in the primary grades.

Children associating sounds of pitches with notation.

Discrimination and Contour Awareness

Although infants are capable of noticing the difference between two pitches or two melodic contours, the task for older children is to begin to describe what they notice. At first, they may use the words "same"/"different" in response to patterns, or "I know that song!" or "I don't know it," in response to questions regarding the familiarity of various songs. Preschool-aged children usually show their recognition of familiar songs simply by joining in and singing along. Around the age of three, children may recognize that the contours of familiar songs are the same, for example, "The Alphabet Song," "Baa, Baa Black Sheep," and "Twinkle, Twinkle Little Star." And, as children between ages four and seven develop relational concepts such as "high" and "low," they can begin to describe the movement of contours and the relationship among different pitches.

The activities in Table 5.2 are designed to increase children's sensitivity to pitch differences and to melodic contour through active experimentation and discovery. Though these are being presented in separate categories of singing, playing, moving, listening, and creating, most children will benefit from multiple approaches. These percepts are basic to the formation of other pitch understandings and need to be developed regardless of the age of the child.

Kodály and his proponents adapted John Curwen's (and Sarah Glover's) nineteenth-century British hand sign system; the technique illustrates the power of a combined perceptual approach for pitch development. In this system, each pitch of the diatonic scale is associated with a hand sign (Figure 5.1). Children use simultaneously the visual, auditory, and kinesthetic modalities as they respond to individual pitches, pitch motion, interval relations, and melodic contours. This system encourages children to use the hand signs when they sing out loud or to themselves, and to model aural perception of various melodic and harmonic events in music.

Pitch Relations and Melodic Motion

Around the age of four, most children begin to demonstrate the ability to categorize specific aspects of pitch as being relatively the same. For example, they might group three relatively high pitches together and two relatively low pitches together. Or, they might recognize that two melodic contours are the same even though they use different pitches to shape them. Often it is easier for them to demonstrate their understandings through pointing, grouping, or playing than through telling.

The words "high" and "low" or "up" and "down," when applied to pitch, are confusing to young children. Because pitches are not high or low acousti-

Table 5.2 Experiences in Pitch Discrimination and Contour Awareness

Mode	Ages Four to Eight	Ages Nine to Twelve
Singing	Learn more songs to use as images of shapes and patterns Echo different shapes with voice or kazoo Find repeated patterns in songs, e.g. "John the Rabbit"	Sing many songs Signal when all voices match pitch Sing familiar songs or patterns on "loo," identify them from their contour
Moving	Shape contour with hands or bodies as children listen or sing—add flashlight for variety Learn Kodály-Curwen hand signs, practice and identify patterns from hand signs	Take "aural dictation" of different melodic shapes by listening, then moving using either levels or Kodály-Curwen hand signs; discover those patterns in songs
Playing	Have children generate contour at keyboard that teacher imitates—label *same;* then teacher plays contrast—label *different* Play single pitch, see if child can match it on another instrument; expand to two, three, and four pitches	Echo-play individual pitches or melodic contours by ear on keyed percussion instruments and/or soprano recorders
Listening	Play two pitches or contours, children show palms down if same/palms sideways if different	Listen to melodies on recordings, shape with body or hand signs or trace on paper
Reading	Present children with various visuals of melodic curves, have them sing or play Have several children hold a long rope with both hands and shape a melody by raising or lowering hands Use computer software programs that connect sight and sound: *Toney Listens to Music; Magic Music Balloons; Toney Music Games*	Give children tracing paper to place over melodies in books, have them connect the heads of the notes in a dot-to-dot fashion; discuss contours Place melodies of familiar songs on bulletin board or overhead—see how quickly children can "name the tune" from the contour Use software programs that connect sight and sound: *Music FUNdamentals*
Creating	Improvise a short piece on keyed percussion, taking melodic contours and displacing them	Compose a piece using contrasting contours: jagged/smooth Compose a piece using a skyline of a city or mountain for a contour

111

Figure 5.1. Kodály-Curwen hand signs. *Reproduced with permission from Choksy (1981).*

Children creating string melody.

Old John the Rabbit

Figure 5.2. "John the Rabbit" (African-American singing game). *Reproduced with permission from* World of Music, Grade 1 *(1992).*

cally and because most keyboards are presented to children on a horizontal plane, children are understandably confused by the vocabulary we use to discuss pitch. In addition, the words "up" and "down" are often used to talk about volume as well as pitch; for example, "Turn down the TV, it's too loud!" Finally, pitch notation is an arbitrary system that is often confusing for learners, because it places pitches in a two-dimensional visual plane that does not match the acoustic sense perceivers have of pitch.

Teachers and parents wishing to help children apply terminology correctly should use words such as "upward"/"downward" or moving "higher"/"lower" to describe pitch motion. Other strategies, using step bells, slide whistles, movement, and vertically oriented xylophones, may also help. Ultimately, because music is more than pitches in isolation, it is desirable to present children with patterns taken from melodies of familiar songs and instrumental works to build their sense of pitch relations.

Table 5.3 gives strategies designed to help children form concepts about discrete aspects of pitch relations such as high/low; upward/downward; stepwise, leaping, or repeating motion; and small, medium, or large intervals. Age-appropriate activities are suggested. Singing, moving, and playing in-

Table 5.3 Experiences in Pitch Register, Motion, and Interval Size

Mode	Ages Four to Eight	Ages Nine to Twelve
Singing	Have children imitate high/low sounds—sing songs with exaggerated differences of high/low Sing scale songs and describe upward/downward motion Develop a sense of interval size and melodic motion through use of Curwen hand signs	Sing upward-moving passages of a familiar song out loud, and downward-moving passages internally Use words upward/downward and high/low to describe passages in songs Sings songs with various kinds of motion—discuss effect of size of leaps, steps, repeated tones
Moving	Make high or low motions in response to individual pitches or pitches embedded in songs Move gradually upward/downward to glissandi and scale songs	Walk forward if melody moves upward, backward if melody moves downward, and step in place when it repeats Refine by stepping if melody steps and leaping if melody leaps
Playing	Place "lower ↔ higher" on body of keyed instruments Have children play high/medium/low sounds in response to cues Suspend a small xylophone vertically on Peg-Board—high pitches on top, connect with staff notation Use step bells to reinforce sense of upward/downward Play various kinds of patterns—stepping, leaping, repeating—to accompany songs	Experiment with tuning bottles in a stepwise tuning, color-code water, and use to accompany various patterns in songs or to play ear tunes—notate using colors As children are prepared to play various ostinati, bourdon, and other accompaniment patterns, discuss the movement of the patterns and the relative size of the intervals
Listening	Show upward motion by pointing upward; downward by pointing downward, and repeated tones with palm flat, facing floor Circle iconic patterns on response sheets that represent different kinds of melodic motion: a) ↗ b) ↘ c) ↗↘ d) ↘↗	Learn to identify melodic patterns within recorded works; read and play or sing them first, then identify them Select patterns on response sheet as numbers are called while listening: a) [musical notation] b) [musical notation]

(continued)

Table 5.3 Continued

Mode	Ages Four to Eight	Ages Nine to Twelve
Reading	Make a score out of dots at various levels in different patterns; have children play on keyboard: Show pitch motion and intervals on a hand staff (palm facing chest) or by placing buttons on a paper staff	Work with software programs such as *Doremi* or *Arnold* to practice the various concepts Notate or highlight various repeated note, stepping, and leaping patterns; play on keyed percussion instrument; begin to associate staff locations and pitch names
Creating	Create a high/low contrast piece; record it and add movement to it Experiment with how to create glissandi on various instruments; create a piece for glissandi using various tone colors	Have children notate a melody as if on a walk, incorporating steps, leaps, and repeats. (Notation could resemble a map.) Perform pieces on pitched instruments.

Children with step bells and vertical glockenspiel.

struments provide the most concrete means of experiencing pitch relations. Listening and reading involve greater intellectual abstraction, and creating allows children to synthesize the new understandings they have developed.

Advanced Pitch Concepts

Around the age of six or seven, children begin to develop a clear sense of tonality, or that a piece of music is centered within a logical system and moves within that system to a final point of resolution or rest. They bring to this an already developing sense of melodic phrase (music is expressed in a series of ideas that have a sense of completeness).

These percepts can be developed into concepts during the primary grades. Then, in combination with concepts of melodic motion, they can be refined into more specific concepts regarding pitch organization during the intermediate years. These concepts include:

1. **Scale:** The underlying set of tones for a melody. It is from the Latin word, *scala*, that means ladder or stairs. Scales use specific intervals as they rise and fall. The size of those intervals varies with the type of scale and the tuning systems used in the culture in which it occurs.

2. **Major and Minor Modes:** The two most commonly used modes in the Western tradition. They are distinguished by a difference in the treatment of the third and sixth tones of the scale. Each is used for different musical effects. The major scale consists of stepwise intervals in the pattern of:

The minor scale pattern is:

3. **Melodic Sequence:** A short melodic pattern repeated at different pitch levels. It is used as a forming device for building melodies.

The activities in Table 5.4 suggest concrete ways of involving children with these ideas. Because many of these activities are dependent on understanding of and experience with foundation concepts, the preponderance of the activities are geared toward the older elementary child. Many of the activities listed here for children aged four to eight could be adapted for older children if necessary.

Growth in Understanding of Vertical Pitch Structures

Musically perceptive listeners are not only aware of what is occurring melodically in music, but are aware of what is going on in addition to the melody. They are aware that sounds occur simultaneously, and that those vertical arrangements of sound result in something called harmony. This harmony can be created by a combination of independent melodic lines (polyphonic texture) or a stacking of pitches (homophonic texture). The progression of harmonies through a piece of music and the choice of harmonic colors create various feelings of tension and release in the listener.

Once again, this awareness builds gradually and is influenced by the cultural and stylistic norms for what constitutes agreeable and not agreeable combinations of sounds and sequences of those combinations. Table 5.5 describes the course of that growth based on current research (see Colwell, 1992; Hargreaves, 1986; and Serafine, 1988).

Table 5.6 suggests a range of ideas for the development of percepts and concepts related to harmony and texture. As in Table 5.4, the majority of the activities are aimed for older children. Many of the activities for younger children can be adapted and used with older children as necessary.

Numerous resources offer additional strategies to develop pitch awareness. Ideas on how to reinforce children's perceptions and build them into concepts can be found in Edelstein et al. (1980), Findlay (1971), and Aaron (1976), as well as many contemporary music series texts. Materials to implement multicultural strategies can be found in Anderson and Campbell (1989) and Jessup (1992). Strategies that extend to creative application of pitch concepts can be found in Thomas (1970), Schafer (1976), or Paynter and Aston (1971).

Helping Children to Think Musically

Research in pitch perception clearly shows that people develop sensitivities to pitch and pitch structures as a natural part of responding cognitively to the

Table 5.4 Experiences in Tonality, Phrase, Scale, and Sequence

Mode	Ages Four to Eight	Ages Nine to Twelve
Singing	Ask children to supply the final note of both familiar and unfamiliar songs; label that as the "home tone"; note strength of home tone in scale songs	Learn to shape phrases expressively, discuss varous effects
		Using familiar songs, notice differences between strong and weak phrase endings
	Have groups of children sing alternating phrases in a song; identify as phrases	Sing a given song in a major key and then a minor key; discuss differences
		Sing songs in other scales: pentatonic; whole tone; chromatic
		Discover sequences in melodic patterns; assign singing of each to different groups
Moving	Move around the room to a melody, coming to rest at the final point	Choreograph various phrases in recorded music; if phrase repeats, repeat movements
	Use arms, scarves, or streamers to shape phrases in air	Learn Kodály-Curwen hand signs for scales; note relationship of minor half step to other tones; discover whole- and half-step differences in major and minor scales
	Move in style to song, changing direction at end of phrases	
		Move major and minor scales through room taking full step on whole step and smaller step on half step; sing or play scales while moving
		Move sequential patterns with body in space; alternate with a partner
Playing	In songs with equal phrase length, play finger cymbals to highlight end of each phrase	Highlight phrases by playing contrasting rhythm instruments on beat or melodic rhythm
	Give each child a set of diatonic octave bells; have them play the tonal center in tonic-oriented songs	Learn to play major and minor scale patterns on piano, chromatic bells, or synthesizer. Begin with C Major and a natural minor; transpose patterns to other

(continued)

Table 5.4 Continued

Mode	Ages Four to Eight	Ages Nine to Twelve
	Have children play the final phrase of songs on keyed instruments; relate sense of close to tonal center	starting points; improvise within those scales
		Play handbell or tone bell to highlight beginning of each occurrence of a melodic sequence
Listening	Trace phrases on paper as you listen to recorded works, compare lengths	Using randomly ordered pitches from the C Major scale, give one tone bell and mallet to each of eight children. Line them up and have them play. Encourage other children to place them in correct order to form a human scale; play scale song
		Use human scale to add black keys, and discover whole and half step relationships for both major and minor scales
Reading	Find beginning and ending pitches in songs that end on do; develop understanding that most songs move toward tonal center at ending though they may not begin there	Take melodic dictation for phrases using Kodály techniques
	Discover repeating and contrasting phrases in songs by looking at notation; listen to confirm your perception	Help children associate different tonal centers with different scales and different keys
		Give pairs of children a familiar melody and some staff paper; extract the various pitches from the melody and notate them; discover whether the melody uses all of the pitches of the scale on which it was based
		Highlight melodic sequences on score
Creating	Once children become aware of tonal center, challenge them to end vocal or instrumental improvisations on do	Improvise using various scales structured on Orff instruments
	Improvise in call-and-response form across an eight-beat phrase	Using a chromatic instrument, invent a scale and compose a four measure melody using it
		Compose a piece using melodic sequences as a structuring device; try inverting them for variety

Table 5.5 Harmonic Development

Age	Percept/Concept	Teacher Action
Five to seven (Kindergarten to Grade 1)	Developing sensitivity to relation between melody and harmony—harmonic fit	Help children distinguish between accompanied and non-accompanied music
	Small number of children beginning to notice separate vertical events	Ask children to indicate when chords need to change as accompaniment to a melody
	May perceptually combine two pitches into one	
Eight to ten (Grades 2–4)	Stronger ability to notice numbers of vertical events	Build triads and add to songs
	Beginning to sense closed or strong and open or weak cadences	Sing songs with combined lines such as ostinatos and rounds
		Add autoharp accompaniments to songs
Eleven to twelve (Grades 5–6)	Able to correctly identify number of simultaneous events	Keep refining perception of simultaneous sounds through listening
	Clear sense of strong and weak cadence	Have them use simultaneous sounds and cadences creatively
	Can harmonize accurately by ear	Give students melodies to harmonize with basic chords

music that surrounds them. The challenge for the teacher is to build on these percepts and expand them into conscious concepts that can be applied through a lifetime of musical experiences.

As teachers strive to make musical learning meaningful, they need to be selective, choosing activities that will stimulate musical growth. However, any activity, done in isolation, runs the risk of simply filling time in interesting or not-so-interesting ways. A well-developed series of strategies involves a variety of modes: singing, moving, playing, listening, reading, and creating. Discussion and reflection will also be a regular part of the process of learning. Strategies carefully selected, ordered, and implemented across time, at levels appropriate to a child's development, have a much greater likelihood of expanding the ability of children to think about music.

Table 5.6 Experiences in Harmony and Texture

Mode	Ages Four to Eight	Ages Nine to Twelve
Singing	Sing songs with and without auto-harp or guitar accompaniment, discuss differences Age 7 and beyond: sing vocal ostinati to accompany songs; keep track of lines	Sing two and three-chord songs, indicating chord changes with I, IV, or V fingers or root of chord with hand sign Sing songs that alternate strong and weak cadences; discuss differences Sing rounds in two, three, and four parts; tape and listen to differences in texture Add vocal chording on I, IV, and V chords to accompany songs
Moving	With a two-chord song, move through general space, changing direction when chords change	Make up different movements, alone or with a partner, to show I, IV, and V chords; move them in response to music Choreograph the melody of a round with simple movements; perform the song and movements in a round; note layers Learn to lead two-part singing with Kodály-Curwen hand signs
Playing	Have children accompany songs with autoharp, bell chords, or automatic chords on a synthesizer; begin with one-chord songs and move to two-chord songs in which they identify changes by ear Accompany melodies with ostinati, bourdons, or descants; discuss texture and harmony	Accompany songs using chords on autoharps, bells, or keyboards by ear and then by sight Play two-, three-, and four-part rounds on recorders or pitched percussion; discuss textures created Build triads on every pitch of the diatonic scale; identify them as major or minor Learn the chord progression for a favorite pop tune or twelve-bar blues, play to accompany songs Learn to perform various African rhythm complexes with rhythmic percussion instruments such as

(continued)

Table 5.6 Continued

Mode	Ages Four to Eight	Ages Nine to Twelve
		from Ghana or on xylophones such as the Mandinka would play; discuss textures created by layers
Listening	Age 6 or 7 on: listen as teacher sings a song with a harmonic accompaniment; raise hands to indicate when chords need to change	While listening, mark beats to a song changing colors when the chords change or hold up different colored cards as chords change (i.e., red = tonic, blue = dominant, yellow = subdominant)
		In a small group, develop a listening map to show the overlapping lines of a polyphonic work; check the map against the music
Reading	Age 7 or after: learn to track chord changes in music while playing accompaniment	Follow the relationship of lines in a two-line polyphonic piece, first on listening map and later with actual music
		Learn to build root-position triads using buttons on a paper staff
Creating	Improvise an accompaniment to a pentatonic melody on an Orff keyed percussion instrument	Improvise an accompaniment using broken chords
		Using the pentatonic scale, compose a piece for three different melodies that are layered to create various textures
		Compose a piece for chords, experimenting with different progressions and rhythms; use different instruments for variety; start with root position triads, later add sevenths, ninths, or elevenths

Questions

1. If children automatically gain perceptions of pitch and pitch structures as a result of growing up in a musically rich environment, why should parents and teachers devote time to expanding those perceptions? List three reasons.

2. What is the difference between a percept and concept? How are the two related?

3. At what point are children developmentally ready to explore ideas related to tonality? What are some ways to reinforce that perception?

4. At what point can children accurately perceive the number of simultaneous sounds in a piece of music? What kinds of tasks might you create to test that ability?

5. Why is it important to have a developmental perspective, beginning from the early childhood years, regarding what children are capable of perceiving? What meaning might that have for an elementary general music specialist?

Activities

1. Create music manipulables such as a dowel staff or magnet board that you can use with children to reinforce various musical concepts.

2. Using the model of moving from concrete activities of singing, moving, and playing instruments to more abstract experiences of listening, reading, and creating, plan a series of activities to teach and extend the concept of upward/downward pitch motion to second-grade children. Work in a team to plan the activities. Use music series texts as basic resources. Feel free to go beyond those sources as needed.

3. Select a perceptual task children should be able to perform at the age indicated in this chapter. Work with another person to devise a way to test whether children have that percept or concept. Implement this test with at least five children to determine where they are developmentally. Bring your results back to class and present your discoveries.

4. Select an activity or a series of activities from this chapter designed to expand understanding of pitch and implement them with children. Modify them as necessary to fit the unique needs of the children involved.

5. Review some of the musical activities suggested in the Anderson and

Campbell book (1989). Select two that could be used to develop pitch-related concepts. List what those concepts are.

6. In one of the books on musical creativity listed in the bibliography, find a strategy related to pitch development and implement it with children.

References

AARON, T. (Ed.). (1976). *Musicbook O*. St. Louis: Magnamusic-Baton.

ANDERSON, W. M., & CAMPBELL, P. S. (Eds.). (1989). *Multicultural perspectives in music education*. Reston, VA: Music Educators National Conference.

Arnold, computer program. (1990). Bellevue, WA: Temporal Acuity Products.

BENWARD, B., & WILLIAMS, D. B. (1992). *Doremi*, computer program. Bellevue, WA: Temporal Acuity Products.

COLWELL, R. (Ed.). (1992). Section D: Perception and cognition. In *Handbook of research on music teaching and learning*. New York: Schirmer Books.

EDELSTEIN, S., CHOKSY, L., LEHMAN, P., SIGURDSSON, N., & WOODS, D. (1980). *Creating curriculum in music*. Menlo Park, CA: Addison-Wesley.

FINDLAY, E. (1971). *Rhythm and movement*. Evanston, IL: Summy-Birchard.

HARGREAVES, D. J. (1986). *The developmental psychology of music*. Cambridge, UK: Cambridge University.

JESSUP, L. (1992). *World music: A source book for teaching*. Danbury, CT: World Music Press.

MONSOUR, S., & KNOX, C. (1990). *Magic musical balloon game*, computer program. Bellevue, WA: Temporal Acuity Products.

Music FUNdamentals, computer program. (1992). Morristown, NJ: Silver Burdett and Ginn.

PAYNTER, J., & ASTON, P. (1971). *Sound and silence*. Cambridge, UK: Cambridge University.

PEERY, J. C., PEERY, I. W., & DRAPER, T. W. (Eds.). (1987). *Music and child development*. New York: Springer-Verlag.

SCHAFER, R. M. (1976). *Creative music education*. New York: Schirmer Books.

SERAFINE, M. L. (1988). *Music as cognition*. New York: Columbia University.

THOMAS, R. (1970). *Manhattanville music curriculum project (MMCP) synthesis*. Bardonia, NY: Media Materials.

WILLIAMS, D. B. (1992). *Toney Music Games*, computer program. Normal, IL: Illinois State.

WILLIAMS, D. B., & FOX, D. B. (1990). *Toney listens to music*, computer program. Bellevue, WA: Temporal Acuity Products.

6

The Singing Child

For the child, to sing is to turn interests, experiences, and feelings into a very personal musical expression. Kimberly sings of flowers, David of trains, and Tony about lions, bears, dogs, and dragons. Michelle chants with Rosalita and Candy the "songs" of their handclapping games. Robert and Charoen trade songs they learned at church and in the temple, making up new words and tunes as they sing them. Lonnie sings before sleep, while Tuyen invents a new tune each morning. Diana sings to the wind's drone, her head tossed out the window of her father's car. Wayne mixes singing with lip-syncing all the latest tunes on MTV. Heather eagerly awaits her weekly choir rehearsals, while Marla sings her solos like the singing star she dreams to be.

The sounds of singing children can bring joy to those who listen, for these sounds emanate from their childlike thoughts and experiences. The quality of children's voices reflects a combined innocence, playfulness, and energy that befits them. Children sing alone and together, with and without the accompaniment of instruments or the electronic media of tapes, television, and radio. They sing spontaneously, and often without knowing it: at meals; while walking to school; and in the middle of an independent school project. As they imitate and personalize the songs they have heard, children bring joy to themselves as well as to those who listen.

In today's high-tech societies, some may say that the singing child is an anachronism—a symbol of days gone by. Some may believe that "children would rather be entertained than to entertain" themselves and others by singing, that "boys beyond grade two do not sing," and that "folk-song singing has been replaced by rock-song shouting." This gloom-and-doom perspective can discourage teachers and parents who recall their own active childhoods as singers, and who wish to incorporate songs within the learning experiences of children.

Are children singing less (and less well) in the contemporary world of high-tech media? While the media may appear to pacify children while it entertains them, children actually begin to sing at or before the stage at which they acquire speech—at a time before they may even be attracted to the media. It follows that children will continue singing when given opportunities to do so. Away from their tapes and television, they sing a great deal. Teachers and parents can provide occasions for singing—before classes and assemblies, at the start and close of the school day, after dinner, before bedtime, or while camping, walking, or riding in the car or on the bus. These are the times for singing favorite songs as well as for learning new ones. As for the media, rather than reducing children's singing, radio, recordings, and television may be stimulating their songfulness as well as adding to their repertoire.

Singing is a phenomenon for all ages, times, and cultures, but it begins and is nurtured in childhood. Children's vocal development can be greatly enhanced through training. The teacher who understands the physiology and capabilities of the young voice will select an appropriate repertoire and instructional techniques for children from preschool through the elementary grades. Contrary to the myth that singing lessons should begin in or after adolescence, vocal technique can be taught from the earliest songs by the knowledgeable teacher.

The Developing Child Voice

As early as infancy, as children begin to discover their vocal capabilities, they are making musical sounds. Playfully, they explore sounds with the vowels and consonants that they have heard before, extending their duration, repeating them rhythmically, and in rising and falling pitch passages. Like the babbling that precedes speech, musical babbling is the vocalization that precedes the performance of melodies (Moog, 1976). As they toddle toward two years, children progress in their vocalizations, producing increasingly longer melodic phrases spontaneously. While young children may seldom use words in their spontaneous songs, they string nonsense syllables together in small intervals of seconds and thirds. By the age of three, children begin to develop the periodic accents of regular rhythmic patterns in their spontaneous songs, and slightly larger intervals may occur. Besides their own invented songs, children reproduce the short songs of nursery rhymes and childhood chants at this age, including the simple movements associated with them. An outline of children's vocal development can be found in Table 6.1.

Children four and five years of age begin to discover the difference between their singing and speaking voices. Their singing may shift from a light, airy sound to a "playground yell" for lively songs. While their spontaneous

Table 6.1   Children's Vocal Development

Age	Developmental Activity
Less than one	Vocalizes (babbles) vowels and consonants
Age one/two	Babbles in irregular rhythmic patterns Imitates the contour of songs' melodic phrases, but not discrete pitches
Two	Babbles in extended melodic phrases Babbles in small intervals of seconds, thirds Imitates occasional discrete pitches of songs
Three	Invents "spontaneous songs" with discrete pitches and recurring rhythmic and melodic patterns Reproduces nursery rhymes and childhood chants
Four/five (Kindergarten)	Discovers differences between speaking and singing voices Shifts song qualities from light and airy to the "playground yell" for lively songs Sings spontaneous songs spanning two octaves Sings in tune within range of five pitches, d-a
Six/seven (Grade one)	Sings in tune in range of d-b Can begin to develop head voice, with guidance Begins to have expressive control of voice.
Seven/eight (Grade two)	Sings in tune in range of octave, about C-c′ or d-d′, with smaller tessitura
Eight/nine (Grade three)	Sings in tune in range of B♭-e♭′, with smaller tessitura Can perform fundamental harmony songs such as melody over vocal ostinato or sustained pitch
Nine/ten (Grade four)	Sings in tune range of A to e′, with smaller tessitura Sings with increasing resonance (grades four, five, and six) May experience first vocal change (boys, beginning age ten) Can perform canons, rounds, descants, countermelodies Can sing with appropriate phrasing, with guidance
Ten/eleven (Grade five)	Sings in tune range of A♭ to f′, with C-c′ octave tessitura Is increasingly selective of song repertoire Prefers songs in middle range Prefers songs without sentimental or babyish texts Can perform two-part songs
Eleven/twelve (Grade six)	Sings in tune range of G to g′, with C-c′ octave tessitura Can perform three-part songs

c = middle c; c′ = one octave higher; and C = one octave lower than middle C.

singing may span nearly two octaves, the range at which they can sing accurately in tune may extend only five pitches, from d to a. As children learn new songs, they progress through five stages, reproducing: the words; the rhythm of the words; a general but inaccurate sense of the melody's contour; a more accurate sense of individual pitches within the melody; and, finally, the tonality of the song across all its phrases. They learn songs through imitation of a model, and require the teacher's step-by-step guidance toward more accurate reproduction.

As children learn to sing a repertoire of songs, they also acquire rhythmic and melodic fragments that spill into their own musical play and invented songs. In many Western cultures, children through the elementary grades may incorporate the descending minor third into their invented songs, often accompanied by a fourth:

"Rain, Rain Go Away" and "Little Sally Walker" are examples of Western traditional children's songs that feature this common melodic pattern. Despite its frequent presence, however, it may be premature to suggest that the minor third is the first or most frequent interval to emerge in children's vocalizations, especially before systematic study of children in other world cultures has been undertaken. As children in the West gain exposure to popular music, the songs they strive to sing and create anew may contain the syncopated rhythms and the melodic patterns characteristic of the popular sound. Similarly, children's extended experience with any other musical style is likely to influence their accumulated repertoire and to flavor their musical expressions.

Children in the primary grades are more apt to sing in tune than younger children. Their singing range widens from d to b for six-year-olds to about an octave by second grade, from B to d', and from about B♭ to e♭' by third grade. Their tessitura, or the average range in which most pitches of a song lie, is somewhat smaller. So although children are capable of a larger vocal range, songs that linger on the lowest to highest pitches should be avoided. Children may continue to sing as they do at play, in their lower chest range, unless their head voice is developed—particularly through pitch-matching exercises. The use of a pure neutral syllable like "loo" will assist children in concentrating on appropriate vocal production through their ranges.

At eight years (or by second grade), children are likely to be able to maintain the same tonality throughout a song. As their musical memory increases, they are able to learn longer and more complex songs. By the age of nine, children may succeed at performing fundamental harmony songs—those with a recurring vocal ostinato, or sustained sounds overlapped by moving melo-

Figure 6.1. Range and tessitura for children's voices, ages 6–12.

dies. Their need for socialization with friends may nurture their interest in singing with others, while at the same time their perceptual development offers them a greater awareness of blending their voices with the ensemble of singers.

In the intermediate grades, when children are showing signs of rapid physical development, their voices are also affected by the maturation process. Their singing quality is fuller and more resonant in the fourth, fifth, and sixth grades than in the primary grades, although some children may feel more self-conscious about singing (especially solos) and thus may sound softer and lighter than their full-volumed capacity. The range of children's voices before the first changes that accompany adolescence typically spans from A to e′ for fourth graders, from A♭ to f′ for fifth graders, and from G to g′ for sixth graders; the tessitura for children ten through twelve years may be limited to about one octave. Some boys will experience a first vocal change by age ten or eleven, although others will sing well into early adolescence with a robust yet pure quality unmatched by children at any other age.

Children begin to manifest the signs of physiological and psychological changes typical of adolescence by the close of their elementary years. Unless they are accustomed to singing, they may lose interest and resist any occasion to sing. While in some societies singing is an act of great pride that brings on admiration by members of the opposite sex, in American schools it is not unusual to find girls who are embarrassed to sing in front of boys, and boys who view singing as a feminine or at least a less virile activity. To many children on the brink of adolescence singing is no longer "cool." Maintaining children's interest in singing requires a careful selection of songs with texts that are meaningful to them (and not too sentimental or babyish), with melodic ranges well within the safety of their tessitura.

The changing male voice is a symptom of the hormonal changes that begin to occur at the onset of puberty. When boys show a sudden growth spurt and a physical awkwardness, they may also demonstrate a heavier quality as they speak and sing. Their voices may occasionally "crack" as they reach beyond their middle range. While experts vary somewhat in their approaches to boys' changing voices, most recommend singing within the middle and most comfortable section of their range, and avoiding register extremes.

As children come to understand the vocal mechanism, they are better able to use their voices productively. Children in the intermediate grades also are capable of performing with appropriate phrasing, diction, and intonation—all important facets of choral singing. Because they can perceive more than one simultaneously occurring musical line at a time, and because their voices are stronger and more independent than earlier, they can sing in harmony the rounds, partner songs, and part-songs that comprise the repertoire of children's choirs. As they mature, children are able to sing expressively and to evaluate their own musical and vocal performance in terms of accuracy and appropriate tone, blend, and style.

Physical Training for the Child Voice

Beyond the natural development that occurs from preschool through the elementary grades, children's voices can be greatly enhanced through training. This is not to say that private singing lessons are advisable for children; lessons may best be reserved for the later years of adolescence and adulthood when vocal development is complete. The astute teacher, however, who knows and provides occasions for exercising children's voices through songs, vocal games, and drills, will quicken the pace of development and extend the capacity for musical expression. Daily or even twice-weekly "group sings" will undoubtedly create more musical singers at an earlier age.

"Perfect singing posture," or PSP, is prerequisite to gaining good breath

"PSP"—Perfect Singing Posture. *Reproduced with permission from* Teaching Kids to Sing *by Kenneth H. Phillips, Schirmer Books, 1992.*

control, producing a beautiful tone, and phrasing a set of tones expressively. Although they are physically active and seldom sedentary, children require regular coordination, conditioning, and postural-development exercises. Imagery and exercise (rather than verbal explanations) can lead to the correct stance (or seating position) for singing.

PSP involves the following bottom-to-top body parts. Suggestions for how to achieve the correct position are noted:

1. Feet should be flat on the floor, about six inches apart, with one foot slightly ahead of the other. The weight is on the balls (not the heels) of the feet. Practice in shifting the weight "from heels to toes" will bring about an awareness of where the weight should be.

2. Knees need to be relaxed and not locked. A light bouncing in place, one knee alternating with the other, and then both knees, can eliminate tightness and tension.

3. The spine is to be lifted up and away from the hips. It should be straight but not stiff. Leading with the arms extended, and hands clasped backward, a spinal stretch can extend down to the toes, outward from the chest to the front, right, and left sides, and then high above the head. A return back to center will move the spine gently into place.

4. The chest should be slightly raised. Movement of the arms in a circular "breast stroke" gesture from the middle of the chest to above the head and down to the side can loosen yet also coordinate the musculature of the chest, rib cage, lungs, and sternum.

5. Shoulders are held back slightly and down. Shoulder rolls are helpful: rotation of the shoulders forward, down, and up will decrease tension; the reverse movement (backward, down, and up again) can also be helpful.

6. The head is held high, as it rises up out of the spine and neck and rests level and well aligned. Head rolls achieve this position, by dropping the head to the chest, rolling it to one side and then the other.

7. Arms and hands should hang easily down at the sides. This can be achieved at the end of the spinal stretch or "breast stroke" gesture, although attention may need to be called to the position of the arms and hands.

One of the most complete means for attaining appropriate alignment of the body parts for PSP is the image and imitation of a marionette puppet. Children begin this exercise by standing tall, and imagining that there are two strings attached to them—from the ceiling to the bottom of their back, and to the top of their head. An invisible puppeteer loosens the string, and the children drop from their waist, with heads and arms hanging down past their knees, to the floor. In that position, they gently bounce. When the puppeteer begins to pull at the strings, the marionette children slowly rise and realign themselves: chest, shoulders, neck, head, and arms fall relaxedly into place.

PSP can be achieved in a sitting, as well as standing, position. The alignment of the middle- and upper-body transfers from standing to sitting positions. Children who sit on chairs should sit on the front half of the seats with their feet flat on the floor. For those whose feet do not touch the floor, they should sit further back on the seats while hooking their feet on the front rung of the chair. Children who sit on the floor can be coaxed to cross their legs, raise themselves out of their hips, and lean slightly forward. No one position should be maintained for too long a time; standing and sitting positions can be taken alternately throughout a singing session.

Breathing for singing is similar to breathing for high-endurance sports like swimming and long-distance running. Children are intrigued when they discover the physicality of good singing, and the parallel of singing to athletic endeavors. With perfect singing posture, their bodies are readied for the deep breathing that must initiate and sustain the vocal sound. The image of filling the feet, the knees, the stomach, and diaphragm (and the lungs) with air shows

Marionette strategy for attaining PSP.

how complete and all-encompassing the breathing must be. Children can come to understand that as they fill themselves with the air of a very deep breath, their lower rib cage expands along with their lungs. Like a balloon or a bagpipe, they have the air within them that can be moved up the windpipe and across the vocal cords causing vibration to occur and sound to be produced.

Breathing exercises should precede singing activity. Children can take in air as they would sip soda through a straw: with puckered lips, they slowly sip the air in a manner similar to drinking. Because sipping is an easy and gentle action, there should be no tension in the exercise. Taking the image of the balloon, children can compare the expansion of their own lungs to the fullness of a blown balloon. They can imitate the roundness of a balloon as they breathe in through their mouths, their arms curved in front of them, fingers touching. The more air they inhale, the wider the balloon becomes; their arms move out more widely so that their fingers can no longer touch. As the air of a balloon is slowly released, they can slowly release the air without producing a vocal sound, and their fingers touch again. The inhaling and exhaling process can challenge children physically, especially when the appropriate vocal sound to which the exercises lead is demonstrated.

Vocal exercises that combine the inhaling, sustaining, and releasing of air develop control essential to good singing. Several suggestions for warming up the voice with attention to the breathing mechanism follow.

1. The Ha-Ha. Imitate the quick, deep breathing of a dog panting at the end of a long and energetic run. Place the hands just under the rib cage at the diaphragm, take a deep breath, and exhale in short "ha-has." Breathe again, and while exhaling, sing the "ha-has" on one pitch. A third variation is to sing the "ha-has" stepwise from do to sol and back again, and then on a triadic do-mi-sol-mi-do.

Figure 6.2. The "Ha-ha."

2. The Cool "OO." Because the [u] vowel, as sounded in "new," resonates well and is a relaxed sound for children to produce, it is commonly used in warm-ups, and to tune voices to one another. Using a descending stepwise pattern that ends in a skip of a fifth up and down, sing an "oo" sound with "the letter "l" interspersed. Care should be taken not to form the lips too tightly; in fact, a relaxed and slightly dropped jaw will allow maximal air flow without changing the vowel sound.

Figure 6.3. The Cool "OO."

3. The "No-ah's Ark." The pure [o] as in "cold" requires the jaw to drop more than in the [u]. It should also have very little of the "vanishing oo" sound of "no"; that is, "no-oo." The [a] of "father" is sounded by dropping the jaw to a space long enough to allow the insertion of two fingers vertically. A slight smile contributes to a brighter [a] rather than "uh" sound. By singing "No-ah's Ark," children exercise two distinctive positions of the mouth and thus two separate vowel and vocal sounds. A smaller- and larger-ranged version of ascending and successive thirds is appropriate for children in the primary and intermediate grades.

Figure 6.4. The "No-ah's Ark."

4. The "Mmmmm" on the Vowels. Using the "m" sound to lead easily to vowel sounds, sing on one pitch the vowels [i] sounded as "ee," [e] sounded as "ay," [a], [o], and [u]. The [i] is like the sound in "green," and is produced with the lips slightly puckered so that the sound does not spread too widely. The [e] is a dipthong similar to the sound in "play," with an emphasis on "eh" that closes on "ee." In this exercise, five vowels are sounded on a single pitch. The transition from the consonant "m" to each vowel and back to the consonant again should be smooth, connected, and all on one sustained breath. The exercise can be accompanied by I, IV, I, V7, I.

Figure 6.5. "Mmmmm" on the vowels.

5. The Echo. The modeling of pitches and pitch patterns by a leader is then imitated by the children. In leader-follower fashion, sing patterns and phrases from familiar songs as well as those yet to be learned. Use neutral syllables like "loo," "noo," "la," and "bee" for tuning voices, and solfège syllables for building understanding of pitches and their relationships.

Figure 6.6. The Echo.

Toward Accurate Singing

Children who can hear and perceive melody are well-equipped for singing accurately. The ability to hear is a physical endowment, but to perceive the melody of a song well enough to sing it requires focused and attentive listening. Children need the teacher's direction to attend to the pitches, phrases, and contours of a melody, as well as its rhythm, text, and formal organization. Some learn best through repeated listenings alone, others learn well when visual means (including color-coded shapes, numbers, pictures, and graphs, staff notation, and the printed song words) are applied, and still others require the use of their bodies to "feel" the melody. One means of focusing children's listening is the use of direct questions, such as: "Listen: does the melody move mostly upward or downward?"; or "Which word sounds the highest pitch of the song?"

Children can draw the melody's movement with their fingers, hands, arms, or even torso. This graphing of the melody's rise and fall is sometimes referred to as "mapping." Such mapping can be broad and involve the entire body, or it can be contained within a very small space. Mapping may consist of a line drawing with the finger that moves each phrase from left to right "in the air," on chalkboards with chalk, or on large pieces of paper with crayon.

Another means of directing children's attention to individual pitches and their relationships is through the use of a hand sign system first developed by Sarah Glover and John Curwen in England in the middle of the nineteenth century. The system was later popularized by proponents of the Kodály approach, and is often referred to as "Kodály hand signs" (see Fig. 5.1). In this system, each pitch of the diatonic scale is associated with a hand sign. Additional signs are used to indicate chromatic pitches, or accidentals outside of the song's key signature. Children can be taught the hand signs with relative ease, as they sing the pitch names of the diatonic scale or as they learn the melodic fragments and tonal phrases of the songs they know. The hand sign system is effective as a technique for teaching melodic direction and shape, and is enjoyed by children as a game that challenges their listening, critical thinking, moving, and of course, singing skills.

Children are more likely to sing accurately when they can discriminate among higher or lower pitches, and when they are presented with occasions for reproducing short melodic phrases. Pitch-matching requires not only listening perception and short-term memory skills, but also the skills of vocal production. Through a series of echo-chants built on neutral syllables, solfège syllables, or word-phrases, children can match the pitches of short melodic phrases that are sung to them. These phrases may be embedded in familiar songs, or songs they will eventually learn to sing, or in a familiar music repertoire. These melodic phrases may also be built into conversational or dialogue phrases, in which the same pitches used for a question may be used by children in their response. Table 6.2 presents a sampling of musical fragments for pitch-matching. When such phrases are accompanied by appropriate gestures to indicate pitch direction and pitch relationships, children may sing them with even greater accuracy.

As children develop the abilities to discriminate pitches and to sing in tune, they should also be developing tonal memory. The teacher can guide children in strengthening their tonal memory by playing "name that tune," in which they identify the title of a familiar song that is sung by the teacher or selected leader without words on a neutral syllable. Another playful approach to strengthening the memory is to lead children in singing a song, and on a prearranged cue (such as a tap on the drum) to sing silently, only to return to singing aloud when given the cue again. Children must retain a sense of pulse, tempo, and pitch while silently performing the melody so that they can join in together again when the cue is given. Tonal memory, like rhythmic memory, requires children's utmost concentration. With it, their musicianship—and their repertoire of songs—can grow.

For every phrase or song that is sung, the pitch and tempo must be set by the teacher. Children need to know on just what pitch they are to begin their singing, or all attempts at accurate singing are foiled. Familiar songs can begin with the teacher's sounding of the tonic or "home tone" of the song, and then the 1-3-5-3-1 (d-m-s-m-d) of the key. A piano, xylophone, guitar, or other pitched instrument may be more helpful to the teacher than to the children, who may need to hear the vocally produced pitch to match it. Even in teaching individual song phrases by rote, the teacher should make a practice of sounding the first pitch, vocally, on a neutral syllable such as "loo" or "la," and then signaling the children to sing that pitch on that syllable before repeating the phrase. The pitch and tempo for familiar and new songs can be set together by conducting the meter while singing an initial phrase on the first pitch of the song. One example for pitch- and tempo-setting at the same time is shown in Figure 6.7.

As children listen to song phrases and fragments, they must also strive to learn and retain their components to sing them accurately. They learn the words, rhythm, and melody of a song through repeated listening, and then by imitating the singer who serves as model for them. Young singers require far more repetition of songs and song segments than they typically receive to grasp all the musical details. For example, an eight-measure melody like that of "Hey, Betty Martin" may require six or eight repetitions before a group of seven-year-olds can retain and reproduce the song with the words, melody, rhythm, and tonality intact. The teacher can sing alone while the children listen or the children can sing while following the teacher's lead. A longer and more complex song like "Tinga Layo" may necessitate as many (or more) repetitions for a group of ten-year-olds to learn it.

Table 6.2 Pitch-matching Samples

Pitch Patterns through Solfège

Dialogue Chants

Table 6.2   Continued

Not all children sing accurately in tune, although the great majority of children are capable of it. Children who sing daily at home or in school develop in-tune singing by the end of the second grade, but for those in environments without regular opportunities to listen to music and to sing, there may be vocal troubles that require attention. Rather than to label the uncertain singers as "monotones" or "nonsingers," teachers may need to devise remedial exercises within class and help sessions before or after school, or at recess. Some children need coaxing to find their singing voice, and may need to sing close to the pitch of their speaking voice. Others need to know that it is "safe" to sing aloud (and possibly solo). This will entail discussing the "rules of etiquette" with the group while singing alone, so that all children can be helped in becoming a part of their singing team. A series of siren-like sound effects can be modeled and then imitated, to extend the range of children who drone on one or two pitches or who sing below the appropriate pitch. The sound of a ghost is another aural image that can assist children in hearing and feeling how their voices can reach registers not usually associated with their own speaking ranges. Likewise, children can imitate the sound of "yoo-hoo" or a train whistle.

These experiences can lead to pitch-matching exercises, and to songs with

Figure 6.7.   Starting a song.

Figure 6.8. Extending voice range.

simple rhythms and small melodic ranges. Unless children have physiological conditions (such as damaged vocal cords or severe hearing deficits) or the rare condition known as "amusia," they can learn to sing accurately. The patient teacher's knowledgeable and inventive remedies can ensure success.

The Vocal Model

Children tend to sing a song in the manner and style in which it was presented to them. Thus, the presence of an accurate vocal model is critical to the instructional process. Whether the teacher, parent, or other adult seeks to teach a song, attention must be paid to musical style and voice quality as well as to the components of the song itself. If children are to sing in a light head tone, then the song must be sung by the model in that way. If a song is to be sung with vigor at high volume, then that model should be presented. If a song is suited for a softer and slower performance, then children must hear it that way. Children will sing a song presented in legato style in that manner, just as they are likely to sing a song in as many phrases (with as many breaths) and as many accents and dynamic nuances as they hear from the model.

The teacher or other singer who models for children should assume a singer's posture: straight and well-aligned, but not stiff. Children need to see and hear what is expected of them. They need to see a singer's facial expression and gestures reflect the mood and text of the song, and hear the singer's energy and enthusiasm for the song, because it is the singer's "performance" that can convince them that this is a song they should know. Most importantly, the singer who models for children should sing the song musically—in tune, in its correct rhythm, and according to its stylistic nuances.

If the voice quality of the model is in many cases imitated by children, then what can be said about the male singer intent on teaching children to sing? Until the fourth grade, even children who sing regularly may have difficulty matching pitches when they hear the male voice sounding an octave below their own register. Some children attempt to sing at the lower octave, while others target a set of pitches somewhere between the model's pitch and that of the higher octave. Male singers working with young children or with children inexperienced in singing make more effective models for children when they sing using a falsetto quality. This falsetto sound should not be forced or at the full volume of a countertenor; instead, the sound should be light and some-what softer than the full dynamic intensity of the "real" voice. As children are able to transfer the sound of a male voice to their own register, often by fourth grade, they can begin to reap the benefit of hearing the male voice in its characteristic register.

Although much of the singing children do can be led by the teacher without the aid of other accompaniment, the use of instruments may well enhance the vocal sound. A tasteful accompaniment for recorder, xylophone ensemble, guitar, or piano can add musical interest, particularly for public performance

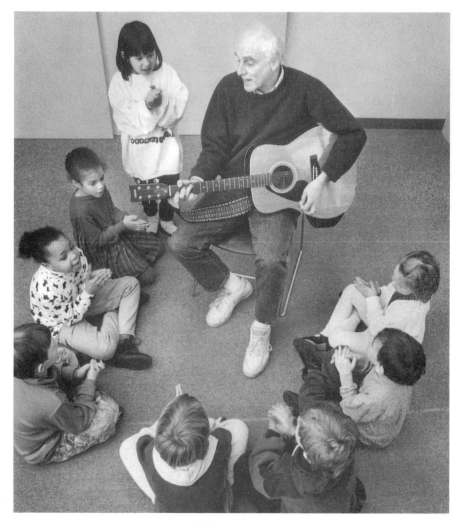

Male singer with children: from light falsetto to characteristic register.

(for the parents' club meeting or a school assembly, for example). A recorder descant played by a small group of children can provide a light contrapuntal line to the voice melody. The percussive quality of xylophone bourdons and ostinatos can provide striking contrast to smooth and well-supported singing. By strumming or plucking a guitar, the teacher can move closer to the children to hear and to help them with singing problems. The piano can provide an excellent support to singing, although it must be played with sensitivity to the vocal balance. However, because school music classrooms are often outfitted with a piano, it is tempting to overuse it in the early stages of learning a song so that children cannot listen to the teacher's (or their own) voice.

Should recordings be used in teaching children to sing? This is an irresistible proposition, and when instruments beyond those of the classroom appear on a recording, there may be greater musical intrigue and possibly greater motivation for children to sing. Some recordings have the advantage of demonstrating to children the ideal aural image of how their own young voices should sound. A recording can make a most acceptable model of a perfected sound, and can be used to introduce a song, or to later reinforce it. Still, it may be largely the task of the teacher to start and stop the song, and to raise and lower the pitch, tempo, and volume of the song, according to the vocal abilities and musical needs of the children. No recording or other electronic apparatus can do this with such ease and immediacy.

Selecting and Teaching Songs

Processes for teaching songs to children range from "rote" to "note," or combinations of the two. Teaching a song by rote is transmitting the song orally, while teaching by note quite clearly involves children's ability to read music. The process depends on the teacher's perspective, the lesson objectives, and the children's skill levels. Yet even before the teaching process begins, initial steps can be taken to ensure children's successful singing. The critical first step is selecting songs that are musically, textually, and developmentally appropriate. Guidelines for song selection are noted in Table 6.3, along with other preparatory issues (see also Table 13.1 for a guide to authenticity in the selection of music).

Song collections are plentiful, with songs of every genre—traditional, patriotic, art/classical, composed, popular, and even songs transmitted and preserved by children. Readers should review the collections of Erdei and Komlos (1974), Fowke (1969, 1977), Lomax (1960), and Seeger (1948) for songs from North America. A good collection of rounds suitable for this age group has been compiled by Finckel (1993). For examples of children's songs from other world cultures, see Adzinyah, Maraire, and Tucker (1986), Brennan (1988), Campbell, McCullough-Brabson, and Tucker (1994), Ellis

Table 6.3 Song Selection and Preparation

---

1. Select a song that is age-appropriate.
    Check the song's range
    Check the song's tessitura
    Check the text:
        Is it too "babyish"?
        Is it too "grown-up" or "lovey-dovey"?
        Will the subject matter interest the children?
        Does it contain offensive language (perhaps unintended)?
        If in a foreign language, can you pronounce it?
2. Select a song in a style that you can sing.
    Check the style: If it is outside your training and experience, can you learn to
        sing it in its appropriate style?
3. Review the song for its musical and textual highlights.
    Check the melody: Are there tonal phrases to sing in isolation?
    Check the rhythm: Are there rhythmic phrases to chant in isolation?
    Check the text: Are there ideas for relating to a story, poem, discussion of a
        historical or cultural issue?

(1990), Nguyen and Campbell (1992), and Sam and Campbell (1992), all accompanied by recordings. The music textbook series published by Holt, Rinehart, and Winston, Macmillan, and Silver Burdett Ginn contain a rich variety of songs appropriate for use with children from kindergarten through the eighth grade.

One of the most popular ways for the teacher to present a song is through oral and aural means, or by rote. In the rote approach, children are given numerous opportunities to listen to the complete song. Fragments of the song are then presented sequentially to the children (oral) in small phrases or "chunks"; children listen (aural) and then echo these fragments. These chunks are sung repeatedly until accuracy is achieved, and then the chunks are combined with other chunks until the whole song is learned. The children's imitation of the model is a necessary strategy in the rote approach, and one that can nearly guarantee the development of a large repertoire of songs.

Another approach to teaching a song involves children in the reading of notation. A selected song may contain melodic and rhythmic patterns that were sung, chanted, and played in earlier lessons. Given the great array of songs in series textbooks and in song collections, children can be challenged to seek familiar notated patterns within the new song, and to perform them. Rhythms can be chanted according to the preferred system, and melodic patterns can be sung on neutral syllables or with solfège syllables. While there may be unfamiliar patterns to be learned by rote, by trial-and-error, or by putting to practice the logical and analytical skills required of reading words or

Table 6.4 Rote and Note Approaches to Teaching "Kookaburra"

By Rote	By Note
1. "Can you keep the steady pulse?" Teacher sings the song while children accompany by patting and clapping	1. Teacher presents notated rhythm patterns: ♫♫ ♫♪ ♪♫ "Take a minute to practice. Silently chant and clap the familiar patterns."
2. "Can you draw the melody's rises and falls"? Teacher sings the song again while children draw in space the melodic contour.	2. "Let's chant and clap as I point to the individual patterns." Teacher and children perform them, using favored chant system (for example, ti-ri-ti-ri, ti-ti-ri, ti-ti ti-ti).
3. "What word is sung on the highest pitch of the song?" Teacher sings the song again, followed by children's answer.	3. Repeat as necessary.
4. "Listen and then sing after me": "Kookaburra sits on a old gum tree." Teacher sings first phrase; children imitate.	4. "Sing with me": s s s s l l l s m s m Teacher and children sing together.
5. Repeat first phrase as necessary.	5. Repeat as necessary.
6. "Listen and then sing after me": "Merry merry king of the bush is he." Teacher sings second phrase; children imitate.	6. "Now, what would happen if we sang that phrase beginning on mi? Shall we try it?" m m m m f f f m d m Teacher and children sing together.
7. Repeat second phrase as necessary.	7. "Let's try singing these phrases with our hand signals AND our musical syllables." Teacher and children sing and signal the two phrases.
8. "Listen and then sing after me": "Laugh Kookaburra, laugh Kookaburra." Teacher sings third phrase; children imitate.	8. "Look at two new rhythm patterns: ♩♫♫ ♪♫♩ Let's clap and chant them." Teacher and children clap and rhythmically chant.

(continued)

Table 6.4 Continued

By Rote	By Note
9. Repeat third phrase as necessary.	9. "What if we added pitches to those rhythms? Could you sing them?" Teacher presents notation for last two phrases.
10. "Listen and then sing after me": "Glad your life must be." Teacher sings final phrase, children imitate.	10. "What's the highest pitch?" (Do.) Listen and follow with your hand signs: ♩ ♬♬ ♩ ♬♬ ♫ ♫ d l t d l s s l s f md d d
11. Repeat final phrase as necessary.	11. "Now sing with me." Teacher and children sing last two phrases with syllables and hand signals.
12. "Let's sing the first two phrases, first me and then you." Teacher sings phrase one and two; children imitate.	12. Repeat as necessary.
13. Repeat as necessary.	13. Teacher presents the notated song. "Can you clap and chant the whole song?" Teacher and children clap and chant together.
14. "Let's sing the last two phrases, first me and then you." Teacher sings phrase three and four; children imitate.	14. "Can you, slowly, sing the melody with our musical syllables and hand signals? Watch me when you get lost." Teacher and children sing and signal together.
15. Repeat as necessary.	15. Repeat as necessary.
16. "Now we're ready to sing the whole song." Teacher and children sing together.	16. "Let's read the words to this song, in rhythm."
17. "Can you sing the song without me? I'll get you started." Teacher sets pitch and tempo; children sing.	17. "Let's sing the song with the words."
	18. Repeat as necessary.
	19. "Can you sing the song without me? I'll get you started." Teacher sets pitch and tempo; children sing.

notes, children can connect the familiar to the new patterns in learning the song. The teacher may eventually sing the entire song to provide them with a coherent image of the song. Children can feel quite accomplished in having the ability to decode the notation themselves. Table 6.4 presents both rote and note approaches to teaching "Kookaburra."

Rote and note are two approaches, although combinations of these approaches are also possible. The immersion process is another means for learning a song, in which children hear the song sung by the teacher, parent, or another child to the extent they individually require before joining in and singing it. When a song is learned, children can then be led to related activities, including playing body percussion on ♩, ♫, and, ♫♫, creating a dance to reflect its phrases and form, accompanying the song with ostinati on classroom instruments, improvising a variation on recorder, or including it in a performance of other songs and chanted poems on similar subjects. However, any possibilities for extending their capabilities for singing expressively requires their full knowledge and skills in performing the song. With this accomplished and with the vocal production capacity in good working order, children can then be taught to sing musically.

How to Teach Singing in Parts

When children have developed the perceptual and productive skills that come with singing in tune, the next natural stage is to sing in harmony. Children in the third grade can be successful in singing songs in two-part arrangements: melodies with drones and ostinati. Fourth grade children perform canons (or rounds), descants, and countermelodies well in two independent groups; three-part canons can be reserved for children in fifth and sixth grades. When music instruction has been consistent and strong, bona fide two-part choral pieces can be read, rehearsed, and perfected for performance in the last years of elementary school.

Old Texas (U.S.)

Hey, Ho, Nobody Home (England)

In testing children's ability to sing in independent groups, songs like "Old Texas" with active melodies sung over the sustained pitch of a second group can be selected. The teacher can lead the singing, sustaining as children sing in imitation. Eventually, two groups can perform this fundamental form of part-singing.

Among the first attempts at singing in parts is the use of a repeated melodic pattern, or ostinato, to accompany the melody, as in "Hey, Ho, Nobody Home" or "Ah, Poor Bird." Ostinato parts are created by examining the melody for its harmonic possibilities, and sampling on a pitched instrument one- or two-measure segments that jell harmonically with each measure of the song. While seconds or sevenths occasionally may sound together in passing, so long as they are resolved to thirds, fourths, or fifths on the strong beats, the ostinato will probably be quite satisfying.

Canons and rounds comprise some of the most fulfilling musical experiences for children in their elementary years. Critical to that fulfillment, however, is the process by which they are taught. First, the teacher should be certain that the children are secure in singing the song's melody as a larger group, and then in smaller groups. Second, the teacher can cue the class to begin singing, and then can begin softly singing the second part "at the canon." The number "2" on the scores signifies the point at which the group must be when the teacher begins singing. Third, a small group of children can be selected to sing with the teacher "at the canon." Finally, the class can be divided equally,

Ah, Poor Bird (England)

Scotland's Burning (England)

Kaeru No Uta (Japan)

Autumn's Here (U.S.)

Viva la musica (Germany)

so that the two groups can maintain their independent parts while performing. "Scotland's Burning," "Kaeru no Uta," "Autumn's Here," and "Viva la Musica" are examples of canons that work with children's voices.

A descant is an independent melody that can be added above a first and usually more familiar melody. It is higher in pitch than the main melody. Conversely, a countermelody can be added below a familiar main melody. Using some of the procedures for teaching a round, children can sing the melody while the teacher softly adds a descant or countermelody; the class can gradually be divided into two groups. The songs "Skye Boat Song" and "Yo Mamana Yo" illustrate the use of the descant and countermelody.

Some musical traditions of the world are best sung in unison if a culturally authentic sound is to be rendered. Still, harmony is an important feature of

Skye Boat Song (Scotland)

Yo Mamana, Yo! (Mozambique)*

As sung by Salamao Manhica. From Roots and Branches. © *1994 World Music Press. Used by permission.*

many songs from Anglo- and African-American traditions, as well as from parts of sub-Saharan Africa, the Pacific Islands, and much of the Hispanic world. Excerpts from three pieces are included below: "Mbube," from South Africa, "Savalivala" from Samoa, and "Ambozado," from Puerto Rico.

Two- and three-part songs for children in the intermediate grades are increasingly available from publishing companies that specialize in choral music. Children's ability to sing in tune, in harmony, and to render songs with musical sensitivity makes singing a pleasure for them as well as for their listeners.

Mbube (South Africa)

Savalivala (Samoa)

Children's Choirs

When children have been raised to enjoy singing, they may be eager for the additional musical experiences that membership in a choir provides. Children's choirs in schools, churches, and community are a growing phe-

Ambozado (Puerto Rico)

1. Am - bo - za - do, ma - ta - ri - le, ri - le, ri - le. Am -
2. ¿Que quie - re us - ted?   ¿Que

bo - za - do ma - ta - ri - le ri - le ron.
quie - re us - ted?

3. Yo quie-ro un pa-je.
4. Ella dice que-lo quie-re.
(Él)

nomenon. When viewed as much as an educational entity as a performance one, the choir can extend the musical goals as well as the vocal development of children. Aural skills can be refined, pitch-matching can be improved, and children can become exposed to a variety of the historical and cultural repertoire. Within the framework of the school curriculum, a twice-weekly choir meeting of forty-five minutes to an hour can greatly enhance children's vocal and musical development.

School choirs often open membership to children of mixed ages beginning in the third or fourth grade, although two or three choirs can be formed according to age and experience. A public performance for parents or at a school assembly may be one of the choir's targeted goals, so that children can know the joy of performing for others. Seasonal, holiday, and graduation programs that feature children from all classes and grade levels can be capped off with a set of songs performed by the school choir. City- or district-wide festivals of elementary school choirs are other occasions for sharing with an audience the results of children's efforts in their rehearsals.

An audition is useful if only to emphasize the commitment of children to singing in a choir, and so that there is an understanding that each child's voice is important in its contribution to the group sound. This is not to say that the choir should be exclusive in its acceptance of only the most talented children. In fact, all children who express interest in singing in a school choir should be given a fair chance to become a member of the singing "team." An audition allows the director to know the vocal quality and musicianship of each child, and helps to guide the type of vocal exercises and repertoire to be used in rehearsal. Children who need remedial work also can be identified through the audition process.

Auditions can take place before or after school or at recess, but preferably not during the music class. To determine range and pitch accuracy, each child can be asked to sing a familiar song like "America" or "Are You Sleeping" first in a comfortable middle-range key, and then in higher and lower keys. Vocal quality and range also can be assessed by singing a descending major scale on a neutral syllable, starting first at c' (c above middle c), then at d', e', and so forth. Another test of pitch accuracy is having each child sing a set of short melodic patterns that are first sung or played by the teacher. Tonal memory can be tested by lengthening the melodic patterns to be imitated from four to six to eight beats. Finally, vocal independence can be evaluated by asking the student to sing a familiar song ("Are You Sleeping?," "Row Your Boat," "Music Alone Shall Live") while the teacher sings it in canon. These tasks offer the information teachers require in selecting and arranging music for the choir, while they challenge children musically and vocally.

A choir rehearsal may progress in several stages, beginning with physical warm-ups and vocal exercises. To maintain attention, a rehearsal should contain a variety of musical selections and approaches to them. One rule of thumb is to efficiently rehearse each song, or song section, for a maximum of seven minutes before proceeding to a new piece. In the case of a part song, those who are not singing should be silently following their part, which they may be directed to sing "on cue" at any given moment. When children show signs of distraction or inattention, a physical exercise or rhythmic pattern can be introduced to restore focus and energy. All rehearsals, regardless of how close a performance may be, should close with a familiar song that is guaranteed to send children on their way with good sounds and feelings about themselves and their membership in the choir. For further advice on organizing a children's choir, see McRae (1991).

Reasons to Sing

Children are still singing despite rumors that the media-rich world in which they live has turned them to passive listeners and "lip-syncers." The voice is the one musical "instrument" that all possess, and for which no rental fee nor elaborate arrangement for private instruction is necessary. For many children, singing is the path that they will choose to experience as participants and performers the great joy of music. Teachers who enjoy singing will further kindle the interests of children, because enjoyment is irresistible; it is contagious.

Teachers and parents may be teaching more than musicianship when they sing with their children. In fact, a great many ideas can be advanced through song. The link between language, speech, chant, and song is undeniable, such that children can expand their vocabulary as well as understand ways in which words fit together as they learn new songs. Cultural values can be advanced through songs, and songs from various cultures and historical periods can present children with glimpses of different worlds and eras. Song texts cover nearly every subject under the sun, so that there are countless songs about animals, food, modes of transportation, flowers, rivers, patriotism, and of course, family, friends, and neighbors. Singing can be combined with other musical activities, too, so that children can sing as they play instruments, move, and create new music.

Questions

1. Trace the development of children's voices from early childhood through the intermediate grades, with special attention to changes in range and quality.
2. What is "PSP"? How is it attained?
3. Cite evidence to support the view of singing as a physical as well as mental endeavor.
4. What is a developmental sequence for children's part-song singing?
5. What are the components of an audition for membership in a children's choir?

Activities

1. Prepare a song to teach: (a) by rote; and (b) by note. How do the approaches differ? How might aspects of each be combined over several lessons?
2. Choose a traditional song and write a vocal ostinato for it.
3. Collect ten songs that you feel all children in preschool and/or elementary school should "know." Analyze the songs for their melodic and rhythmic content, order them from less to more complex, and determine the grade level at which you would teach these songs.
4. Visit a music store specializing in choral scores, and begin a card file that

gives the song title, composer/arranger, publisher, range and tessitura, songs and part-songs for use in (a) music class; and (b) the school choir. Select a set of songs that could conceivably comprise an autumn, winter, or spring program.

References

ADZINYAH, D. M., MARAIRE, D., & TUCKER, J. C. (1986). *Let your voice be heard.* Danbury, CT: World Music Press.

BRENNAN, E. V. (1988). *The singing wind: Five melodies from Ecuador.* Danbury, CT: World Music Press.

CAMPBELL, P. S., MCCULLOUGH-BRABSON, E., & TUCKER, J. C. (1994). *Roots and branches.* Danbury, CT: World Music Press.

ELLIS, K. (1990). *Domino: Selected songs from the Virgin Islands.* Nazareth, PA: Guavaberry Press.

ERDEI, P., & KOMLOS, K. (1974). *150 American folk songs for children to sing and play.* New York: Boosey and Hawkes.

FINCKEL, E. A. (1993). *Now we'll make the rafters ring: 100 traditional and contemporary rounds for everyone.* Pennington, NJ: A Cappella Books.

FOWKE, E. (1969). *Sally go round the sun.* Garden City, NY: Doubleday.

———. (1977). *Ring around the moon.* Englewood Cliffs, NJ: Prentice-Hall.

LOMAX, A. (1960). *The folk songs of North America.* Garden City, NY: Doubleday.

MCRAE, S. W. (1991). *Directing the children's choir.* New York: Schirmer Books.

MOOG, H. (1976). *The musical experience of the pre-school child.* C. Clarke (Trans.). London: Schott.

NGUYEN, P., & CAMPBELL, P. S. (1992). *From rice paddies and temple yards: Traditional music of Vietnam.* Danbury, CT: World Music Press.

PHILLIPS, K. H. (1992). *Teaching kids to sing.* New York: Schirmer Books.

SAM, S.-A., & CAMPBELL, P. S. (1992). *Silent temples, songful hearts: Traditional music of Cambodia.* Danbury, CT: World Music Press.

SEEGER, R. C. (1948). *American folk songs for children.* New York: Doubleday.

CHAPTER 7

The Listening Child

Courtney concentrates happily as her mother sings a new song to her. When her mother stops, she says, "Sing it again, Mommy, sing it again!" Her mother sings it over several times and, finally, Courtney joins in, singing the song accurately. Josh walks down the street, almost dancing, as he listens through his headphones to his latest purchase, a tape of his favorite pop group. Ofewe sets a rhythm pattern on his synthesizer, focuses on its flow, then begins to improvise a melody to it. Michiko practices a phrase from her latest piano piece, shakes her head in frustration, tries it again, then smiles with satisfaction.

Each of these children is engaged in the perceptive activity that is at the heart of all we do with music whether singing, dancing, creating, or playing. That activity is listening. Music is an aural art that stimulates our ears and challenges our minds, usually bringing a pleasure and satisfaction that transcends much of what we experience in life. Most music is received through the ear, not the eye. And most music performed throughout the world is aurally transmitted and will never be written down. Therefore, development of the ear is crucial to development of musicianship.

Learning to listen perceptively is a skill that can grow as surely as the gourmet can learn to detect the ingredients in a dish from a single taste. The reward of developing that skill is the same as any person feels at being sensorily alive, at being able to notice the subtleties and nuances present in an experience. Indeed, of all the musical abilities teachers try to help children develop, the ability to listen with focus and insight is perhaps the most important and long lasting. Of all the ways we interact with music, the most frequently used lifelong skill is through listening.

To help children develop their aural perceptive abilities, teachers and parents need to engage children in what R. Murray Schaefer (1976) calls "ear

158

cleaning." This is difficult to achieve in a world in which we are constantly bombarded with sounds, and quiet is virtually impossible to find. To counter the effects of noise pollution, we need to open children's ears and minds to events in all aspects of music making: singing, playing instruments, moving, conducting, composing, and reading. Children need to learn to reflect on the quality of their own and other's performances.

Increased sophistication in listening also can be developed through listening to recorded music. This does not mean the kind of functional listening most people do when they use music as a background to help them celebrate, relax, clean house, or study. In most of those instances, the music is a kind of tonal bath, which surrounds and washes over them, but is not seriously attended to. The teacher needs to foster *active listening*, in which the learner focuses on musical events such as patterns that repeat and contrast, the creative use of tone colors, or the shaping of the music through dynamic change. Increased sophistication also comes through exposure to and development of a wide repertoire of music of various styles, cultures, and genres: from Bach to rock; or from Indonesian gamelan music to Native American flute music.

The Development of Perceptive Listening

Key to the development of listening skills is the ability to perceive sounds and to form thoughts about those sounds. The auditory sense develops early and is remarkably keen in most children. Infants at birth can differentiate between pitches and quickly learn to identify the sound of their mother's voice. All babies go through a "babbling" stage in their first six months of development, in which they become increasingly sophisticated in matching vocal and mouth sounds that their parents generate. It is through this listening and corresponding vocal play that children are forming the mental constructs for language production and for the music of their culture.

Children as young as three months, perhaps younger, can vocally match sustained pitches. Children as young as six or seven months appear to have acquired a sense of musical phrase, and by eight months a sense of what constitutes a "good fit" melodically in their culture. By the time children are in preschool they are developing vocabulary to describe what they hear. Concepts of tone color, dynamics, tempo, and style seem to emerge early. Concepts of pitch, rhythm, and form later emerge, around the age of four or after. Children grow in their perceptiveness through about the age of eight or nine, when they seem to reach a plateau. Older children are able to recognize and apply a wide range of concepts to musical listening experiences, provided they have had a strong foundation in music education (for further detail on the development of these skills see Scott-Kassner, 1992; and Haack, 1992).

The Development of Attitudes Toward Music

Most teachers are eager to have their children "love" music. That often translates into the selection of works for performance and listening that have an immediate appeal, but may not have lasting value. Many complex factors besides the music itself enter into the development of attitudes toward music. A number of these factors are outside the teacher's control. A child's gender, ethnic background, age, personality, socioeconomic status and the ensuing beliefs, feelings, and values that emerge all contribute to the formation of attitudes toward music. Teachers, families, peer groups, the media, and other adult authority figures also have an influence.

Young children from preschool through the age of eight are usually remarkably open to all kinds of music. This period of children's lives seems to be a good time to introduce them to a wide range of excellent music of many styles, genres, and cultures.

About the age of nine or ten, children begin to exhibit much more sensitivity to peer culture and the influence of the media, often rejecting, on a surface level, music that is not endorsed by that culture. Tests of preference show that children of this age prefer music that is loud rather than soft, fast rather than slow, and music that has a strong beat rather than less intrusive music. They are also drawn to humorous music. Teachers need to encourage children of this age to be receptive toward music that they do not necessarily prefer, so that they can learn about and from that music.

As most people mature, they will once again open themselves to a wider range of music than what they were attracted to during their teenage years. At the same time, music they associate with certain times or events may continue to appeal to them throughout a lifetime.

Teachers can take heart in the knowledge that, in spite of children's preferences and tastes in music, they can be helped to understand a wide range of music through active involvement in listening. Because the area of attitude development is so complex, teachers cannot guarantee that experiencing a work of music will cause a student to "like" that work. However, there is some evidence that as human organisms we: (1) are drawn to complexity; (2) tend to value what is familiar, and feel uncomfortable with the unfamiliar; (3) can learn to focus our perception on subtle changes; and (4) can change our attitudes through learning, in spite of what our enculturated tastes might be. These findings should challenge teachers to formulate an approach to active listening in which children are:

1. Regularly presented with music that is more complex and intriguing than most of the music they are exposed to in their daily environments

2. Allowed to listen to various pieces of music enough times so that those works become familiar and no longer seem exotic

3. Given the conceptual tools for discussing and analyzing music and regularly helped to perceive and respond to musical events in increasingly refined fashion

4. Encouraged to discuss their preferences (a choice between two different events) and/or attitudes (a more generalized network of beliefs, values, and feelings) without being told that their choices or feelings are incorrect

Once children express an attitude about a piece of music, whether positive or negative, they need to be encouraged to go to the next step and describe what about the music makes them feel that way. A fifth grader, Steve, said he "loved" the song, "Bridge over Troubled Water" as sung by Simon and Garfunkel. All of the other students agreed. The teacher played the recording again, asking the children to connect their feelings to what was happening musically. At the end, Steve eagerly raised his hand and offered a detailed analysis of the dynamic and melodic shaping of the A section of the piece that built emotional tension, then released. This was in contrast with the B section that was all on one level dynamically and melodically. He then went on to discuss the lyrics in each of those sections and how they fit expressively with what was going on in the music. Steve had clearly connected his affective response with actual musical events.

Building Skills of Aural Perception

A program in active listening has several goals:

1. Build heightened aural perception and sensitivity to music and musical events (aural skills development)

2. Illustrate and reinforce/expand concepts of music

3. Build an aural repertoire that represents a wide range of styles, cultures, and genres of music

Although these may seem to be discrete activities, they are actually interdependent; growth in one area affects another. For example, the greater your ability to perceive musical events, the more likely you are to form concepts about those events, and the richer your experience of listening to all kinds of music becomes. Hopefully, growth in one or all of these skills will lead to greater aesthetic satisfaction through listening.

Learning to listen perceptively demands focus and attention. Teachers can use a variety of techniques to help children become aware of sounds:

1. Have children close their eyes. Drop a familiar object such as keys or a pencil, and have children name the object.

2. Have children close their eyes. Drop a piece of chalk from a certain height and ask children to show that height with their hands above a desk. Try this with several different heights.

3. Have children hide behind a screen and play different rhythm instruments while other children name what they hear.

4. Ask a child to close his or her eyes and then identify the voice of a classmate, after hearing a sung phrase.

5. Have children shape the upward/downward sounds of a slide whistle as they listen with their eyes closed.

Each of these perceptive listening activities helps children focus on the aural aspect of the stimuli by eliminating visual cues. This training leads naturally to the more difficult task of listening for specific events in recorded music. This task is more difficult because the music is usually more complex. Many things are occurring, not just one. To help children focus, teachers need to develop active listening strategies.

Active listening to recorded music means involving more than the ears and the mind. To help children focus on a particular aspect of the music, teachers may use some physical means, such as having students perform, read, or move as they listen. In many instances, only a segment of a recorded work will be played. Sometimes, an entire work or section of a work will be used.

Tables 7.1 through 7.6 suggest a variety of active listening strategies designed to focus attention on different aspects of music: tone color, rhythm, pitch, texture, dynamics, form, and style. These strategies are designed for use with a broad variety of recorded music, and with "live" performances by children, teachers, and guests. Specific concepts appropriate to the elementary curriculum are listed in the left-hand column, and ideas to focus children's perception by using movement, performing, or reading are listed in their respective columns.

In addition to the strategies that follow, music series texts often provide listening maps and call charts to help children track musical events, both aurally and visually. Samples of those can be found in Figures 7.1, 7.2, and 7.3. Teachers and, eventually, students can develop their own maps and call charts.

Table 7.1 Active Listening to Tone Color

Concept	Moving	Performing	Reading
Voices or instruments alone Voices or instruments in groups	Raise your hand when you hear the first trumpet; tap your head when you hear the first trombone Clap to the pattern the bass drum plays Pretend to play the violin whenever you hear it In a group of four, assign each person to listen for a different instrument in a movement in a string quartet, and decide how to move when they hear the sound of their instrument	Sing with the pattern of the two-toned bell Sing with the female voice only—listen to the male Identify the pitches of the marimba ostinato, and play it on the bass xylophone while listening to the recording Select a rhythmic percussion instrument that would fit stylistically with a given piece, and improvise a rhythm to accompany the recording	Circle the names or pictures of the instruments you hear in this piece List in order of entrance the instruments you hear Make a simple score of entrance and exits and relationships of the instruments in a work featuring three contrasting timbres Visually follow a simple score, and cue the instruments or voices as they enter

Integrating Listening into Concept Teaching

Active listening plays a key role in concept teaching. Active listening strategies, such as those suggested in Tables 7.1 through 7.6, can be implemented throughout the initial stages of lessons designed to teach concepts.

Ultimately, concept teaching aims to help children transfer or generalize their knowledge and apply it to new works of music. Listening used in this context is more reflective, calling on perception and analysis skills, rather than physically involving children in moving, performing, or reading. This application of aural awareness more closely represents the kind of listening musicians and other sophisticated listeners do. Giving listening tests, such as suggested in the "What Do You Hear?" illustration in Figure 7.4, helps to determine whether children can transfer their new-found understanding to unfamiliar music.

Table 7.2   Active Listening to Rhythm

Concept	Moving	Performing	Reading
Beat Rhythm Meter Tempo Syncopation	Tap the beat, off-beat, or rhythm on various parts of the body	Selecting instruments that complement a recording:	Learn to read the rhythm of the main motivic pattern in a piece of music—find that pattern whenever it enters (aurally and visually)
	Move around the room to the rhythmic flow of a piece—change directions at the ends of phrases	Add an accompaniment that highlights the beat, rhythm, and/or meter	Read and/or notate the rhythm patterns in a work that features layered rhythms
	Create a movement pattern using different body levels (stomp, slap, clap, snap) to accompany patterns in a recording	Create a rhythmic ostinato to accompany the music	Read and interpret by conducting the various meters in works in single meters and works that change meters
	Pass a ball around a circle to the beat, changing direction when the tempo changes	Identify a repeated pattern in the music; play with it whenever it occurs	Read and maintain a rhythm pattern as an accompaniment to the music
	Work with a partner to show meter through movement; make the downbeat a strong motion		
	Bounce a ball on the accented beat, catch/roll/hold on the weak beats		

The following activities highlight the essential elements of concept teaching, and show how integral listening is to the process.

1.   Select musical examples and activities that focus attention on the critical attributes of the concept being studied: for example, the feeling of a steady, even, underlying impulse in the music.

(*Text continues on page 169*)

Table 7.3 Active Listening to Pitch

Concept	Moving	Performing	Reading

Horizontal
  Upward/
    downward
  High/low
  Step/leap/
    repeat
  Melodic curve/
    patterns
  Phrase
  Scale
  Tonality
  Range/register
 	
Vertical
  Chords
  Cadences
  Clusters
  Layers
	Shape the general curve of the melody alone and with a partner
	
	Show the highest and lowest notes of the recorded work by using high and low movements
	
	Shape phrases
	
	Develop discrete movements to show steps, leaps, and repeats in a melody
	
	Discover the main theme or motives in a work; develop a movement to represent each motive; perform the appropriate movement when you hear each theme
	
	Move through general space, pausing at cadence points; make contrasting motions to show half and full cadences
	
	Change motions each time a chord changes
	
	In a group of three, have one person move on the I chord, a second on the IV chord, and the last on the V chord
		Sing along with the melodic line of a work using words or a neutral syllable
		
		Play the melodic line with the recording
		
		Play or sing motives or melodic themes with the recording
		
		Develop a melodic ostinato to play as an accompaniment to a pentatonic melody
		
		Play chord progressions on a synthesizer along with a pop/rock piece
			Look at the melodic shape or notation of a motive, pattern, or theme—note each time it occurs in the music
			
			Draw the shape of the melody as it unfolds
			
			Read through the melody on a score ahead of time—note its shape: smooth/angular; its register: high/low; its range: low to high; its use of steps, leaps, and repeats—imagine what it will sound like, then listen to test your perception
			
			As you listen, notate the chord changes and number of beats on each chord of a blues or pop song
			
			Circle the cadence points on a score as you listen—listen again, and mark them as half or full

Table 7.4 Active Listening to Texture and Dynamics

Concept	Moving	Performing	Reading

Texture
  Monophonic
  Homophonic
  Polyphonic
  Mixed
	Move the line of a single melody; upper body in personal space, then through general space
	
	In a group of three or four, have each person move to a different line in a polyphonic piece
	
	Show the layers of a round or canon by moving in concentric circles to the lines as they enter (each circle represents a different part)
	
	While one group moves to a melody, have another show the pattern of the underlying chords
	
	Create different movements to show that you hear various textures
		Sing or play in unison with the melody of a monophonic work
		
		Sing or play with various lines or chords of other works, adding to the texture; fade the volume to listen to students, then increase volume
		
		Add a countermelody or ostinato to a recording to create a polyphonic texture
		
		Add chords to a recording of a melody to create a homophonic texture
		
		Shift textures in your accompaniment to create mixed textures
			Trace the line on a score of a monophonic melody as you listen
			
			Draw or notate the line as you listen
			
			Visually track the entrances and exits of lines in a polyphonic work as you listen
			
			Using different colors, draw the separate lines as you listen
			
			Follow the notation of a homophonic work noting the relation between the melody and the chords
			
			Follow a call chart that outlines the textures in a mixed texture work
			
			Invent your own call chart

Dynamics
  Loud/soft
  Dynamic accent
  Gradual change
  Sudden
	Show changes from loud to soft through changes in energy and flow
	
	Show dynamic accents through angular movements
	
	Develop group crescendo/ decrescendo
		Clap or play a rhythm instrument on selected or all dynamic accents
		
		Play rhythm instruments to accompany gradual and sudden changes
			Follow the dynamic markings on a score, gesturing or conducting to show changes
			
			Draw a score of the dynamic changes while listening

Table 7.5   Active Listening to Form

Concept	Moving	Performing	Reading

Repetition/ Contrast
  Phrase
  Unitary
  Binary
  Ternary
	Make up one motion for initial idea, contrasting motions for other idea(s); perform motions solo or in groups	Select different instrumental or vocal timbres to accompany various phrases or sections of a work	Order simple shapes such as triangles, squares, and circles at your desk to show the structure of a piece as you listen (AA, AB, ABA, ABACABA)

Rondo theme and variations	Change directions with each new phrase, showing repetition and contrast in phrases with specific motions	Using only hands as a sound source, accompany a recorded rondo changing the playing technique with each theme (clap, rub, snap, etc.)	Follow the score as you listen; label each section as it occurs
Through composed Tone poem Program music	Show a rondo by using different colored scarves and movements; assign each section to different groups	Learn to perform the theme by playing or singing, then identify it in each of its incarnations	Read the theme before you hear the music; note the contour and rhythm; discuss ways it might be varied; chart the variations on a piece of paper as you listen
	Have one group pattern the theme through movement while additional groups pattern the variations, incorporating the theme	Play or sing the main themes of the characters or sections before listening	Follow or draw a storyboard of a piece as you listen
	Develop creative movements or dramas to tell the story or convey the mood as a piece unfolds		Follow story in book, with puppets, or illustrate storyline or mood

Table 7.6 Active Listening to Style

Concept	Moving	Performing	Reading
Style is the result of the combination of the elements of music reflecting cultural or personal choices	Change the quality of movement to reflect the style of the music (flowing, curved movements vs. sharp, short, angular movements) Learn specific dances or patterns of movement from dances of various times and cultures; add them to show style of music (grapevine step, arms at shoulders [from Greece]; knees bent, arms bent slightly, palms down, eyes downward, movement toward ground, feet toward ground, upper body move in and out [from some parts of Africa])	Add a clapping or percussive accompaniment that fits the style of the music on the recording, i.e. $\|\!:\ \downarrow\ \textbf{?}\ \downarrow\ \downarrow\ \|\ \textbf{?}\ \downarrow\ \downarrow\ \textbf{?}\ :\!\|$ for clave in a calypso piece Imitate through singing or playing the vocal or instrumental style used on a recording (blue notes, chest resonated voice, open sound toward front of facial mask)	Select from a set of style cards that match the music being played: *Set #1 (touch)* Velvet Gravel Steel wool Lima beans Bubble plastic Plush rug Fake fur *Set #2 (art)* Impressionist Baroque Classical Romantic Abstract *Set #3 (images)* Houses from different periods Costumes from different periods *Set #4 (cultures)* Native American African-American Latin-American Sub-Saharan African East Asian Select from a set of style cards that match the music being played Children should be able to describe why they made a certain style choice in terms of the music

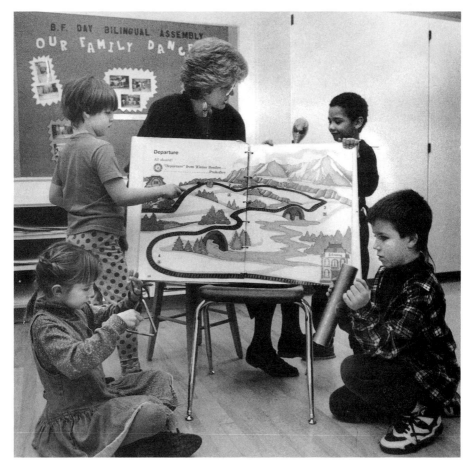

Active listening strategy with listening chart.

2. Have the children experience at least two examples of music that embody those qualities (for example, two pieces with a steady beat) and one example of music that does not have those qualities (e.g., one piece with no beat). This latter example helps to clarify the concept. This is called the "two plus one rule" of concept teaching.

3. Lead children to discover the attributes of the concept through active involvement including aural perception. Have them describe the qualities that they hear in their own words, *then* introduce the musical term for that concept and, later, its visual representation. For example, children perceive and respond to the steady, even feeling in a musical work. The teacher labels this the steady beat and later introduces ways to notate it. Concepts cannot be taught by stating a rule or definition, for example, "Today we are going to

1. Introduction—full orchestra; *ff;* fast.
2. Low strings, low brass; *f,* then *mf;* slow.
3. English horn, clarinet, strings, tambourine; *mp;* slow.
4. Clarinet and piccolo solos, strings accompany; *mf;* slow.
5. Horns, woodwinds, tambourine; *f;* fast.
6. Strings, tambourine, brass; *ff;* slow.
7. Oboe, clarinet, low strings pizzicato (plucked); *mp;* slow.
8. Woodwinds, strings, brass, percussion; *ff;* very fast.
9. Full orchestra, brass section predominates; *ff;* fast.
10. Full orchestra to end; bass drum "stinger."

Figure 7.1. Call chart for "Sailor's Dance" from *The Red Poppy* by Reinhold Glière. *Reproduced with permission from* World of Music, Grade 7, *Silver Burdett Ginn, 1992.*

learn that music can be organized around a steady, even feeling called a steady beat. Does everyone understand?" Concepts must be taught through experience and discovery.

   4.   Children are taught to apply their knowledge of a particular concept to other pieces of music. These examples should become more and more subtle to challenge their perception. For example, you might start with works that have a clear use of the steady beat such as disco or other pop music, much folk and ethnic music, and gradually move to jazz and art music. (This latter process may occur across several years as the children mature.)

   Table 7.7 illustrates a possible sequence for teaching the concept of beat. These eight- to ten-minute lessons should be presented during portions of a class period, and spread over several days. Listening and responding to recorded music plays a key role throughout this sequence.

Building an Aural Repertoire

Teachers often will want to play a work of recorded music across a series of lessons or several times throughout a year. This approach helps children take works into long-term memory, so they become internalized references for a lifetime of musical learning and valuing. Repeated hearings help children become "friends," not simply "acquaintances," with the music that teachers, parents, and/or the children themselves find significant.

Theme 1

Figure 7.2. Notated listening guide for "Prelude" from *Carmen* by Georges Bizet. *Reproduced with permission from* World of Music Grade 5, *Silver Burdett Ginn, 1992.*

One approach to repertoire building is to take a gestalt or holistic point of view. This allows the children to hear the entire piece, section, or movement in the initial listening. Subsequent listenings may concentrate on smaller parts for a particular focus. A final listening returns to the whole. This whole-part-whole approach to listening can take advantage of many active-listening techniques already discussed in this chapter.

The repertoire ideally should come from a wide range of music of the highest aesthetic quality, well-crafted and well-performed. This could include masterworks from the Western art music tradition, as well as folk, traditional, and popular music from a broad variety of cultures. Teachers may wish to set a goal of building knowledge of six works each year. Works could be organized around themes such as composer, artist, or culture of the month. At the elementary school level, children can become acquainted with individual

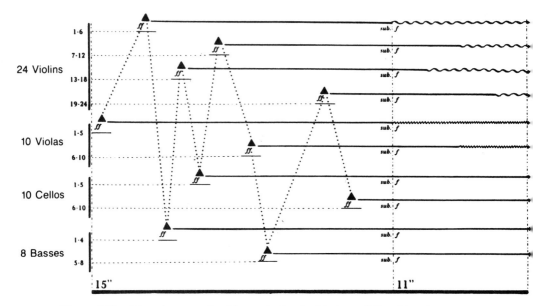

Figure 7.3. Listening map for *Threnody for the Victims of Hiroshima* by Krzysztof Penderecki. *Reproduced with permission from* Music and You, Grade 6 *(1989).*

styles within the Western art music tradition, but are not yet ready for a historical approach to that music.

Resources for listening are abundant, as close as the nearest record store. Recordings and listening lessons are also incorporated in music series texts. Visuals, such as charts and overheads, often are included to assist learning. Recordings that incorporate a range of listening activities are often found in elementary school texts, including *Music Smart!* by Hotchkiss (1990). Other delightful recordings about the lives of composers are available from Classical Kids Productions in Toronto. More and more children's books are being written to tell the stories of recorded works and composers. Many of those examples, along with music videos to enhance listening, can be found in such sources as the *Music in Motion* catalog or in local music stores that feature materials for teachers. The Metropolitan Opera in New York publishes *The Metropolitan Opera Boxes*. The Smithsonian Institution in Washington, D.C., publishes a wide range of educational recordings including folk and traditional music from throughout the world.

In addition, listening lessons can be developed by teachers using any available recorded music. In the pop and jazz fields, it is often advisable to purchase "Best of . . ." albums from artists who have demonstrated staying power in constantly changing fields.

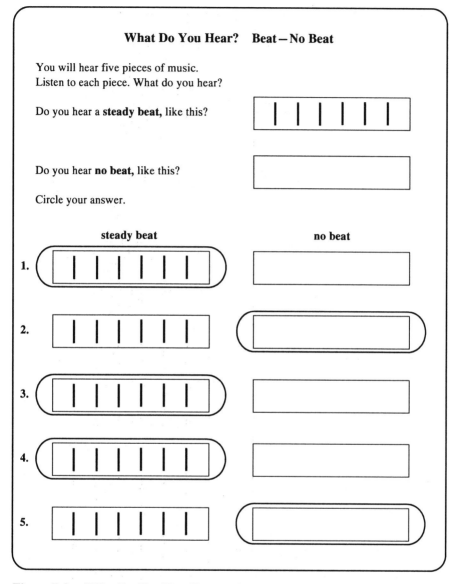

Figure 7.4. "What Do You Hear?" *Reproduced with permission from Silver Burdett Ginn, 1992 World of Music, Gr. 1.*

Table 7.7 Conceptual Lessons That Integrate Listening

Day 1 Introduction	Day 2 Expand	Day 3 Cement	Day 4 Examine	Future Application
Respond to steady sounds in surroundings. Sing song with steady beat. Tap various body parts in imitation of teacher. Discuss feeling in children's own words. (Words such as steady, even, repeating might emerge.)	With the help of the teacher, find the steady feeling in a disco or pop piece. Move to the music with entire body. Play instruments to the beat while accompanying a familiar song. Label the steady feeling as "steady beat."	Ask children to find the beat in a familiar song or a recording. Play a piece with no beat (Japanese Shakuhachi music). Have children describe what they notice about the lack of beat.	Either: Have children describe steady beat in their own words and illustrate it. or Have children complete "what do you hear" exercises that asks them to identify whether recorded works of music have or do not have a steady beat.	Over time have children: Show the beat in new pieces of music. Discuss the importance of the beat in new pieces of music. Compose and perform pieces that are centered around a beat or no beat.

Listening Sequence

A listening sequence, whether completed in one day or spread across many class periods, needs to include several steps:*

Step 1: Prepare

Children need to be prepared to listen. The preparation will depend on the purpose of the listening. They could listen to a story such as *The Nutcracker*; they could be told the background of the culture the music is from, and find the region on a map; they could view a painting or picture that helps establish a mood or sense of style; they could hear a story of the composer, composition, or of the lives of the people from whom the music originated; or they could sing a melodic theme or sing/clap a pattern or motive they are to notice (this could be taught by rote or from a score). It is very important to give children something specific to listen for and a way to show that they hear it. These should be quiet responses such as raising hands, pointing, or writing so that all children can concentrate on the music. (Ideas for directing and monitoring perception are listed in Tables 7.1 through 7.6.)

Step 2: Listen

Play the recording, and check student's perceptions or feelings through class discussion.

Step 3: Activate/Participate

Listen again, while actively involving students in performing or moving in some way to the music. These exercises can be repeated more than once and over time. It is a wonderful way to build a work into children's internal repertoire. For example, young children never seem to tire of moving like dwarfs to *In the Hall of the Mountain King* by Grieg.

Step 4: Question/Discuss

Discussion should take place throughout this sequence, and can address the music, portions of the music, the activities the children are doing, or their emotional response to the experiences or the music.

---

*Adapted from work by Sandra L. Stauffer.

Step 5: Listen Again

Listen to the recording quietly, simply to notice familiar moments, expand insight into the music, and to reestablish the work as a whole.

Step 6: Extend the Listening

Use this listening as a stimulus to have the children:

1. Compose music in similar forms or with similar characteristics.
2. Listen to other music by the same composer or culture that has similar or contrasting characteristics.
3. Listen to other music by other composers or cultures that has similar or contrasting characteristics.

The sample lessons shown in Tables 7.8 through 7.10 illustrate these principles and suggest possible ways to approach repertoire building with selected works. Music teachers who see children only once or twice a week may wish to enlist the help of classroom teachers in reinforcing listening experiences with children. (Remember that dubbing tapes or CDs and distributing copies to others is illegal under the copyright law. However, tapes and CDs owned by the school or district may be used in any classroom.) Table 7.9 is adapted from suggestions in the book *Multicultural Perspectives in Music Education* by Anderson and Campbell (1989). This is one of many resources now available to help build listening repertoire from multicultural sources. Table 7.10 is an example of a listening strategy developed from a recording by contemporary artists.

Keys to Listening

Opening ears and minds to the sounds and subtleties of music and watching the discoveries children make and the excitement they feel bring great satisfaction to the teaching of music. To do this successfully, teachers need to continue listening themselves: not just to familiar works but to unfamiliar ones, and to the comfortable and uncomfortable. Teachers need to bring attitudes of openness, curiosity, and discovery to the act of listening. They need to be willing to engage in focused listening, not just passive listening.

Teachers who actively nurture their own musical growth through listening have growing riches to offer their students. The keys to listening can be developed and, through them, worlds of pleasure unlocked. To paraphrase philosopher Harry Broudy, teachers need to develop their own connoisseurship to help their students engage in a lifetime of *enlightened cherishing*.

Table 7.8   "Minuet in G" by Ludwig van Beethoven

Grades: Second to fourth
Repertoire Goal: To internalize Beethoven's "Minuet in G," and to gain a sense of style typical to that period.
Concept Goal: To understand that ABA form can exist in an orchestral work. To verbalize differences between the sections.
Skills Goals: To perceive the differences in the sections. To coordinate movements to the sections.

Day #1: Show a picture of Beethoven. Ask the children if they have ever heard his name. (Discuss what they know about him.) Explain that he wrote many kinds of music including music to be danced to. A popular dance of his day was called a minuet. Tell them you are going to play a particular minuet called "Minuet in G." Listen to this music and try to imagine the dancers. What kinds of motions might they be making and why? (Play recording. When it is finished, have children demonstrate some motions and discuss their choices.)

Day #2: Put "Minuet in G" on chalkboard. Have children tell you what they remember about that piece. Tell the children they are going to help invent a dance to do to the music but first they need to develop a sense of the way the music is organized. Review AB and ABA form. Ask them to listen to the music and to discover which pattern best fits its structure. Once children have discovered ABA form, show pictures of people dancing the minuet. Discuss the style of dress and hair. Discuss the elegance of the posture. Have them suggest stylized motions to do during the A section and contrasting motions during the B. Try those with the music. Note whether they change movements with the change in sections. Have them discuss how effective their choices were in terms of the music.

Day #3: Play "Minuet in G" as a mystery tune on a recording or on the piano. See how long it takes the children to name it and the composer. Put two words on the board, "even"/"uneven." Tell them you want them to clap the rhythm of the melody of the "Minuet in G" as they listen and decide which word best fits the A section and which best fits the B. Later, help them to discover other ways the two sections contrast.

Further Extensions
1. Play the audio or video tape of the program *Beethoven Lives Upstairs* by Classical Kids Productions from Toronto. Have the children select other works by Beethoven they want to know.
2. Invite a guest artist in to play some Beethoven and discuss why the children are attracted to his music.
3. Learn actual steps from the minuet and practice dancing them to the Beethoven selection.
4. Compose an ABA form piece for instruments in which each section is sixteen beats long.

Table 7.9   "San Antonio" from *In Praise of Oxala and other Gods: Music from Colombia, South America*, Nonesuch Records

---

Grades: Fourth to sixth

Repertoire Goal: To internalize the piece "San Antonio," gaining a sense of style represented by African-derived music from Colombia.

Concept Goal: To understand that this music is created by the use of layers of various percussion instruments playing ostinati plus voices singing in call-and-response fashion. To understand the context in which the piece is used.

Skills Goals: To perceive the layers and specific rhythm patterns of the instruments. To be able to replicate by ear at least one of the patterns. To name the instruments being played. To play and sing the parts with accuracy. To add vocal harmony.

Day #1: Find Colombia on a map of South America. Discuss the fact that a large part of the country is a tropical rain forest, and much of it can be reached only by boat because the vegetation is so thick. Most of the people are very poor and make their money from growing bananas and catching fish. African slaves were brought to this region to work in the gold mines. The people who brought them left, and the blacks stayed. There are about 5,000 living there today. Though Colombia is a Spanish-speaking country, much of the music has been influenced by the music that the African people brought with them.

Tell them that in the religious music that comes out of the Catholic church, the people often sing songs to saints. The song "San Antonio" is a song to Saint Anthony and is usually sung on Christmas Eve as a lullaby. It is sung in Spanish but there are some African influences including the instruments used. (Review some of the traditional African instruments learned in an earlier unit.) Listen to "San Antonio," and notice the instruments used. Be ready to name them. (Discuss the use of marimba, rattles, and drums.) Listen again and notice the relation between the two voices and the instruments. Focus particularly on patterns that repeat. (Discuss the call-and-response vocal form, and the instrumental ostinato.)

Day #2: Show children the notation for the call-and-response section of "San Antonio." Teach them the response pattern. Sing the call, and have them respond. Play the recording and have them join in each time they hear the response. (They may be able to sing this in harmony.) Ask for volunteers to learn the call. Take turns using different leaders. Other children may wish to add the rattle or drum part, learning it aurally.

Day #3: Echo clap the rhythms for the call and response in the marimba part for "San Antonio." Have children discover those patterns in the score of the marimba part. How are they similar to the sung line? Teach some children to play those patterns on the marimba or keyboard. Put the whole piece together.

(continued)

Table 7.9 Continued

With	With
Call	Response

Further Extensions

1. Listen to other music on this recording, and compare and contrast the use of elements such as call and response and ostinato.
2. Research and report on other aspects of the importance of music in the Colombian culture.
3. Discover and perform some African-American songs based on the call-and-response form. How are they similar/different?
4. Using a pentatonic scale, compose a call-and-response form piece with a contrasting marimba ostinato.

Table 7.10 "Hush Little Baby" from *Hush* by Yo-Yo Ma and Bobby McFerrin, Sony Masterworks SK 48177

Grades: Pre-K to second
Repertoire Goal: To internalize a sense of style that comes from an improvised version of a familiar song.
Concept Goals: To review the meaning and traditional style of a lullaby. To understand that improvising is a way to be musically playful.
Skills Goals: To physically and vocally respond to the flow and mood of the music. To aurally perceive ways that a familiar work has been altered. To experiment with musically altering other familiar works.

Day #1: Read the picture book *Hush Little Baby* as illustrated by Aliki (Simon and Schuster, 1968). Discuss the sequence and the predictability of the rhymes. Learn to sing the folk song "Hush Little Baby." Sing it as you follow the pictures in the book.

Day #2: Bring in a doll or stuffed animal. Pretend to put it to sleep by rocking it. When it resists falling asleep, suggest that a lullaby might help. Have the children listen carefully to see if they can help rock pretend babies and also sing the lullaby. Begin to sing "Hush Little Baby" on the neutral syllable "loo." Watch to see when children recognize the song, and enter in. Have them name the song and then sing it while they pretend to rock their babies and put them to sleep.

(*continued*)

Table 7.10   Continued

Day #3: Put the words "word/bird," "sing/ring," "down/town," etc. on the board. Have children help to "read" them. Ask them what song the words are from. Sing the song using soft, soothing voices. Discuss the flow (gentle) and dynamic quality (soft) of the lullaby. Tell them you are going to play a recording of two men performing "Hush Little Baby." Ask them to listen to decide whether they think this will put the baby to sleep or not. Listen and discuss their responses as to why this would not put the baby to sleep. (It is loud and fast.) Have the children stand, face a partner, and hold hands. Play the recording again while the children rock back and forth to the flow of the music, creating an imaginary cradle.

Day #4: Introduce children to the names of the two musicians who performed "Hush Little Baby." Show them their pictures. Discuss the fact that they are both very famous musicians who love to experiment or play with sounds. (Children may have seen them on *Sesame Street*, *Mr. Rogers*, or TV ads.) Listen to their arrangement of "Hush Little Baby" to discover what they did to make it different from the original. Discuss those ideas (faster, louder, different words, higher pitches, sliding, mouth sounds, clapping). Have children join in vocally with the recording, trying some of the techniques. Discuss the delightful character of this style of singing. Read the book *Hush Little Baby* illustrated by Margot Zemach (E. P. Dutton, 1976). Does its quality "fit" more with the original version of the song or the Yo-Yo Ma and Bobby McFerrin version? Why or why not?

Further Extensions

1. Develop their own vocal improvisations (playing with sounds) using familiar nursery rhymes as a basis.
4. .Find out more about Bobby McFerrin and Yo-Yo Ma (videotapes from PBS, other recordings). Build their names into the children's vocabulary. Compare the style of cello playing used by Yo-Yo Ma in "Hush Little Baby" to a more traditional style. Discuss the differences.
2. Take another lullaby, and turn it from a gentle piece to an upbeat piece by improvising.
3. Listen to other selections from *Hush* such as "Flight of the Bumblebee" by Rimsky-Korsakov. Discuss how the various effects were created.
4. Find out more about Bobby McFerrin and Yo-Yo Ma (videotapes from PBS, other recordings). Build their names into the children's vocabulary. Compare the style of cello playing used by Yo-Yo Ma in "Hush Little Baby" to a more traditional style. Discuss the differences.

Children playing marimba to accompany recording.

Teacher with young children and dolls, singing "Hush Little Baby."

Questions

1. How would you justify spending class time having children listen to recorded music?

2. What is the difference between active perceptive listening and passive functional listening? What are three techniques to enhance active listening?

3. At what age/stage are students likely to form strong preferences for particular kinds of music? How might that influence what recordings are used with them?

4. How might a teacher respond to older elementary children's requests to bring pop-music recordings to music class?

5. What is necessary for concept learning to occur? How can active listening strategies enhance concept learning?

6. What are useful steps for planning listening lessons?

7. How can teachers nurture their own ongoing growth as perceptive listeners?

Activities

1. Discuss with others in your class the validity of the following statement: "A teacher can make children like music that the teacher likes."

2. Interview two kindergartners, two second graders, two fourth graders, and two sixth graders about what kind of music they like and why. Are their stages of preference similar to those outlined in this chapter? Summarize and report your findings to your class.

3. Select a piece of recorded music you find exciting. Determine why you find it exciting. Using the steps outlined for a listening sequence, plan a series of activities to share this music with children.

4. Develop a set of materials that children can use to enter more actively into the listening experience. These could include ideas from the "reading column" of Tables 7.1 through 7.6 or others.

5. Develop a listening map to help children track events in a recorded work.

6. Closely examine different music series texts to see how they incorporate listening to music. What literature have they chosen? How have they helped get children actively involved? How have they helped to build

repertoire, if at all? Teach one of those lessons to your class or to a group of children.

7. Actively listen to a recording that you own and enjoy. As you listen, write down things in the music that you might wish to highlight for children. Look at a scope and sequence chart on the development of musical concepts (MENC, 1991), and decide what age child might be ready to notice the things you noticed. Develop a series of active listening procedures for that recording that would appeal to children at those ages.

References

ANDERSON, W., & CAMPBELL, P. (1989). *Multicultural perspectives in music education.* Reston, VA: Music Educators National Conference.

CAIN, T. (1988). *Keynote.* Cambridge, UK: Cambridge University.

EDELSTEIN, S., CHOKSY, L., LEHMAN, L., SIGURDSSON, N., & WOODS, D. (1980). *Creating curriculum in music.* Menlo Park, CA: Addison-Wesley.

HAACK, P. (1992). The acquisition of music listening skills. In Colwell, D. (Ed.), *Handbook of research on music teaching and learning* (chap. 29). New York: Schirmer Books.

HOTCHKISS, G. (1990). *Music smart!* Reston, VA: Music in Motion.

Music Educators National Conference. (1991). *Teaching general music.* Reston, VA.: Music Educators National Conference.

Music and you, Grades K-8. (1988). New York: Macmillan.

SCHAEFER, R. M. (1976). *Creative music education.* New York: Schirmer Books.

SCOTT-KASSNER, C. (1992). Research on music in early childhood. In Colwell, D. (Ed.), *Handbook of research on music teaching and learning* (chap. 45). New York: Schirmer Books.

The World of Music, Grades K-8. (1991). Morristown, NJ: Silver Burdett Ginn.

Catalogs/Resources

Classical Kids Productions. 1988. *Beethoven Lives Upstairs.* The Children's Group, 561 Bloor St. W., Suite 300, Toronto, Ontario, Canada M5S 1Y6.

Claudia's Caravan (a catalog of multicultural/multilingual materials). P.O. Box 1582, Alameda, CA. 94501; (510) 521-7871.

The Metropolitan Opera Box for ages 11–18. Education at the Met, 1865 Broadway, New York, NY 10023.

Music in Motion (a music education and gift catalog). P. O. Box 833814, Richardson, TX 75083-3814.

Roots and Rhythm Mail Order (A catalog of blues, folk, world music, and pop recordings and books). 6921 Stockton Ave., El Cerrito, CA 94530; (510) 525-1494.

The Whole Folkways Catalog (a catalog of historic Folkways recordings). Smithsonian/Folkways, Center for Folklife Programs and Cultural Studies, 955 L'Enfant Plaza, Suite 2600, Smithsonian Institution, Washington, DC 20560; (202) 287-3262.

World Music Press/West Music (A catalog of world music resources). West Music, 1208 Fifth Street, PO Box 5521, Coralville, IA 52241.

8

The Moving Child

In the world of children, music and movement are nearly inseparable from one another. Clear the room, set the rules, start the music, and watch the movement begin: Rochelle pirouettes like a ballerina to the light and whirling music of the flute. Alley glides like a swan to the cello's melody. Nicolas hops, then jumps in one place to the dialogue of the clarinet and bassoon. With the entrance of the brass instruments, Sally marches with her knees high and her toes pointed. Sean, Li, and Tommy strut forward with long legs overlapping, arms stretched across each other's shoulders. Jimmie jogs with a "pretend" basketball to the pulse of the percussion section. Consuela and Trina find the pulse and clap hands, forward, backward, and upside down. Anna stands at the center of it all, conducting.

Children love to move. With the sound of the music, they release their bundles of energy. Heads nod; toes tap; bodies rock; arms swing. Even without music, while children play, they often move in some semblance of a musical rhythm. Moving children skip, hop, walk, run, slide, gallop, jump, twist, and turn. Movement—of all kinds—is one of their favorite things to do.

The foundation of music for children is ultimately and intimately entwined with their physical selves. Music, the aural art, is also music, the kinesthetic art. Children develop their musical abilities through a combination of what they experience through their ears, eyes, and bodies. As children listen, sing, or play instruments—even as they read music—their aural, visual, and kinesthetic senses are activated. Movement is thus vital to their musical development, and basic to all that they do.

Music classes for children in elementary schools and in early childhood settings are animated affairs. The teacher's task is to harness, shape, and direct the spontaneous and natural movements of children toward an understanding of rhythm, melody, phrasing, texture, dynamics, and form. Under a teacher's guidance, children combine their movement with body sounds: stepping, clapping, patting, or snapping. They sing songs with associated actions or games. They practice the preparatory movements that ease them toward the playing of musical instruments. They move creatively to express what they hear and feel. They learn the structured steps of a dance. For all of these experiences, the teacher uses logic and creativity to steer children through their movement toward musical understanding.

Movement helps children to internalize musical concepts. It is also used by teachers to allow children to let off steam, and to change the classroom pace from a sit-down activity to a move-around exercise, to reward children for hard work that was well done. Movement gives opportunities for socialization and cooperation through singing games and dances. It offers children a means for understanding other cultures through folk dances. It stimulates thinking, including musical thinking. It is an important means by which children can express themselves. Movement balances the academically passive parts of the school day with the children's characteristically active nature. Movement can successfully merge children's energies, attitudes, and ideas.

Movement responses to music may be instinctive and natural, but children's instincts can be further developed and refined through instruction. When children are receptive to musical sound, the rhythm or melody will inspire them to actively participate in the music through the movement they imitate or invent. They are capable of responding to music with motion and emotion: It evokes in them both kinesthetic and aesthetic reactions. Children's natural movements can be used as avenues to music learning when lessons are designed by teachers to match movement to musical concepts.

Movement and Child Development

From infancy, children listen attentively to music and respond by moving to its rhythm. Moog (1976) noted that by the age of six months, when infants are increasingly able to coordinate the actions of their sense organs, they move their whole body in a generalized—albeit not a very synchronized—manner. By two years, toddling children are seen rocking from side to side, bouncing up and down, and waving their arms in "conducting" patterns. As children begin to listen more attentively to music at the age of three to four, the variety of their movements declines and they enter into a period of practicing and perfecting the movements they already know. Their physical coordination improves as they enter kindergarten, when four- to six-year-olds are able to move more often than not to the pulse of the music.

Children develop their capacity to use their large muscles necessary for such locomotor activities as walking, running, and hopping before they can control the small muscles they need for writing, drawing, or playing such in-

Children mirroring movement patterns.

struments as the recorder or keyboard. By the time they are in kindergarten, children have usually developed the coordination that enables them to hop, gallop, skip, and jump rope. They enjoy physical activity, and move successfully to singing games and action songs, simple folk dances, and opportunities to respond freely to recorded and live music. They enjoy creating movements to music in individually expressive ways.

There is little doubt that movement ability and the psychomotor skills necessary for performance improve with advancing age. Petzold's (1966) classic study found that by third grade, most children can accurately maintain a steady beat through tapping. Developmental patterns are apparent, in that when children in the primary grades are asked to reproduce rhythms, they do so most accurately by chanting the rhythms, moderately so by clapping, and least accurately when stepping them. Children show a gradual but marked increase in accuracy through the first three grades in these types of rhythmic movement, with girls generally outperforming boys who may lag about a year behind. While children's larger muscles develop earlier than their small muscles, the extent to which they can fine-tune coordination of the torso, the arms, and the legs to express themselves musically improves gradually through the age of ten or eleven years. This complex perceptual-motor coordination is vital to reading and performing music. See Table 8.1 for a summary of children's movement development.

Table 8.1   Children's Movement Development

Age (yrs.)	Developmental Skill
Less than six months	Responds to music through generalized body movement; movement not yet synchronized to rhythm
Two	Responds by rocking, bouncing, waving arms to rhythm
	Develops walking and running skills
	Attempts to imitate clapping and "patty-cake" movements
Three/four	Practices known movements by repeating them
	Invents and imitates new movements
	Begins to develop large muscle coordination for jumping, hopping
	Can perform simple action songs and game songs
Five/six (Kindergarten)	Begins to develop rhythmic clapping and patting
	Begins to develop skills for galloping (one-sided skip) and jumping rope
	Can perform simple folk dances in circles and lines
	Begins to develop small muscle coordination for drawing and printing (writing)
Six/seven (Grade one/two)	Begins to develop skipping skills
	Responds (frequently) to music through hand-clapping; achievement of "beat competence"
	Can "follow" the pulse and dynamics of music, and respond to gradual changes through movement
	Can perform beat on drum, rhythm sticks; can play sustained bourduns on xylophone (but requires preparatory movement to precede performance)
Eight/nine (Grade three)	Can maintain a steady beat while tapping, patting, clapping
	Can accurately reproduce rhythms by chanting, tapping, patting, clapping, or stepping
	Can perform ostinatos on xylophones (but requires preparatory movement to precede performance)
	Develops small muscle coordination for playing recorder, keyboard
	Can respond quickly and accurately to musical changes (in tempo, rhythmic patterns, texture) through movement; (quick reactions)
	Can perform more complex folk dances in circles, lines, squares, and partners
	Can conduct meters with rhythmic accuracy

(continued)

Table 8.1 Continued

Age (yrs.)	Developmental Skill
Ten/eleven twelve (Grades four to six)	Girls begin to show early signs of physical maturation
	Develops small muscle coordination (and dual coordination of breathing and fingers) for performing wind and brass instruments
	Enjoys active physical involvement; may prefer sports to dance
	Can perform rhythmic "canons" by moving to music that is previously sounded (four beats earlier) while listening to other music
	Can respond to two distinctive features of music through simultaneous movement (stepping the rhythm while conducting the pulse)

Through the primary grades, as children develop strength, agility, and flexibility, they increase their ability to play with some control percussion instruments such as the drum, tambourine, claves, and maracas. They can play simple accompaniments on xylophones and bells, including sustained bourdons and simple ostinato patterns. Preparatory movements performed initially without the instruments will provide children with the motor patterns necessary to play them with rhythmic accuracy and fluency of movement. The motor coordination necessary for the performance of wind, brass, stringed, and keyboard instruments is usually not well developed before the age of eight or nine years. However, there is little doubt that those children presented with opportunities to play these instruments will develop the necessary muscles to do so, should they be motivated to heed the adage that "practice makes perfect."

From the perspective of child development, movement is more than just the motor coordination necessary for the performance of a musical instrument. It is the essence of children's play and the manner through which they come to know their world. From early childhood, children move playfully as they sing songs associated with games, actions, and dances. The melodies of *action songs* and *singing games* draw from children the movements they have naturally encountered in their free play. These movements are recalled and organized by children to express the song's rhythmic and expressive qualities. Even in the upper elementary grades, carefully selected songs to appeal to the interests of older children can provide the orderly release of physical energy that the music requires.

Eurhythmic activities, in which children are encouraged to "do what the music tells you to do," can be designed to be in step developmentally with children's physical capacities. Children from preschool through the sixth grade can be motivated to use their bodies to illustrate music's salient features. By stepping the pulse, conducting the meter, tapping the melody's repeated rhythmic pattern, or drawing the melodic contour or shaping the phrase length in the air, children can demonstrate without words their understanding of musical concepts. Through eurhythmics, the body becomes a personal instrument for realizing the music from the simplest to the more challenging exercises.

While the development of feeling for a steady beat may be one among many musical goals, it may not always be necessary that children synchronize their movement with others or to a unifying pulse. In *creative movement*, children may be guided to develop their own repertoire of movements to express loud or soft, slow or fast, high or low, or choppy or smooth. They may explore a single movement, repeating it and expanding it, or take the movement modeled for them and vary it. By imitating the teacher or another student, children build their movement vocabulary for later recall and use. Music supplies the impetus for children to assemble new and familiar movements in ways that are personally expressive.

The structured movements of *dance* requires the basic skill of keeping time with the music. Even in the primary grades, children frequently are able to perform simple folk dances in a synchronized manner, although this is partly dependent on their physical development. The synchronicity required for perfecting the structured steps and formations of circle, square, partner, and line dances should not necessarily delay the teaching of these dances; the very practice of doing the dances will provide children with the exercise for developing their sense of rhythm and time.

Movement for tight spaces and confined areas.

Precepts and Principles of Movement

In designing lessons and experiences for children that unite music with move-ment, the teacher will want to include musical concepts and genres of move-ment that children potentially can develop. The teacher with musical training will recognize the musical concepts as fundamental to children's understand-ing of "what makes music tick." The teacher who has observed children at play will recognize that the movement genres describe the natural inclinations of children toward physical activity (Table 8.2). The challenge is how to match musical concepts with movement genres. How can these repertoires be merged? How does movement "teach" a musical concept? How does a musi-cal concept motivate movement?

Movement and music are both concerned with time, and so the concepts of pulse, duration, accent, and tempo figure prominently in each. Of all the pos-sible combinations of movement with music, then, the most obvious is the ways in which these rhythmic (pulse, duration, accent) and expressive (tempo) concepts might be expressed through movement. But melody, tim-bre, form, and texture can also be expressed physically by children through various locomotor and nonlocomotor movement styles, and through varia-tions in space, time, and energy. The action songs, singing games, eurhyth-mics, creative movement, and dance lessons suggested below will illustrate precisely how.

For movement-based musical experiences to be educationally sound, the teacher also needs to consider a set of precepts and physical arrangements to ensure the success of these exercises with children. The following items are intended to guide the teacher in the planning of music-and-movement lessons for children.

Precepts/Observations

1. Observe children at play during recess, noting their energy, speed, di-rection, levels, and various locomotor and nonlocomotor genres of their movements. Note the distinctions in the movement of boys and girls, and among children of various age groups.

2. Consider ways in which the movement qualities of athletic activities, sports, and playground games can be brought into lessons that explore musical concepts.

3. Be prepared to model a variety of movement possibilities for children's imitation and eventual variation and personal interpretation. Also, take note of children who move with ease and flair, who can serve as models of movement for their peers.

Table 8.2 A Repertoire of Musical Concepts and Movement Genres

Musical Concepts	*Movement Genres (cont.)*
Rhythm	Shake
Pulse (beat)	Push
Duration	Pull
Accent	Sway
Meter	Rise
Patterns	Collapse
Melody	Locomotor (across space)
Pitch: high/low	Walk
Contour	Run
Repeat/step/skip	Jump
Timbre	Hop
Musical sound and "not-musical"	Gallop
sound	Skip
Voices (type)	Slide
Instruments (type)	Leap
Alone	Lunge
In groups	Strut
Form	Movement variations
Repetition	Space
Variation	Shape (round, angular, bodily
Contrast	designs)
Texture	Size (large, small)
One line	Level (high, middle, low)
Multiple lines: simultaneous	Place (in place, through space)
Multiple lines: independent	Direction (forward, backward,
Expressive qualities	sideways, turning)
Tempo: fast/slow	Pathway (straight, curving)
Tempo: changing	Time
Dynamics: loud/soft	Pulse (beat)
Dynamics: changing	Duration (long, short)
Movement Genres	Accent (force)
Nonlocomotor (in place)	Tempo (fast, slow)
Stretch	Energy
Bend	Attack (sharp, smooth)
Swing	Weight (light, heavy)
Twist	Flow (bound, free)
Bounce	Strength (tight, loose)

4. Encourage children to explore the variety of ways in which the various body parts can be moved, including experiments with the energy, speed, directions, and levels in space.

Physical Arrangements/Considerations

5. Make room for movement. Move chairs and desks to the side of the room, go outdoors in the good weather, and use cafeterias, gyms (although acoustics *can* be a problem), lobbies, and hallways.

6. Explore the possibilities for movement in tight spaces, in chairs, and at desks. Some of the most fulfilling movement can be done sitting down by snapping, clapping, patting, stamping, and "conducting."

7. While allowing children the freedom to express musical ideas through movement, set movement "rules" (move without touching anyone; listen before moving) that will contain what might otherwise prove chaotic to the classroom.

8. Choose live music (on piano, for example) and recorded music in a variety of styles that will motivate children to want to move in various expressive ways.

Prelude to Movement-based Musical Experiences

In beginning to develop a sensitivity to music through movement, children need to be aware of: (1) the potential of their bodies to move in place (non-locomotor) and across space (locomotor); (2) the relationship of their bodies to people and objects in the room; and (3) the related qualities of space, time, and energy found in both music and movement. Exploratory movement ideas suggested in Table 8.3 act as a prelude to movement-based musical experiences, and can be performed with and without musical accompaniment.

Exploratory movement experiences can be initiated or further developed by the classroom teacher or physical education instructor. Nonetheless, the music teacher may use these suggestions for movement as a means of warming up children's physical selves in preparation for musical exercises that require agility, grace, flexibility, and the coordination of thinking with doing. Children enjoy the discovery of the capacities of their bodies to move as suggested and to "act on command"; such exercises are inherently motivating. Presented as questions or as creative imagery, children can be led toward problem-solving as they present solutions through the most personal of entities: their bodies. For the music teacher, however, the end product of all

Table 8.3   Exploratory Movement With and Without Music

Goal	Exploratory Tasks
Body awareness	Find different ways of moving your fingers, hands, arms, elbows, shoulders, feet, legs, head, and hips.
Body relationship	Walk your own path without touching anyone. Walk around every (chair, block, hoop) placed on the floor.
	Touch two fingers to the two fingers of your neighbors as you pass them.
	Follow teacher across the floor in exactly the same way (but *after* teacher has completed movement).
Time (speed)	Move a body part: fast, faster, slow, slower, gradually faster or slower.
Space (direction)	Walk forward, backward, sideways, toward the door, toward the windows.
Space (levels)	Walk high, low, medium; alternately high and low.
Energy (weight)	Make yourself heavy, light, strong, limp.
Energy (flow)	Walk without stopping. Stop suddenly, or gradually.
Nonlocomotor movement	Draw (with your hands, elbows, head, feet) a straight line, a curved line, a zigzag, a loop. Shape your body into a box, a triangle, a "T," a "V." Move from one shape to the next within four beats, or seven beats.
Locomotor movement	Walk, leap, lunge, run, jump, hop, gallop, skip, strut, slide.

movement experiences is the development of children's musical understanding, skills, and values.

Action Songs and Singing Games

For young children from the toddling stages through the primary grades, action songs and singing games help develop coordination and synchronized rhythmic movement, and the singing voice. Many children's songs that are performed in schoolyards during recess are oriented toward actions and games. The movements of these songs offer a release for pent-up energy, and may serve as a memory cue for learning the words of those songs. The songs provide avenues for channeling children's energies toward meaningful movement.

Action songs are those to which rhythmic gestures are added, often to co-incide with the meaning of the song text. These songs can usually be performed with little previous training and without movement exercises preceding them. As a lullaby, "Suogan" suggests the rocking of a baby to sleep, while the texts of "Johnny Works with One Hammer" and "Teddy Bear" tell the young singers to hammer with one or more hammers, and to turn around touch the ground, respectively. Beyond the traditional action songs, children may enjoy inventing gestures for familiar songs.

Song: "Suogan"

Level: Early childhood through grade one

Movement: Cradle "the baby" in the arms, rocking it back and forth to the musical pulse

Suogan (Wales)

Song: "Johnny Works with One Hammer"

Level: Early childhood through grade one

Movement: Verse 1, Pound one fist on knee
Verse 2, Pound two fists on knees
Verse 3, Pound two fists and one foot
Verse 4, Pound two fists and two feet
Verse 5, Pound two fists, two feet, and nod head
On "then he goes to sleep," rest head on hands.

Johnny Works with One Hammer (U.S.)

2. two hammers, then he works with three.
3. three hammers, then he works with four.
4. four hammers, then he works with five.
5. five hammers, then he goes to sleep.

Song: "Teddy Bear"

Level: Early childhood through grade one

Movement: Act out the words of the text

Teddy Bear (U.S.)

Many children's traditional songs incorporate games. Singing games may have survived many generations because of the joy they bring to children. The games typically require children to gather in circles, lines, small groups, or with partners, and the movement they perform is often matched to the pulse or melodic rhythm of the song. Counting songs and hand-clapping songs are singing games as well, and children enjoy the excitement of songs that have a "game goal" in mind. "Ring around the Rosy" and "London Bridge" are well-known singing games in English-speaking countries. From Cambodia, "Leak Kanseng" involves a scarf and a chase around the circle. "Guru Ndiani" is a children's singing game from Zimbabwe. Like action songs, the children's own singing provides the necessary accompaniment to the movement and the game.

Song: "Ring around the Rosy"

Level: Early childhood through grade one

Movement/game: Children hold hands while walking in a circle. At "ashes, ashes," they clap their hands twice. On "down," they all jump down. The last one to go down must sit in the middle.

Ring Around the Rosy (England)

Ring a-round the Ro-sy, a pock-et full of po-sies, Ash-es, Ash-es, we all fall down.

Song: "London Bridge"

Level: Early childhood through grade one

Movement/game: Two children form a bridge by raising their hands high so that other children can walk under it. On "half built up" only one hand of each child is raised. On "through the chopper" the bridge is brought up and down on the backs of children passing. On "to prison" one child is caught and taken away. On "take the key" the child is pushed back and forth between the set of arms.

London Bridge Is Falling Down (England)

2. Build it up with sticks and stones
3. Sticks and stones we do not have   London Bridge is all built up
4. Build it up with iron bars   Through the chopper you must go
5. Iron bars we do no have   Off to prison you must go
6. Build it up with silver and gold . . .   Take the key and lock her up

Song: "Leak Kanseng"

Level: Early childhood through grade two

Movement/game: In an open space, children gather to sit in a circle and place their hands on their knees. One child holds the scarf as he or she walks on the outside of the circle while all repeatedly chant. After two or three trips around the circle, the "scarf-hiding" child places the scarf behind the back of one sitting child. If the "sitting child" is aware of the scarf placed behind her or him, she or he picks it up and chases the "scarf-hiding" child around the circle. The "scarf-hiding" child takes the space of the former sitting child, and the game begins anew.

Leak Kanseng (Cambodia)*

As sung by Sam-ang Sam. From Silent Temples, Songful Hearts: Traditional Music of Cambodia, © 1991 World Music Press. Used by permission.

Song: "Guru Ndiani"

Level: Early childhood through grade two

Movement/game: In the center of a circle, two children hop on one leg, hands behind their backs, trying to bump the other onto two legs. The winner chooses a new child to challenge him or her. The circle of children are divided into two halves to sing the two interlocking parts.

Guru Ndiani (Zimbabwe)

There are historical collections of action songs stemming from the late nineteenth century, and a wide variety of Kodály- and Orff-based published materials. Forrai with Sinor's (1988) collection of action songs and singing games is especially noteworthy for those teaching younger children.

Children engaged in Dalcroze Eurhythmics, with teacher at the piano.

Dalcroze Eurhythmics

Principles developed by Swiss musician Emile Jaques-Dalcroze provide the single most complete system of rhythmic training to appear in the twentieth century. He recognized movement as the foundation of a thorough musicianship, and so developed a means of communication linking the ear, the brain, and the body. He established eurhythmics (i.e., good rhythm) as an alternative to dance and gymnastics, developing in his students a fuller musical consciousness through directed and improvised physical responses to music. While few teachers today submit to the rigorous training of the Dalcroze approach, partly because of the challenges of learning the keyboard improvisation that Dalcroze used to accompany these movement exercises, eurhythmic experiences can be integrated within music classes for children in modified ways, using drums or prerecorded music as the impetus for movement.

Eurhythmics has been misinterpreted frequently as physical conditioning exercises, creative movement, or dance; it is none of these. Still, eurhythmics requires children to be limber, quick, and controlled. It requires them to express the music they hear through a creative reorganizing of the movements they already know. It sets their bodies to "dance" (in a figurative sense) to the musical sounds they perceive.

Elements of music, including basic sound awareness, pulse (beat), tempo, articulation, style, dynamics, accent, meter, melody, phrases, anacrusis (upbeat), duration, proportional relationships, and timbre can be taught through Dalcroze eurhythmics. Little is needed to bring children into contact with music through eurhythmics: a large space, a drum, a piano, a stereo, and rules for "boundaries" and acceptable behavior that all children understand. Table 8.4 presents a sampling of suggestions for eurhythmics experiences; the creative teacher will use these as springboards for further development into ten-minute experiences, full lessons, and experiences that extend for days, weeks, or months.

At times, recorded music can be used to stimulate movement, but the live and partly spontaneous music played by the teacher on piano or percussion instrument is best. Children learn at different paces. Some need to hear a musical idea many times, and with the teacher's access to an instrument, the music can be easily slowed down, repeated, or given more emphasis. Whatever the instrument, the teacher should feel comfortable with it. Basic rhythms, melodies, and harmonies can stimulate sensitive movement when they are played musically.

Short composed piano pieces also provide the impetus for teaching musical concepts through movement. In planning a lesson that emanates from a composed piece, the teacher should thoroughly analyze its rhythmic and melodic

Table 8.4   Sample Experiences in Dalcroze Eurhythmics

Musical Concept	Experience
Sound versus silence	Children move when music is heard and freeze during silences.
Pulse (tempo)	Children step to the pulse of one child (no music). As teacher calls out the name of another child, children step the tempo and quality of that child's walk.
Pulse (tempo, timbre)	Children step to the beat of the drum. When the drum stops, children stop. When teacher taps the rim of the drum, children change the direction of their walking. (Variation: children continue walking to the same beat even when the drum has stopped, testing their internalization of its sound.)
Articulation	Children hop or jump to choppy, staccato music, and glide, slide, or sway to legato, smooth music.
Dynamics	Children improvise strong movements for loud (forte) music and quiet, subtle movements for soft (piano) music. As music crescendos, children gradually enlarge their movements, diminishing them for diminuendo parts.
Style (tempo, dynamics, articulation)	Children clap/step/follow teacher's improvisation on piano or xylophone. They should be encouraged to use as much variety of space, time, and energy as is necessary to kinesthetically realize the music.
Tempo	The room is divided into two parts: a slow and a fast half. Without music, children move from one side to the other using the designated tempo of each half. When teacher plays music, children resolve their movement to that new tempo. Teacher demonstrates a movement that children imitate. Then, as music in various tempos is played, children perform the movement slower or faster.
Accent	Children (walk, run, skip) through the forest. On accent, they jump behind a tree to hide from a bear.
Phrase	Children move in response to musical phrases. After several listenings, they use the same movements for the repeated phrases and change the movement for contrasting phrases.
Timbre	As teacher plays piano in various registers, children clap the high melodies and step the low melodies. Challenge them to coordinate the two when both treble and bass parts are sounding.

(continued)

Table 8.4 Continued

Musical Concept	Experience
Meter	Children walk the pulse and clap on the first beat of each measure to teacher's improvised music in twos, threes, fours, fives, sixes, sevens, etc. Choose a number, and while teacher plays music, children clap, pat, step, and rest for that number of beats. Challenge children to respond to the call of other numbers with the same sequence of movements. (For example, on "four," children clap, pat, step, and rest for four beats each, and on "seven," children clap, pat, step, and rest for seven beats each.) In partners or a circle of children, choose a way to demonstrate a meter of two, three, four, five, six, seven, etc., by rolling, tossing, or passing a ball. (For example, in a $\frac{2}{4}$ meter, partners might bounce and catch the ball. In a $\frac{3}{4}$ meter, a circle of children might bounce, hold, and pass the ball.)
Melody	As ascending music plays, children rise like the sun. They fall slowly like the sun setting on the horizon with the sound of descending music. Children move forward to ascending melodies, backward to descending music, and stand in place for melodies of static and unchanging pitch.
Anacrusis	Children step the pulse and conduct the meter. On music with an upbeat, or anacrusis, they step counterclockwise and on music with a downbeat, or crusis, they step clockwise.
Duration	Children walk the quarter notes of teacher's improvised music on drum or piano, and stop and clap when eighth notes are played. Children sit in a circle. As the teacher improvises music on piano or drum, children "walk" the quarter notes by patting their laps, "run" the eighth notes by clapping, pat the half notes on their head, and tap the whole notes on the floor in front of them.
Proportional relationships	Children step the pulse of the music. When a verbal or musical cue is given, they step twice as fast or twice as slow.

nuances, phrasing, and overall formal organization, as well as the expressive markings that indicate tempo, dynamics, and articulation. The piece may require concentrated practice in preparation for the lesson, so that the composer's musical intentions are artfully presented to the children. When the teacher has reached a level of familiarity and confidence that will allow her or him to occasionally glance away from the instrument so as to be able to evaluate the movement responses of the children, then that piece is probably ready for teaching. A sampling of technically easy piano pieces is presented in Table 8.5, with suggestions for musical concepts that can be highlighted through eurhythmics.

The teacher who incorporates Dalcroze eurhythmics in music lessons will find that children become astute listeners for musical elements to meet the challenges of these movement games. While specialized Dalcroze training will shape the teacher's ability to improvise at the piano, a good musician who takes time out for practice will be capable of facilitating fundamental eurhythmics experiences into classes. Further information on eurhythmics can be found in the writings of Abramson (1973), Aronoff (1969), Findlay (1971), and Mead (1994).

Creative Movement

Creative movement is a form of dance that is personal, interpretive, and expressive. It can be used to socialize children, to provide entertainment to an audience of parents, and to communicate ideas and feelings more directly or deeply than words. Unlike most dance forms, creative movement lacks authoritarian structure. There is no one "right" way of doing things, and there are no specific steps to learn. It is inspired by verbal and musical imagery, and is an extension of exploratory movement experiences. It primes the kinesthetic impulses for responding to a stimulus. It may spring from a musical source, but it is not as closely united to specific musical concepts as required by eurhythmics. Creative movement links children's emotional and inventive selves with the kinesthetic skills of their bodies to utilize space, time, and energy in a unique dance.

The concepts to be taught should be presented as questions and challenges that inspire individual solutions. The Socratic method should be prominently used when the teacher guides children's movement through such questions as the following. How do squirrels scamper? What parts of the squirrel's body moves? Can you swing like a puppet blowing in the wind? Can you swing high or low? Can you swing while you walk, run, or skip? Can you swing in an even rhythm or uneven rhythm? Children should be encouraged to explore and discover the concept of breath, body parts, sounds, shapes, accents, lev-

Table 8.5 Sample Piano Pieces for Eurhythmics Experiences

Schumann: The Wild Horseman (measures 1–8)

Musical concepts

  Pulse; tempo; style

  (Gallop like a horse) ♩ ♪♩ ♪

  Triplet figure of melody

  (Clap the continuous trotting sound) ♫♩

  Two-measure accompaniment figure

  ("Hop, hop – – step, hop, hop") ♪𝄾𝄾 ♪𝄾𝄾 | ♩ ♪♪ 𝄾𝄾|

  Melody and accompaniment

  (Group one trots while group two hops)

  (Group one plays on woodblock,

  Group two plays on drum)

Beethoven: Ecossaise in G (measures 1–8)

Musical concepts

  Steady eighth-note accompaniment pattern ♫♫

  (Lightly step the steady accompaniment pattern)

  Two similar four-measure phrases: A A'

  (Change direction at the end of each phrase, but retain same quality if the phrase
    is the same)

  Two-measure crescendo, two-measure decrescendo < >

  (Enlarge movements for crescendo, and decrease size and space for descrescendo)

  Anacrusis ♫ | ♩

  (Make a movement that "leans into" the first pulse, of measure one and five)

  Staccato and legato ♫ ♫♫

  (Glide on legato and give a slight hop to the staccato sounds)

  Accent

  (On measures two and six, hop and land on the accented pitch (e'))

  Rhythmic pattern in treble ♫♫♫ ♪ ♩

  (Step the rhythmic pattern, with attention to articulation, accent, dynamics, and
    anacrusis)

Schumann: Soldier's March (measures 1–16)

Musical concepts

  Pulse; tempo; style

  (March like a soldier)

  ♫. ♪ pattern, measures 1, 5, 9, 13

  ("Skip-ty, step" [binary] or "step-hop, step")

  Four-measure phrases: A B A B

  (Change direction at the end of each phrase, and move at distinct levels for A
    and B phrases)

  (In partners, create movements for A and B)

---

els, and pathways rather than to be told or shown what to do. The teacher may lead children in preparatory movement experiences, select and present the stimulus for creative movement, direct attention to the concept through imagery that may be verbal, visual, or musical, and shape the final form of the experience through suggestion and approval. The learning, however, emanates from the child's own willingness to discover the expressive potential of her or his body.

Creative movement can be inspired by a word, a picture, a poem, a story, a song's melody, a rhythmic pattern, or a symphonic work. Teachers who strive for the development of musical understanding through creative movement may begin with any of these stimuli, but will be certain to reinforce a selected concept as an aid to the children's realization of an image, or by incorporating music at the culmination of the exercise. To ensure learning, the teacher must be certain that the lesson is based on a preset goal, that children are informed of the goal, that they are presented with a variety of questions, problems, and stimuli, and that they are encouraged to achieve the lesson goal (if they do) through particular attention to the strengths of individual children as well as the group as a whole.

Suggestions for experiences in creative movement are found in Table 8.6. Some will encompass complete lesson periods, others can be included as short segments within a lesson, and still others may require several periods and much practice to fulfill. The creative teacher will likely extend, vary, and develop these experiences to suit the needs of children.

Creative movement generates enthusiasm among children. It gives them permission to explore and express freely and playfully the ideas that are brought to mind by poems, pictures, music, and stories. It gives them freedom to experiment with their own space, time, and energy, leading them to a discovery of the language of movement. The use of music as a stimulus for movement, as part of the learning process, or as a component of the final product provides a more fulfilling and integrative experience for children. In this manner, children learn music as they also learn to speak through their bodies. For additional ideas on creative movement, see Joyce (1980).

Dance

Dance is a purposeful, choreographed, and much-rehearsed movement to music. Dance knows many forms: classical ballet; modern dance as inspired by Martha Graham; classical court dances of Southeast Asia; theater dances of China and Japan; martial arts-inspired dances of Latin America; and ballroom, break-dancing, and folk dances. To dance well, these forms involve physical training that is dependent on technique, knowledge, and experience.

Table 8.6 Experiences in Creative Movement

Goal	Experience
To portray words in movement and sound	In partners or small groups, present children with words to be turned into movement and sound pieces: Yawn, tramp, spin, shuffle, ooze, flutter, drip, explode, crack, spurt, swish, ripple, crunch, stir, sprinkle, plunge, slither. In a presentation to the class, these pieces may be moved silently and then presented with vocal, body, and instrumental accompaniment.
To portray musical terms in movement	Assign groups of children various musical terms, and ask that they express them through movement: legato; staccato; forte; marcato; sforzando; cantabile; piano; piacere; lento; allegro; appassionato; doloroso. (First they must learn the meanings of these terms as applied to music.) They may later invent a melody to express the term, and to coincide with the movement.
To depict a musical in movement	Play a recording of Camille Saint-Saëns' "The Lion" from *Carnival of the Animals*. Direct children's attention to pitch register and direction in the lion's growl. Through repeated listenings, ask that they move "like a lion" (large, strong, forceful), stopping to growl at the appropriate time. Ask children to listen to a recording of Aaron Copland's *Fanfare for the Common Man*, to note the sounds and the silences, to identify the long and sustained sounds, the instruments, the melodic leaps, the changes in dynamics. Play the opening forty-five seconds of the recording repeatedly, giving children the task of finding their own individual movements to personify the piece.
To create a movement-and-music version of a visual image	Show children a copy of a painting or a photograph. In small groups (depending on the number of figures), encourage them to "make the visual image come to life." They will need to discuss what the people are doing, where they are going, and how they are moving. Their tableau should begin as a still image, and can proceed through a movement piece that communicates without words. Vocal, body, and instrumental music may be improvised by another group of children to accompany the tableau. Paintings such as George Caleb Bingham's "Raftsmen Playing Cards," Frederic Remington's "Howl of the Weather," or John Steuart Curry's "The Mississippi" may inspire movement.

(continued)

Table 8.6 Continued

Goal	Experience
To create a movement piece from a collection of individual movements	Gather children into groups of four to eight. Ask that each child invent a movement to be included in a movement collection; each group should have as many movements as there are children. As a group, they practice their collective movements until one flows easily to the next. As an extension, they can choose to allow each movement one, two, or four pulses, or repeat some or all of the movements. Children can develop different levels of energy and space for these movements, should they wish to express them as "tired," "intimidated," "angry," or "gentle." Musical accompaniment can be suggested, selected, or created.
To express a poem through movement	A poem paints a visual image that can be realized through movement. Children can choose to follow the rhythm of the words, or move more freely to the images that strike them.

The Puzzled Centipede (Anon.)

A centipede was happy quite,
Until a frog in fun
Said, "Pray, which leg comes after which?"
This raised her mind to such a pitch,
She lay distracted in the ditch
Considering how to run.

The Animal Dance (P. S. Campbell)

The owl, the skunk,
The bull, and the bear
Went dancing one evening.
They let down their hair.
The owl did waddle.
The skunk gave a twirl.
The bull hopped on two feet.
The bear took a whirl.
Closing in on a circle,
They turned to their right.
Holding paws, hoofs, and feathers,
They took off as in flight.
The skunk set the speed
For all three of his friends.
Fast. Faster. They circled
And spun to the end.

(continued)

Table 8.6   Continued

Goal	Experience
	With centrifugal force, *They did laugh and then scream,* *"We're the animal dancers!* *We dance in your dreams!"*
To express a story through movement	Action stories inspire movement. Collections such as Joanna Cole's *Best-Loved Folktales of the World* provide many examples for dramatization. One story, with potential for both movement and musical accompaniment, is "A Crocodile's Tale" from the Philippines.

A Crocodile's Tale

A little boy named Juan saved the life of a crocodile by untying a rope around his neck. But instead of thanking him, the crocodile sweeps little Juan up with his tail and wraps it around him. He wants to eat the boy. While the crocodile catches fish from the river as "appetizers," Juan cries for help. He is heard by a monkey sitting in a tree on the bank of the river. The monkey shouts to the crocodile, "What are you doing with Juan?" To which the crocodile replies, "I'm going to eat him." The clever monkey shouts "Can't hear you! What did you say? Come a little closer." The crocodile swims to the middle of the river, with his tail wrapped around Juan. "I'm going to eat him, and maybe you, too." Again the monkey shouts "Can't hear you! Come a little closer." The crocodile swims to the bank and shows his teeth to the monkey in the tree. In an instant, the monkey lunges down with a rope to tie the crocodile's snout tightly shut, and Juan frees himself from the tail and jumps to safety. The monkey and Juan celebrate by joyfully dancing the Tinikling, a traditional dance of the Philippines (see page 212 for Tinikling instructions).

Unlike other types of movement for children, dance is an art. It is structured and premeditated movement that demands concentration in learning the postures, positions, and steps, and that requires practice to keep the specific movements in the memory.

For children through the elementary grades, folk dance is one of the best avenues for experiencing music, cultures, and movement all at once. The first dances attempted should be those with simple and repetitive footwork set to music with a clearly defined pulse. Line and circle dances are often easier for beginners than partner dances, so that they can focus on the steps rather than on their relationship to their partner. Weikert (1982) suggests a progression for learning folk dances, taking into account physical education goals. When the emphasis is the development of children's musical understanding, the following sequence is more effective.

1. *Listen.* As an introduction to the musical style of the dance, the teacher should guide children to listen carefully to the music. Children can attend to musical details. What instruments are playing? Which are the melody instruments? Do you hear repeated rhythmic patterns? Can you chant, clap, or write them? Is the melody wide or narrow in range? Can you sing the melody? Is the texture of the combined instruments chordal, unison, or heterophonic (simultaneous variations played by several melody instruments)? Concentrated and repeated listenings will create a more comfortable dance experience, and the music will become better understood and appreciated.

2. *Respond.* The teacher should direct children to listen to the recording (or to the song as it is sung or played), and respond to the underlying rhythm in the bass line, the chordal accompaniment, or the percussion instruments. By patting the accented beats on their laps, children are responding to the dance rhythm. When learning a dance to a song, rather than a recorded musical piece, the teacher can nonetheless present the steps as a clapped or patted ostinato rhythm for all to follow.

3. *Chant/pat.* Ask children to chant descriptive words to indicate the motion of the dance. By chanting "step," "hop," "pause," "left," "right" and the like, children will more easily perform the necessary rhythmic movement of the feet. The words are spoken in the rhythm of the steps, which are "danced" with the hands on the lap.

4. *Chant/step.* The transfer of movement from the hands to the feet occurs next. The repeated rhythmic chant should continue, so that the children match the steps to the descriptive words. This speech-action activity is initially more successful without the music, which may confuse some students who will be distracted by other musical aspects such as timbre and melody.

5. *Step/internalize.* In the final stage, the music returns to accompany the movement. Children begin to internalize the rhythmic chant, thinking and doing the steps. As a result of earlier stages in the sequence, children develop an inner hearing for the rhythm and a kinesthetic ease in performing the movement.

Table 8.7 presents instructions for a selection of folk dances, along with their associated melodies and references to accessible recordings. Melodies played on classroom instruments by children can provide the culminating performance for programs and for children's own pleasure.

The movements of folk dance are natural and unaffected, stylized but not stilted, offering a means of socialization, enrichment of school programs, and exposure to the folkways of world cultures. As a movement-based musical experience, folk dance makes a meaningful contribution to the musical development of children. Weikert's (1982) folk-dance collections, with their accompanying recordings of dance arrangements, are useful for teachers who can modify the instructional sequence to suit their musical goals.

Movement for Musical Development

Teachers are sometimes hesitant to initiate movement experiences. What if the music room is too small? Explore the school building and schoolyard for alternative spaces. Modify the size and scope of some of the movement experiences. What if the children don't know their left from their right? Most action songs, singing games, eurhythmics, and creative-movement experiences don't require a knowledge of left and right. In learning folk dances, children can tie a ribbon around their left (or right) wrists. What if the children aren't "getting" a musical concept? Focus their attention. Repeat the melody, the rhythm, the chant, and the directions. Model the movement. Sequence the activity, breaking it into smaller segments. Give them time to practice. What if they get rowdy? Set the rules at the start, remind children of the penalties for broken rules, and follow through on them. What should the rules be? That depends on the activity, your goals, the space, and the age of children. Keep the rules simple and straightforward; sometimes "no-touch" and "stop-when-the-music-stops" rules are enough. What if they won't move? Determine whether the movement is age-appropriate. For older children, opportunities for teaching each other and working in small groups may be more readily received than too many teacher-directed lessons.

Movement is more than an occasional experience. It is an integral part of children's musical education. Children develop musical sensitivity when their natural movements are channeled toward the discovery or reinforcement of musical features and components. The musically trained teacher who recognizes children's movement capacities is critical to advancing their musical knowledge, skills, and sensitivities.

Table 8.7 Folk Dances

Table 8.7 Continued

Sakura (Japan)

Sa - ku - ra, Sa - ku - ra, ya - yo - i - no so - ra___ wa, Mi - wa - ta - su

ka - gi___ ri, ka - su - mi - ka ku - mo___ ka, Ni - o - i zo

i - zu___ ru; I - za - ya, i - za - ya Mi___ ni yu___ ka - n.

Level: Grades 2 to 6

Title/Source	Sequence	
Sakura	Independent, in lines or circle (Phrase = 4 beats)	
Japan	Phrase 1	Arms extended, "Nod Right, Nod Left"
Art of the Koto:	Phrase 2	Make "Right arm circle, Left arm circle"
The Music of Japan	Phrase 3	Move "R arm side-front, L arm side-front"
	Phrase 4	"Hands pat Right lap, Hands pat Left lap"
	Phrase 5	Repeat 3
	Phrase 6	Repeat 1
	Phrase 7	"Right, left-elbow, Left, right-elbow"
		(Raise right arm, fingers skyward, left
		hand below right elbow, then left arm)

La Raspa (Mexico)

La ras - pa yo bai-lé al de -re-cho y al re-vés. Sí

quie - res tú bai - lar, em - pie-za a mo - ver los pies

Brin - ca, brin - ca, brin-ca tam-bién, mue - ve, mue - ve mu-cho los pies. Que la

ras - pa ras a bai - lar al de - re - cho y al re - vés.

(continued)

Table 8.7   Continued

Title/Source	Sequence

Level: Grades 3 to 5
La Raspa   Partners, facing each other, hands on hips
Mexico   Phrases 1–8
Folk Dance Fun
(Kimbo 7037)

R   L   R   L R L
"Step Step Step Clap Clap St St St Cl Cl"
Measures 9–10   Link right elbows, skip once around
Measures 11–12   Link left elbows, skip once around

Tinikling (Philippines)

Level: Grades 3 to 6

Title/Source	Sequence

Tinikling   Two long poles (of 6–10) feet on the floor; child holding
Philippines   two poles at each end
                   Pole movement: Count 1 Strike poles together
                                       Count 2 Poles apart, strike floor
                                       Count 3 Poles apart, strike floor
                   Dance movement: Count 1 Jump out, spreading feet apart
                                       Count 2 Jump in, with feet together
                                       Count 3 Jump in, with feet together

Schottische (Sweden)

Fine

D.C. al Fine

Table 8.7   Continued

Title/Source	Sequence

Level: Grades 4 to 6
Schottische
Sweden
Folk Dances for
All Ages (RCA
Victor 1622)

Phrase 1 — Move apart: R L R R — "Step Step Step Hop"
L R L L — Step Step Step Hop"

Phrase 2 — Move together: R R L L — "Step Hop Step Hop"

R R L — — "Step Hop Step Pause"

Gerakina (Greece)

Ger - a - ki-na's at the fair, Ger - a - ki-na with her gol - den ban-gles on,

There's mu-sic ev -'ry-where.   Ring,   pre-tty gol-den ban - gles, jin-gle, jin-gle,

jan - gle. Sing   in the   air,   Ger-a - ki-na danc - ing at   the   fair.   All the vil-lage

boys will come to the square For the jin-gle   jan - gle dance   at the   fair

Level: Grades 4 to 6
Gerakina
Greece
Dances of the
World's People
(Folkways FD 6501)

Line, all join hands
Shoulder hold
Two-measure repeated pattern:

R R L   R L   —
"Step Step Step   Step Behind Pause"

Alternate repeated pattern:

R L R   L R   R
"Step Step Step   Step Toe-in Toe-out"
    behind

Questions

1. Discuss the musical and social outcomes of including movement in a music lesson for children.

2. Define the movement components of space, time, and energy.

3. At what age would action songs be appropriate for use with children? Singing games?

4. How are eurhythmics and creative movement related? How are they different?

5. List musical goals for teaching folk dance to children. How would they differ from the goals of a physical education instructor who teaches folk dancing?

Activities

1. Visit a school or park playground to observe the movement of children at play. What games do they play that include songs and movement? What movements can older children perform for which younger children have not yet mastered the coordination? Make a list of your observations regarding children's use of space, time, and energy.

2. Begin a collection of songs, including game, dance, and action songs, that require or suggest movement. Organize them chronologically according to the level of kinesthetic development necessary to enable children to successfully perform them.

3. Choose a musical concept and prepare a set of movement experiences appropriate for children in kindergarten, grade 3, and grade 6.

4. Select a sample experience in Dalcroze Eurhythmics, and prepare a ten-minute lesson to teach in class. Develop that same idea into a thirty-minute lesson.

5. Listen to recordings of music from various historical periods and cultures. Select one or more musical concepts from each, and consider ways in which movement can be applied as a vehicle for developing children's understanding of the concept(s).

6. Write a letter to your principal to explain how the movement experiences she or he observed in your music class were educationally justified. Include an explanation of which specific musical concepts were learned by children through the movement demonstration.

References

ABRAMSON, R. (1973). *Rhythm games.* New York: Movement Press.

ARONOFF, F. W. (1969). *Music and young children.* New York: Turning Wheel Press.

FINDLAY, E. (1971). *Rhythm and movement: Application of Dalcroze eurhythmics.* Evanston, IL: Summy Birchard.

FORRAI, K. (1988). *Music in preschool.* J. Sinor (Trans.). Budapest, Hung.: Corvina Press.

JOYCE, M. (1980). *First steps in teaching creative dance to children* (2nd ed.). Palo Alto, CA: Mayfield.

MEAD, V. (1994). *Dalcroze eurhythmics in today's classroom.* New York: Schott.

MOOG, H. (1976). *The musical experience of the pre-school child.* C. Clarke (Trans.). London: Schott.

PETZOLD, R. G. (1966). Auditory perception of musical sounds by children in the first six grades. *Cooperative Research Project No. 1051.* Madison, WI: University of Wisconsin.

WEIKERT, P. S. (1982). *Teaching movement and dance.* Ypsilanti, MI: High Scope.

9

The Playing Child

Strike up the band, and the child is captivated by the colorful sounds of musical instruments. As the instruments thump, soar, chime, rattle, slide, shimmer, ring, bellow, and shake, the various timbres are as stimulating to children as they are spellbinding. And when children are given the chance to play, they do so with great pleasure. Janie beats the drum at a snappy and spirited speed. Julie shakes the maracas, first with her right hand, then with her left, and then both at once. LaToya concentrates on the different sounds she can make on a tambourine. Andrew and José hammer out melodies together on wooden xylophones. Ellen sings a song she knows while pushing chord keys on an autoharp. Franz practices two guitar chords over and over, creating new rhythmic strums as he goes. Rex and Evan are at the keyboard, playing a blues progression that matches a popular song's harmonies.

Children of all ages are players of musical instruments, or would like to be. Infants shake rattles, toddlers bang on cardboard boxes, tables, chairs, or pots and pans. Toy pianos, flutes, and guitar-like instruments make popular birthday gifts for preschoolers. In early childhood centers, the highlight of any day is music making—especially when it includes the playing of drums, jingle bells, wooden sticks, and tambourines.

As children mature, pitched instruments available at home and in their elementary school classrooms can offer them challenging and gratifying musical experiences. Some instruments, such as xylophone, recorder, and tone bells are for playing melodies; some, such as autoharp and guitar, primarily produce harmonies or chords. Ensembles of xylophones or recorders provide both melody and harmonic accompaniment. Keyboard instruments such as piano, organ, MIDI synthesizers, and small tabletop or lap pianos provide musical challenges to older children. Children continue to be fascinated by nonpitched rhythm instruments through the elementary years, particularly by drums of all sizes and shapes—kettle, bongo, conga, and hand drums. Whether they play alone, in small groups, or full ensemble, children will play to be heard, and to hear themselves play.

Developmental Sequence

Children's abilities to play musical instruments are closely related to their physical development. An example of this relationship might be seen in the playing of maracas or gourd rattles found in much African and Latin-American music. Infants in their fourth and fifth months master the task of grasping toys and other objects, including their own baby rattles, and are already on their way to making music. By the time children are three years old, they have usually developed the muscle control that goes with playing and silencing the rattle at will. Primary-grade children have the coordination as well as the perceptiveness to keep the musical pulse and to play basic rhythmic patterns. Children in the intermediate grades can become quite adept at playing a host of rhythms on maracas, due to their physical maturation, musical perception, and cognitive understanding of the characteristics of the music they are making.

While rhythmic skills are usually the first to emerge—as early as the first year of life—the muscular coordination essential to playing musical instruments may develop much later. The early rhythmic rocking of an infant leads later to the swinging of the arms (about age three), which progresses to the alteration of one hand and then the other for playing two mallets on a drum (about age five or six). The more sophisticated eye-hand coordination skills begin to be refined from the age of seven onward, becoming more perfect through practice. For example, eye-hand coordination allows the child's visual sense to signal and set in gear his or her neurophysical system in the complex operation of striking a xylophone key. Something so seemingly simple as playing a melody on piano requires motoric machinery that involves the eyes, ears, and multiple muscles of the finger, hand, and forearm. Add to that the coordination of the breathing apparatus in the playing of wind instruments, and it is no wonder that recorders are only introduced to children in the third or fourth grade, with instruction on orchestral wind and brass instruments initiated at the close of the elementary school years, in fifth or sixth grade.

The pedagogy of Shinichi Suzuki has been widely recognized for the manner in which it develops listening skills and performance techniques at an early age. While the image of pint-sized violins comes to mind, it is the philosophy and practices of the Suzuki approach that attracts parents and their children. Suzuki called the method "Talent Education," and based it on the premise that all children are born musical. The tenet that children learn musical instruments in the same way they learn to speak is reflected through seven principles of Suzuki's method: (1) begin early, with listening at birth and lessons from about two-and-a-half years onward; (2) delay music reading until musical skills and performance techniques have developed; (3) involve parents in lessons and home practice; (4) use excellent music literature that is developmentally appropriate; (5) balance private lessons (for attention to technical skills) with group lessons (for motivation and socialization); (6) repeat, review, and reinforce the performance of previously learned music; and (7) accentuate self-development while de-emphasizing competition. The Suzuki method maintains that children will develop musically through their instrument, when they are given occasion to develop the motor abilities necessary for performance on violin (or cello, piano, flute, and numerous other instruments).

But because the motoric development of children progresses naturally and is largely unassisted by such specialized instruction as Suzuki, they will learn best when presented with experiences in playing musical instruments that match their developmental abilities. This is not to say that the exploration of assorted sounds that musical instruments can produce cannot be initiated in earlier stages; in fact, such discovery learning should be encouraged at every age. Still, children are likely to cultivate performance techniques on an instrument when they are physically ready to do so, thus the importance of matching motoric development to instruments. Table 9.1 provides a sequence for the formal introduction of musical instruments into children's performance experiences. Playing techniques introduced at a given age will, of course, require practice for refinement.

The Body as a Percussion Instrument

The body can be viewed as a musical instrument; clapping, slapping, tapping, snapping, stamping, and patting the shoulders, head, elbows, knees, and stomach produces various sounds that delight children everywhere. In some cultures, the body is considered one of the primary sources of musical sound. For example, African-American sacred songs, particularly folk spirituals and gospel, often feature clapping, just as African-American folk songs frequently include "hand jives" of slaps, claps, and snaps. The potential for timbral variety through "corpophones," the body's sound producers, has frequently gone unnoticed in some cultures, but can nonetheless be successfully brought into the culture of the classroom.

Children at play often create their own original body-percussion pieces. They can also learn through imitation body-percussion sounds that can en-

Table 9.1 Developmental Sequence for the Playing Instruments

Age (yrs.)	Musical-Motoric Development	Instruments; Instrumental Techniques
Less than 2	Rocking, nodding, swaying Capacity to grip/grasp	Rattles (shaking) Jingle bells (Shaking)
2–3	Short periods of rhythmic regularity	Hand drum (hand tapping) Sticks (striking)
3–4	Longer periods of rhythmic regularity Sensitivity to pulse Swaying of arms	Claves (striking) Sticks (rubbing) Woodblock (M* striking, rubbing) Sandblocks (rubbing) Tambourine (shaking, striking) Guiro (rubbing) Maracas (shaking) Gong (M striking) Cowbell (M striking)
5–6 (Kindergarten/ Grade 1)	Maintenance of pulse Alteration of hands Basic eye-hand coordination	Finger cymbals (striking rim to rim) Bongo drums (hand striking) Timpani (M striking) Cymbals (striking) Triangle (M striking) Keyboard (one hand)
7–9 (Grades 1 to 3)	Eye-hand coordination	Finger cymbals (striking; attached) Slit log drum (M striking) Temple blocks (M striking) Conga drum (hand striking) Goblet drum (hand striking) Double iron agogo bells (M striking) Tone bells (M striking) Xylophone (simple drone, bourdon, ostinato; two M striking) Keyboard (both hands/melody w/chords) Recorder (g-b) Autoharp (chording)
10–12 (Grades 4 to 6)	Increased facility of eye-hand coordination Finger flexibility Control of breathing apparati	Xylophone (moving drone, ostinato, melody; two M striking) Keyboard (both hands/two moving parts) Recorder (c-g′) Guitar (chording) Orchestral wind/brass

*M, mallet.

The body as a percussion instrument.

hance their rhythm skills, increasing their vocabulary of internalized rhythms. With guidance, children can be led to perform ensemble pieces that feature the rhythms of body percussion, one pattern layered on another. Body percussion makes for an exciting performance piece for audiences of parents, other children, and people in the community.

Body-percussion exercises can also be used to prepare children for their performance on nonpitched rhythm and barred instruments. By patting the rhythm of an ostinato on their laps, children are then better able to play the pattern on a drum, a woodblock, or a xylophone. Even guitar and autoharp strums can be played first in the air, while fingers can play "imaginary" re-corders and piano keyboards on the arm, the floor, or a tabletop. A reward for initially working out the rhythm through a body percussion exercise is the opportunity to play it on the instrument itself. Examples of body percussion pieces and exercises that can stand on their own, or be transferred to instruments, are found in Table 9.2.

Nonpitched Percussion Instruments

Also known as "rhythm instruments," nonpitched percussion instruments are found nearly everywhere that children are gathered: from preschools to public schools, from child-care centers to churches and temples. Rhythm instru-

Table 9.2 Experiences in Body Percussion

1. Teach the rhythms through measure-by-measure imitation, with the intention of engaging all children to perform all parts in body percussion.
2. Transfer rhythms to instruments, to be performed by four different groups of children.

3. Transfer these complete rhythm phrases to xylophones to be played on any keys of the pentaton according to children's personal choice.
4. Teach the following rhythms through imitation. Practice to perform the parts in three groups that gradually combine, overlap, repeat, increase in volume, and conclude on cue.

(continued)

ments can be played alone or in groups, with or without pitched instruments such as xylophones or keyboards, to accompany songs, chants, poems, or stories. They can accent and interpret narratives, and provide leitmotif-like sounds to represent story characters. They provide colorful timbres in improvisations and pieces composed by small groups of children. When played together in polyrhythmic fashion, they provide a fascinating complex of sound.

Nonpitched percussion instruments may be classified as *membranophones*, which are various sizes and shapes of drums that produce sound through a vibrating skin or membrane, and *idiophones*, instruments of wood, metal, and gourd that are struck, shaken, scraped, or tapped. They may also be categorized according to the material from which they are made: woods, skins, metals, and gourds.

Table 9.2   Continued

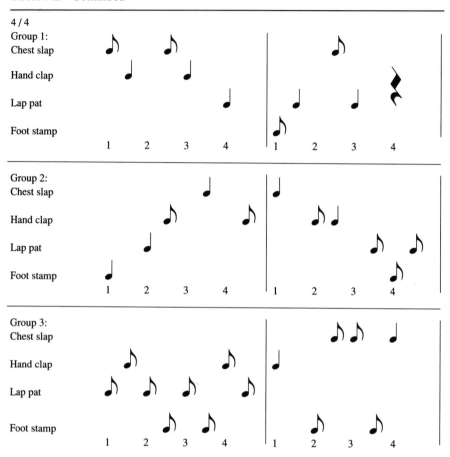

Possible Performance Plan: Arrange children in three groups of equal numbers, to be placed in three circles, one long line, or an open-ended, three-sided square. The director may wish to use claves to keep a constant pulse, and to aurally signal changes, additions, or deletions of groups in some preplanned way. Group one begins performing its rhythm, continuing as group two enters, followed by the entrance of group three. A previous form can be determined, so that groups perform, wait out several cycles, and return again; one such form is given below. The director can cue louder and softer cycles, while the pulse remains the same throughout. Basic movements (such as changes of direction toward which the children face) may be added for visual impact, although the major objective is the performance of polyrhythms through body percussion.

Suggested form: (numbers stand for group, one complete rhythm cycle per number)

(continued)

Table 9.2   Continued

1	1	1	1		1	1	1	1		1	1	1	1		1	1	1	1
	2	2			2	2				2	2			2	2			2	2
		3	3	3		3	3	3			3	3	3		3	3	3	
p		mf	p	f		p	f	mf		f	mf			f				

Alternative plan: All parts are combined into a six-measure pattern, and learned. The six-measure rhythm is then performed in canon, with group two entering one measure after group one, and so forth.

Children enjoy exploring the possible sounds that rhythm instruments can produce, either informally and independently or as stimulated by words of a poem or story. They should also be led by demonstration to learning the traditional ways of holding and playing the instruments, to obtain the greatest resonance from them.

The musical quality of commercially available instruments varies somewhat, but many of them produce pleasant and resonant sounds that are attractive to children through their elementary years. A set of classroom instruments typically includes sticks, flat and notched woodblocks, cymbals, triangles, tambourines, jingle bells, and sandblocks. Additional rhythm instruments in these sets frequently include gongs, finger cymbals, cowbell, and claves. Of the many varieties of drums, those most typically found in well-stocked classrooms include hand drums, bongo drums, conga and goblet drums, and timpani. Still other nonpitched percussion instruments, including those from various world cultures, are the Latin American guiro, claves, and maracas, West African double iron agogo bells, East Asian temple blocks, and the slit log drum, commonly found in West and Central Africa. Some of these instruments can be made by a teacher or parent, or by children as an art project, although their musical quality may be questionable. A number of nonpitched percussion instruments are described below, along with techniques for playing them.

Gourds

Maracas   (also rattle, shekere, honsho, cabasa). Found throughout Latin America, maracas are pairs of dried gourds with seeds inside, and are shaken like rattles. Those played in Mexico, the Carribean, and South American countries are related to the rattles of Native American and West African cultures. The shekere, honsho, or cabasa, found throughout much of Sub-Saharan

Wood, metal, skin, and rattle hand percussion instruments.

Africa, is covered with a beaded netting that is moved by the hand, providing a scraped, "rattling" sound.

Woods

Sticks.   Played in pairs, one stick is struck against the other. Ridged sticks rubbed against each other produce an alternative sound.

Claves.   Typically made of rosewood, claves are "thick sticks" of about one inch in diameter. They are played by holding one clave in the "cup" of one hand, and striking it with the other. Of the many rhythms, one of the best known Latin-sounding pattern for claves is: | ♩. ♩. ♩ | ♪ ♩ ♩ ♪ |

Woodblock.   A partially hollowed block of wood. The most resonant sound is produced by striking a wooden mallet over the slot on the wide surface. The tone block is a variant of the woodblock, with ridges around its hollowed cylindrical shape. It can be struck or rubbed with a mallet.

Temple blocks.   Similar to woodblocks, colorful temple blocks of about four or five sizes are positioned horizontally on a stand at about waist level. When struck by a wooden mallet, they produce sounds that are nearly (but not quite) "pitched." These East Asian instruments can be used to accent songs from China, Taiwan, Japan, Korea, and Vietnam.

Sandblocks. The friction of rubbing together two blocks of wood that are covered with sandpaper produces the swishing sound of sandblocks. Sandblocks can effectively instill in preschool- and primary-grade children the feel and sound of pulse and meter.

Slit log drum. Often just larger than a shoe box, the classroom version of the Sub-Saharan African slit log drums consist of slits cut into the flat top side of a hollowed log or block of wood. The longer and shorter wooden slits are played with mallets, producing lower and higher sounds. Not really a drum at all, the slit log provides a set of colorful timbres in an improvisation or composition.

Guiro. Pronounced "gwee-do," the ridged surface of this wooden instrument is scraped with a stick. Much of Latin America's music features its sound.

Skins (Drums)

Hand drum. Named because it is held at the rim by the hand, the hand drum is played by striking its head with the other hand or with a mallet. On some, the skin can be tightened or loosened by adjusting the screws at the rim. The hand drum is useful for keeping the pulse, and for playing rhythm patterns.

Bongo drums. A pair of drums, usually connected by a wooden crosspiece, held on the lap or between the knees. Bongos are played with the fingertips, the palm, and the thumbs. They play an important rhythm role in Latin American music, particularly from the Carribean.

Conga drum. A long upright drum in the shape of a narrow barrel with a skin head stretched across one end, the conga drum produces a variety of resonant timbres when the player strikes its center, edge, or wooden side with the palm and heel of the hand, the flat and cup of the hand, the fingertips, or even with sticks (at the side). Sounds reminiscent of Latin American and Sub-Saharan African cultures emanate from the conga drum. It may be played alone or in pairs.

Goblet drum. An important Middle Eastern instrument, the goblet drum is wide at the head and narrow at the base. It is played with fingertips and the palm of the hand at the center and edge of the head.

Timpani. Similar to the symphonic timpani in function, the children's version can be tuned to the tonic, dominant, subdominant, or other prominent pitch of a musical piece by adjusting the screws at the rim. Timpani sit at about waist level on stands with metal legs, and are played with padded mallets. They come in various sizes, so that several pitches in a piece can be sounded as a percussive bass line.

Metals

Cymbals. Two concave, metal disks (with knobs for holding); cymbals can be struck or rubbed together. They can also be played separately with a mallet or wire brush.

Finger cymbals. Smaller versions of the hand-held cymbals; elastic loops are used to attach the cymbals to the middle finger and thumb of the same hand. Finger cymbals produce ringing and muted sounds, and are commonly heard in the performance of Middle Eastern music. They can also be played without attachment to the fingers, by touching the rim of one to the rim of the other.

Triangle. This three-sided instrument of metal or steel hangs from a string, and is played by striking it with a metal or wooden stick. Its bright timbre is useful for sounding accents.

Tambourine. A tambourine features pairs of metal disks attached to a circular wooden rim that make a jingling sound when shaken. Those tambourines with a drumhead are similar to a hand drum. Most of the countries bordering the Mediterranean, including Spain, Italy, Greece, Turkey, Israel, and Egypt feature the tambourine in their songs and dances.

Jingle bells. Small bells on a stick or a plastic ring worn around the wrist or ankles, jingle bells can be added to seasonal music and to the sounds of some Native American Indian groups.

Gong. The flat brass gong found in orchestras is also an important percussion instrument in the music of China, Korea, Japan, and other parts of East Asia. Played with a padded mallet or wooden stick, various sizes of gongs are capable of playing different pitches, providing bright and long, sustained sounds. These flat gongs are not to be confused with the mellow-sounding knobbed gongs of Southeast Asia, including Indonesia.

Cowbell. Literally a bell found hung around the necks of cows, the cowbell produces "open," lower sounds when struck by a mallet near its opening and "closed" higher sounds when struck at the top near its handle. It is an important instrument in much Caribbean and South American dance music.

Double iron agogo bells.   Found in the West African iron-culture countries of Nigeria, Ghana, Dahomey, and the Ivory Coast, these connected iron bells of two sizes produce a higher- and lower-pitched sound when struck by a mallet. A polyrhythmic layering of patterns played simultaneously adds an authentic timbral color with agogo bells.

These nonpitched percussion instruments provide an array of timbres for children's musical growth. They can develop children's aural awareness, and can motivate children to learn to read rhythmic notation. A "rhythm band" approach (common in the 1930s and 1940s) is to be avoided: children are capable of far more than merely striking, tapping, rubbing, or shaking instruments without direction or a coherent musical concept in mind. Rather, experiences such as those described in Table 9.3 allow children to sample timbral qualities and also to match the durations they hear with how they are symbolized.

Pitched Instruments

There are many instruments on which children can play melodies and accompaniments. Among them are the barred instruments, including xylophones, metallophones, glockenspiels, and tone or melody bells; wind instruments such as recorders and the closely related song flutes; the chording instruments such as guitar and autoharp; and keyboards (pianos, lap pianos, synthesizers, and organs). A number of these pitched instruments are likely to be found in schools and in the home. They are described here, along with suggestions for their use in developing children's musical understanding and fundamental performance skills. Instructional resources are available for those who wish to teach or to learn these instruments, which also provide children with skills, techniques, and repertoire beyond the beginning levels.

Barred Instruments

The barred instruments developed by German composer Carl Orff are widely known for their exceptional tone quality. These are often referred to as "Orff instruments," and consist of larger and smaller wooden or metal bars laid across a frame, which are struck by mallets made of wood, plastic, felt, wound yarn, or cloth. There are also other styles of metal xylophones consisting of

Table 9.3   Experiences with Nonpitched Percussion Instruments

1. Gather all of the available instruments together. Experiment with the possibilities for sound on each of them. Seek answers to these questions: Which ones produce pitched or nonpitched sounds? How many different sounds can be produced? What are the traditional ways of sound production? Can you invent new ways? Categorize the instruments according to material (gourd, wood, skin, and metal) or manner of sound production (struck, shaken, rubbed).
2. Read a poem together. Ask children to choose instruments that can aid in the expression and interpretation of the poem.

   The Diesel Engine (P. S. Campbell)

   About half past eight,
   I like to hear the diesel engine daily.
   Once,
   it whirred, purred, and clicked,
   ticking track after track in a pre-arranged pulse.
   Now,
   it rattles, and coughs,
   spewing smoke in white puffs out its stumpy red stack.
   Still,
   I like to hear the diesel engine daily,
   About half past eight.

3. Play a Latin-flavored rhythmic piece with these instruments and their ostinato patterns. First chant the mnemonic syllables and word-phrases of the rhythms, then play by gradually adding one instrument after another. Play the piece with a recording of salsa music.

Table 9.3   Continued

conga									
	heel	tips	flat	heel	tips	heel	cup	cup	(repeat)
	L	L	R	L	L	L	R	R	

(Strike conga drum with left hand heel or finger tips; strike with right hand either flat or cupped.)

4. Divide children into small groups. Ask them to select a scene (the seashore, a forest, a busy downtown street, the building of a house, the last day of school), and to create the aural image of the scene by making a sound-piece performed by nonpitched instruments. Encourage free rhythms as well as pulsive pieces.
5. Encourage children to invent notation for their rhythmic compositions. Allow their own graphic notations to lead (or return) them to the reading of standard rhythmic notation of the Western staff.

colored bars, or black-and-white chromatic bars similar to a keyboard that predate the increasingly popular Orff-style instruments.

Orff instruments were developed to complement the Orff-Schulwerk approach to teaching music to children. Still, they can be employed by all who wish to offer children instrumental experiences. The sounds are pleasing to

Selected "metals" and "barred" instruments.

the ears, and are attractive to children who enjoy playing with sound, developing their playing skills, and expressing themselves through improvised and composed pieces they create. Whether played alone, in ensemble, or as an accompaniment for singing, the Orff instruments greatly enrich children's musical experiences.

The barred instruments of the Orff-Schulwerk consist of xylophones made of wood, and metallophones and glockenspiels made of metal. The xylophones and metallophones come in three sizes (soprano, alto, and bass), while there are soprano and alto glockenspiels. All contain a pitch range of a C to A octave (an octave and a sixth), in various registers. The instruments can be played in combinations of different registers or groups of metals and woods.

Barred instruments are usually placed on the floor in front of the musicians, the larger, lower bars to their left, with the players sitting comfortably on the knees or cross-legged. (Glockenspiels can be elevated on a stack of books for easier access, eliminating the need to bend over.) There should be room for movement of the arms and elbows while playing. The mallets are held as in holding a hammer, hairbrush, or toothbrush. Some experimentation and practice may be necessary before the right spot to strike on the bar is found; eye-hand coordination is critical for mastery in playing. For the best resonance, children should be encouraged to "pull out" the sound, rather than to hammer it in; the mallets should bounce away from the bars rather than rest on them.

The bars are removable, so that only those pitches necessary for a particu-

Figure 9.1. Ranges of instruments.

lar melody or accompaniment may be played. For example, if a pentatonic melody is to be played, then two bars per octave are removed, making it easier to play the melody. In the case of a repeated accompaniment pattern, or ostinato, all bars not a part of the pattern are removed, clearing the way for the ostinato. Additional bars provide the chromatic pitches for G-major (F♯) and F-major (B♭); these are provided with the initial purchase. Other accidentals may be purchased, however, as well as fully chromatic instruments.

Barred instruments are most frequently used to supply an accompaniment to a song, using a wide array of musical techniques, from drones to ostinatos. Examples of techniques for accompaniment are ordered from simple to more complex in Table 9.4. While not all-inclusive, these examples convey the flavor of the potential for instrumental accompaniment. These techniques require preparation before playing; children should pat the patterns on their laps that they will eventually play on the instruments. The success with which these accompaniments are played will depend on children's motoric development. Similarly, the extent to which they can be used to accompany folk songs and children's songs will depend on the teacher's musical ear and training. In particular, Orff-Schulwerk training offers lessons in orchestration and mastery of the performance techniques and the pedagogical process. A number of sources on Orff-Schulwerk describe and illustrate the various barred instruments, including Frazee (1987), Steen (1992), and Warner (1991).

Of course, barred instruments also function as melody instruments, and as means for improvisation. Children can play songs they know on xylophones, either "by ear" or by reading notation. A host of familiar songs like "Little Sally Walker," "Suogan," "Hey Betty Martin," "Kookaburra," and "Scotland's Burning" are excellent selections to challenge children to play what they already know, while they also master the instrument.

From imitative devices to expressive tasks, children can develop creative musical thinking and improvisatory skills through playing these instruments. For example, as children hear a rhythmic pattern of four or eight beats clapped by the teacher, they can then play it back on the instruments, choosing pitches as they play. As they hear a short musical "question" played for them by a leader, children can then play back an invented short musical "answer." In another task, children can be directed to listen to a simple melody, and then to play it back as closely as they can to the way they heard it—without delay. They can experiment with playing the simple melody softer or louder. They can also attempt to play it twice as fast or twice as slow. With partners, children can play musical dialogues, questioning and answering each other every four, six, or eight beats. They can take a known melody and vary it, adding an ostinato pattern. Alternately, they can take a drone and invent a melody for it. The possibilities for building their musicianship through instrumental improvisation is nearly endless, and the rewards are great.

Table 9.4   Accompaniment Techniques on Xylophones, Metallophones, and Glockenspiels

Simple Drone, in place

Simple Drone, in different registers

Simple Drone, in a different rhythm

Simple Drone, broken

Simple
Moving Drone, treble pitch

Simple
Moving Drone, lower pitch

Double
Moving Drone, drone 5th

Double
Moving Drone, 5ths / 6ths

Double
Moving Drone, broken

(*continued*)

Table 9.4 Continued

Several ostinati can be combined to provide for colorful textures.

Tone bells, also known as melody bells, also belong to the family of barred instruments. They are separate metal bars attached to a resonating box, which are played with a plastic or rubber mallet. Tone bells are kept in a large box and can be played as a xylophone, or can be distributed to a group of children for playing a "collaborative melody" similar to the manner in which a hand-bell choir may function, with each child contributing separate pitches to the melody. The tone quality is soft and bell-like; thus, tone bells function well as harmonic accompaniment to children's voices. In this function, children can contribute the root, third, and fifth (and seventh) of tonic, dominant, and sub-dominant chords to accompany a vast selection of folk and popular songs.

The Recorder

The recorder was a popular instrument of the European Renaissance period; it is also among the most common melody instruments played by children in the elementary grades today. Various other instruments are related to the re-corder, using the same playing techniques and featuring a similar pure, clear

Recorder playing position.

tone quality, including song flutes, flutophones, and tonettes. When children have been singing, listening with discrimination and in directed ways, and playing percussion instruments in their early years at home and in school, a logical next step is reading and playing melodies. When they show the physical development that enables them to move their fingers with ease, they are ready for the coordinated tasks of reading, breathing, and finger dexterity that are required to play the recorder. Beginning at about the age of nine, children in the third, fourth, and fifth grades are able and eager for the recorder, a pathway for furthering their musical understanding.

Children often relish the chance to play the recorder. For some, the recorder is an important precursor to the study of band instruments, and is used to give them the feel of fingering the wind instruments they may later choose to study. The recorder is also an important means of understanding melody—

its highs, lows, contours, and intervallic pitch relationships. In typical ensembles of Orff instruments found in elementary classrooms, the recorder is the only nonpercussive instrument (with the exception of the voice). The smooth and sustained melodic flow of the recorder is complementary to the more static and percussive sounds of the barred instruments.

Soprano recorders are best for beginners, and alto recorders can be added after fundamental playing techniques are learned, and when fingers are long and wide enough. Professional recorder musicians play wooden instruments, but those made of plastic are inexpensive and offer a surprisingly mellow tone when played gently. Most beginners' recorders come with a soft or plastic tubular case. The mouthpieces can be sterilized with hot water or with aerosol spray sanitizers. Instructional books are available for playing recorder, although a chart of fingerings, musical exercises, and familiar songs are all that you may be needed to introduce children to the instrument.

Children will follow the model of the teacher in finding the correct playing position. The top of the mouthpiece is placed in front of the teeth between the lips. The left hand is placed above the right hand, and its fingers cover the back hole and the top front three holes. The right hand's fingers will cover the bottom front four holes (including the bottom two double holes). Children must meet the challenges of: (1) feeling the holes that they cannot easily see; (2) balancing the recorder with the thumbs at the back, the fingers at the front, and the mouth at the tip; (3) curving the fingers and placing the fleshy finger "pads" on the appropriate holes; and, (4) blowing gently while forming the sound of "doo" with the mouth and tongue. Fingerings are shown for the c-d" in Table 9.5. When the sounds are incorrect or piercingly painful, the most common problems will be resolved by "blowing more lightly" and "covering the (appropriate) holes."

One way to teach the recorder involves singing a familiar song, then singing it with letters, numbers, or solfège syllables while fingering it on the recorder, and finally playing it. Because children know many songs, they may be more quickly able to play them in that they have already mentally processed the rise and fall of the melody and the repeated patterns. Songs like

Table 9.5 Recorder Fingerings

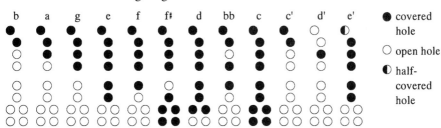

"Hot Cross Buns," "Mos! Mos!," "Polly Wolly Doodle," and "Hey, Betty Martin" feature limited ranges and repeated patterns that children may find more easily transferable to their recorders. The second stage of singing while silently playing is a critical one, because it links the sound with the kinesthetic feeling. During this stage, which may be repeated numerous times until the fingers move easily, children may hold their recorders at their chin to ensure that no tones are sounded.

The recorder is not a toy, nor is it limited to playing simple folk songs and exercises. An exciting repertoire is available for children who learn the fundamental performance techniques, stemming from fourteenth-century Europe through the seventeenth century. Further, the music of other cultures, particularly some East Asian and Native American genres, can be played on recorder. Children can continue to play songs they know on recorder, as well as to invent their own. Those children who continue past the introductory lessons can eventually play the sophisticated music of a Renaissance consort. Recorders combined with other timbres can be very beautiful and aesthetically pleasing. Also, many songs that students hear on the radio, on their cassettes, or CDs are simple enough to play on the recorder. Children can develop quite high levels of skill on recorder when challenged to learn "high-interest" songs as extra-credit projects on their own time. There are several recorder books noteworthy for classroom use, including those by Cox and Richard (1985) and Etkin (1975).

Harmony Instruments

While all melody instruments are capable of producing a melody that functions harmonically in playing an ostinato or descant against a melody (such as xylophones, metallophones, and recorders), several instruments are known for their primary function as accompaniments for singing. The autoharp and the guitar are chordal instruments found at school or at home. Both are social instruments arising from American musical heritages steeped in evening sing-alongs on the back porch, around the campfire, and in the parlor. While the guitar has long been an important part of the American pop and rock music scene, it still remains, along with the autoharp, an important means of producing chords for any folk, popular, or personal music that children may wish to sing and play.

The Autoharp

As recently as the 1950s, one of the most important instruments for the accompaniment of folksingers in the Appalachian hill-country, the Ozark Mountains, and Anglo-American communities elsewhere was the autoharp. It

became useful to teachers who wanted a portable instrument to provide harmony to songs sung by children in the classroom or outdoors, one that could
be easily learned by teachers and children alike. Its sound is soft enough to
support children's singing voices without overwhelming them. By following
chord markings in songbooks and music series texts, the autoharp functions as
a bona fide musical instrument almost immediately.

The autoharp is actually a zither, commonly equipped with twelve, fifteen,
or twenty-one chord bars that are depressed by pressing on buttons. When a
button on the chord bar is pushed, the felts on the bottom of the bar are
pressed against the strings that are not part of the chord, which silences those
pitches. The chord names are printed on the buttons. The autoharp player
reads the chord names found above the melody line of notated songs and
presses the corresponding chord bars with one hand while strumming the
strings with the other. Different strumming patterns can be used to enhance
rhythmic characteristics of a variety of songs.

While the autoharp is generally easy to play, there are two challenges to
consider. One is in the player's adjustment to the traditional Appalachian
playing position, in which the autoharp is held upright and somewhat diago-
nally, with the left hand pressing the buttons and the right hand crossing over
the left to strum the strings. Alternative positions for children include laying
the instrument flat on the lap, on a tabletop, or on the floor.

The second challenge is tuning the autoharp, a very time-consuming task

Autoharp playing position.

even for those with a "good ear." The instrument is affected by weather conditions, thus tuning is necessary almost daily—and sometimes more frequently than that. How? A metal tuning key is provided for tightening the string to raise the pitch, and for loosening it to lower the pitch. By pressing one chord button (for example, G-Major) and then slowly brushing across each G, B, and D string from highest to lowest, flat and sharp pitches can be heard and adjusted with the tuning key. At the very least, all pitches in chords of the song(s) to be played should be tuned. If the autoharp is not in good tuning, it should not be played or it may lead to out-of-tune singing. Electronic tuners greatly simplify this chore.

The advent of the Omnichord, a type of electronic autoharp, eliminates the tuning difficulties of the acoustic instrument. The Omnichord has no strings, but retains the push-button chord system. Additionally, the Omnichord plays rhythmic ostinati, waltz, and rock-style rhythms, and can be set at various tempi, volumes, and timbres that include piano, guitar, brass, banjo, and chimes.

The autoharp and its newer cousin facilitate children's awareness of harmony, of major and minor chord qualities, the function of chords in their support of melody, and the relationship of tonic, dominant, subdominant, and mediant chords to one another. For children in the primary grades, the teacher may wish to press the chord buttons while one child strums the strings. Just as children in the intermediate grades are beginning to hear harmonic changes, they can also play the instrument by themselves. Familiar songs with one chord ("Are You Sleeping?," "For Health and Strength," "Row Your Boat"), two chords ("Sandy Land," "Down in the Valley," "Polly Wolly Doodle"), and three chords ("Red River Valley," "Knick Knack Paddy Whack," "Old McDonald") can be played by reading chord charts—or by ear, providing children with exercises in hearing harmonic changes as they sing. Further information on the autoharp is available in Peterson (1966) and Carlin (1982).

The Guitar

Children are eager to learn the guitar long before they are able to play it, motivated by seeing and hearing it in many popular styles of music, from rock to country to folk, on TV, radio, recordings, and films. When their hands are sufficiently large to stretch around the neck to the strings, they are ready to play; for most children, that occurs around fourth grade.

There are many types of guitars, but the nylon-strung folk or classical guitars are easier on the fingers than the steel strings found on larger acoustic instruments. Nonamplified electric guitars can also be played by children because, despite the steel strings, their necks are narrow and thus easier on the hand and finger expanse.

As a chording instrument, the guitar can accompany songs with as few as one, two (I, V), or three (I, IV, V) chords. The right-hand strums can be as basic as one chord per measure or per pulse, to syncopated rhythms and patterns that combine plucking with strumming. While there are many manuals for playing guitar, children often learn to play through observation and experimentation. Time spent in practice pays off, so that children who play at home or who come to the music room before or after school can become quite proficient. The use of a capo, a plastic-covered bar that is clipped across the strings, extends the possibilities for playing song accompaniments in practically any key.

Children can be playing guitar accompaniments to songs they know even in their first lesson. Once they find a comfortable way of holding the guitar, imitating the teacher's seated position with the guitar resting on the crossed leg, they are ready to play their first chord: e-minor. Table 9.6 presents tablature, or fretboard diagrams, of e minor, E major, G major (simplified and more sophisticated versions), C major, and D major (and D7) chords. When they are played correctly, the left-hand fingers are curved, their tips pressing the designated strings to the fingerboard. Children should be checked and reminded to avoid touching other strings that are not a part of the chord configuration.

Once the fingers of the right hand are comfortable in their chord positions, and in changing chords, then children can begin to learn strumming patterns. Several common patterns are featured in Table 9.7; they are best learned by saying "down" and "up" in rhythm before and while playing. Down refers to the downward brushing of the thumb from the lowest string to the highest, while up is the thumb's upward brush across the higher to lower strings and toward the player's face. Strumming patterns add distinctive flavors to songs, and soon separate beginners from the more proficient players.

Children who have mastered a few chords and their strums can be playing the harmonic accompaniment for a great variety of songs. The e-minor chord alone enables children to play "Shalom Chaverim," "Hey, Ho, Nobody Home," and "Zum Gali Gali." The great majority of children's songs often require no more than three chords, and often only the tonic and dominant. Guitar accompaniment is often especially appropriate for such Latin American songs as "Arroz con Leche" (Puerto Rican), "De Colores" (Mexican), and "Santo de Otavalo" (Ecuadoran). Collections of folk and popular songs are readily available with guitar accompaniment.

Tuning the guitar can present still another challenge, and it is often the parent or teacher who matches the pitches of the six strings (E, A, D, G, B, e) to each other, to a pitchpipe, piano, or the guitar's special tuning pipes. Most instructional manuals feature tuning along with a great variety of chord tablatures, and strumming and picking patterns. For a sequential handbook on playing folk guitars, including chording and picking patterns, see Kuhn and Reid (1984); for classical styles, see Noad (1994).

Table 9.6   Guitar Tablature for the Left Hand

Keyboards

Either at home or in school, children are bound to have opportunities to play a keyboard, that is, pianos, organs, synthesizers, MIDI instruments, and lap pianos. Keyboards are the most popular type of instrument in American homes; over half of American families today own acoustic and electronic pianos, or organs.

Some electronic keyboards are very inexpensive to own individually (e.g., models made by Casio), and come with color-coded notation for playing fa-

Table 9.7 Guitar Strums

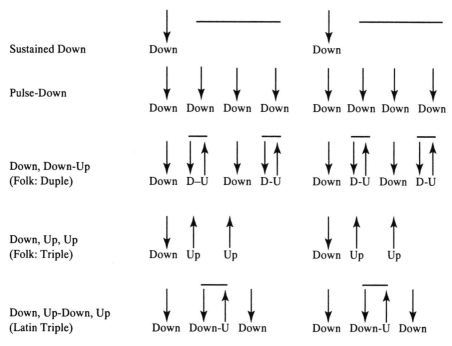

Sustained Down	Down	Down
Pulse-Down	Down Down Down Down	Down Down Down Down
Down, Down-Up (Folk: Duple)	Down D–U Down D-U	Down D–U Down D-U
Down, Up, Up (Folk: Triple)	Down Up Up	Down Up Up
Down, Up-Down, Up (Latin Triple)	Down Down-U Down	Down Down-U Down

miliar melodies and their chords. Frequently, children play with these or other types of pianos at home, and are likely to have explored the black and white keys to "figure out" familiar songs. Keyboard instruments are often responsible for children's first chance to "play music," and may be the source of their growing interest in music. Some children have sampled chords and timbres with the press of a button. They may even have access in their homes to more sophisticated keyboard technology, including MIDI and assorted attachments that allow the sounds of rain forests, windstorms, and outer space to be mixed with violin, guitar, koto, and talking drum timbres.

Most schools are likely to have available at least one classic grand or upright acoustic piano. The music room, auditorium, or assembly space are the most likely locations for the piano. When in tune and played well, the piano can bring unity to the group-singing of patriotic and traditional songs as well as add to the artistic quality of a choral performance. Yet it is far more than an accompaniment instrument. It can stimulate eurhythmic movement to music through its percussive quality and its broad spectrum of expressive capacities. It can illustrate musical features, from pitch to duration to dynamic intensity. It can add color and interest to stories and poems. The piano can also underscore and reinforce musical learning for children of every age.

Whether the music is initiated by the teacher to stimulate musical responses in children or whether the music is read and performed or invented by children themselves, keyboards provide an effective avenue of music instruction. Children can learn by observing the teacher play or by exploring on their own the concepts of scale, intervals, register, range, ascending and descending pitches, melodic contour, repetition, and sequence. They can experiment with tone-matching (playing and then singing pitch patterns), and can come to terms with the function of the staff, treble and bass clefs, and notation when they take it to the piano. Children enjoy experimenting with the piano's potential as both a melody and a harmony instrument. For those who develop basic facility at the piano (or any keyboard), it will become an important channel for personal expression in the original music that they create.

In some schools, pianos are purchased as keyboard laboratories. Such a music room may thus be equipped with ten, twenty, or more electronic pianos on stands, with student headphones. The student pianos are linked to a teacher's station that includes piano and audio facilities for listening to the performances of individual students, small groups, or the entire class. Beginning in the intermediate grades, children can learn to read notation as well as basic piano technique through instruction manuals that progress from one-hand melodies, to song melodies with simple chordal accompaniments, to full-fledged piano pieces from the classical and popular repertoire. Group piano classes in the schools are generally focused on learning about music—its structures and sonorities—through performance. See Chapter 3 for a discussion of Yamaha's Music in Education program, and Chapter 12 for descriptions of MIDI and other technologies for making music and aiding music instruction.

Music teachers may be an important link to children's further training and development as pianists, and as musicians. Because they have presented children with musical problems and have observed the nature of each child's capacity to solve them, music teachers are in a position to evaluate and recommend further instruction. They have noted the rhythmic capacity, aural acuity, and eye-hand coordination of individual children in group piano lessons or in other musical activities, and can thus predict with reasonable accuracy the prognosis of children who wish to study piano (or other instruments) privately. For those children who enjoy playing piano, classroom instruction in keyboard laboratories is ideal. For those few who aspire to become pianists, the music teacher may offer a pathway.

The Benefits of Instrumental Study

For some children, making music is equivalent to playing musical instruments. The appeal of tapping, striking, shaking, blowing, and strumming musical instruments is one of the great joys in their lives. Because musical instruments are extensions of the musical self, when children play they are often demonstrating what they know and can express musically. To play a musical instrument is to deliver to others ideas that are not easily expressed verbally.

Musical instruments enhance the development of musical understanding. Why count rhythms when they can be felt and played? Why learn staff notation unless the symbols can be realized musically? Along with the singing voice, classroom instruments are teaching aids for experiencing musical concepts such as high and low, loud and soft, long and short, fast and slow, and choppy and smooth. The practice of playing a minor third, a perfect fourth, a legato phrase, or a chord progression underscores principles of music theory. Until children can be engaged in the practice of music-making, they are not likely to fully understand the musical structures behind the sound. The playing of a musical instrument can precede, and later coincide with, the reading and writing of notation.

Teachers and parents who are aware of children's attraction to musical instruments, and of their capacities for playing them, can facilitate their musical growth. Children can develop performance skills quite rapidly when they are developmentally ready, that is, when they have arrived at the motoric and perceptual stages required for successful performance. There is the danger that when instruments and their performance techniques are introduced before children are capable of playing them, they may experience frustration and failure that may result in negative attitudes and demotivation. Teachers should recognize the importance of preparatory experiences that set in motion the physical skills necessary for playing with rhythmic accuracy, and should allow children repeated opportunities to "practice their parts" while avoiding the possibilities for boredom by delivering a variety of rapid-fire rehearsal strategies.

The old adage, "practice makes perfect," should be reinforced for children who hope to develop their performance skills on instruments such as the recorder, piano, or guitar. Daily practice at home will undoubtedly result in marked improvement. At school, the teacher may wish to institute an "open-door policy" for children to spend before- or after-school time practicing. Where there is interest in the study of a musical instrument, the motivation to become a proficient player may be awaiting general encouragement of the teacher and parent.

Questions

1. Why are xylophones recommended for use by school-age children rather than by kindergarten and preschool children?
2. What is a corpophone? How many corpophones can you demonstrate?

3. How can classroom instruments be categorized, so that children can understand similarities among instruments regarding (a) their function and (b) the materials from which they are made?

4. What are children's challenges for playing recorder? What direction can the teacher provide to meet these challenges?

5. How is an autoharp tuned? A guitar?

6. Discuss the contributions of the piano in reinforcing children's musical learning.

Activities

1. Create a body-percussion piece. Begin with a poem or song that can serve as the stimulus for the rhythm, and which can then be performed together with or as an alternate to the body percussion piece.

2. Collect a set of children's songs from various cultures that can be performed with one or two nonpitched percussion instruments. Determine which instruments are representative of the cultural tradition.

3. Experiment with various accompaniment techniques for xylophones, metallophones, and glockenspiels. Arrange or orchestrate one folk song to feature each of the following techniques on Orff xylophones: simple drone; moving simple drone; moving double drone; ostinato; layered ostinato.

4. Practice guitar strums as provided in Table 9.7, and invent three new strums for $\frac{4}{4}$, $\frac{3}{4}$, and $\frac{6}{8}$ meter.

5. Write a letter of appeal to the parents of your children, in which you inform them of the importance of home practice in learning a musical instrument. Choose recorder, guitar, or keyboard. Be persuasive in your support of the educational value of playing a musical instrument—individually and in the class ensemble.

References

CARLIN, R. (1982). *How to play autoharp.* New York: Music Sales.

COX, H., & RICHARD, G. (1985). *Sing, clap, and play the recorder* (bks. 1 and 2). St. Louis: Magnamusic-Baton.

Diagram Group. (1976). *Musical instruments of the world.* New York: Paddington Press.

ETKIN, R. (1975). *Playing and composing on the recorder*. New York: Sterling.

FRAZEE, J. (1987). *Discovering Orff: A curriculum for music teachers*. New York: Schott.

KUHN, T. L., & REID, H. D. (1984). *Modern folk guitar*. New York: Alfred A. Knopf.

NOAD, F. M. (1994). *Solo guitar playing, Book I* (3rd ed.). New York: Schirmer Books.

PETERSON, M. (1966). *The many ways to play autoharp*. Union, NJ: Oscar Schmidt-International.

STEEN, A. (1992). *Exploring music*. New York: Schott.

WARNER, B. (1991). *Orff-Schulwerk: Applications for the classroom*. Englewood Cliffs, NJ: Prentice-Hall.

Sources of Classroom Instruments

Andy's Front Hall, P.O.B. 307, Wormer Road., Voorheesville, NY 12186.

Elderly Instruments, 1100 N. Washington, Lansing, MI 48906.

House of Musical Traditions, 7040 Carroll Avenue, Takoma Park, MD 20912

John's Music Center, 4501 Interlake North #9, Seattle, WA 98103.

Magnamusic-Baton, Inc., 10370 Page Industrial Blvd., St. Louis, MO 63132.

Music Education Group, Oscar Schmidt, 230 Lexington Drive, Buffalo Grove, IL 60089.

Rhythm Band, Inc., P.O. Box 126, Fort Worth, TX 76101.

The World of Peripole, Inc., P.O. Box 146, Lewiston Road, Browns Mills, NJ 08015.

Yamaha Music Corporation, U.S.A., P.O. Box 6600, Buena Park, CA, 90620.

CHAPTER **10**

The Creating Child

To a great extent, everything the young child does musically comes out of his or her creative imagination and exploration. Anna engages in the typical vocal sound play of the infant with her "bahs," "duhs," and "gurgles" throughout her range. Juan rhythmically strikes a wooden spoon against a pan, and Marianne laughs and claps with joy when she discovers she can make sounds on the piano. All of these responses represent a satisfaction of the inherent desire children have to generate and manipulate sounds and, eventually, to place them into meaningful structures.

This desire continues through the elementary years and beyond as children eagerly invent words and rhythms for a rap, improvise a pentatonic melody on a soprano xylophone, or work in a group to choreograph a favorite musical selection. The creative impulse is alive in children of all ages, and the music classroom is an ideal setting to stimulate the growth of that creativity *beyond* the initial stages of exploration and discovery.

The arts come into being through the creativity of individuals and groups. To deny children the opportunity to work creatively with the materials and structures of music is to limit their capacity to think artistically, and, ultimately, to limit the full exploration of what it means to be musical. Teaching music without allowing children to compose would be like teaching art without allowing children to draw or paint, or teaching writing by having children copy other people's work. Including composition and improvisation as sequentially developed aspects of a general music program provides the third element of a balanced program of listening, performing, and creating.

Developmental Sequence

The development of musical creativity, both conceptual, and practical, appears to be the result of the interaction of factors of environment, musical thought or cognition, and individual intellectual and personality traits. As children grow in their musical experience and their capacity to physically manipulate or control the sounds of their instruments or voices, they can move to higher levels of creative production. If they are in environments that encourage them to improvise and to compose, they will perceive these activities as natural and as part of what one does to express musical ideas. Some children may feel more comfortable with this process than others and express more musically sophisticated ideas. However, all children can benefit, both musically and intellectually, from active involvement in the creation, not just the recreation, of music.

Several interesting theories have been proposed about the development of creative thinking and creative production in music. Though these theories have yet to be tested extensively, they are included in Table 10.1 to give some models of the growth of creativity during preschool as well as the elementary years.

Creative Thinking

Much of the thinking teachers ask children to do is *convergent* thinking, the type of thinking that results in a single, correct answer. When children are asked to name things such as signs, symbols, composers, or pieces of music, they are directed to think convergently. In performance, children are asked to conform to the correct pitches and rhythms of a song, although often creativity is encouraged in the area of interpretation.

At the heart of creative thought is a different type of thinking, *divergent* thinking. This is when teachers ask children for many possible answers. For example, children could be challenged to discover how many different sounds a percussion instrument makes or how many techniques might be used in playing it.

Webster (1990) has developed a theory of creative thinking in music. According to that theory, qualities of divergent thinking include musical extensiveness (how many ideas are generated), flexibility (the ease of shifting within parameters such as high/low or loud/soft), and originality (how unique the musical ideas are). (In the area of originality, for example, creative children may generate their own songs and themes rather than use more familiar

Table 10.1 Development of Creative Production

Age (yrs.)	Flohr (1985); Kratus (1985, 1991)	Tillman & Swanick (1989)	Teacher Action
Birth to 4–5	Driven by motor energy. Highly individualistic in approaches and patterns. Lacking musical syntax.	Mastery of materials and range of sounds through sensing and manipulating.	Provide age-appropriate instruments to explore. Encourage and reinforce discovery and respect individuality.
4–5 to 9 (Kindergarten to Grade 4)	Predictable rhythmic and tonal patterns, influenced by familiar music. Changing meters and emerging sense of tonality. Lack strong sense of phrase structure and cadence.	Imitation of both personal and vernacular ideas occurs with greater expressive quality. Meter emerges, greater use of dynamic expression, ostinati.	Encourage growth of ideas and craftsmanship. Build musical concepts and awareness of many conventions. Build skills of self-evaluation.
10–12 (Grades 4–6)	Music becomes organized according to cultural "rules" or "structures." Use of melodic and rhythmic motives. Increased use of sounds and patterns of familiar music. Often less original.	Imaginative play in which surprise is an element but using more references to popular-music idioms. Concern for form and structure, use of harmony emerges.	Keep expanding the repertoire of conventions for structuring music. Help students to avoid becoming too critical of their or other's works. Encourage self-expression.

ones.) These qualities interact with others such as a child's musical understandings and sensitivities, ability to imagine pitches and rhythms, and ability to craft a piece to effect the final product of the creative effort.

From the standpoint of the teacher, the key is to establish an environment where these various skills and understandings are consciously developed rather than ignored or left to happenstance. The following ideas should help in designing such an environment.

Exploration and Discovery

The first stage in the creative process for all students is to explore and discover possibilities that exist for manipulating sounds. Children need to have the freedom to explore the range of sounds an instrument or voice might make in terms of *color* (ringing, thunking, raspy, rattle, etc.); *techniques* (scraping, shaking, striking, rubbing, blowing, plucking, strummimg); and range of *dynamics* (loud/soft), *pitch* (definite/indefinite, high/low), and *duration* (long/short/sustained impression).

In the process of free exploration, children are building a repertoire of sound possibilities and techniques from which they can later draw to make musical/artistic decisions. As a stimulus for exploring sounds, the teacher might give every child a piece of paper and say, "Discover as many different sounds as you can make with this piece of paper in the next two minutes. The signal for you to stop and look at me will be when I flash the lights." When the two minutes have passed, students share their discoveries. During this time, the teacher can guide by asking questions that help the children to compare sounds or group them into categories. "Who has rattling sounds?" "Whose sound was almost like that sound?" The teacher can use this time to build musical vocabulary such as high/low or loud/soft: "Play that sound

Young children exploring sounds.

again but change from loud to soft"; "Make your buzz swoop from low to high"; "Repeat the sound of the 'thunk' five times, letting it fade gradually."

Over time, children should be encouraged to explore the sound possibilities of a wide range of sources and to use those sounds creatively. Some suggestions are found in Table 10.2 with additional suggestions in Biasini, Thomas, and Pagonowski (1971).

Once children have discovered what their instruments or voices can do, they can move into either a mode of improvisation or of composition. Whichever mode the strategy involves, the teacher's role is to establish the parameters for the piece.

Table 10.2   Sound Sources

Found Sounds
Paper
Objects (rulers, cups, pens, keys)
Kitchen implements (egg beater, whisk, grater, spatula)
Garage sounds (hammers, saws, nails, drills, tin cans, wood, springs)

Mouth Sounds
Voiced (hum, shout, sing, sigh, shriek, buzz, animal sounds, machine sounds)
Nonvoiced (pop, click, whistle, slurp, hiss)

Room Sounds
Pencils, notebooks, rulers, grates, shades, doors, music stands

Body Sounds
Hands, fingers, feet, arms, legs, chest, head

Toy Sounds
Whistles, hummers, drums, xylophones, music boxes, rattles, doll, kazoos,
Zube-Tube

Environmental Sounds
Birds, animals, machines, vehicles, water, wind, waves

Instrumental Sounds
Classroom (nonpitched percussion, xylophones and metallophones, autoharps,
recorders, pianos, guitars)
Electronic (keyboards, synthesizers, tape recorders)
Ethnic (membranophones, chordophones, idiophones, aerophones)
Band/orchestra (brass, strings, woodwind, percussion)

Student Invented or Constructed Instruments
Give students simple materials (canisters, string, wood, beans, paper, tape, nails,
metal, glass) and have them invent an instrument.

Improvisation

Improvisation at a beginning level allows children to play with sounds and with musical syntax (or putting those sounds together). Improvisation at the highest level, such as that used in jazz or certain world traditions like Indian sitar and tabla duos, Nigerian drum ensembles, or Chopi (Mozambique) xylophone ensembles, involves advanced performance technique combined with deep knowledge of the idiom being used. Regardless of the age or musical sophistication of the improvisers, this process is essential to developing an ease and flexibility in manipulating the language of music. Opportunities to improvise should occur throughout children's development, stimulating them to "converse" in music in the same way they converse using words, freely and spontaneously with meaning.

Generally, an improvisatory piece or section of a piece is invented spontaneously and is not formalized or refined. The following examples illustrate typical structures for improvisation that a teacher might use with children.

A whole-class improvisation with the paper sounds that the children have discovered could include:

1. Asking each person to select three paper sounds they found the most interesting
2. Performing each sound once during the period of one minute, distributing the sounds across the time
3. The teacher or a student could conduct the work, marking the passage of time visibly, with the arm acting like the second hand of a clock
4. The piece could be recorded and the results listened to and discussed in terms of musical interest and success

Children might be asked to improvise a melody to a given rhythm or place a melody on top of a chord sequence. Older children might improvise using scat syllables and/or pitches from a known scale.

An improvisation characteristic of Orff-inspired instruction might feature children's invention of the B section of an ABA or ternary-form piece, where A is a composed or known section. The children, using soprano xylophones, would be directed to invent a melody on a C pentatonic scale, fitting it into an eight-beat frame. Rondo form (ABACA, ABACADA) would allow multiple sections for solo or group improvisation.

In a Kodály setting, children might be asked to generate four-beat rhythm patterns for echo clapping, or pitch patterns using sol, mi, and la for echo singing. Once children have built an internal collection of rhythm and pitch patterns, they might be asked to improvise a longer melody, a melody with additional pitches, or, perhaps, the "answer" to a "question."

Question   Answer

The Dalcroze tradition also uses improvisation as an important component in its pedagogy. Children may listen to their teacher's improvisation at the piano, and then be expected to complete or continue the piece, retaining the same style in the extension. They could perform melodically using the piano or voice, or rhythmically on a hand drum or through movement. Through this process they learn to improvise within an established musical quality.

Children should also be called on to improvise: accompaniments to songs using body rhythms or classroom instruments, movements to music, and music for dramatizations and storytelling. The possibilities for improvisation are endless.

Kratus (1991) suggests that there are seven levels in learning to improvise. These levels could be used as a means of stimulating as well as evaluating and tracking student growth.

1. Exploration: The student tries out different sounds and combinations of sounds in a loosely structured context.
2. Process-oriented Improvisation: The student produces more cohesive patterns.
3. Product-oriented Improvisation: The student becomes conscious of structural principles such as tonality and rhythm.
4. Fluid Improvisation: The student manipulates his or her instrument or voice in a more automatic, relaxed manner.
5. Structural Improvisation: The student is aware of the overall structure of the improvisation and develops a repertoire of musical or nonmusical strategies for shaping it.
6. Stylistic Improvisation: The student improvises skillfully within a given style, incorporating its melodic, harmonic, and rhythmic characteristics.
7. Personal Improvisation: The musician is able to transcend recognized improvisation styles to develop a new style (p. 39).

Improvisation can play several valuable roles in the creative process. It can help to develop and expand musical ideas; it can help children attain a sense of structure, form, and style; it can be used to introduce and reinforce concepts and technical skills; and, at the highest level, it provides an opportunity for the synthesis of these concepts and skills.

Though not typically included as a part of the improvisational process, children can be asked to reflect and comment on the musical effectiveness of the improvisation. Questions could focus on whether it met the requirements of the limits imposed, what was inventive or interesting about the ideas, and how it might be improved. Further suggestions for improvisation in classroom settings can be found in Konowitz (1970, 1973), Aebersold (1972–1988), P. S. Campbell (1991), L. Campbell (1985), and Chatterley (1978).

Composition

A more planned realization of the creative process is the act of composition. It differs from improvisation in that it involves the opportunity for crafting a piece, for reflection and revision. Once again, the teacher serves as catalyst by establishing the limits of the composition. (See Table 10.3 as well as chapter references for ideas to inspire student compositions.)

With very young children, the teacher may participate throughout the compositional process, pulling ideas from the group and helping the students refine their thinking. From late first grade on, children may work in groups of four to five to solve a composition problem with the teacher serving as a resource person (see Tables 10.4 and 10.5). Once the compositions have been performed and taped, the teacher helps to guide the students in evaluating their work. Building skills of critiquing or reflective evaluation is crucial to the compositional process. Finally, the teacher helps students generalize their learnings by bringing in examples of other recorded music that illustrate ideas

Table 10.3 Motivations for Compositions

Themes: "Life and Death of a Mosquito"; "Clouds"; "A Day in a Factory"

Emotions: angry; happy; sad; excited; etc.

Pictures or images: photographs from magazines; paintings; designs, maps, scores

Stories: "wordless" books; children's own stories; fairy tales

Poetry: sound or melodic setting of their own or other's poetry

Sounds: families of sounds; individual sounds; contrasting sounds

Patterns or cycles: "The Seasons"; "A Day"; "A Storm"; "The Butterfly"; "The Water Cycle"; "The Life Cycle of a Salmon"

Musical elements: melody; rhythm; harmony; tone color; tempo; dynamics

Aesthetic ideas: density; texture; tension/release; repetition/contrast

Musical structures: ostinato; phrase; motive; ABA; rondo; layered; theme and variations; blues; free form

Table 10.4 "A Trip to the Zoo"

Teacher Role	Student Role
Ask children to notice the qualities of movements of various animals during their field trip to the zoo.	Carefully observe movements such as smooth/jerky, fast/slow, even/uneven, continuous/random, upward/downward.
Review with the children what they noticed about the movement qualities of the animals. Help them generate sample rhythms that might illustrate those qualities.	Share what they noticed. Generate various rhythmic responses.
Divide children into groups based on the animal they wish to represent, and provide instruments for them to play.	Develop a short piece that conveys the sense of movement of an animal. Practice and refine it.
Select a child to conduct by walking to a temple block from animal to animal. Tape record the results.	Perform your rhythm pattern as long as the conductor is standing in front of your group.
Play tape recording and lead children in a discussion of the results. What animal did each group represent? How could you tell? What could be done differently?	Listen to tape. Respond to questions. Evaluate their own performance. Suggest ideas for revision.

or techniques the children have developed. Books by Thomas (1970) and Paynter and Aston (1971) illustrate clearly this process.

Aural Plans

The first stage in the formal compositional process is to help children structure aural plans for their pieces. This simply means that they will work together to refine a piece, trying many different ideas, selecting and rejecting, and finally reaching consensus on the end product through an aural plan. No graphing or notation will be used to record their work. To a certain extent, aural plans are improvisational because, even though the children may rehearse their piece several times, surprises usually occur.

An example of a whole-group composition for primary children with teacher guidance is given in Table 10.4.

Extensions of this composition would be to use the tape of the music as a basis for creative movement. Another day, listen to the *Carnival of the Animals* by Saint-Saëns and discuss the ways the composer conveys a sense of

Table 10.5 "Layers of Long and Short Sounds"

Teacher Role	Student Role
Assign composition limits: Compose a piece for contrasting patterns of long and short sounds in which the texture never gets thicker than three sounds. Group students and provide instruments. Serve as resource person to groups if necessary.	Select instruments that will play long and short sounds (xylophones, sticks, metallophones, drums, woodblocks, temple blocks, triangles, etc.). Experiment with various patterns. Select the most interesting ones. Structure the piece, deciding when the various patterns will sound and what creates a sense of completeness. Refine it so it is ready to share.
Make either audio or visual recordings of the pieces.	Perform own piece and listen to others.
Guide children in assessment of their own work and the work of others. Expand thinking and vocabulary as the opportunity arises.	Assess the work of their group and their role in it. Assess the composition and suggest ideas for refinement. Help assess the compositions of other groups.
Encourage students to expand/refine compositions. Help expand their thinking by bringing in recorded works that use the same principles. (*Daphne of the Dunes* by Harry Partch is a good example.)	Refine their own work to make it more satisfying. Listen to other works, including recorded works that illustrate the same principles.

the various animals. Identify and discuss similarities, if any, to their compositions. Discuss differences, such as the use of animal sounds. Add creative movements to sections of the Saint-Saëns work.

Because older children can work with less teacher guidance, compositions are often best crafted by groups of children; the ideal group size is four to five. The same assignment can be given to each group if the goal is to discover or reinforce a particular concept or theme via composition (see Table 10.5). It is exciting for children to discover the variety of solutions that can be generated by a single idea. Different assignments can be given to various groups if the goal is a multimovement composition with each group contributing a part (i.e., types of clouds), or if the goal has more to do with the process of composing than with a particular outcome. Table 10.5 gives an example of an aural plan that could be developed by children from the age of eight or beyond.

Older students in small-group composition.

This particular strategy could expand into a unit where children invent and construct their own instruments out of unusual and found materials, then tune them in unique scales in the style of American composer Harry Partch.

Notational Systems

Children grow gradually in their ability to utilize aspects of music notation. Research on children's self-constructed notational systems suggests that they move from pictorial or iconic means of representing their music to more discrete or symbolic means of notating rhythm and pitch, means which may use numbers or letters. Later they move to actual or discrete notation. Figures 10.1 and 10.2 (Upitis, 1990) show two examples of children's invented notations.

Once children have a sense of the compositional process through creating aural plans, the use of notation can be introduced. Initially, children should be free to devise their own systems. Ideally the initial system should be a representation of a piece they have already crafted with an aural plan. For example, second graders are each asked to compose a "one-tone-tune," lasting as long as one breath. They experiment with varying the tone color, dynamics, pattern, and vowel and consonant sounds. Once the piece is refined and shared, each child devises a means of notating the ideas in a way another person could

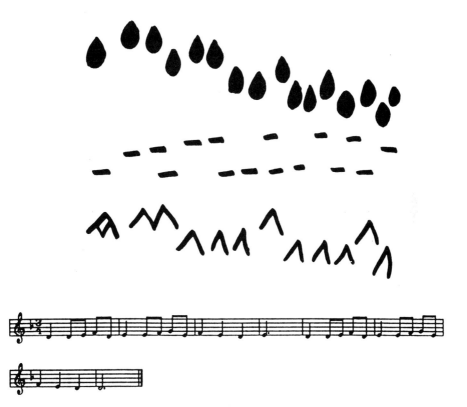

Figure 10.1. Invented notation using abstract symbols. "Explanatory Notes: This piece is notated with tear drops to show that it is in a minor key. Other symbols are used as well, but it is not possible to reproduce the piece from the notation itself." *Reproduced with permission from Upitis, 1990, p. 66.*

understand. They then share their notation with another child and ask that child to interpret it. Dialogues between composer and performer about notation as a means of communication result in interesting insights. A sample notation of a "one-tone-tune" is:

As children experience standard notation through the use of music texts and training in reading, they will want to incorporate it in notating all or part of their compositions. They might start by notating rhythm patterns using stick notation or pitch patterns on a three-note staff:

Figure 10.2. Invented notation using letter names of pitches. "Explanatory Notes: The backwards '2' means 'with two hands and two times.' The knife next to the F indicates the note F♯ ('It is a pirate's knife, and a pirate's knife is *very sharp*')." *Reproduced with permission from Upitis, 1990, p. 63.*

Compositions using notation can also be tied in with skills children are acquiring. For example, once children have learned to play B, A, G on a soprano recorder, they could be asked to compose and notate a four measure melody in $\frac{4}{4}$ time using B A G, ♩ ♫ 𝄽 rhythmic values, and ending on G.

Older children will be stimulated to use notation programs available on computer such as Melody Studio (1992), Ballade (1990), or Personal Musician (1990), and those attached to a MIDI-synthesizer setup such as Encore (1992). A series of exercises using technology to write melodies can be found in Chapter 12.

Children need to remain free to create aural plans, invent devised systems, and use discrete notation. Exposure to performing contemporary works that use devised systems will help children to understand that notation is malleable and must convey what the composer intends.

Song Writing

In a teacher-guided setting, young children can work to create a song using the following procedures.

1. Select a topic. Create a word bank of descriptive words generated by the children. The children suggest phrases for a poem that the teacher transcribes on the board.

2. When the poem is completed, children chant it together, getting a feel for its rhyme and rhythm. The teacher then could play a tonic chord on an autoharp or keyboard and have different children sing melodies for the first line of the poem.

3. After trying several ideas, the class votes on their favorite melody, and it is sung by all and tape recorded.

4. The process continues with the teacher supplying underlying chords, which support the harmonic structure of the melody. (An alternative is to provide a harmonic structure in which children create the melodies.)

5. Children listen to the entire song and suggest changes. The song is sung and tape recorded in its entirety. The teacher can notate it at a later time and share it with the class in that form.

The following song, "Freckles," was composed by a group of second graders in collaboration with their teacher, Jackie Wiggins (1990, p. 45).

Freckles

Second Grade Class

Older children can use a similar process but can work more independently. They might be given a poem with the rhythm notated and encouraged to experiment with different melodic shapes on a keyboard, staying within a single tonal center. They could experiment with stepwise motion, small leaps, and repeated tones. Later, build in concepts of repetition and contrast and melodic sequence. As children grow in their abilities, use ideas of tone-painting, and have students compose their own words and melodies. Other devices such as a twelve-bar blues progression could be provided as an underlying framework for melodic composition:

I	I	I	I
IV	IV	I	I
V	IV	I	I

When children are ready to start notating their own rhythms, they can be shown how the rhythm of the lyrics fits within the framework of a meter, paying special attention to downbeat and upbeat functions. (They might need to practice this first with familiar nursery rhymes, then advance to notating the rhythms of unfamiliar poems or song lyrics.) The computer program Band-in-a-Box (1992) is helpful in this process.

Individualized Plan

As children mature, many prefer to work on their own or in small groups. Teachers can structure the classroom with learning stations where children develop skills by working on their own with keyboards, guitars, synthesizers, and recorders, as well as areas dedicated to listening and composition. In each learning center, folders are provided that tell students the requirements for that center.

Folders for a composition center could be color-coded and numbered for type of assignment and level of complexity. Instruments, blank tapes, and tape recorders are made available for the students. File folders have the title on the outside; the left inside pocket contains pictures, scores, maps or other images; and the right pocket contains the chart shown in Table 10.6.

Assessment

Any creative individual learns to critique his or her own work using objective as well as intuitive standards. Building skills in self-assessment and evaluating the work of others is crucial to the compositional process. This can be done verbally with the teacher guiding the entire class, individually, or within peer or small group settings. Assessment sheets could be kept by individual students as a part of a portfolio project along with selected compositions on tape.

Regardless of the method used, critiques need to focus on the following questions:

1. How well did the composition meet the requirements of the assignment?
2. Did you revise? What did you change? How did you change it?
3. Did you hear music inside your head? When and how did this happen?
4. What "worked" or was "interesting" musically about the composition?
5. If you had more time to spend on the composition, is there anything you would change?
6. How successful was the process? Does anything in it need to change?

Should the teacher wish to keep a written record of student progress in composition, Harris and Hawksley (1989) suggest assessing compositions on qualities of musical features, general style and effectiveness, originality, and performance directions. Their assessment form also records student growth in attitudes, commitment, interpretation, confidence, and discretion. Other ideas for student and teacher assessment of compositions and the compositional

Table 10.6 Format for Independent Compositions

Problem: State the limits of the composition.	Compose a sixteen-beat piece in duple meter for autoharp and nonpitched rhythm instruments.
Materials: State the size of the group and the materials and equipment needed.	Four students One autoharp and pick Various rhythm instruments Tape recorder Blank tape
Procedures: State the steps to be followed in a logical order.	1. Experiment with various chord progressions until you find one you like. 2. Write the progression down, indicating each of the sixteen beats and the chord changes. Make sure the final chord is one that gives a sense of resolution. 3. Select rhythmic percussion instruments that will enhance your piece and add the rhythmic accompaniment. 4. Use an interesting strum to create a rhythm on the autoharp. 5. Practice your piece, refining as necessary. 6. When you are satisfied, tape record the piece, label the tape with your group name and the folder name, and place the tape in the box on the composition table.
Assessment: List questions they need to answer as part of the process of reflecting on their composition and the process.	Each group member answers the following questions separately and submits them with your tape. 1. How satisfied are you with your composition and why? 2. Did you change anything? Is there anything else you'd like to change? How might you change it? 3. What contributions did you make to the process of composing this piece?
Challenge: Ideas for further compositional work, reflection, or transfer into listening.	Listen to the tape in your composition folder. These ideas represent other people's solutions to this problem. Compare them with your own. Discuss your responses with other members of your group.

process can be found in Winner, Davidson, and Scripp (1992) and Paynter and Aston (1971).

Any of these ideas could be adapted to fit the teacher's criteria for creativity, commitment, and skill development. Formal evaluation would not need to be used each time a student composed but could be used several times a year to keep track of the quality of a given student's work. Along with tapes of various compositions, the assessments could become a part of documentation included in student portfolios.

The Rewards of Nurturing Creativity in Music

A challenge in teaching music is to implement a curriculum that balances performing, listening, and creating. Teachers are naturally drawn to teach those things with which they are the most familiar. Because so much of their own musical training required the development of sophisticated performance skills, teachers are drawn to emphasize performance with children. Yet, teachers who are willing to develop the processes of listening and creating with children will find the rewards gratifying.

Quality programs in composition and improvisation will foster many important skills. Children will develop a sense of control over the materials of music as they engage in aesthetic decision making. The result is a feeling of pride and of ownership of their ideas. They will develop a musical vocabulary of sounds, patterns, and concepts with which to create musical syntax, assisting them in thinking musically. They will learn to apply critical and creative thinking skills to the process of making musical decisions. These skills will transfer from composing to listening and performing. Children will learn to work cooperatively with others in the composition process. They will learn to assess their own work and the work of others. They will discover that effective composition involves craft, not just inspiration. Children will grow creatively, critically, musically, and aesthetically. As Pablo Picasso remarked, "Every child is an artist. The problem is how to remain an artist once she grows up."

Questions

1. What is the difference between composing and improvising? What is the difference between convergent and divergent thinking?
2. How is the type of thinking developed during creative activities different from the type of thinking in most of the rest of schooling?

3. What are the benefits to children of improvising? Of composing?

4. What role(s) does the teacher play in the composition process? What role(s) does the student play?

5. Discuss the importance of building skills in evaluative or critical thinking as a part of the composition process.

6. List several ways you and your students could keep track of their growth as composers.

7. Why are music teachers often reluctant to include composition and improvisation as a regular part of their music activities for children?

Activities

1. Find some nonconventional sound sources and work with a group of children to help them explore and discover the sound possibilities. Help guide them through a simple improvisation using those sound sources.

2. Find a composition assignment from one of the books listed in the chapter references and implement it with a group of children or with college classmates. Try to include all of the elements of the compositional process listed in this chapter. Discuss your response to this process and the response of the participants.

3. Write three composition assignments for older elementary children using the format given under "individualized plans." Share your assignments with a classmate to check for clarity and logic.

4. Develop a two-paragraph rationale to be used with parents for having composition as a significant part of your general music program.

5. Read and review one book on composition or improvisation from the bibliography. Note a minimum of five ideas you would want to use with your students.

6. Find a picture from a magazine that might be a good "start" for a composition. Write a composition assignment to go with it.

7. Review a text with activities oriented toward Orff-Schulwerk, Dalcroze, or Kodály methods. Discover strategies that promote improvisation and those that promote composition.

8. Examine through experimentation any of the computer programs listed in this chapter designed to encourage children to develop songwriting skills. Decide which would be most appropriate for your setting, and develop a plan for its use.

References

AEBERSOLD, J. (1972–1988). *Play-a-longs*. New Albany, IN: Aebersold.

Ballade, computer program. (1990). Foster City, CA: Dynaware.

Band-in-a-box, computer program. Buffalo, NY: PG Music.

BIASINI, A., THOMAS, R., & POGONOWSKI, L. (1971). *MMCP interaction*. Bardonia, NY: Media Materials.

CAMPBELL, P. S. (1991). *Lessons from the world*. New York: Schirmer Books.

CAMPBELL, L. (1985). *Sketching at the keyboard*. London: Stainer & Bell.

CHATTERLEY, A. (1978). *The music club book of improvisation projects*. London: Stainer & Bell.

DENNIS, B. (1975). *Projects in sound*. London: Universal Edition.

Encore, computer program. (1992). Half Moon Bay, CA: Passport Designs.

EVANS, D. (1978). *Sharing sounds*. London: Longman.

FLOHR, J. (1985). Young children's improvisations: Emerging creative thought. *The Creative Child and Adult Quarterly, 10*(2), 79–85.

HAMANN, D. L. (Ed.). (1992). *Creativity in the music classroom: The best of MEJ*. Reston, VA: Music Educators National Conference.

HARRIS, R., & HAWKSLEY, E. (1989). *Composing in the classroom*. Cambridge, England: Cambridge University.

KONOWITZ, B. (1970). *Vocal improvisation method*. New York: Alfred Publications.

———. (1973). *Music improvisation as a classroom method*. New York: Alfred Publications.

KRATUS, J. (1985). The use of melodic and rhythmic motives in the original songs of children aged 5 to 13. *Contributions to Music Education, 12*, 1–8.

KRATUS, J. (1991). Growing with improvisation. *Music Educators Journal, 78*(4), 35–40.

MARSH, M. (1970). *Explore and discover music*. Toronto: Macmillan.

Melody studio, computer program. (1992). Fairfield, CT: Queue.

ORTON, R. (1981). *Electronic music for schools*. Cambridge, England: Cambridge University.

PALMER, M. (1974). *Sound exploration and discovery*. New York: The Center for Applied Research in Education.

PAYNTER, J. (1972). *Hear and now*. London: Universal Edition.

PAYNTER, J., & ASTON, P. (1971). *Sound and silence.* Cambridge, England: Cambridge University.

Personal musician, computer program. (1990). Activision.

SCHAFER, R. M. (1976). *Creative music education.* New York: Schirmer Books.

THOMAS, R. (1970). *Manhattanville music curriculum project (MMCP) synthesis.* Bardonia, NY: Media Materials.

TILLMAN, J., & SWANICK, K. (1989). Towards a model of development of children's musical creativity. *Canadian Music Educator, 30*(2), 169–74.

UPITIS, R. (1990). *This too is music.* Portsmouth, NH: Heinemann.

———. (1992). *Can I play you my song?* Portsmouth, NH: Heinemann.

WEBSTER, P. (1990). Creativity as creative thinking. *Music Educators Journal, 76*(9), 22–28.

WIGGINS, J. (1990). *Composition in the classroom: A tool for teaching.* Reston, VA: Music Educators National Conference.

WINNER, E., DAVIDSON, L., & SCRIPP, L. (1992). *Arts propel: A handbook for music.* Cambridge, MA: Harvard Project Zero and Educational Testing Service.

CHAPTER **11**

Curriculum Design and Evaluation

In early May, Ms. Santiago finished a production of the Broadway musical *Cats* with her elementary children. Her principal and the parents of the children were thrilled to see the children "in lights." Ms. Santiago was pleased with their reactions, because the entire school year had been spent preparing for this event. Each year she does a different musical, and her reputation for high-quality productions has spread throughout the region. Some talented children have become the "stars," although all children are involved in some way, many behind the scenes.

In a neighboring school, Mr. Congdon also just completed his annual spring concert to the acclaim of parents, other teachers, and administrators. During April, the children voted to share with parents two or three things they had done in music class during the year. The choices were wide-ranging. First graders sang and dramatized some songs they had learned during their unit on bears; second graders sang and shared a dance they had invented to go with a folk song; third graders played their soprano recorders accompanied by orchestrations on Orff xylophones and metallophones; fourth graders performed some partner songs that they accompanied on various instruments; fifth graders sang a medley of songs related to American history and small groups performed their own compositions; and sixth graders sang a song in three-part harmony and shared a short film they had made, accompanied by electronic music they had composed. Students from each grade level introduced their selections and explained why they had chosen those pieces and what they had learned from involvement in music.

In a third elementary school in the same district, Ms. Solecki's students presented a theme concert called "Our Musical World." Students from each grade level performed music and dances from cultures they had studied during the year. Children dressed in simple, but representative costumes from each culture. Some classes created instruments that they incorporated into the performance. Children's artwork, reflecting styles and techniques from the various cultures, decorated the gymnasium. Slides of specific artworks were projected during the performances. During the final number, all of the children joined hands and voices to sing a song about world peace. The entire audience sang with them on the last chorus.

The Nature of Curriculum

These spring concert vignettes are presented to illustrate the wide differences among music programs and the freedom individual teachers have in determining the content of their own curriculum. Curriculum can be thought of as the activities that occur in the classroom. It is usually hoped that those activities promote significant musical learning. Though spring concerts rarely represent an entire year's work, they do reflect what teachers value and what they have emphasized out of the myriad of possibilities existing in music education.

It is clear from these examples that the operational curriculum, or that which is actually implemented, is dynamic rather than static, and is subject to such variables as teacher attitudes and training, parental and administrative expectations, and current trends in education. It is also clear that the experiential curriculum, or that which the students receive, can differ remarkably, even within the same school district.

The curricular goals for Ms. Santiago appear to revolve around achieving a quality and entertaining performance, with certain students receiving a high level of recognition. Mr. Congdon's curriculum reflects an emphasis on student leadership and clear development of a range of musical performance skills in singing, dancing, and instrument playing, as well as composition. In addition, children are encouraged both to think about what they are learning in music and to make values choices about what they have produced. Ms. Solecki's curriculum appears to be stimulated in part by its connection to the rest of the school program, particularly social studies. It also reflects attention to issues of multiculturalism and societal values. Students learn to express ideas through several art forms and experience an integration of those within and across cultures.

None of the preceding choices is inherently "right" or "wrong." Each curriculum could be justified based on different philosophies and circumstances. However, some reflect more closely than others what the profession of music education has come to value as a comprehensive and balanced approach to the early childhood and elementary curriculums. This is called the ideal curriculum.

Types and Sources of Curriculum

Curriculum plans exist in many forms at many levels, and are available from a range of sources (Table 11.1). Most are highly structured and suggest a logical sequence of concepts, skills, and attitudes to be achieved through the scope of an entire music program. A formal curriculum helps to provide all the teachers in a school or district a frame for their plans and helps to assure that some consistency exists within a program. It helps provide for articulation as students move from one level to another, such as elementary to middle school. Most importantly, a formal curriculum helps establish clear goals or outcomes and becomes a structure for directing teacher and student activity and for musical learning to be measured.

A quality formal curriculum establishes large goals, competencies, and/or outcomes, leaving teachers free to develop an instructional curriculum for their own classroom and a personal method for attaining the goals. A quality formal curriculum reflects the nature and content of music; is balanced, comprehensive, and sequential; and reflects what is known through research about musical development in children.

A music curriculum may be established for teachers by a school district or state, and teachers may be held accountable for teaching to the curriculum goals. Such documents generally are created by committees made up of music teachers and administrators. Usually these curricula are revised every seven to ten years to reflect current trends in education, research in learning, and changing national standards in music education. They may or may not be followed by every teacher in a school district. Successful implementation is usually dependent on training teachers in how to use the curriculum.

In private schools, teachers often create their own curriculum. These tend to be much more idiosyncratic, reflecting the values and training of the teacher(s) and the values of the school. They are more likely to be followed because they are determined locally. They may or may not be formally assessed.

Many sources are available for individual teachers and committees to consider in determining their own curriculum. These sources range from formal to informal and are highlighted in Table 11.1.

Planning a Curriculum

Teachers need to be responsible for thinking through what they wish to accomplish each year in their instructional curriculum. If there is an established formal curriculum for music where they are working, they should follow its guidelines in establishing their own program. If there is not a curriculum, they may wish to use state or national goals in music education as a guide.

Table 11.1 Types and Sources of Curricula

Ideal	Formal	Instructional	Operational	Experiential
National Standards; MENC: Kodály; Orff; Dalcroze	Individual states, school districts, and schools; consultants and other outside experts	District or school guides; music series texts; technology; individual teachers; outside experts; school curriculum	Individual music; teacher and methodology chosen; students; other teachers; school administrator; music administrator; parents	Students; parents; other teachers; administrators; school boards
Highly formal ⟵				⟶ Less formal

Abbreviations: MENC, Music Educators National Conference.

Table 11.2 shows how a general program outcome on the state level becomes increasingly specific as it is realized in the classroom.

A curriculum should be balanced, appropriately sequenced, and comprehensive. It should reflect what musicians do with music, should help children discover the nature of music, and how music is put together. It should challenge the children to grow artistically, creatively, and aesthetically, and should give them a wide repertoire of vocal and aural literature that they can enjoy through a lifetime.

One possibility for organizing a year's curriculum would be to establish comprehensive, age-appropriate goals and procedures for attaining:

1. *Skills* of singing, moving, listening, playing, reading, creating, and critical thinking

2. *Concepts*, including: elements (melody, harmony, rhythm, tone color, and expression); form (how the elements are put together); style and genre (what emerges from structure and culture); and context (the relationship of music to culture, history, and the other arts)

3. *Attitudes* about music, their own preferences for various kinds of music and commitment to involvement in music; increasing aesthetic sensitivity

4. *Repertoire* of vocal music including American heritage and folk songs, composed songs, and songs from various parts of the world; and a listening repertoire of a wide range of quality works that students can identify, discuss, and evaluate

Table 11.2 Relationship between Levels of Outcomes

State Level	District or School Level	Specific Grade Level Year
Students will use the conceptual language of music to organize musical concepts, ideas, and sounds.	Students will develop and apply musical concepts of rhythm, melody, harmony, tone color, expression, form, and style through listening, performing, and creating.	First graders will understand the concept of beat as an organizing device, be able to recognize it in a variety of settings, and use beat as a basis for composition and improvisation.

General ←——————————————————————————————→ Specific

These four curriculum elements are implemented differently reflecting how they are developed in the learner. Skills must be developed gradually, moving from simple to complex tasks. For example, the skill of singing expressively and confidently across a wide range needs to be developed in small steps (see Chapter 6). Skills must also be practiced regularly to be retained. Reasonable goals can be established for children's vocal growth during a given year, and attainment of each step measured throughout that year. Chapters 6–10 will help in formulating developmentally appropriate skill sequences in each of the major processes of music.

Concepts, once learned, do not need to be practiced. A person either does or does not understand a concept. However, once a concept is attained, it does need to be applied to new situations or used in new ways. During a year, a teacher might introduce a short unit that teaches the concept of beat, go on to teach several other concepts, then return to beat, applying that concept to new pieces of music at a more sophisticated level. Once the concept of beat is understood, then children have the basis for understanding concepts of rhythmic durations and metric organization (see Chapter 7 for a model of a concept unit). Chapters 4 on rhythm, 5 on pitch, and 7 on listening are sources for specific concepts typically taught at the elementary level.

All music should be placed in a cultural and stylistic context when taught, and children should be helped to perform in the appropriate style as they learn new pieces. Very young children are not ready to understand the history of music, but they can learn about certain composers, and they are very sensitive to style. Older elementary children can begin to gain a conscious understanding of the attributes of music that come together to create specific musical styles, periods, and genres.

Children working on skills of aural dictation.

Attitudes do not need to be taught in a separate unit but, rather, should emerge from the musical experience itself. The kinds of questions the teacher asks the students throughout the year will help them to grow in their valuing of and sensitivity to music. Asking questions such as these will help the children to consciously make musical decisions and will build patterns of aesthetic thinking. "What did you find interesting about that piece of music?" "How shall we shape the song this time when we sing it?" "What do you want to change in your composition, now that you've heard it?" "How were those two pieces similar or different?"

Repertoire develops from engaging children in quality music through singing, playing, and listening. Concern here is for having children internalize key works so there is a sense of mastery and ownership. Such internalization results from many experiences with a work of music. Excellent literature is available in music series texts with recordings that use authentic instruments from various cultures and represent stylistically correct interpretations. Also many separate song collections of contemporary music are available in music stores. Numerous Kodály-inspired books provide collections of American folk music. The Orff-Schulwerk American edition books include many songs, chants, and instrumental works (see Chapter 3 for names of resources). There are various published collections of songs and listening experiences from throughout the world (see Chapter 13). Other ideas for building a listening repertoire can be found in Chapter 7.

Table 11.3 provides a suggested framework for a year's plan. Teachers need to adapt it to their own setting and to put in specifics for each grade level. Units of study can be superimposed on the framework.

How much can realistically be accomplished will depend on the contact time the teacher has with the children. An ideal would be thirty minutes daily with each class. Much more common is two to three times a week for thirty to forty minutes each. An inadequate program is thirty minutes per week or less.

Table 11.3 Planning Map for a Year's Curriculum

	Sept.	Oct.	Nov.	Dec.	Jan.	Feb.	Mar.	Apr.	May	June
Concepts										
Melody										
Harmony/texture										
Rhythm										
Tone color										
Expression										
Form										
Style/genre										
Skills										
Singing										
Moving										
Listening										
Playing										
Reading										
Creating										
Thinking										
Attitudes										
Musical judgments and preferences										
Programs	Autumn PTSA		Holiday				Spring			

Repertoire
Vocal works to be mastered_____ (at least 15 per year)

Recorded works to be internalized_____ (At least 6 per year)

Additional considerations are: (1) the number and type of programs or concerts to be given each year; (2) the structure of the school and goals for the integration of the music program with the rest of the curriculum; (3) expectations of administrators and other members of the community; and (4) whether there is more than one music teacher involved in implementing the music curriculum in the school.

Other factors that often influence the successful implementation of the curriculum include: (1) teacher attitudes, priorities, and training; (2) facilities and equipment; (3) socioeconomic status of the community; and, (4) the stability/transience of the student population. Of these, the most important factor is the first. It is discouraging for a teacher to be spend more time disciplining than teaching; to adjust to a yearly turnover of one third in student population; or to teach by going from room to room with equipment on a rolling cart. However, if a teacher truly cares about connecting children with music, a great deal can be taught, even under adverse conditions. With dedication and innovation, most challenges can be met.

Implementing a Curriculum

Once the yearly curriculum has been established, individual lessons can be planned. Lessons weave together the strands of the yearly plan. Skills, concepts, and attitudes merge as the imaginative teacher decides how to achieve the goals established. Key considerations to effective implementation are: (1) children and their learning needs; (2) the yearly curriculum; and (3) method (how to reach curriculum goals with a particular group of children). This aspect of the curriculum often provides teachers with the greatest satisfaction, because it requires their creativity and musicianship as well as their insight into what children need.

Effective lessons can be thought of in three parts: (1) *objectives*, or what this lesson is trying to achieve in terms of student growth in music (these come directly from the curriculum goals/outcomes); (2) *strategies*, or what procedures and materials will be used to achieve the objectives (this is where personal method and technology enter); and (3) *evaluation*, or reflecting on whether the objectives were achieved, and whether the strategies were effective. This can include assessments of the children as well.

This model is shown more specifically in Tables 11.4 and 11.5. Movement, as shown by the arrows, is from left to right, then back again. Another model of lesson planning that shows the flow through a lesson can be found under Instructional Strategies in Chapter 2.

Regardless of the model selected, it is important that teachers develop clear goals and objectives that are supported by classroom activities. Some teachers

Table 11.4 Three-Legged Model of Lesson Planning

Objectives	Strategies	Monitor and Evaluate
Concepts, skills, and attitudes specific to the curriculum. Most music lessons have multiple objectives rather than one.	All of the materials and activities, in logical order, that will help children to achieve the lesson's objectives. Questions can be listed. Processes from specific approaches to music education as well as technology can be incorporated.	Monitor whether students understand the task to be done and where they are in their understanding or skills at the end of a lesson. Evaluate whether objectives were realistic and whether strategies were effective.

get so caught up in selecting appealing materials or in following an approach, that they lose sight of the larger reasons for what they are doing. It is as if they have entered the process of planning, as noted in the middle column of Table 11.4. When asked to state their goals, such teachers often reply, "to learn the song" or "to have fun," rather than to build a foundation of musical skills and concepts children can carry through their lives.

Table 11.5 takes this planning model and illustrates how it can be used for a music lesson in the first or second grade. Note the relationship between the columns and the variety and flow of the activities through the lesson.

Pedagogies such as Orff-Schulwerk and Kodály often provide detailed sequences of concepts and skills along with materials and processes for how to achieve those goals. Some even suggest specific lesson plans based on curriculum as well as process. Key to thoughtful use of these or other pedagogies is to reflect on whether the resulting musical learnings constitute a comprehensive and balanced approach. Books by Choksy, Abramson, Gillespie, and Woods (1986), Choksy (1981, 1988) and Frazee (1987) provide useful models for incorporating various pedagogies within the framework of a comprehensive curriculum.

Evaluation

One of the most important and often challenging tasks educators engage in is evaluation. Evaluation involves making a value judgment about something or someone. According to law, principals must formally evaluate teachers each

Table 11.5   Specific Application of Planning Model

Objectives	Strategies	Monitor and Evaluate
1. To develop skills of pitch matching, sight singing, interval awareness, and inner hearing.	1. Warm up with sight-singing exercise, drawing pattern of sol, mi, do from song, "Mouse, Mousie." Use hand signs. Work on internal hearing of pattern.	1. Listen for intonation and accuracy. Correct as necessary. Ask child to give indication for inner singing.
2. To discover sol, mi, do pattern in song and to add a bourdon accompaniment.	2. Find "Mouse, Mousie" in books. Put fingers on sol, mi, do pattern. Sing song. Sing again while patting an F, C bourdon on laps. Select children to play bourdon on xylophones.	2. Watch to see that everyone is pointing to pattern in books. Monitor accuracy of playing. Note on file cards who performed and how well they did.
3. To begin focus on concept of binary or AB form.	3. Sing the song "Jubilee." Clap hands on the A section, pat laps on the B section. Once children get a sense of where to switch, have them suggest other contrasting movements. Have children discuss why the movements changed.	3. Watch to see that children switch movements at the B section. Monitor responses to question.
4. To review one or two repertoire songs and refine sense of style in singing them.	4. Have child draw repertoire song from sack. Experiment with interpretation.	4. Watch to see what children are still having problems with words or melody.

year. Teachers constantly evaluate their students, sometimes formally, sometimes informally. Teachers also evaluate their administrators, often based on how supportive they are, how well they communicate, and how well they lead. Parents evaluate the success of the music program based on the attitudes of their children toward the music classes and on the musical quality of the concerts. Ideally, teachers evaluate their own curriculum on a regular basis and reshape it as necessary. Table 11.6 illustrates a variety of ways, both formal and informal, that evaluation of curriculum and of teachers occurs.

Mouse, Mous - ie, lit - tle mous - ie, hur - ry, hur - ry do.

Or the kit - ty in her hous - ie will be chas - ing you!

Figure 11.1. "Mouse, Mousie." *Reproduced with permission from* World of Music, Grade 1 *(1992)*.

As can be seen from these illustrations, evaluation is often subjective or highly personal, lacking in objective or measurable standards. A complete lack of objective standards could be troublesome. It would be distressing to have the music curriculum evaluated solely on how well the students performed in a spring concert, or teachers evaluated on impressions principals received from faculty room discussions over coffee.

Ideally, evaluation involves collecting a combination of objective and subjective data as well as affective or feeling responses. The best evaluation

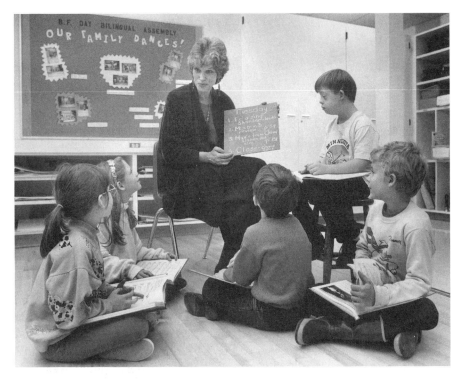

Teacher pointing to goals on chalkboard.

Figure 11.2. "Jubilee!" (singing game from Kentucky). *Reproduced with permission from* World of Music, Grade 1 *(1992).*

is constructive, helping the learner, administrator, teacher, or program to grow.

Evaluation is often used as an umbrella term to describe taking stock of a program or the people in it. However, other terms such as assessment, measurement, and testing may be used to describe specific tools in the evaluation process. Each of these tools can help to increase the base of objective information to use in making evaluative decisions.

Assessment is often used synonymously with evaluation. However, it can also mean a more deliberate collection of information for specific purposes. It does not necessarily involve numbers. Through it, students receive and participate in continuous feedback on both process and product. It may be subjective within the framework of standards. For example, children might be asked to assess the quality of their own performance (self-assessment) or that of others (peer assessment). Criteria related to expression, tone, phrasing, and rhythmic and pitch accuracy could be used. Teachers could assess a child's progress in playing the autoharp or xylophone. Children could assess their own musical growth by writing about their progress in a music journal.

Table 11.6 Evaluation of the Curriculum

Ideal	Formal	Instructional	Operational	Experiential
National testing of student achievement; accreditation of teachers and programs	Statewide or district-level testing; school or program accreditation	District testing; individual teacher testing and tracking of students and ongoing assessment of curriculum	Individual teacher testing and tracking of students and ongoing assessment of goals and procedures; student self-assessment and peer-assessment; evaluation of program and teacher by administrators	Student attitudes and growth; teacher reflections and comments; parent observation of student achievement and attitudes
Highly Formal ⟵				⟶ Less Formal

Testing involves the systematic observation of a person's behavior, and then quantifying that behavior in a numerical scale or by placement in a category. A teacher might test children's knowledge of basic musical terminology through a written test, or understanding of a concept through administering a test of aural perception. Attitudes could be formally sampled via a rating scale using a like-to-dislike continuum or an interest inventory. Skills might be tested by rating performance accuracy. To be valid, the test needs to be specific to the behavior it is measuring, and it must be constructed so it is consistent across different sets of students. Tests can be constructed by the teacher, or a standardized test such as those available to test musical achievement could be used.

Measurement also involves assigning a range of numbers to individuals or events but is less specific to a particular behavior than a test. It allows the comparison of individuals or groups, and often involves statistical treatment of the data collected. Teachers might measure individual student progress across time in a variety of ways and compare the data with each other or compile it for a final grade. Also, teachers might measure all the students in a class and compare the results with those of another class.

One of the more provocative questions in evaluating music learning is how to get at what is happening inside a student's head. Success in music, a performance art, is most often measured by performance. That is something tangible that can be seen and heard. However, the comprehensive elementary general music program is not based solely on musical performance, but also attempts to help children attain a variety of concepts and skills.

Musical behaviors can be overt (observable to others) or covert (internalized and private). Overt behaviors most commonly developed at the elementary level are singing, moving, playing, reading, identifying, and creating. Covert behaviors are such things as listening, conceptualizing, perceiving, discriminating, recognizing, imagining, feeling, and valuing.

Developing techniques for measuring overt behaviors is relatively simple; all you have to do is observe what children produce. Developing techniques for measuring covert behaviors is more challenging and needs to reflect as much as possible what is happening mentally and emotionally. Table 11.7 suggests some ways teachers might help make internalized responses externally observable.

Tracking Student Growth

To both document how each child is growing in music and to measure the effectiveness of instruction, it is valuable and important to develop a system for tracking student growth. Often preschool or elementary teachers rely solely on informally gathered impressions of children, and fail to take the time to establish a system that will provide a more objective basis for evaluation.

Systems for gathering and recording data may vary from simple to elaborate, depending on the teacher's preference, how many students are in each class, student contact time per week, what reporting system(s) are used, and how much technical and physical support the teacher gets for accomplishing this important task. For instance, it would be virtually impossible for a teacher assigned to two schools, seeing 1200 students one time each week, to do much more than instruct, whereas, a teacher assigned to one school with 350 students, seeing them two or three times a week, should be able to establish a more formal system.

One method is to identify key behaviors or markers to follow, consistently measure, and record. This might include skills such as singing accurately, expanding vocal range, performing a bourdon on the beat, or playing an ostinato using a crossover pattern. It might also include recording attitudinal responses or age-appropriate understandings. A separate file card for each child in a class could be made with key behaviors listed. File cards could be color-coded for different classes or grade levels. The file cards should be randomly ordered and selected from the top of the pile as those students are asked to demonstrate skills or understandings in the context of a lesson. Notes could be made immediately about level of understanding or skill and the card placed on the bottom of the pile. This system assures that, over time, every child in the

Table 11.7 Measuring Covert Behaviors

Covert Response	Overt Response
Listening: a complex aural response to music that depends on attention and perception and is influenced by attitude and past experience.	Ideas presented in Chapter 7 suggest how to focus perception and how to assess what children perceive. Some options are telling, diagramming, pointing, sequencing, circling, listing, moving, singing, playing.
Perceiving: to notice something through one or more of the senses. Auditory perception is the most important in music, but reading music and following a conductor demand visual perception and performing music demands muscular and touch perception.	Children could identify, discuss, shape, draw, diagram, notate, point to, circle, order, sing, play, conduct, or move to what they perceive.
Discriminating: telling the difference between two things, people, or events.	Present children with two musical events and have them tell you, verbally or through thumbs up (same) thumbs down (different), whether those events are the same as or different from each other. It could be two pitches, two patterns, two phrases, or two melodies.
Recognizing: knowing that something is familiar.	Children could point or circle or talk about what they recognize. The next level would be to have them identify or name what they recognize, such as a song or a recorded work, a composer, or country from which a work comes.
Conceptualizing: to form a generalized understanding based on grouping similar but different objects or events into a category based on their commonalities; depends on skills of discrimination and perception.	Children can group sounds based on commonalities, such as all high sounds, all ringing sounds, etc. They can group patterns such as similar melodic shapes, or types of music such as rock or folk. Once they attain a concept, they could: (1) define it in their own terms; (2) bring in examples that illustrate it; (3) perceive it in unfamiliar music (i.e., that piece does have a beat, that piece does not); (4) compose using that concept (i.e., compose a short piece that illustrates beat/no beat. *Warning*: People can understand concepts without being able to

(*continued*)

Table 11.7   Continued

Covert Response	Overt Response
	demonstrate them through accurate performance. Do not assume that because a child cannot perform a chromatic scale that the child does not understand what one is.
Imagining: the ability to internally image musical ideas or to image other ideas that are stimulated by music.	Aural imagination can be examined through sight-reading or sight-singing; strategies using internal/external responses within a piece; improvising, and composing. Other images could be shared through telling, writing, drawing, moving.
Feeling: the emotional or affective response to music. This is influenced not only by the music itself, but by experiences the listener may associate with that music. Feelings are not right or wrong.	Have children discuss or write down their responses. They could also dance/move or draw responses.
Valuing: the value people attribute to a piece or style of music or to musical experiences. Values cannot be imposed, as in, "You will like this music" but, rather, emerge from active involvement with music. Values can be influenced by other factors including families, peers, and the media.	Observe students' responses to a variety of music, and have them discuss or write down their responses. After they state a value response, such as "I really like that music" or "I hate that music!," encourage them to discuss *why* in terms of the music. Observe what recordings they purchase, concerts they attend, or what pieces they want to sing or perform over and over. Allow them to make preference choices and to discuss them.

class gets to play instruments or lead a game or a song, and in turn be carefully observed by the teacher. Grades on tests could be entered on the card, in a grade book, or on a computer database where all of the data are finally compiled.

Another system might be to have a file folder for each class. Duplicate charts with student names, listed alphabetically, could be pasted inside on both halves of the folder. On one chart, the teacher could track student behaviors regarding attitude, attendance, and participation. On the other chart, skill and concept goals for various segments of the year could be listed, and individual student growth toward or attainment of those goals could be marked using a rating or checkoff system.

Teachers could record information about children's musical behaviors directly onto a computer database. Advantages of this system include the ability to: (1) sort in each category; (2) group information for measurement; and (3) generate detailed personalized reports for parents.

Some models focus less on outcomes and more on the ongoing process of assessment. This process includes what students are able to learn from assessing themselves, and their own and other's products. In these models, each child is given a portfolio to record evidence of their work, including drafts. Portfolios must reflect the domain in which the child is working. Because music is a discipline that involves performance, perception/cognition, and creativity, evidence that reflects those dimensions must be included. Table 11.8 indicates means of collecting and recording data in music.

Also key to portfolios is student reflection on their own artistic growth and the growth of the groups in which they participate. Through reflection they become active in the learning process, and learn to apply musical standards to production, be more inventive, and generate ideas for new work. Reflection can be done in journals and on forms developed for those purposes. Projects are long-term and portfolio work ongoing. Portfolios can be assessed by teachers, students, and parents. Sources for assessment ideas in music come from Winner (1991) and Winner, Davidson, and Scripp (1992). Additional ideas for alternative assessment including how to structure a system can be found in Herman, Aschbacher, and Winters (1992).

Table 11.8 Portfolio Contents in Music

Musical Behavior	Evidence	Context
Performance	Videotapes and/or audio tapes	Individual and ensemble performances
Perception/cognition	Tests, journal entries, charts, grids, interviews, discussions	Individual growth and reflection
Creation	Drafts of ideas in journals, scores, recordings of compositions and improvisations	Individual and group efforts

Reporting to Parents

School systems, whether public or private, usually establish standards or procedures for reporting to parents both about the curriculum and about student progress. A variety of methods are typical to the early childhood and elementary levels for reporting about the curriculum, including:

1. Autumn open house or curriculum night: teachers describe program to parents
2. Informal programs at the end of units to which parents, other classes, and administrators are invited
3. Descriptions about the program that go out in brochures or in school or music newsletters
4. PTSA meetings that feature the music program; these can be informances where teachers and children discuss the curriculum and model actual lessons
5. Music in Our Schools Week (MIOSW), an international celebration with children, teachers, and community. Support materials are available annually from MENC.
6. Parent observation in the classroom during MIOSW or throughout the year

There are also many methods to report to parents about student progress and achievement. With the exception of concerts, these are specific to each child and usually involve a dialogue that helps to educate parents, not only about their child or children but about the music curriculum:

1. Parent/teacher conferences. These are usually with the classroom teacher and rarely involve the music teacher. In schools where the arts are central to learning, arts specialists may also hold conferences with parents.
2. Concerts for the community. These are important vehicles for recognizing student achievement in music. They are most useful when they feature all students, although individuals may be recognized.
3. Student contracts that are signed by students and parents outlining what the student hopes to achieve in music.
4. Student projects that result in a culminating event and in sharing of student portfolios.

5. Individual conferences any time during the year as requested by the parent or the teacher. This could include IEP conference about children with special needs.

6. Report cards that could include:

   (a) Letter grades or satisfactory/unsatisfactory in music, assigned by music teacher

   (b) Comments about each child's performance in music written by the music teacher

   (c) Checklist in music that shows progress in specific skills areas, attainment of understandings, and attitude toward music

   (d) No acknowledgment of the music program on report cards

Music teachers need to consider how to make those communications as effective as possible so that parents understand that the purpose of the music program is to educate children, not simply to entertain them. Grades and comments, if required by a system, need to be based on systematically collected and broadly based data about musical growth, not just about attitudes or behavior in the music classroom. Teachers who rely only on a "big show" to impress parents or who grade strictly on whether a child is cooperative in music limit the purposes of music education.

Distilling the Essence of Curriculum and Evaluation

At a time when the role of the arts in education is being questioned, it is essential that music educators be clear about the importance and value of music. One of the best ways to convey that is by having a clearly stated curriculum with a sense of direction in which students are growing. Many excellent sources are available to provide that structure. Thoughtful and creative instruction by dedicated teacher/musicians will help to assure that the journey is meaningful and the destination worthwhile.

Effective evaluation, whether of individual students, groups of students, teachers, or programs can be accomplished with greater ease if it is based on a clearly articulated curriculum and substantive data. Information that has been gathered regarding student learning and teacher effectiveness should be drawn from a range of sources, both formal and informal, subjective and objective. Parents, administrators, and the broader community will respond supportively to programs that offer both substance and results.

Questions

1. What is a curriculum, and why is it important to have one?

2. Describe the differences among an ideal curriculum, a formal curriculum, an instructional curriculum, an operational curriculum, and an experiential curriculum. Give sources for each type.

3. What constitutes a balanced and effective curriculum in music?

4. What role(s) does the individual teacher have in regard to the curriculum? Where does personal method fit in?

5. What considerations are important when establishing a curriculum? What factors might influence its successful implementation?

6. What are the elements of a three-legged lesson plan, and how do they relate to each other?

7. Where do specific lessons fit into the curriculum?

8. What are some effective techniques for measuring student behavior and growth in music?

9. What is the difference between overt and covert behaviors? What are some behaviors from each category that are developed in general music?

10. What are some ways to keep track of student development in music?

11. What role does the music teacher have in communicating about the music curriculum to parents and administrators? What are some ways of accomplishing that?

12. How should the giving of report cards in music relate to the music curriculum?

Activities

1. With another person, review and discuss at least two music curriculums, preferably from different levels such as national and local. Notice their similarities and differences. Determine how comprehensive they are in light of the standards set forth in this chapter. Discuss how useful they would be as a frame for your teaching. Would they help in assessing student growth?

2. Review an instructional curriculum, whether it be in a music series text or from a specific pedagogy. Determine what goals/outcomes are being emphasized in skills development, conceptual development, attitudes and

values in music, and listening and vocal repertoire. How are these being developed? How are they being assessed in the lessons provided?

3. Observe a model music lesson based on a three-legged model. Follow the lesson and assess how effective it was and how the parts related to each other. Observe another model music lesson without knowing the goals and objectives. See if you can determine what the teacher was trying to accomplish. Discuss that with a partner and with the teacher.

4. Find two different goals or outcomes from a formal music curriculum. Write specific goals for an operational curriculum that would come out of the general goals. Develop a lesson plan using a three-legged model to achieve those goals.

5. Review different systems for tracking student growth in general music. Discuss with others which one or ones seem the most effective and why. Develop a system for your own classroom.

6. Interview music teachers from three different school systems about how they evaluate their children in music and how they are expected to report to parents. Discuss with them their perceptions of that process.

References

ABELES, H. F., HOFFER, C., & KLOTMAN, R. H. (1993). *Foundations of music education* (2nd ed.). New York: Schirmer Books.

BOYLE, J. D., & RADOCY, R. E. (1987). *Measurement and evaluation of musical experiences*. New York: Schirmer Books.

CANGELOSI, J. S. (1991). *Evaluating classroom instruction*. New York: Longman.

CHOKSY, L. (1981). *The Kodály context*. Englewood Cliffs, NJ: Prentice-Hall.

———. (1988). *The Kodály method* (2nd ed.). Englewood Cliffs, NJ: Prentice-Hall.

CHOKSY, L., ABRAMSON, R. M., GILLESPIE, A. E., & WOODS, D. (1986). *Teaching music in the twentieth century*. Englewood Cliffs, NJ: Prentice-Hall.

FRAZEE, J. (1987). *Discovering Orff: A curriculum for music teachers*. New York: Schott.

HERMAN, J. L., ASCHBACHER, P. R., WINTERS, L. (1992). *A practical guide to alternative assessment*. Alexandria, VA: Association for Supervision and Curriculum Development.

MAGER, R. F. (1973). *Measuring instructional intent*. Belmont, CA.: Fearon.

Music Educations National Conference. (1993). Music education standards: A draft. *Music Educators Journal* (September), center pullout.

PASCH, M., SPARKS-LANGER, G., GARDNER, T. G., STARKO, A. J., & MOODY, C. D. (1991). *Teaching as decision making: Instructional practices for the successful teacher.* New York: Longman.

WINNER, E. (1991). *Arts propel: An introductory handbook.* Boston: Harvard Project Zero and Educational Testing Service.

WINNER, E., Davidson, L., & Scripp, L. (Eds.). (1992). *Arts propel: A handbook for music.* Boston: Harvard Project Zero and Educational Testing Service.

CHAPTER 12

Technology for Music Instruction

Some children have trouble matching pitches and singing in tune. Technology can help with this, as well as many other musical skills. Kevin was a typical representative of the out-of-tune singers group until he went through the first five exercises on the *Pitch Master.* When he sang the correct pitches into the *Pitch Master's* microphone, the indicator needle stayed in the "acceptable" band and he heard a reinforcing tone in one earphone and his own voice in the other. When he sang too sharp or flat, the needle showed him how far off he was, and the reinforcing tone stopped. For the first time in his life, Kevin received sufficient, specific, and immediate reinforcement to help him hear what correct intonation was and to help him control his voice for in-tune singing. His newly found self-confidence showed radiantly in his face like a prisoner released from bondage. He was a singer now!

Mr. Badillo had seen remarkable success in developing inner hearing with his fifth-grade music class using the *Doremi* computer program. The children begged him to play the *Doremi* game every class, and, after four sessions, almost all his children could identify "mystery pitches" and indicate them with their solfège hand signs. Many children could identify four "mystery pitches" played sequentially, and do it accurately time after time. Throughout the rest of the year, Mr. Badillo noticed the spectacular ripple effect *Doremi* had on the children's ability to learn new songs quickly and accurately and to remember motives and melodies when listening to and analyzing classical music. He also noticed that their compositions were using more interesting melodies and harmonies: the children seemed to have moved beyond the experimental stage of sound exploration to a stage of intentional design.

Pitch Master. *Courtesy Temporal Acuity Products.*

They were "hearing" the sounds in their heads before writing them down on paper.

Although it may seem like magic, the success of technology in music classes is simply the result of good instruction: giving proper materials at the time they are needed; and proper feedback and positive reinforcement of children's efforts as they approximate the desired musical behaviors. Human teachers are absolutely essential for teaching music, but are limited in the amount of time and attention they can spend on each child. Luckily, the technological revolution has ushered in the information age, bringing music teachers the assistance they have long desired. Higgins (1992) explained that "the term *technology* is derived from two Greek words: techne, meaning 'art,' and logos, meaning 'discourse'—'the art of discourse.'. . . Technology has become a vital part of education because it increases our ability to communicate with the learner, and thus our effectiveness as teachers" (p. 480). Even though technology has many advantages, it does add another layer of complexity (and sometimes anxiety) to the teacher's many tasks. Four important issues about technology for teaching music to children will be considered. Why use technology? What is available? How can it be used? What is likely to happen in the future?

The Uses of Technology for Teaching Music

For some kinds of music learning, Technology-Assisted Instruction in Music (TAIM)[1] is far more efficient than human teachers in helping children learn. Behavioral psychologists, such as B. F. Skinner (1968), found that children remembered more when instruction was frequently followed by immediate reinforcement. Skinner believed that reinforcement sufficient for optimum learning was impossible to achieve by one teacher in a classroom of children, and he advocated the use of teaching machines, which provided reinforcement much like a private tutor.

Shrader (1970) pointed out an opposite, but equally beneficial characteristic of TAIM: the benefit of limiting human observation. He believed that, in traditional methods of learning, it was necessary to expose the learner's deficiencies, and that this often embarrassed children and caused them to conceal their weaknesses, thereby making it more difficult to diagnose misunderstandings and provide corrective instruction. By using TAIM, where the child's mistakes are not brought to the attention of the entire class, the learning task can be focused in a nonjudgmental, anxiety-free environment.

Learning through TAIM has many other benefits:

1. Children work at their own pace, taking just as long as they need to learn the material

2. Computer programs patiently repeat drills as many times as needed, thus relieving children from being hurried and allowing human teachers to concentrate on teaching things that technology cannot yet teach

3. Drill programs check children's understanding and offer frequent feedback on their progress

4. Tutorial computer programs are usually well-sequenced, taking children in small steps from the known to the unknown

5. Open-ended technology (such as CD-ROMs and videodiscs) allow children to follow their own interests, instantly access, and randomly explore a vast amount of musical information

6. Most children enjoy learning with TAIM, due to its highly interactive nature and multimedia audiovisual appeal

7. Children may interact with TAIM individually, in small groups, or in full classes

---

[1]TAIM is a newer, more inclusive term replacing CAIM (computer-assisted instruction in music). Technology has grown far past computers and now includes many ancillary music-learning devices used alone or in connection with computers.

8. Using MIDI devices and sequencing/writing programs on the computer, children can create and notate their own music without encountering the traditional music-theory barriers

9. Comprehensive and thoroughly trained musicianship can be developed in children by combining several TAIM resources into a course of study

Music educators have long recognized the power of technology to enhance music learning. The Tanglewood Symposium of 1968, for example, established technology-assisted instruction as one of the Music Educators National Conference's important goals, and the professional literature on music teaching and learning abounds with articles advocating music technology. However, the actual implementation of TAIM in real classrooms poses several problems and questions:

1. Which equipment and software are available and most effective for teaching which skills and concepts?

2. How can technology be smoothly integrated into the curriculum?

3. How can just one or a few computers, CD-ROMs, etc. serve a whole classroom of children?

4. How can children's learning with technology be made accountable?

5. Which types of children benefit most from technology and how often should it be used?

6. How can children be motivated to stay on task while working with technology?

7. What are the psychological and social advantages and disadvantages of learning with technology?

8. How can funds be obtained for purchasing TAIM equipment and programs?

The solutions to these problems are as varied as the educational settings from which they arise, and require thoughtful teacher innovation and resourcefulness. The following ideas provide a point of departure on the journey toward harnessing technology for teaching.

Technology Available for Teaching Music

In the broadest sense, technology includes all kinds of communication devices and products, such as clarinets (and other acoustic instruments), radios, televisions, audio recordings (records, tapes, and CDs), audiovideo recordings (slides, filmstrips, motion pictures, videocassette recordings, videodiscs, and CD-ROMs), synthesizers, computers, computer software programs, MIDI devices, and interactive programs that link two or more technological devices. Each application of technology has its important uses in music education, but, because other devices are discussed in other books, this discussion will concentrate on the use of synthesizers, computers, software programs, and interactive programs and hardware.

The term "computer" has come to represent an entire system of electronic parts, known as "hardware," including a central processing unit (CPU), random-access memory (RAM), read-only memory (ROM), input devices (keyboards, disk drives, MIDI devices, sampling devices, modems, mouses, light pens, touch pads, joysticks, trackballs, scanners, etc.), and output devices (monitors, printers, digital-to-analog converter [DAC], sound systems, modems, fax machines, MIDI devices, etc.).

Musical Instrument Digital Interface (MIDI) is an especially important component of technology for music. MIDI is a set of specifications regarding the connection of and communication among various types of digital equipment capable of generating, sampling, controlling, recording, altering, or re-

Composer Marvin Sanders in his music studio. Equipment includes computer with monitor and mouse, MIDI synthesizers, hard-disk recorder, digital-audio tape machine, laser printer, mixer, and sound amplification system. *Reprinted with permission from* Electronic Musician, *January 1994.*

Computer with monitor, keyboards, and mouse. *Courtesy Temporal Acuity Products.*

producing sound. MIDI was the result of the collaborative efforts of thirteen independent manufacturing companies in the early 1980s to standardize their products so that they could be used interchangeably or together. The specifications were first published in 1983, and developments since then in digital music have been astounding. MIDI-compatible instruments are equipped with specific hardware for information receiving, transmitting, or both, and are connected to each other by five-pin cables. A precise code has been established that specifies information about musical data such as pitch, note on, note off, channel, key velocity, aftertouch, program change, etc. Through this code, MIDI allows a wide variety of equipment to communicate with and control each other including computers, synthesizers, sequencers, pitch-to-MIDI converters, drum units, and signal processors.

Computers and MIDI devices do what they do because programmers have written lists of instructions, called "programs" or "software," telling the equipment exactly what to do and in what sequence. Educational software programs for music learning divide into five different application categories: tutorial; skill and drill; games; simulation; and utilities. Most older programs concentrate on the first three categories and use closed-format, deductive sys-

Sound board. *Courtesy Temporal Acuity Products.*

tems. That is, they contain a series of stimuli to which children are expected to respond with only one "correct" answer (the lower thinking skills of knowledge, understanding, and application on Bloom's Taxonomy[2]). Tutorial programs are designed to introduce children to new musical concepts and skills. Skill and drill and game programs reinforce learning through repetition. In these programs, children generally are involved with linear progressions of skills or concepts until a predetermined level of mastery is reached.

Simulation programs use open-format, inductive systems in which children simulate actual musical performance, and there is no single "correct" answer (the higher thinking skills of analysis, synthesis, and evaluation on Bloom's Taxonomy). Another type of simulation program is the integrated multimedia software that allows children unstructured exploration of musical compositions, musical representation systems (symbols for pitch, rhythm, form, expression, etc.), and information related to music (composers, cultural and historical influences, etc.).

Utility programs are those that help children and teachers organize and store information or control various output devices. Of the many types of util-

---

[2]Bloom (1956) developed a taxonomy of cognitive skills, which organized thinking processes into six hierarchical levels: knowledge, understanding, application, analysis, synthesis, and evaluation.

ity programs, five are especially useful for musicians: word processing; databases; sequencing; music printing; and multimedia controllers. Word processing and database programs are useful for organizing and communicating ideas about music. Sequencing and music-printing programs organize and communicate actual musical sounds. Multimedia controller programs give children and teachers the capability of organizing and communicating linguistic ideas, visual representations, and musical compositions in the same package.

Some TAIM software in wide use today turn microcomputers into teaching machines for cognitive and/or psychomotor learning. *Note Blaster* and *Pick the Pitch* are examples of programs that reinforce the cognitive skill of naming pitches. The *Pitch Master* single-use computer, illustrated in the opening of this chapter, samples children's singing and reinforces correct pitch input by showing a needle in the "correct zone," awarding points, and sounding a reinforcing tone. The *TAP Master* system teaches rhythm reading and performance from the level of basic beat-maintenance through sophisticated polymetric rhythmic études. Several MIDI programs track actual musical performances, reinforce correct work, and show errors.

In its 1993–94 *Technology Directory*, the Association for Technology in Music Instruction listed 287 software programs whose specific purpose was teaching music concepts and skills. The directory also included many other programs that were not designed specifically for instruction, but could be used as powerful instructional resources. As with any other teaching resource, teachers need to choose TAIM programs based on their overall curriculum goals. Most school districts and states, as well as professional organizations and textbook publishers, have established written curriculum guidelines to define and describe the goals and objectives of music education for children in preschools and in the elementary grades. Music teachers should review these guides and choose only those programs that can teach these skills and concepts better than human teachers. Curriculum guides often divide music learning into a three-way (cubic) matrix with the three axes being: (1) musical elements such as pitch, rhythm, harmony, form, and expression; (2) musical processes such as listening, playing, singing, moving, creating, reading/writing, and valuing; and (3) specific grade or age levels at which skills and concepts should be introduced or refined. Once teachers know what they want to teach, they need to become familiar with the particular software programs available for teaching each skill or concept.

Of special note regarding technology and music curriculum are two outstanding technology-integrated music curricula: the *Music in Education* package available through the Yamaha musical instrument company; and the *Master Musician Music Literacy Curriculum* available through Temporal Acuity Products. In both these systems, the authors have developed a careful sequence of software to take students from music novices to masters. They are both relatively expensive to implement, but have shown impressive results in building music skills, concepts, and attitudes.

Becoming familiar with technology and keeping up with the latest developments can be done in several different ways:

1. Attend college classes or workshops specifically designed to acquaint teachers with many programs and equipment

2. Attend software and equipment demonstration sessions at professional in-services and other conferences

3. Attend demonstrations by technology producers and dealers at conferences or in their plants or stores

4. Obtain demonstration disks through the mail (most companies offer this free service)

5. Read descriptions of technology in the catalogue of theAssociation for Technology in Music Instruction

6. Read descriptions in trade catalogues, such as Temporal Acuity Products's *Music Education Solutions* or Micro Music, Inc.

7. Read software reviews in periodicals such as the *Music Educators Journal*

8. Discuss technology with colleagues who currently use TAIM

9. Enroll in a computer network, such as Internet or Pepper, to research and discuss through e-mail the latest developments in TAIM

Usually, the software chosen will determine the kinds of equipment needed. Sometimes, however, the kind of computer has already been selected by previous teachers or the school district, and teachers will need to confine, at least temporarily, their software choices to the platform(s) available. There are good reasons for using more than one kind of computer, but financial considerations often restrict teachers to one kind.

Table 12.1 presents a short sample list of software, from which teachers might choose to establish a basic music technology library. The list by no means represents all the software available, nor are the particular programs cited necessarily the best for all applications.

There are several other lists given in other books that might be helpful to the novice technology user, including Rudolph's (1984) *Music and the Apple II* and the guidebook, *Integrating Technology into K-12 Music Classroom* (1990), published by the Washington State Superintendent of Public Instruction. The most complete source is the latest edition of the *Technology Directory* of the Association for Technology in Music Instruction (ATMI).

Table 12.1 Selected Computer Software for Teaching Music Skills and Concepts

Skill/Concept	Software	Computer
Rhythm reading and performing	Rhythmacity	IBM
	Courseware II, III	Several
	TAP Master	TAP Master
	Elementary Series	
	Intermediate Series	
	Advanced Series	
	MiBAC Music Lessons	Macintosh
Sight-reading/sight singing	Pitch Master	Pitch Master
	First-Read Series	
	Diatonic Series	
	Music Lab	IBM
Ear training	Toney Listens to Music	Apple II
	Doremi	Apple II
	MiBAC Music Lessons	Macintosh
	Arnold	Apple II
	Melodious Dictator	Apple II
	Harmonious Dictator	Apple II
	Music Lab	IBM
Identifying Written Pitches	Music Made Easy	Several
	Note Blaster	Apple II
	Pick the Pitch	Apple II
	MiBAC Music Lessons	Macintosh
Scales/Key Signatures Harmony	Music Made Easy	Several
	Allvin Basic Musicianship	Apple II
	Courseware III.5	Several
	Swan Key-read	Several
	Key Signature Drills	Apple II
	Theory Sampler	Apple II
	MiBAC Music Lessons	Macintosh
	GUIDO	IBM
	Explorations	Macintosh
Interval Recognition	MiBAC Music Lessons	Macintosh
	Interval Mania	Apple II
	GUIDO	IBM
	Explorations	Macintosh
Error detection/intonation	Courseware III.1	Several
	Sebastian II	Apple II
	Swan Tune-Up	Several
Instrumental Fingering Transposition	Swan Fingerings	Several
	Micro Brass Series	Apple II
	Swan Transpose	Several

298

(continued)

Table 12.1 Continued

Skill/Concept	Software	Computer
Sequencing/printing	Music Printer Plus	IBM
	Finale, Nightengale	Macintosh
	Deluxe Music	
	Construction Set	Several
Technology-integrated music	Yamaha Music in Education	
	Master Musician Music	
	Literacy	
Piano pedagogy	PianoWorks	IBM
	Music in Education	
	Miracle Piano	
Music appreciation/history	Deleware VideoDisks	IBM
	CD-ROMs	Macintosh, IBM

In evaluating music-instruction software, teachers should actually run the programs to determine:

1. What skills or concepts are being taught and what ages would they be suitable for?
2. What procedures and techniques are being used to convey information (i.e., is there simply a lot of text on the screen, or are there interesting graphics and musical illustrations)?
3. What is the quality of the sound (and are extra funds required for special equipment needed, such as a digital-to-analog converter [DAC] or MIDI boards)?
4. How easily do children interact with the program?
5. What kinds of feedback are given to children (especially when they make errors)?
6. Does the program review appropriate information if children respond incorrectly?
7. Can teachers and/or children easily control the scope and sequence of the lessons?
8. What kinds of positive reinforcement are used?
9. Can the software be used in a variety of instructional settings (individual, small group, whole-class)?

10. How expensive is the software relative to the amount of learning material supplied?

Teachers should also evaluate the printed documentation, which comes with most software, in terms of its helpfulness in planning and executing lessons.

Because there are many important considerations to make before purchasing software, teachers are strongly encouraged to write formal evaluations of programs as they go through the review process. A consistent form or database should be used for these evaluations, so that complete information can be collected and compared easily. It is difficult to remember all the details about each piece of software without written evaluations. Table 12.2, adapted by permission from the ATMI Directory, presents a sample evaluation form.

Using Technology to Teach Music

Even in teaching situations where all the curriculum and software/hardware decisions have been made, questions still arise about how technology is actually used in music classrooms. To use technology, most teachers need to make a paradigm shift—a new way of thinking—about music learning and music instruction. Traditional music instruction for children usually includes: (1) grouping for instruction by whole class, with some instruction given in small groups and very little, if any, individual instruction; (2) pacing of instruction at the whole-group level with virtually no individual pacing; (3) when the teacher needs to give special instruction to a section or individual, other children are not actively engaged in learning, which reduces time on task and creates opportunities for behavior problems; (4) individual children are not often tested and given specific feedback about their progress; and (5) TAIM is very rarely used, if at all.

In contrast, instruction with technology has the following characteristics: (1) grouping for instruction is by individual or small group, with only a small amount of time spent in whole-class instruction; (2) most pacing of instruction is at the individual and small-group level; (3) when the teacher gives instruction to some, others are usually productively engaged in learning activities; and (4) individual child responses are tested often and given much corrective feedback. The use of technology allows for individual differences in background, motivation, aptitude, and learning rate.

Many strategies have been developed for organizing and integrating technology instruction into typical elementary general music settings, and each is useful for meeting specific needs. Some teachers send individuals or small groups of children to the media center or computer lab to "graze" randomly in

Table 12.2   Sample Product Evaluation Form for TAIM

Product name: _____

Current version: _____

Product author: _____

Publisher name: _____

Publisher address: _____

_____

_____

_____

Telephone: _____

Contact person: _____

Copyright date: _____

ISBN/ISSN: _____

Cost (individual copies): _____

Cost (multiple copies): _____

Demo disk available/cost: _____

Description of contents: _____

_____

_____

_____

Hardware required (include types of computers): _____

Hardware suggested: _____

Additional software required: _____

Reviews/field test data: _____

_____

_____

_____

Suggested grade/ability level(s): _____

_____

whatever programs interest them at the moment; other teachers have developed more directed and integrated sequences using individualized or cooperative learning settings. Tyler (1949) suggests that "continuity, sequence, and integration" (p. 86) are very important considerations when structuring learning experiences. When several different computer programs are available, children may use them haphazardly, not in a logical sequence that builds from one skill or concept to the next (Adams-Nepote, 1991).

There are some important pedagogical principles to consider when designing strategies for using technology:

1. Decide who will use the technology
2. Sequence learning in small steps
3. Do not isolate children
4. Consider using a Mastery Learning approach

Decide Who Will Use the Technology

Shrader (1970) and Hofstetter (1979) found that high-ability students were least likely to enjoy and learn from drill programs, while low-ability students were the most likely to enjoy and learn from them. Canelos, Murphy, Blombach, and Heck (1980) suggested that CAI drill can be especially effective when used by learners who have not yet acquired good study habits. Kulik, Kulik, and Bangert-Drowns (1985) found CAI to be especially effective at the elementary school level and less so as children grew older. Mc-Greer (1984) supported the use of technology by two distinct populations: students with special interests; and students who need remedial tutoring.

Technology can also be used for entire classrooms to introduce or reinforce musical skills and concepts. Network systems can be used to serve several computers, and effective instruction can also be provided by having an entire class take turns running a program on a single computer (this is easier with a large-screen monitor or a projection panel on an overhead projector). Tutorial programs, videodiscs, and CD-ROMs work well in whole-group situations, much like a film or videotape resource, except children have more control and interact more with computers. For example, the HyperCard application program for Schubert's *Der Erlkönig* can be projected on a large screen, rather than having children crowd around a small computer monitor. Children can control the pace and progression through the HyperCard screen pages (called "stacks") by clicking the mouse when the cursor is over preprogrammed screen areas, called "buttons." Children are able to command the software to play the music, show the story's translation, show visual representations of the three "characters" in the song, display information about the composer, and display the music score and the structure of the composition.

Teachers can also invent game formats for adapting drill or game programs to whole-class reinforcing activities. The *Doremi* program, for example, is an ear-training drill program that plays a major scale, then plays a "mystery note" (a randomly selected note from the major scale) that the children must identify. This software was designed to be used by one or two students working at a computer, but can be adapted for use as a game for the entire class: (1) divide the class into teams of three or four children; (2) have each team send one member to the computer for a turn to select the answer; (3) award three points to the team whose member gets the right answer on the first try, two points for the correct answer on the second try, and one point for the correct answer on the third try; and (4) keep the rest of the class focused on the "game" by giving a bonus point to the first student to show the correct solfège hand sign of the mystery note. The game can be continued over several classes in a "tournament" and a prize awarded to the team earning the most points. In this way, all children learn from the technology at the same time, rather than cycling through TAIM sessions individually or in pairs.

Sequence Learning in Small Steps

Learners prefer well-organized, logically sequenced instruction (Canelos et al., 1980). Bloom (1971) advocates dividing the total curriculum into small, easily learned units that children must master before going on to the next step. Most tutorial and drill programs incorporate these principles within their design, and the music educator also needs to keep these principles in mind when incorporating TAIM into the overall curriculum goals for musical skills and concepts. This can be easily accomplished by matching Student Learning Objectives (SLOs) itemized in curriculum guides with SLOs described in the printed documentation included with most software programs.

Do Not Isolate Children

Try to invent strategies that encourage child-to-child interaction. In the process of working together, children are required to discuss, explain, interpret, demonstrate, relate, generalize, compare, and justify their understandings. Hooper and Hannafin (1988) believe that it is probably unnecessary and unwise to assign a computer to each child individually, because children who explain to others will develop descriptions that also help them in the learning process. In an interview with Brandt (1988), Slavin reports that students working alone on individualized materials often fail, because they no longer received explanations and motivations from qualified teachers. Bloom (1971) strongly advocates cooperative learning strategies. Johnson, Johnson, Holubec, and Roy (1984) believe that increased motivation and greater understanding result from group discussion. This is especially important in music performance groups, which are not simply collections of individuals making music together, but highly integrated groups (Kassner, 1992).

Consider Incorporating Mastery Learning

Mastery Learning is an instructional delivery approach, developed by Bloom (1981), in which the curriculum is divided into small parts and children are allowed to take as long as they need to learn each part to a mastery level as measured by frequent tests. Children who do not achieve mastery in the first exposure to new material are retaught with ancillary materials and approaches, and then retested until they achieve mastery.

Research on mastery learning has demonstrated significantly improved learning of music skills and attitudes toward music learning, increased speed of learning (particularly in low achievers), and quick learning of psychomotor skills (especially with low aptitude children). From their meta-analysis of research in mastery learning, Guskey and Gates (1986) found several main effects of mastery learning:

1. Better student achievement
2. Higher grades
3. Higher standardized test scores
4. Better ability to learn complex and abstract ideas
5. Better ability to apply ideas to new problems
6. Longer retention of ideas
7. More positive attitudes and greater interest in the subject matter
8. Better motivation for further learning

TAIM combined with mastery learning holds children ultimately responsible for the learning and provides opportunities for exchanging machine success with human approval and recognition (children report scores to the teacher, who marks criterion mastery on wall charts).

How to Fund Technology-Assisted Instruction in Music

Several strategies have been used to obtain the money necessary to buy equipment and programs. In some enlightened school districts with adequate funding, teachers are encouraged to buy and use technology. These districts seem to be in the minority, however, and, more often than not, teachers need to be proactive to get their technology needs funded. Many districts have grant money available to teachers who write grant proposals. Teachers new to a district should investigate the grant programs their district promotes. Parent-Teacher Associations, local businesses, and service organizations often will also entertain grant requests. To get money through the grant process, teachers need to include clear information about: (1) what they want to buy; (2) exactly how much the technology will cost; (3) why they want to buy the technology (what can it do); (4) how the technology will fit into the existing curriculum; (5) which children will use the technology; and (6) some technology-use background of the teacher. Some districts or organizations employ people to help write effective grant requests and/or provide forms for this purpose.

Another means of obtaining money for technology is fund-raising projects. This often is the choice of last resort, but may be the only way to get technology in the classroom. Many companies exist to provide goods or services for fund-raising projects, and they advertise widely in educational journals. Teachers need to choose a company with a good reputation, good product that sells itself, and a high return for effort with a minimum of bookkeeping and product management. Be sure to check with the school district to get permission and follow the proper process adopted by the district for fund-raisers.

The Likely Future of Technology for Music Teaching

Technology for teaching music is rapidly expanding and improving. There has been a revolution in the use of technology in the last two decades, and this will undoubtedly see much more expansion and development in the future. Computers have become faster, able to store and manipulate more information, and more able to interact with humans in a variety of ways. Future programs will most likely continue these trends and also become more interactive; that is, they will become more sophisticated in not only stimulating us with high-quality audiovisuals, but respond to our attempts to acquire the skills of music making. Artificial intelligence, digital sampling, and high-definition television, for example, will probably be incorporated in more software as the technology improves and the cost becomes more affordable. Networking throughout the world will become commonplace. Teachers will never reach the end of their learning about new technology, and need to keep themselves informed. Technology cannot replace the music teacher, because technology is only the method of communication, not the creative, thinking, musical force that can be provided only by humans. Technology can, however, provide new, more powerful means of support for music educators and children.

Questions

1. Give the terms from which the following acronyms are coined: TAIM, CAIM, CPU, RAM, ROM, CD-ROM, MIDI.

2. Name the five types of software programs.

3. List as many sources as you can from which to learn more about technology for music teaching (at least five).

4. Circle the letters of the statements that are NOT true regarding TAIM: (a) children work at their own pace; (b) computer programs patiently repeat drills as many times as needed; (c) computers will probably replace human teachers within twenty years; (d) open-ended technology (such as CD-ROMs and videodiscs) allow children to explore randomly a vast amount of musical information; (e) a single computer should never be used to instruct an entire class; and (f) because it is so complicated, teachers should begin using technology in their classrooms only after they understand it completely.

5. Visit a music classroom where technology is being used; ask the teacher and children what they like about using technology, what they don't like, and how effective they think it is for music instruction.

6. Visit a music store that sells the latest electronic music equipment. List in categories that most interest you the equipment available for music instruction. Establish an organized notebook of descriptive (promotional) materials and price lists.

7. Discuss the rationale for combining cooperative learning techniques with TAIM.

8. Discuss the rationale for combining mastery learning techniques with TAIM.

9. Discuss the important considerations that a teacher must think about when evaluating software.

10. Imagine you are in an interview for a music teaching job and the principal informs you that the district has just passed a technology levy that will provide matching funds for money raised by each building. The principal desires to improve instruction in his or her building by getting as many of these matching funds as possible. The prospective employee must be knowledgeable about technology, and the principal asks you to explain how you will help raise funds for and use technology in your music instruction. Write an outline of ideas for your response (include your past experiences with technology, reasons why you think technology is important, what technology you would like to purchase and use first, how you will incorporate technology into your curriculum, and your plans for earning the money for matching funds).

References

ADAMS-NEPOTE, S. 1991. Enhancing mastery learning with instructional technologies. *Outcomes, 10*(3), 17–20.

ALLVIN, R. L. (1985). *Basic musicianship: An introduction to music fundamentals with computer assistance,* computer program. Belmont, CA: Wadsworth Publishing.

BENWARD, B., & WILLIAMS, D. B. (1985). *Doremi,* computer program. Bellevue, WA: Temporal Acuity Products.

BLOOM, B. S. (Ed.). (1956). *Taxonomy of educational objectives.* New York: David McKay.

————. (1971). Mastery learning and its implications for curriculum development. In E. W. Eisner (Ed.), *Confronting curriculum reform.* New York: Little, Brown and Company.

————. (1981). *All our children learning: A primer for parents, teachers, and other educators.* New York: McGraw-Hill.

BRANDT, R. (1988). On research and school organization: A conversation with Bob Slavin. *Educational Leadership, 46*(2), 22–29.

CANELOS, J. J., MURPHY, B. A., BLOMBACH, A. K., & HECK, W. C. (1980). Evaluation of three types of instructional strategy for learner acquisition of intervals. *Journal of Research in Music Education, 28*(4), 243–49.

ELLINGER, J. (1991). *MiBAC Music Lessons,* computer program. Northfield, MN: MiBAC Music Software.

FELDSTEIN, S. (1984). *Music Made Easy,* computer program. Sherman Oaks, CA: Alfred Publishing.

GUSKEY, T. R., & GATES, S. L. (1986). Synthesis of research on the effects of mastery learning in elementary and secondary classrooms. *Educational Leadership, 43*(8), 73–80.

HIGGINS, W. (1992). Technology. In R. Colwell (Ed.), *Handbook of research on music teaching and learning.* New York: Schirmer Books.

HOFSTETTER, F. (1988). *Note Blaster,* computer program. Bellevue, WA: Temporal Acuity Products.

HOFSTETTER, F. T. (1979). Evaluation of a competency-based approach to teaching aural interval identification. *Journal of Research in Music Education, 27*(4), 201–213.

HOOPER, S., & HANNAFIN, M. J. (1988). *Cooperative learning at the computer: Ability based strategies for implementation.* New Orleans: Association for Educational Communications and Technology. (ERIC Document Reproduction Service No. ED 295-647).

HyperCard, computer program. (1992). Santa Clara, CA: Claris.

JOHNSON, D. W., JOHNSON, R. T., HOLUBEC, E. J., & ROY, P. (1984). *Circles of*

Learning. Washington, DC.: Association for Supervision and Curriculum Development.

KASSNER, K. (1992). Effects of computer-assisted instruction in a mastery learning/cooperative learning setting on the playing abilities and attitudes of beginning band students. Doctoral dissertation, University of Oregon, 1992.

KOOZIN, T., & JACOBSON, D. (In press). *Der Erlkoenig*. HyperStack computer program. Grand Forks, ND: University of North Dakota.

MCGREER, D. M. (1984). The research literature in computer-assisted instruction. *Update: The Applications of Research in Music Education, 3*(1), 12–15.

MOORE, B. R. (1985). *Pick the pitch*, computer program. Bellevue, WA: Temporal Acuity Products.

MURPHY, B. (Ed.). (1993). *Technology directory*. East Lansing, MI: Association for Technology in Music Instruction.

RUDOLPH, T. (1984). *Music and the Apple II*. Drexel Hill, PA: Unsinn Publication.

———. (1993). *Teaching music with technology*. Champaign, IL: Electronic Courseware Systems.

SHRADER, D. L. (1970). An aural approach to rhythmic sight reading based upon principles of programmed learning, utilizing a stereo-tape teaching machine. Doctoral dissertation, University of Oregon, 1970. *Dissertation Abstracts International, 31*, 2426A. (University Microfilms No. 70-21576).

———. (1974). *Tap Master*, computer program. Bellevue, WA: Temporal Acuity Products.

SKINNER, B. F. (1968). *The technology of teaching*. New York: Appleton-Century-Crofts.

SMALL, D., project coordinator. (1990). *Integrating technology into the K-12 music classroom*. Olympia, WA: Superintendent of Public Instruction.

SWAN, P. D. (1989). *Swan Fingerings*, computer program. Provo, UT: Swan Software for the Arts.

———. (1989). *Tune-Up!*, computer program. Provo, UT: Swan Software for the Arts.

THOMAS, R. B. (1985). *Pitch Master*, computer program. Bellevue, WA: Temporal Acuity Products.

————. (1991). Musical fluency: MMCP and today's curriculum. *Music Educators Journal*, *78*(4), 26–29.

TYLER, R. W. (1949). *Basic principles of curriculum and instruction*. Chicago: The University of Chicago.

Catalogs

Micro Music. Atlanta, GA: Micro Music.

Music Education Solutions. Bellevue, WA: Temporal Acuity Products.

Journals

Electronic Musician. 6400 Hollis Street, #12, Emeryville, CA 94608

13

Music, Multiculturalism, and Children

Children come in many sizes, shapes, hues, and views. The music they know well and can perform derives from the rich cultural traditions of their homes and ethnic communities. Mikael hums the songs of his grandmother's Russian childhood. Maisa sings the way she does with her Norwegian relatives, adding harmonies in parallel fourths and fifths to the melodies she hears. Ramón comes to school with the tunes of his uncle's Mexican mariachi band in his ears, with the Spanish words at the tip of his tongue. Luis claps and pats the sophisticated syncopations of Puerto Rican claves and congas easily, never missing a moment in time. Shirelle sways as she sings, because "that's the way it's done" in the gospel choir in which she performs on Sundays. Bisi sings a duple-metered melody while clapping in three, performing with ease the typical cross-rhythm of a Nigerian game song. With encouragement, Jarenchai performs the graceful ramvong dance of Laos, Li-Chen demonstrates the ribbon dance of China, Joseph steps the circle dance of the Sioux, and Saroda communicates through the gestural language of the South Indian classical dance, the Bharata Natyam. A gathering of children like Mikael, Maisa, Ramón, Luis, Shirelle, Bisi, Jarenchai, Li-Chen, Joseph, and Saroda is an occasion for a microcosmic classroom experience, a reflection of the world's multiethnic variety.

The circle of uniform and evenly measured three-by-three foot carpet squares often found in a school music classroom belies the rich cultural diversity of American schools and society. Diversity is apparent in the faces of children in schools, on playgrounds, and in neighborhoods. It is apparent in the various perceptions of the world they share, in their languages, dialects, and variations of English, in the holidays they celebrate, and in the customs they choose to share with their friends and schoolmates. The cultural traditions of so many varieties of children do not melt into some all-American "people-pot." Rather, the classroom is like the image of a quickly changing multiethnic society: a mosaic of many colored tiles that comprise the new America.

Should current trends in immigration and birth rates in the United States persist, by the turn of the century our population will be 14 percent African-Americans, 12 percent Hispanic or Latin Americans, 5 percent Asian-Americans, 1 percent Native Americans, with the remaining two thirds of European heritage (1990 U.S. Census Report). Projections are that by 2020, the number of U.S. residents who are nonwhite or Hispanic will have more than doubled to about one third of the American people, while the white population will not be increasing at all. By midcentury, the "average American" will trace his or her roots to Africa, Asia, the Hispanic world, the Pacific Islands, and the Middle East—almost anywhere but Caucasian Europe. Americans are living in a fast-changing society, with the statistical charts on race and ethnicity turning upside down and inside out.

Definitions

If schools are the vehicles through which children are presented with the knowledge and values of a given nation, then the music program should offer to children: (1) opportunities to experience a broad sampling of the world's musical traditions; and (2) more thorough-going journeys into selected musical cultures. While this stance seems logical enough, sometimes the prospects of teaching music from a multicultural perspective may seem overwhelming. One reason for this is the all-encompassing definition of multicultural education, which includes the study of groups distinguished not only by race or ethnic origin, but technically also the music of people of different ages, social classes, genders, religions, lifestyles, and exceptionalities (Banks, 1992). Within this framework, the tasks of multicultural music education are enormously broad, and perhaps too comprehensive to be applied to the actual curricular changes that are occurring.

"Multiethnic" is a label applied to curricular developments that focus exclusively on the study of groups distinguished by ethnic origin. Music programs that focus in depth on musical styles of a group of people united by national or ethnic origin, such as the music of the Chinese, Filipinos, Nigerians, and Brazilians, are referred to by the rubric "multiethnic music education." While "multicultural" is the term featured prominently in curric-

Cambodian children dancing in costume.

ulum and instruction materials, "multiethnic" refers more directly to ethnicity rather than age, social class, gender, or other issues.

The term multiethnic suggests an intensive study of music from more than one ethnic group. Fourth-grade children who are learning to sing Japanese and Chinese songs, to listen analytically to the music of the Japanese koto and the Chinese zheng (zithers), and to play Japanese shakuhachi and Chinese di (flutes) melodies on recorders, are reaping the benefits of a multiethnic curriculum. First-grade children who are learning the melodies, movements, and functions of singing games from Zimbabwe and Venezuela are also being served a multiethnic-flavored music curriculum. Even an intensive study of one new and less familiar musical culture begins to approach the mission of multiethnic music education, because children are already making subconscious comparisons of their "mother-tongue music" acquired in their homes with the music of the teacher's choice. The intent of multiethnic music education is, in addition to the provision of a variety of musical experiences (singing, listening, moving, playing instruments, and creating), to offer children an understanding of how the music reflects people's lifestyles and ways of thinking across cultural boundaries.

Another curricular concept in music education programs for children is "world music education." As distinguished from multiethnic music education, world music education features the study of musical components as they are treated in various musical styles across the world. For example, preschool children may learn to clap or step the steady pulse to the music of an African-American blues song, a Chinese luogu (percussion ensemble), an Indonesian gamelan piece, and a Latino salsa number. Third-grade children may learn about timbre by listening to fiddles and musical bows from Ireland, Pakistan, Malawi, Cambodia, and Mexico. Sixth-grade children may come to understand syncopation as a prominent characteristic in the music of Ghana, Cuba, China, and African-American gospel music. Like the term multiethnic, world music education suggests another type of comparative approach to music. Unlike multiethnic music education, world music education is concerned with cross-cultural comparisons that span a great many musical styles, rather than concentrating more narrowly and more deeply on a smaller selection of ethnic groups. World music education may also allow less contextualization of musical experiences, as the emphasis is placed on more extensive (rather than intensive) musical (rather than cultural) experiences.

Which is best: to teach a small selection of musical traditions thoroughly, as in the case of multiethnic music education, or to teach music conceptually through cross-cultural examples, as in the case of world music education? There may be room for both within the design of musical experiences for children. In the scope of a year's plan, children can learn aspects of melody, rhythm, timbre, texture, and form by engaging in active listening to many samples of the world's musical styles and genres. Just as the examples of a musical concept can be historically broad—from the music of Monteverdi through Messiaen—they can also be culturally broad, chosen from Bulgaria, Bali, and Brazil, for example. Within the same year, a series of lessons on one musical tradition or genre—for example, dance music of the Pueblo Indians of New Mexico and/or the Macedonians of Yugoslavia—can lead children into a knowledge of people and their musical ways of thinking. Side-by-side in a single school year, children can experience the best of both musical and multiethnic understanding. There is no limit for ways in which many musical styles can be brought to children to develop their understanding of music.

One thing is certain, as products of a multiethnic and multiracial society, children must be led to listen and to respond to the aesthetic components and cultural meanings of more than a single musical tradition. They are living in a less-homogenized world than any earlier generation, one that demands their understanding of many people. Ideally, through their musical experiences sensing its ebbs and flows, learning its logical structures, and feeling its power, children may come to understand not only the music, but also the music makers. They may learn to take note of not only the differences among people and their musical expressions, but also the similarities that transcend all people.

Uncertainties in Teaching "New" Musical Styles

There are misgivings, uncertainties, and well-founded questions to consider in offering a broader palette of musical "colors" and styles. Consider the often quoted statements both for and against offering children the musics of many cultures.

"My kids are not ethnic; they are white." In fact, everyone is ethnic, including European-Americans. All music is ethnic, too, including the masterworks of Mozart and Mahler, of Charles Ives and Paul Simon. Each song and instrumental piece manifests the characteristic musical components of the culture from which it derives. Even those rare teachers who still teach homogeneous groups of children whose ancestors arrived from Europe generations ago know that those children will venture beyond their neighborhoods. They will have the opportunity to associate with people in diverse ethnic communities in an increasingly pluralistic American society. It may be that by knowing about other ethnic groups' values, their traditions, and their artistic and musical expressions, children will also come to know the world's people better.

"My schedule is too packed to include multiethnic music." According to definitions of multiethnic and world music education, it may be unnecessary to offer additional classes to explore a variety of music traditions. Rather, teachers can inject the new or less-familiar musics into their lessons to illustrate musical elements.

Musical experiences intended to bring about multiethnic understanding may also require new ways of teaching across the curriculum. Teachers of music, art, and classroom subjects can team together to develop monthly and quarterly units on a given country, cultural region, or ethnic group. Colloquial expressions can be spoken, customs can be practiced, stories can be told, read, and re-enacted, visual arts and crafts can be viewed and copied, songs can be sung, and traditional instrumental pieces and dances can be performed. In a collaborative and thorough way, music teachers can join together with others to enlighten children about the "worlds" of people and their cultural expressions.

"I don't know the languages of the foreign songs." Although foreign-language songs challenge teachers and children, the cultural experience can be very powerful. There is an added dimension when the original language of a song intermingles with the song's rhythm and melody, rather than singing an English translation. Music teachers whose ears are fine-tuned to discriminate fractional sound variations can often easily learn the phonemes of new languages as well. A foreign-language song is best learned by listening—at home, in the car, and at school—with the ears perceiving the music and language as one. Once it is aurally channeled and internalized, there is a growing confidence in transmitting the song to children. The song becomes a part of the listener's and singer's repertoire.

Children can also be initiated to a musical culture through music listening experiences, movement, and opportunities to play instruments of the culture. Listening can be active, engaging children to gesture the rise and fall of a Japanese shakuhachi (flute) melody, or to snap, clap, pat, and stamp the ostinato of a Cuban bomba drum. Basic circle and line dances of the Middle East, Eastern Europe, and Native American cultures can be performed by young children as early as first or second grade. Children can play West African polyrhythms on various nonpitched percussion instruments, and selected melodies from many cultures on recorders. They can play the melodies and polyphonic textures of selected Southeast Asian and sub-Saharan African music on xylophones, if in a somewhat modified manner. Occasionally, listening, movement, and instrumental performance can be combined with songs, a four-dimensional experience for children.

The Musically Competent Teacher

Increasingly, courses within collegiate music and teacher education programs expose students to musical styles beyond Western European art music. Prospective teachers can gain initial acquaintance with musical cultures through one or more broad-based world music survey courses, and can follow that with specialized seminars for the in-depth study of the musics of African, Asian, European, Latin American, Native American, Australian and Pacific Island cultures. Although these may be offered only as elective or optional courses in collegiate music programs, they are nonetheless invaluable for teaching music to children from multiethnic and global perspectives.

In addition to full-fledged courses, workshops are also occasions for learning the musics of other cultures. These workshops are commonly offered through summer-school programs by musicians from various traditions, by ethnomusicologists with considerable study of one or more musical cultures, and by music educators with a commitment to multiethnic education. For those who cannot squeeze additional courses into their undergraduate program, these workshops can be taken during the summer interim period soon after teaching certification is completed. In addition to courses and workshops, musicians in the community may offer lessons on traditional instruments and singing styles for a moderate fee.

Many teachers have chosen to learn to play or sing music other than Western European art music. Those who are competent in a musical tradition or style are the ones who are best able to teach it accurately and easily. The musical competence they achieve through specialized training includes aural competence, or the ability to listen to and understand the structural components of a musical style. Ideally, musically competent teachers also attain a measure of performance proficiency, vocally or on an instrument. Children are fascinated with the music that is performed live for them, and are eager for opportunities to "play" instruments or sing in the style of a confident performer. When fundamental instrumental techniques and pieces can be demonstrated by the performing teacher, and when songs can be sung using their original language and appropriate vocal timbre and inflections, the music becomes more appealing to children. The performing teacher also gains credibility in the children's eyes.

Gaining proficiency within a musical tradition requires time and effort. Just as aural and performance competence in Western European art music requires many years of listening, reading, and practice, it is also the case in knowing well the music of the Zulu of South Africa, the Han Chinese, the Sephardic Jews of Spain, or African-Americans. Those who take the time to sing or study an instrument of a "favorite" other culture, and then build a school or personal library of recordings, writings, and videotapes on the music and culture, are well on their way to gaining proficiency within that tradition. By becoming musically competent in a style, they have the skills, knowledge, enthusiasm, and confidence for presenting it to children.

Teachers of music usually become competent in Western European art music through their training, but they can also progress to the study of another musical culture. Those with aural and performance competence in more than one music are said to be "bimusical"; it is this quality that approaches the goals of bicultural and eventually multiethnic (multicultural) education. A modified bimusicality is a goal to be achieved in children as well, so that they can listen to and perform the music of more than one culture. Becoming musically competent in more than one tradition may develop an appreciation for the complexities of other musics, as well as the recognition of their validity and logic. Of course, performance proficiency is not necessary for selecting examples of a pentatonic piece, a triple-metered song, or a polyrhythmic texture from a variety of musical traditions (a curricular tactic featured in world music education). Still, any attempt to know musical traditions more than superficially will excite both teachers and their children.

New Repertoire for Familiar Pedagogies

Teaching music from the perspectives of multiethnic or world music education does not mean negating or discarding the old or the well-established pedagogical approaches. Techniques such as speech rhythms, rhythmic syllables,

Young child playing West African shekere. *Photo by Patricia Shehan Campbell.*

movable do, stem notation, melodic mapping, instrumental performance, listening grids and call charts, part-singing, eurhythmic movement, and improvisation may be readily used in teaching nearly all music traditions. In fact, three of the classic methods associated with teaching music to children may find new freedom in the repertoire that is introduced.

Orff-Schulwerk provides children with experiences that are as social as they are musical. Many of the world's music traditions beautifully suit its components. Many music traditions are inseparable from poetry, stories, and movement, because their musical events are comprehensive and integrated. The music of West African cultures such as the Ibo and the Yoruba offer call-and-response songs, layered polyrhythmic compositions on nonpitched percussion instruments, stories replete with music in choral response, and movement created to follow the repeating and contrasting phrases. The xylophone cultures of Indonesia, Cambodia, Laos, and Thailand, much of sub-Saharan Africa, and some Latin American-Caribbean cultures are natural repositories of music that can be performed on Orff's familiar xylophones and metallophones. The possibilities for exploring the world's musical styles through one or several of Orff's components are rich, readily available, and ripe for experimentation.

Proponents of the Hungarian approach that Kodály inspired consider folk and traditional music to be at the heart of music instruction. Unadulterated folk music is alive and well in every culture and applicable to children's learning of both music and their national heritage. The child-centered Kodály sequence for teaching melodic and rhythmic concepts can extend to many of the world's musics. Indeed, transfer of the tools of the method—movable do, rhythmic syllables, hand signs, and the shorthand notation of stems and solfège initials—from Hungarian to Anglo- and African-American songs occurred as early as the 1960s. Given the goal of the Kodály approach to foster musical and cultural understanding, such tools could transfer to the traditional and art music of Asian-, African-, Latin-, and Native-American cultures as well. The musical vocabulary used by a culture in its children's songs, folk and folk dance music, and instrumental and choral works may be better understood through the application of Kodály techniques.

If rhythm is the primary element of almost all music, and the source for musical rhythms is contained within the natural movements of the body, then the techniques of the Dalcroze approach should be suited to the development of a thorough understanding of music from many cultures. The eurhythmics techniques of "follow," "quick reaction," and "canon" can apply aptly to styles as diverse as the rhythmically dynamic Jamaican soca (soul calypso) style and the rhythmically subtle Japanese koto concert repertoire.

Walking the pulse, conducting the meter, and changing directions as each new phrase appears are Dalcrozian responses for music of any style, period, or form. When an unfamiliar selection from a little-known tradition becomes the stimulus for movement, the challenge to respond correctly to a different but equally logical musical structure is considerable. The reward, however, is greater intimacy through natural body movements that express musical understanding. The Dalcroze approach may provide the difference between simple exposure to, and integral, intensive experience of, the world's musics.

The application of classic pedagogical techniques to a new repertoire of music is an appropriate balance for achieving the aims of a multicultural music education. Like Orff, Kodály, and Dalcroze, other approaches also can serve as frameworks for the development of musical and multicultural understanding: the eight-step learning sequence of Edwin E. Gordon; the perception, performance, and creativity processes of MMCP; and the integration of performance with the study of theory and literature as espoused in Comprehensive Musicianship. Whatever the approach, possibilities exist for infusing a greater variety of music into classes for children.

The Aural/Oral Transmission Process

One of the marks of Western thinking is the tendency to emphasize the end, or product, rather than the ways and means, or process, by which the product is achieved. Children can be guided to bring music they study to concert-level perfection in their performance, but product-oriented instruction without attention to process is only half the musical and cultural experience. The emphasis on *how* music and music learning evolves is central to valid experiences for children in the various musical styles the world can offer them.

An emphasis on process also distinguishes many of the world's great music traditions: the classical music of India; the African-American gospel song; the gamelan music of Java; the Chopi (Mozambican) xylophone and drum ensemble; the Bulgarian polyphonic song; the rock, reggae, and rap music of North America; and the siku (panpipe) music of the Bolivian Andes. While musicians strive for a finished musical work in any tradition, their interaction with each other and with the musical components in the process of learning and rehearsing together is critical in defining both the music and the musical culture.

If authenticity is to be taken seriously, the transmission of much of the world's popular, traditional, and even art music can only be delivered orally—as it can only be received aurally. Notation, a marvelous technological invention, is not pervasive, nor can it replace direct contact with the musical sound. Teachers and children can best become familiar with unfamiliar music through listening, the most direct route.

How then should the teaching of the world's musics proceed? The transmission process by which the teacher can facilitate both musical and multiethnic understanding involves familiar teaching and learning practices. The use of teacher modeling, student imitation, and exploration and improvisation are important components of the transmission of music in many cultures, just as they are often integral to any well-planned lesson. When a traditional song or instrumental piece is transferred from a listening mode into the realm of performance, an aural/oral delivery system can be easily applied. The teacher as transmitter of a musical piece owes it to the tradition to maintain the authenticity of the transmission process as well as of the finished musical product. Notational literacy is an important goal of music instruction, but for achieving the goals of cultural literacy and understanding, the oral/aural process by which music is taught and learned may temporarily override the more traditional curricular objectives. See Campbell (1991) for further discussion of classroom teaching in light of world music transmission systems.

Children performing in an African drumming ensemble.

Curricular Design

Many established curricular programs are undergoing revitalization to meet the needs of children growing up in a changing American society. Education in social studies, language arts, math, sciences, and the arts is becoming more inclusive of African-American, Asian-American, Latin-American, and Native-American cultures. Music is no exception; a study of textbooks over the past few decades underscores the tremendous leap the profession has taken to teach a broader variety of musical styles that are more fairly represented as they are also more authentically presented. Curricular change comes slowly, however, and both the revision of pedagogical materials and the infusion of a more comprehensive perspective on music and music making into classes for children take the time, effort, and creativity of the teacher.

In the pioneering efforts to achieve the curricular goals of multiethnic music education and world music education, there are several important determinants to be considered: (1) Many of the instructional materials, and the longer-range curricular plans, are not written down, so that they must be invented through the teacher's own cultural immersion, musicality, and knowledge of how children learn; (2) An understanding of children's learning styles and attitudes can guide the teacher in designing a curriculum that provides active participation in music-making experiences along with initial exposure to selections of a culture's music; and (3) Arrangements with members of particular ethnic communities to sing their traditional songs, play folk instruments, and tell traditional tales can provide children with the human interaction so vital in understanding music and culture. These considerations can be supported, although not replaced, by the recorded, filmed, and printed materials that are becoming available, so that children become more broadly experienced in the musics of many cultures.

Table 13.1 offers questions as a guide to choosing recorded and printed music that brings the world of music to children. Both listening and performance experiences in a variety of music traditions can be selected in accordance with these principles. Affirmative responses to these questions indicate that the teacher's selection is a probably a wise one.

The design of an all-inclusive music curriculum can take several directions. Multiethnic music education is likely to be packaged within a curricular unit of several weeks, a month, two months, or longer, and will feature a variety of experiences in the music of a selected culture or country. In the larger realm of year-long curriculum design, the intensive study of one musical culture can lead to the study of further cultures (including the music of the teacher's training, or the "mother tongue music" of the teacher or of the ma-

Table 13.1   Guide to Authenticity in the Selection of Music*

1. Is the recorded music performed by a musician from within the culture? Is the printed music notated, transcribed, and/or attributed to a musician from within the culture? Is a scholar with training and experience within the culture involved in the recording or notating of the score?

2. Are notated instrumental pieces characteristic of the musical style, rather than arrangements for instruments outside the tradition?

3. If a song contains lyrics, are they in the original language? Is it accompanied by a guide to its pronunciation? Is an English translation provided? Is it literal, or amended to "fit" the melodic rhythm?

4. If a song involves a game, dance, or movement, are the instructions clear for how to perform it? Is there a photograph, a diagram, an illustration, and/or a clear outline of how to perform the game, dance, or movement?

5. Is there a recorded version of the song or instrumental piece to be performed, so that the "real" music can be heard, used as a model, and later compared to the children's version?

6. Is a cultural context provided for the music? Are there accompanying notes or a book to offer a description of the culture—values, customs, historical, geographic, and economic issues that may add to an understanding of the music? What is known of the function and meaning of the music to the people who make it?

*Adapted from Judith Cook Tucker

jority of the children within the classroom or school). The phrase "multi-ethnic music education" suggests that more than a single musical culture will be explored, and that comparisons will be made among several musical cultures.

In a study of China's music, for example, a unit may begin with samples of instrumental sounds, followed by exposure to the appearance and sound production capacities of the huqin (fiddle), pipa (lute), zheng (zither), di (flute), and luogu (drum and gong ensemble) through live demonstration or videotapes. The unit may unfold to include vocal music, with opportunities to perform several traditional children's songs and chants, and to view videotapes of the premiere Chinese performing art, Peking Opera. Maps, slides, transparencies, posters, and photographs of China, and its people, places, and paintings can provide a cultural context for the music, along with occasions for reading Chinese traditional poetry and folktales. With ample experiences in listening analytically to Chinese music, children can be guided to create music in the "Chinese style," using recorders, cymbals, gongs, and drums to render pentatonic melodies with syncopated rhythms in duple meter. Table 13.2 presents a calendar of events in a study unit on Chinese music for children in the intermediate grades, to provide one of several pathways to realizing the goals of multiethnic music education.

In designing lessons that incorporate the goals of world music education, the teacher may choose from among several pathways. The "musical components" avenue was highlighted in the earlier definition of world music as a curricular concept, where cross-cultural comparisons are made regarding specific aspects of melody, rhythm, timbre, texture, and form. The "music material" approach features a study of similar musical instruments across cultures, for example, the incidence of lutes in Europe, Asia, and the Middle East, or the spread of bamboo and bronze instruments in Southeast Asia. Still another approach is "parallel genres," the study of theater, dance, orchestral, wedding, or opera musics (to give a few examples) in a variety of cultures. Table 13.3 presents examples of these directions in world music education for children of various ages and grade levels. Note that Western European art music is not abandoned in these approaches, because it is one of the important world music traditions.

There are many resources available for use in teaching the world's musical traditions. Community resources, including traditional performing artists, are rich and waiting to be tapped for assembly programs, long-term residencies, and contractual teaching. Readers may wish to collect a set of ethnomusicology references, including books by Malm (1977) on Asian music, Nettl (1991) on European, African, and Latin American musics, and May (1982), Nettl, Capwell, Bohlman, Wong, and Turino (1992), Titon (1992), and Fowler (1994) on these and other selected world musical traditions. Lessons for children are found in books by Anderson and Campbell (1989) and

Table 13.2 Multiethnic Music Education: Calendar for Chinese Music Unit for Fourth Graders

	Weekly Class Meetings: Two at thirty minutes each (Note that suggestions are oriented toward student rather than teacher behaviors)

Lesson One	*Enter class while listening to Chinese music
	Listen to tape of Chinese instrumental music selections
	    1. How do you play these instruments?
	    2. What do these instruments look like?
	See illustrations (photos, slides) of instruments
	Find China on a map; discuss geography
	*Depart class while listening to Chinese music

Lesson Two	Match listening samples to illustrations of instruments (huqin, pipa, zheng, di) Play "Jasmine Flowers of the Sixth Moon" (Liuyue Moli) on recorder Read and discuss text of "Jasmine Flowers" Sing "Jasmine Flowers" See photos of China's people and places Discuss lifestyles of people in China
Lesson Three	Review by identifying instruments by sight and sound Review "Jasmine Flowers" on recorder Add woodblock and bells on "Jasmine Flowers" Match listening samples of illustrations of instruments (luogu ensemble of gongs, cymbals, drums) Play luogu parts for "The Flower Drum Song" (Huagu Ge) See videotape clip of Chinese instruments
Lesson Four	Review luogu parts for "The Flower Drum Song" Sing (or play on recorders) "The Flower Drum Song" Sing and add luogu parts for "The Flower Drum Song" See photos of Chinese festivals; describe festivals Review "Jasmine Flowers" for recorder, woodblock, bells

Lesson Five	Listen to tape of Chinese instrumental musical selections (presented in first lesson)
	    1. Can you tap the steady pulse?
	    2. What is the meter? [duple]
	    3. Can you hum the melody?
	    4. How many pitches are there? [five]
	Sing "Jasmine Flowers" and "The Flower Drum Song"
	Repeat questions 1–4; summarize meter/melody concepts
	Tell the Chinese folktale "Money Makes Cares"

Lesson Six	Watch videotape clip of Peking Opera Review "The Flower Drum Song" with luogu Review "Jasmine Flowers" for recorder, woodblock, bells

(continued)

Table 13.2 Continued

　　　　　1. Do you hear uneven syncopated rhythms?
　　　　　2. Can you clap them as you sing the songs?
　　　　Discuss syncopated rhythms, pentatonic melodies, and duple
　　　　　meter as characteristic of Chinese music
　　　　Review/retell the Chinese folktale "Money Makes Cares"

Lesson Seven　Review characteristics of Chinese music
　　　　Review tale of "Money Makes Cares"
　　　　Children are assigned to groups to prepare
　　　　　1. narration of tale
　　　　　2. dramatization of tale
　　　　　3. creation of incidental instrumental music for tale (on record-
　　　　　　ers, gongs, drums, woodblock, bells)
　　　　　4. performance of "Jasmine Flowers" and "Flower Drum Song"
　　　　　　for inclusion in tale

Feng Yang Song

(continued)

Table 13.2   Continued

Jasmine Flowers of the Sixth Moon (Liuyue Moli)

| Lak | gei — | mo | li — | jin | jian — | shui. | Long | gun — | si(n) | zui — |
| Lahk | gay — | moh | lee — | jin | john — | shwee. | Long | gun — | see(n) | zwee — |

| jin — | go | zhui. | Ho | hui | lan — | die — | xien — | xiang — |
| jin — | goh | zhwee. | Hoh | hwee | lan — | dee — | zhehn — | zhahng — |

| dui — | Xin | bin(n) | mou — | gun | xiung — | ka | kui. |
| dwee — | zhin | bihn | moo — | gun | zhung — | kah | kwee. |

Lesson Eight	Rehearse performance project in individual groups
Lesson Nine	Continue rehearsal
	Integrate groups into performance/production of tale
Lesson Ten	Perform tale
	Teacher-directed evaluation to determine children's understanding of Chinese music/culture

*All classes start and close with the sounds of Chinese traditional music
Sources: Anderson & Campbell. (1989), "Jasmine Flowers of the Sixth Moon"; Cole, (1982), "Money Makes Cares"; Han & Campbell, (1992), "The Flower Drum Song" and "Jasmine Flowers"; and JVC, (1989) China.

Dunbar-Hall and Hodge (1991). Books accompanied by recordings of children's songs from various world cultures include collections by Campbell, McCullough-Brabson, and Tucker (1994), East (1989), and Vanaver (1990). Recordings are plentiful, and those on the Smithsonian/Folkways, Nonesuch, Lyrichord, Monitor, and Rounder labels are among the most accessible. Ethnic-flavored instruments and a host of videocassettes and films complete the basic package of instructional materials for delivering a quality program of world music to children.

Many Musical Worlds

Multiculturalism is a big word and a broad concept, but certainly, the objectives of multicultural education can be at least partially met through children's

Table 13.3   Directions in World Music Education

Grade: Any   Suggested Listening or Song Experience

Musical Concepts

   Triple Meter   Korea: "Ahrirang." *JVC World Sounds.* JVC 1009.
                             Austria: Mozart, Symphony 40, K 440, Movement 3.
                             Sweden: "Vals from Orso." *Folk Fiddling from Sweden.*
                             Nonesuch 72033.

Tritonic Melody

   (d, m, s)   Hopi, Native American: "Mos', Mos'!"

Zimbabwe: "Sorida."

(continued)

Table 13.3 Continued

(s, l, t) Japan: "Yuyake"

Yu - ya - ke   ko - ya - ke   A - shi-ta ten - ki - ni   na ____ re!
[Yoo - yah - keh   koh - yah - keh   Ah - sheetah ten - ke - ne   nah ____ reh]

Cambodia: "Leak Kanseng"

Leak   kan - seng   chma kaim   keng   oh   long   oh   long
[Lee ahk   kahn sahng   chmah kahm   kehng   oh   long   oh   long]

Syncopation	Ghana: "Chalala Eh" and "Wateh Eh." *Mustapha Tetty Addy: Master Drummer from Ghana.* Lyrichord 7250.
	China: "The Hero's Defeat." *China's Classical Masterpieces.* Lyrichord 7182.
	Cuba: "A Los Rumberos de Belen." *Sabroso! Havana Hits.* Virgin/Earthworks 91312.
Music Material	
Lute	'Ud (Egypt, the Middle East). *Music in the World of Islam.* Tangent 131-136.
	Sitar (India). *The Sounds of India: Ravi Shankar.* Columbia 9296.
	Shamisen (Japan). *Japan: Kabuki and Other Traditional Music.* Nonesuch 72084.
	Pipa (China). *Floating Petals, Wild Geese, The Moon on High: Music of the Chinese Pipa.* Nonesuch 72085.
Bronzes in Southeast Asia	Balinese metallophones/gongs. Music from the Morning of the World. Nonesuch 72015.
	Javanese metallophones/gongs. *Javanese Court Gamelan, Vols. 1–3.* Nonesuch 72044, 72074, 72083.
	Cambodian metallophones. *Silent Temples, Songful Hearts.* World Music Press.
	Vietnamese coin clappers. *Music of Vietnam.* Lyrichord 7337.
	Filipino gongs (kulintang). *Philippine Gong Music.* Lyrichord 7322.

(continued)

Table 13.3 Continued

Parallel Genres

Theater Music	Italy: Puccini, "Gianni Schicchi."
	China: Peking Opera. "Hu Hung-yen: Aspects of Peking Opera" (videocassette). The Asia Society.
	Japan: Kabuki. "Martial Arts of Kabuki from the National Theater Institute of Japan" (videocassette). The Asia Society.
Suite	Peru: Suite of dances. *Music of the Incas: "Ayllu Sulca."* Lyrichord 7348.
	Iran: Suite in Dastgah Mahour. *A Persian Heritage.* Nonesuch 72060.
	Bach: French Suite.

---

exposure, experience, and education in music. The world of music offers a comprehensive view of the sounds, functions, and meanings of music globally and within the many ethnic groups of a single nation. The musical expressions of groups of people are the focus of multiethnic music education, where children are offered intensive study of one and then another musical culture. Likewise, world music education provides children with knowledge of how groups of people organize the elements of music in unique modes of musical expression.

Formal as well as informal experience in listening and (ideally) performing the music of another culture increases children's understanding and thus appreciation of unfamiliar musical styles and music makers. Carefully planned experiences in the musics of many cultures can bring about improved musicianship, increased preference for "new" musical styles, and a deeper understanding of people and their music. Through the intermediate grades, children are open to changing their values and attitudes, so that the palette of musics offered to children in their early years can be a powerfully awakening and broadening experience.

Questions

1. Define "multiethnic music education" and "world music education." How are their goals distinguished from one another? In what ways are they similar?

2. What uncertainties may have slowed the curricular advances in the teaching of world musics?

3. Describe ways in which classic methods of music for children can be used in teaching world-music traditions.

4. What are some of the important issues to consider regarding authenticity and representativeness in the selection of music for children?

Activities

1. Launch a demographic study of the city/district in which you may teach. Study the recent changes in the ethnic composite of the school population, as well as projections for the future.

2. Choose a "favorite culture." Develop an annotated list of books, recordings, and videocassettes useful in teaching the music of this culture.

3. Develop a month-long curricular plan in teaching children the music of a "favorite culture."

4. Choose one avenue of world music education (musical components, music material, parallel genres), and collect songs and listening experiences from various musical traditions to illustrate selected features within that category.

5. By listening to a recording, prepare to teach a song or instrumental performance from an oral tradition, with careful attention to rendering an authentic sound.

References

ANDERSON, W. M., & CAMPBELL, P. S. (Eds.). (1989). *Multicultural perspectives in music education*. Reston, VA: Music Educators National Conference.

BANKS, J. (1992). *Multiethnic education: Theory and practice* (2nd ed.). Boston: Allyn and Bacon.

CAMPBELL, P. S. (1991). *Lessons from the world*. New York: Schirmer Books.

CAMPBELL, P. S., McCULLOUGH-BRABSON, E., & TUCKER, J. C. (1994). *Roots and branches*. Danbury, CT: World Music Press.

COLE, J. (1982). *Best-loved folk tales*. Garden City, NY: Anchor Press/Doubleday.

Diagram Group. (1976). *Musical instruments of the world: An illustrated encyclopedia*. New York: Facts on File.

DUNBAR-HALL, P., & HODGE, G. (1991). *A guide to music around the world*. Marrickville, NSW, Australia: Science Press.

EAST, H. (1989). *The singing sack: 28 song-stories from around the world.* London: A & C Black.

FOWLER, C. (1994). *Music! Its role and importance in our lives.* New York: Glencoe.

HAN, K.-H., & CAMPBELL, P. S. (1992). *The lion's roar: Chinese luogu percussion ensembles.* Danbury, CT: World Music Press.

The JVC Video Anthology of World Music and Dance. (1989). Washington, DC: Smithsonian/Folkways.

JESSUP, L. (1992). *World music: A source book for teaching.* Danbury, CT: World Music Press.

MALM, W. P. (1977). *Music cultures of the Pacific, the Near East, and Asia.* Englewood Cliffs, NJ: Prentice-Hall.

MAY, E. (Ed.). (1982). *Music of many cultures.* Berkeley, CA: University of California.

MENC Sounds of the World. (1986–1991). Reston, VA: Music Educators National Conference.

NETTL, B. (1991). *Folk and traditional music of the Western continents* (2nd ed.). Englewood Cliffs, NJ: Prentice-Hall.

NETTL, B., CAPWELL, C., BOHLMAN, P. V., WONG, I. K. F., & TURINO, T. (1992). *Excursions in World Music.* Englewood Cliffs, NJ: Prentice-Hall.

TITON, J. T. (Ed.). (1992). *Worlds of Music* (2nd ed.). New York: Schirmer Books.

VANAVER, B. (1990). *Sheaves of grain: Songs of the seasons from around the world.* Danbury, CT: World Music Press.

Musical Instruments

ABA Music for Children, 221 Madron Avenue SE, Salem, OR 97302.

Andy's Front Hall, P.O.B. 307, Wormer Road, Voorheesville, NY 12186.

Elderly Instruments, 1100 N. Washington, Lansing, MI 48096.

John's Music Center, 4501 Interlake North #9, Seattle, WA 98103.

House of Musical Traditions, 7040 Carroll Avenue, Takoma Park, MD 20912.

Magna-Music Baton, 10370 Page Industrial Boulevard, St. Louis, MO 63132.

Music and Instruments for Children, 2430 South University #103, Denver, CO 80210.

14

Music For Exceptional Children

Malinka, age eight, loves to sing; she does so with great enthusiasm but has a difficult time controlling her voice and her impulse to sing constantly. Trebon, age ten, is an active composer; he can replicate, by ear, challenging piano pieces he has heard two or three times. Jessica, age eleven, is withdrawn; she comes to music class but sits there, looking downward. James, age six, seems to need constant attention; he moves all the time, hits the children next to him, talks out of turn, and rarely sings without shouting, but he loves to play the African drums.

Each one of these children has unique needs and abilities, some of which are being met through special education and some through regular education. All attend music classes with children of their own age in a regular education setting as a part of their school's goal to place them in an environment where they can achieve their maximum growth. This is called the *least restrictive environment* or LRE. Though these children have been labeled *exceptional*, they are more like other children than they are different.

The music teacher who works with these children is part of a *child study team* that helps to determine the best placement for each special-needs child. As a team member, the music teacher is able to communicate with the others the goals of the music program to make sure each child can be successful. She or he also learns from the other team members how to help meet the unique needs of each of these children and what support can be expected in the process. She or he helps decide how mainstreaming in music can help achieve goals set forth in each child's annual *individualized education program* or IEP.

The following descriptions outline the factors that the child study team considered in placing Malinka, Trebon, Jessica, and James in a music setting.

Malinka is a Down's syndrome child, moderately retarded, with a gift for relating with joy to the people around her. Though she has some problems inhibiting her responses, she is developing increased control. Her performance in school suggests she should be able to live in a group setting as an adult and hold a job provided there are some supports for her. The committee decided that she would benefit from the structure of the music setting, the challenge of learning to match her voices to those of the children around her, and the intellectual and physical stimulation of being with children who learn more quickly than she does. Though she will largely learn music by rote, her participation is immediate and feeling of success immense.

Trebon is a highly gifted child, particularly in music, although he is also a part of his school's pull-out gifted program where he receives additional instruction. When the music specialist recognized Trebon's exceptional gifts in music, she encouraged his parents to get him private lessons. Though they wanted that for him, they could not afford the cost. The music specialist contacted the district music supervisor who had begun a program, funded through a combination of school funds, PTSA grants, and community corporate grants, to give private music lessons to economically disadvantaged children. Members of a local private music teachers association agreed to come to the schools to offer lessons at reduced rates as part of their dedication to public service. In her music class, the specialist offers Trebon opportunities for leadership as an accompanist and a teaching assistant, helping her when she divides the class into smaller groups for guitar instruction and for composition assignments.

Jessica is a child who has been emotionally and physically abused by her parents. She is now living in a foster home and is receiving counseling. She has coped with her abuse by withdrawing, and her self-esteem is at a very low level. She has normal intelligence but poor social skills. Her teachers are eager to help her learn to express herself and to trust and interact with others in group settings. Because the music classroom is based on group expression of musical ideas, the team decided to place Jessica with a class of fifth graders. Though Jessica withdraws during group singing, she is willing to play accompaniments on Orff xylophones. She is also starting to express some ideas, both verbally and musically, in the small group composition sessions. (The music specialist has elected to form cooperative groups that retain a stable membership for three months.) As a result, Jessica is beginning to trust the other students in her group and is making some friends. Her teachers report she is increasingly eager to go to music class.

James has been diagnosed as having attention deficit-hyperactivity disorder or ADHD and some learning disabilities. His parents have decided not to control his behavior with Ritalin because they are concerned about the negative effects of continued medication. James comes to music from a resource room where teachers are working with him on specific academic and social skills. The resource-room teachers have worked with the music specialist to implement a behavior-management procedure that is consistent with the one they are using with James. Some of the musical goals for the year include reducing the amount of energy James uses in singing, building accuracy in reproduction of patterns through techniques of echoing, and having James notate and then read and perform his own patterns.

Who Are Exceptional Children?

Though it could be said that on some level every child is exceptional, with unique abilities and needs, current practice defines exceptional children as "those whose physical attributes and/or learning abilities differ from the norm, either above or below, to such an extent that an individualized program of special education is indicated" (Heward and Orlansky, 1992, p. 27). This generally includes children who are gifted learners, children who have learning and/or behavior problems, and children who have physical disabilities. Categories of exceptionality include:

- Mental retardation
- Learning disabilities
- Behavior disorders (emotional disturbance)
- Communication (speech and language) disorders
- Hearing impairments
- Visual impairments
- Physical and other health impairments
- Severe handicaps
- Gifted and talented

Exceptional children may or may not have a *disability*, or "the reduced function or loss of a particular body part or organ" (Heward and Orlansky, 1992, p. 27). Children who cannot perform tasks involving seeing, hearing, or moving the way others can may be said to be disabled. Persons with disabilities may or may not be *handicapped*, referring to the "problems a person with a disability or impairment encounters when interacting with the environment" (Heward and Orlansky, 1992, p. 28). A person using a wheelchair may be handicapped when trying to go to the second floor of a building without elevators, but not handicapped intellectually in the school classroom.

A new category of *at-risk* children is emerging in the literature. Though these children are not currently identified as disabled or handicapped, they run a greater-than-usual chance of developing a problem. They are often preschoolers whose conditions of birth (such as premature birth, or fetal drug or alcohol syndrome) or home environment (such as abuse or economic deprivation) suggest that they may be at risk for developmental problems and may need special help. At-risk children are those in the primary or intermediate grades who demonstrate learning problems in the regular classroom and are at risk for placement in special programs or, if older, for school dropout. These children are not currently classified as exceptional but their needs are real, and early intervention by schools and social agencies is becoming common.

Educating Exceptional Children

In 1975, Congress passed Public Law (PL) 94-142, the Individuals with Disabilities Education Act. This legislation was instrumental in changing the ways schools had historically dealt with children who have special needs. It requires that schools offer free public education to all students regardless of the severity of their need; that individuals and families of individuals with handicaps have a say in their education; that an annual plan (IEP) is developed for each individual that helps to place him or her in the least restrictive environment (LRE) for growth. Gifted children are the only group of exceptional children not covered in this act but may be included in corresponding state laws for the education of the handicapped.

Since 1975 schools have responded in various ways to this legislation. Increasingly, schools have moved away from isolating or even warehousing handicapped children to mainstreaming them throughout the entire school program with support from resource rooms and teachers trained in special education. Some schools have integrated all handicapped children, including those designated as severely retarded, into the regular classroom using a model called *inclusion*. In such schools, children and faculty are taught to assist these children as needed, and support is usually provided to meet the additional physical and educational needs of these mainstreamed children. In other schools, mainstreaming largely occurs in areas typically taught by specialists: music, physical education, and art. Though mainstreaming is not mandated by PL 94-142, that has been the most frequent response to the call for placing children in the least restrictive environment.

The federal government encourages but does not require states to create and fund special programs for gifted and talented students. Forty-eight states have such programs, but the relative amount spent on them is minimal compared to that spent on children with disabilities. Many models exist for serving gifted and talented children; one of the most common is to pull them out of their regular classroom for enrichment classes. Entrance into these classes is usually a measured IQ of 130 to 135. Some schools teach the most intellectually gifted children (the top 1 percent) in completely separate programs. Other schools, particularly at the secondary level, screen students based on specific gifts in math and science, humanities, or the arts. Selected students are placed in magnet schools that stimulate them to achieve advanced levels of performance in the area(s) of their gifts.

Of the children in special education (about 9.4 percent of the total population), 48 percent are diagnosed as having learning disabilities; 23 percent with speech and language impairments; 14 percent with mental retardation; and 9 percent with emotional disturbance. Two thirds of these children receive at least part of their education in a regular classroom with the support of a resource room, and the remainder are in self-contained classrooms. The most severe are usually educated in special schools. Ninety percent of children receiving special education are mildly handicapped (Heward and Orlansky, 1992).

Mainstreaming and the Music Classroom

The decision to mainstream a child in music is often justified for a variety of positive reasons that relate directly to the nature of music and of music learning:

1. Music taps into nonverbal ways of knowing and allows children to express ideas regardless of verbal abilities. At the same time singing can help children to develop vocabulary and understanding of language.

2. Music is multimodal in nature, stimulating the eyes, ears, and muscles along with the mind. Children who have a disability in one sensory area may still participate in music via other senses. The joy of producing sounds and movements draws children actively into the process of music making rather than requiring them to be passive receptors of new ideas.

3. Music can be performed at very sophisticated levels by rote. It is not necessary to be able to read music to perform it well. Though an important outcome of a quality music program is the skill of music reading, children who have difficulties with abstract symbols, such as reading words or translating numbers, can enjoy success in music.

4. Music making is generally a collaborative endeavor. Music is usually made and learned in groups rather than alone. This is particularly true of preschool and elementary general music programs. Therefore, chil-

dren can gain a sense of belonging and commitment to a group that is important to social development.

5. Music, as a performing art, allows for the expression of a wide range of emotions, and it can communicate on very deep levels without the use of words. It stimulates and challenges us to grow aesthetically.

6. A single activity in a music classroom can be adapted to a wide range of ability levels.

7. Music, as a temporal art, challenges the mind to recognize patterns across time, a skill that often needs to be developed in children with patterning and memory deficits.

Yet, in spite of the many potential benefits of mainstreaming children in music, such decisions need to be weighed carefully for each child in terms of: (1) his or her unique needs and abilities; and (2) the demands of the music classroom. The purpose of the LRE is to place children in a situation in which they can succeed and grow, not where they will be ignored or fail.

The goals of a quality music program for children are many but largely focus on the development of musical skills and musical thought. Children who have been through such a program should be able to perform, create, read, and discuss music. There are many demands on complex motor-coordination skills and on thinking at the critical and creative levels. A quality music program is far more than a series of activities designed to help children have "fun" musical experiences together.

Also, though it is tempting to focus on the possible therapeutic values of musical involvement for exceptional children, general music teachers are rarely trained as music therapists. Therefore, they do not have the background or credentials to plan for placement of children in music classes for therapeutic reasons nor to systematically implement therapeutic uses of music.

The most effective decision to mainstream a child in music will result from clear communication and cooperation among the members of the team involved. One of those members should, by law, be the music specialist if he or she is being asked to receive a child. The music specialist needs to consider whether a child with a particular set of needs can succeed in the context of a particular classroom, and needs to gain insight from the team members about how best to work with each mainstreamed child.

Regrettably, many schools ignore this requirement and simply send the children to music classes without any warning, a practice known as *dumping*. Results of such decisions have led to anger and confusion on the part of music teachers, lack of acceptance of the mainstreamed child by the other children, and, ultimately, a more, rather than less, restrictive environment.

The Music Educators National Conference (MENC) has clearly stated standards for mainstreaming in *The School Music Program: Description and Standards* (1986). This booklet can be used to communicate with administrators the national standards for a quality music education program. It reads:

> When handicapped students are mainstreamed into regular music classes:
>   a. Music educators are involved in placement decisions
>   b. Placement is determined primarily on the basis of musical achievement
>   c. Placement does not result in classes exceeding standard class size
>   d. Placement does not result in a disproportionate number of handicapped students in any class.
>   Music instruction is provided in special education classes for those handicapped students not mainstreamed for music.
>   Special education music classes are no larger than other special education classes, and teacher aides are provided for special education music classes if aides are provided for other special education classes (pp. 25–26).

As part of a successful placement in music, the music teacher will need to join other members of the child study team to make sure that the IEP for that child reflects realistic goals for musical attainment. By law a child study team must include at least: (1) the child's teacher(s); (2) a representative of the local school district other than the child's teacher; (3) the child's parents or guardian; and (4) whenever appropriate, the child herself or himself. Other specialists, including music specialists, can be added as necessary.

Each IEP is required to contain basic information about and goals for the child, and must be established at the beginning of the school year and reviewed once during the year. Local school districts have usually developed their own forms. Ideally these plans should help identify the student's level at the beginning of the term, goals for the class, how these goals will be achieved, and how the student's progress will be evaluated. Figure 14.1 is an example of an IEP in music.

Though involvement in this process clearly takes time, music specialists need to understand that their right to participate is protected under the law, and that doing so can help create a more positive environment for the mainstreamed child. Specialists also need to know that schools should be committed to educating all students in music whether they are mainstreamed or not.

1. Student James King

School Paxton Elementary

Grade III

Current Placement Resource Room   Age 9

Date of birth 8/7/69

2. Committee

	Position	Initial Date
Ms. J. Strong	Music Teacher	
Dr. T. Forman	Assistant Principal	
Ms. J. Kane	Resource Teacher	

3. Present Level of Functioning

Strengths: Plays rhythm instruments quite well, maintains rhythm most of the time. Can imitate simple sounds.

Needs: To improve use of his singing voice. To improve his ability to respond to music rhythmically in a less inhibited manner.

4. Annual Goal

Will imitate short phrases in songs.

Will respond by running, synchronizing his steps to the drumbeat.

5. Instructional Objective

Will imitate a short random phrase.

Will respond to a fast drumbeat by running, though not necessarily synchronizing steps with beat.

6. Assessment Procedure

Will imitate the phrase accurately in pitch and rhythm in two of three consecutive sessions.

Will run to the drumbeat (sixteen measures of $\frac{2}{4}$) with 80 percent accuracy

7. Educational Service to be Provided

a. Services required

A full-frequency-range hearing aid. Music in a regular classroom having a hard surface floor.

Sixteen twenty-minute sessions with the music therapists to develop the singing voice and synchronize running movement with the drumbeat

b. Date initiated

10/1/78

c. Duration

8 weeks

d. Individual response

Joan Reed

e. Extent of time in regular educational program.

Placed in the regular third-grade music class one thirty-minute period per week.

f. Justification for placement

Placement based on music-assessment instrument.

8. I have had the opportunity to participate in the development of this individualized education program.

Parent's signature _____

Figure 14.1 Individualized Education Program. *Reproduced with permission from Graham and Beer, 1980, p. 87.*

The Music Classroom and Exceptional Children

Whether teachers work with exceptional children in a mainstreamed classroom or self-contained setting, the key to success is the willingness of the teachers to adapt instruction to meet the needs of those children. Each category of exceptionality has unique characteristics as does each child within a category.

For some students, teachers need to adapt the pace and clarity of instructions, slowing down what they do, repeating directions, and modeling tasks. For some children, teachers will need to adapt the complexity either of the task, of the music, or of the level of thought required, sometimes simplifying it and other times making it more challenging. For other students, teachers will need to adapt the materials and instruments, making print larger, using sequencing cards, or adding velcro fasteners to gloves so children can hold bell mallets. And for others, teachers will need to adapt the processes they use to have children learn, using student partners and cooperative groups, allowing students to experience instruction (seeing, hearing, moving) and demonstrate knowing (telling, singing, playing, writing, moving) through multiple rather than single modalities.

Ultimately, deciding how to adapt instruction can be an exciting and challenging process, which will increase a teacher's repertoire of strategies designed to meet the needs of all children. The following ideas should provide an initial base. Other resources include the special education teachers and specialists (hearing, speech, and psychologists) assigned to work with exceptional children, the parents, the children themselves, print resources such as those listed in the references for this chapter, and classes in mainstreaming.

Mentally Retarded

Children who are classified as mentally retarded (MR) are significantly below average in general intellectual functioning, which either results in or is associated with deficits in adaptive behavior (average Intelligence Quotient [IQ] is 100). Some children with low IQs are able to function well in school and society. Those children would not be classified as mentally retarded. However, if a child has a low IQ and does not meet age level standards of personal independence and social responsibility, then he or she will be labeled mentally retarded.

There are typically four levels of mental retardation that are defined in terms of levels of IQ.

Mild Retardation (IQ of 50–55 to approx. 70)

This group is the most likely to be mainstreamed into music classes with the assistance of a resource-room teacher to meet individual their needs. Often these children are not identified until they begin schooling. Many do well in school and function independently as adults.

Moderate Retardation (IQ of 35–40 to 50–55)

These children have usually been identified at an early age and often have other handicapping conditions and physical abnormalities. They are usually taught in a self-contained classroom where focus on daily living and functional skills usually outweigh academics. Many of these children have Down's syndrome or are brain damaged. They continue to need support as adults.

Severe Retardation (IQ of 20–25 to 35–40); Profound Retardation (IQ below 20–25)

Most children in these categories are identified at birth and have significant central nervous system damage. They usually have not been taught in schools, although that is beginning to change. New technologies are helping to reach children who are profoundly retarded. Most of these people will need care, some twenty-four hours a day, throughout life. However, some may be able to function semi-independently as adults.

Music teachers are most likely to be asked to work with mildly and moderately retarded students either in mainstreamed or self-contained settings. The following list of characteristics of mildly retarded children is accompanied by specific teaching strategies to meet their special needs.

1. MR children may have problems with focusing attention or distinguishing the important from the unimportant. They may also be unable to generalize learnings to new settings.
   - Use color highlighting of notated melodic and rhythmic patterns
   - Notate their part (such as an ostinato) separately; use color highlighting
   - Teach songs without recordings or other accompaniment
   - State lesson goals clearly, and repeat during the lesson
   - Speak in short simple sentences without talking down
   - Ask them to perform one musical task (e.g., chant/sing or maintain a steady beat or ostinato) rather than multiple tasks

2. MR children may have problems with memory from one lesson to another and also short-term memory of patterns within a lesson.

- Repeat materials, skills, and concepts across several lessons
- Keep musical patterns for echo clapping or singing short, simple, and slow; repeat them if necessary
- Break tasks down into small units and teach with simple directions; use hand movements to practice dance patterns ahead of time or patschen (patting the lap) to practice instrument patterns
- Use visual cues such as pictures or movements to help them remember the order of events in a song; for example, "I Know an Old Lady Who Swallowed a Fly"
- In learning a new song, have them join in on the part that repeats; for example, "Sandy Land"

3. MR children may have trouble with cognitive organization of ideas and abstractions.

- Use iconic notation to represent patterns
- Teach ideas by rote rather than note
- Let them develop their own way of writing music down
- Help them "chunk" or group information using visual, verbal, or movement cues; for example, music charts that come with music series or bulletin boards that highlight or review concepts

4. MR children may have trouble singing in tune across a wide range or may sing with too much energy.

- Work to expand their tessitura upward (often it is low, from B to g)
- Have them sit next to an effective singer and encourage them to match that singer's voice

5. MR children's mental age (MA) is behind their chronological age (CA) yet they often identify with same-age peers.

- If mainstreamed based on CA, adapt instruction per suggestions above; have them work with a partner who can monitor and assist
- Respect their CA when selecting song and listening materials; don't treat older students like little children
- Discover something they do well in music, and let them offer leadership

Trevor playing the drum.

Learning Disabled

The area of learning disabilities is perhaps the most difficult to define of all of the areas of exceptionality. Generally children identified as learning disabled (LD) are of normal intelligence but have "significant difficulties in the acquisition and use of language, listening, speaking, reading, writing, reasoning, or mathematical abilities" (Heward and Orlansky, 1992, p. 137). It is assumed that these limits are intrinsic and due to some problem in the central nervous system, and not a result of other handicapping conditions or extrinsic influences such as environment or lack of education.

By far, the largest number of exceptional children served in schools today are identified as learning disabled, though the form(s) that the disability takes varies greatly. The majority are males (a three-to-one ratio), identified in the elementary grades, who are more deficient in spelling and reading than in mathematics, and who have increased difficulty in learning with increased age.

Because learning disabilities is an umbrella term covering a wide range of behaviors, it is difficult to state principles that will apply in every case. A careful dialogue with the resource room teacher and a review of each mainstreamed child's folder should help the music teacher to better meet individual needs.

1. LD children may have difficulty receiving and translating input from one or more of the senses used for learning:

a) Visual (verbal and nonverbal)

b) Auditory (verbal and nonverbal)

c) Tactile (touch) or kinesthetic (muscle movement) (verbal and nonverbal)

- Develop strategies that allow them to hear/see/move or touch either simultaneously or sequentially
- Highlight visuals using large print, color, frames that isolate patterns on overheads or in their books
- Slow down verbal input and recordings; teach difficult parts separately
- Use concrete manipulables to reinforce musical ideas such as notation: magnet boards or hand staffs for pitch work; popsicle sticks for rhythm work; and also felt or sandpaper notes
- Separate the reading of rhythms from pitch
- Learn songs by rote, then add the tracking of words; print one line of words under a song, not multiple verses
- Practice instrument parts kinesthetically away from the instrument first

2. LD children may have problems cognitively integrating all of the different information they receive during a music lesson. Depending on the complexity of the task, they have to move from paying attention to what it is the teacher is emphasizing, to perceiving the place in the music, to forming an image of what that is, to interpreting a symbol of how it is represented, to conceptualizing it in terms of other similar musical events or in terms of the task. This is particularly challenging in music because even a simple folk song printed in a music book is full of information. Most of the musical tasks children are asked to perform involve complex coordination of the mind and the body.

    a) Perform a task analysis of the skills or concepts children are expected to do or understand

    b) Teach LD children to perform something in a series of smaller steps: how to hold a mallet and how to strike it; later how to coordinate with complex patterns, later how to read; later to understand an ostinato

    c) Know that motor coordination may be a problem; simplify motor tasks

3. LD children may have difficulty showing what they know through writing or reading—provide alternative means of showing what they know: pointing; circling icons such as arrows or lines; matching; manipulating; singing; moving; and telling.

Behavior Disordered

The term *behavior disordered* (BD) is increasingly used to apply to children who might have previously been labeled emotionally disturbed, socially maladjusted, or psychotic. Health impaired or autistic children are also placed in this category. The behaviors may have either a biological or a psychological cause.

Children identified as BD are usually either very aggressive and act out (externalizers) or are shy and withdrawn (internalizers). The level of their behavior puts it consistently outside of the social norms. As a result of that behavior, they are often socially isolated and in trouble academically. Happily, most of these children have normal intelligence and can be helped to gain needed social skills in the regular classroom and at home.

Because the range and variety of behaviors in BD children is so broad and potentially disruptive, it is *essential* that the music specialist communicate with the resource teachers and/or school psychologists to know how best to adapt their teaching for successful mainstreaming of these children. This planning needs to be done ahead of time because BD children need: (1) consistency in expectations; (2) clarity in the communication of those expectations; (3) options or choices rather than mandates; and (4) extrinsic guidelines and support for behavior modification.

Music teachers need to anticipate places in their lessons that might be difficult for behavior disordered children and implement procedures that will

result in successful rather than inappropriate behaviors. The classroom procedures and adaptations highlighted in Table 14.1 are relevant to the teaching of
all children, and build on suggestions presented in Chapter 2 coming from the
work of Skinner and Madsen.

Sensory Handicaps

Hearing-impaired students are often assumed to be incapable of perceiving
sounds or of learning to make music, but nothing could be further from the
truth. The term, *hearing impairment*, refers to a wide range of hearing losses.
Most students who are hearing impaired are capable of hearing some musical
sounds and responding to and performing music. Even deaf children can perceive vibration and pitch changes through their sense of touch, and can learn
to play various percussion and wind instruments as well as dance in time to
music.

   A person who is *deaf* may perceive some sounds, but not clearly enough to
understand speech either with or without a hearing aid. It is very hard for deaf
children to communicate aurally; rather, they rely on vision. A person who is
hard of hearing can perceive enough sounds to be able to understand speech
and communicate similarly to the normal hearing child. Most hearing-

Counting out to choose a leader.

Table 14.1 Classroom Management Procedures

Classroom Procedure	Possible Adaptation
Entering and leaving classroom and finding place to sit	Lines with leaders, single file, no talking, assigned seats or carpet squares—make it more musical by moving children to a drum, piano, or recorded signal
Distributing, holding, and collecting books	Include BD children as leaders for the day or week to distribute and collect books—one book per child so there are no difficulties with sharing. Establish clarity on respect for the books.
Distributing and playing instruments	Model correct way to hold mallets or other instruments and correct playing technique. Have children imitate teacher's model. Move around, not over, Orff-barred percussion instruments, mallets left in holders or on top of instruments. Distribute instruments one at a time to add color to a piece rather than taking a "rhythm band" approach. Place hand percussion instruments under chair when finished, or collect immediately by instrument type, e.g., placing all tambourines on the front table. Develop silent "freeze" signal if noise gets out of hand, e.g., hand on chin or lights out. Immediately remove instrument from possession of student who is not respecting it.
Selecting a partner for a dance or giving an instrument to another person	Avoid saying, "choose a partner." Use colored tags, shapes, numbering off, or letters signifying individuals. "Everyone with a red tag stand with someone with a blue tag. Move to the drumbeat for eight beats."
Forming a circle or other formation for a dance	Place Xs on floor with tape or white (washable) shoe polish in the proper formation. Stand on the X with no touching until given the signal.
Working in small groups for composition or other projects	Establish cooperative groups of four to five with a balance of different types of children in them. Keep the groups consistent for at least three months. Let them select a group name. Always have them work in the same area of the room.
Establishing and reinforcing behavior standards	Have student generate a list of class rules (or teacher does so if necessary). Keep the list short and clear. Post it in front of room. Discuss the rules to make sure children understand what their responsibilities are. Refer to them regularly. Have children understand consequences of not following the rules such as warnings, time-outs, or discussion with the teacher or parents. Try to use praise and positive reinforcement as much as possible. Be patient and calm. If a BD child is on a behavior modification plan, follow its guidelines in teaching music.

346

impaired children do not require special services. Most deaf children are now being served in regular schools, rather than in special schools for the deaf.

In effectively working with hearing-impaired children in music, the music specialist would benefit from knowing answers to the following questions:

1. What is the degree of the hearing loss?
   a) Mild (20–55 decibels): can understand conversation from three to five feet, gets confused in groups, may speech read (read the movements of the mouth of a speaker)
   b) Moderate (55–70 decibels): can understand loud conversation only. May have impaired speech and language comprehension
   c) Severe (70–90 decibels): may hear loud sounds about one foot from ear, may identify some environmental sounds, probably has difficulties with speech (consonants) and language, uses vision to understand
   d) Profound (90–110 decibels): may hear some loud sounds but mostly senses vibrations, difficulty with speech and language; relies on vision rather than sound for communication;

2. How are they receiving information?
   a) Through auditory learning (learning to listen to actual sounds)
   b) Through amplification instruments: hearing aid; microphone and hearing aid; or cochlear implant (find out what frequencies they can hear)
   c) Through speech reading (trying to understand through careful attention to a speaker's face)

3. What methods are being used to teach them?
   a) Oral approaches: emphasis is placed on auditory, visual, and tactile means of reaching children; speechreading; amplification; and talking (will need to sit where they can read speech)
   b) Total communication: use of speech reading, signing, and finger spelling (may need an interpreter or a note taker and must sit where they can read speech)
      Adapting for the hearing-impaired student may involve some or all of the following suggestions:
      - Seat the child at the front of the room and make sure light falls on your face
      - Face the child and speak directly to him or her
      - Speak clearly but not too fast
      - Don't shout or raise the level of your voice

- Cue children if you are going to ask them a question
- Assign a note taker for older children
- Use visual communication such as pictures, icons, charts, over-heads, chalkboards, written notes (e.g., place the page numbers for songs and words representing key concepts in order on the chalkboard)
- If you are wearing a microphone, be sensitive to the potential of distortion from ambient noise and instruments. Have students adjust hearing aids accordingly
- Model fingerings and mallet techniques for playing instruments
- Have children touch instruments to feel vibrations: piano sounding board; body of the guitar; frame of a drum; the body of Orff bass bars (good for pitch discrimination)
- Give children instruments that have low frequencies or can be felt through the hand such as rhythm sticks. Avoid instruments that have bright, piercing sounds
- Do not expect that children in the moderate to profound loss categories can hear recorded music clearly
- Use instruments such as alto recorders or Melodicas (with or without extensions) to work on pitch motion, articulation, breathing, and rhythm
- Tap patterns on desks or other sound conducting surfaces to help children feel meter and rhythm
- When possible, teach music in rooms with wooden floors so that vibrations can be felt; a wooden platform increases the resonance potential of sounds from instruments like pianos and xylophones
- Place stereo speakers on the floor of a gymnasium, select music with a strong beat such as popular dance music, and encourage hearing-impaired children to dance with their shoes off, feeling the music through vibrations in the floor
- Help *all* children learn to sing some songs by signing. It is important for all children to understand that there are many ways to communicate

Visually impaired children constitute a very small percentage (0.1 percent) of the school-age population. The causes of visual impairment and the degrees of loss of sight vary greatly. Some children have blurred vision, or poor peripheral vision, are very near sighted, can only see light and shadows, or see nothing. Many (about 30 percent) have other handicaps. Most attend regular classes with peers.

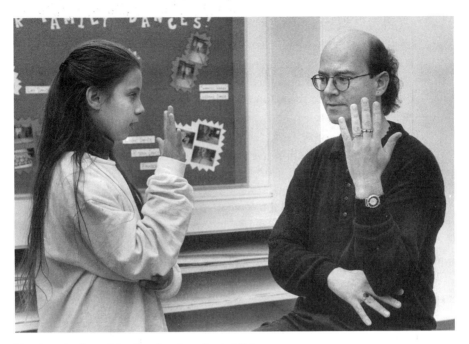

Teacher signing with a hearing-impaired child.

Again, the key for the music teacher is to understand the type of visual impairment a child has and to learn how to maximize use of any residual sight that might exist. Children who are legally blind (20/200 vision in best eye with correction) will probably be learning through a Braille system. Other visually impaired students may use technological devices such as the Optacon that enlarge and raise regular print for easier reading.

Music, an aural art, is readily accessible to the blind child through listening and imitation. Even if reading notation is involved, children can learn through a variety of concrete manipulables (such as tongue depressors for rhythm patterns or magnet boards with raised staff for melody work) or through Braille notation. The following ideas may help in adapting for the visually impaired child.

1. Develop manipulables to use for sensing through touch: sandpaper or felt notes; notes outlined in string; individual staffs to use at seats with staff raised up with layers of Elmer's glue or tape; tongue depressors for rhythm work; listening maps with raised patterns using glue or string; Braille notation or labels if necessary

2. Enlarge notation through: patterns notated with black pen on tagboard; blowing a song up to a larger size through magnification on a copy

machine; large notation on chalkboards or overheads; chart books available with music series using an Optacon

3. Use auditory sense by: recording on tape lessons or song materials; explaining unusual noises; training auditory perception of sounds in foreground and background; verbally cuing when they are to play instruments or change chords; using balls with bells for activities using balls in music; identifying persons who are speaking by name

4. Increase confidence in movement by: consistently placing chairs and instruments in room; using sighted partners for dancing or hula hoops/ropes tied in circles/parachutes for circle dances; talking students through patterned movements for dances or instrument playing; guiding individual movement in personal space in time/flow with music; helping children move by walking next to them while supporting with a hand under their elbow (do not push or pull children)

Physically Handicapped

Children who are physically handicapped may have an orthopedic impairment (involving the skeletal system and muscles) or a neurologic impairment (involving the nervous system), or both. Cerebral palsy (CP) is a major cause of physical handicaps. In addition to CP, a whole range of accidents and diseases can result in physical handicaps. Some of them result in limited physical functioning because they affect breathing (asthma) or energy (diabetes or AIDS). Usually, focus in treatment and schooling is on what parts of the body are involved (one or more limbs) and whether the motor and/or perceptual motor handicaps are mild, moderate, or severe.

Children with mild handicaps are usually able to improve motor and perceptual functioning with intervention, and are able to keep up with peers in academic work. Children with moderate and severe handicaps may have some academic delays as well as motor-coordination problems that keep them from achieving age-level expectations. Physical and occupational therapists can help the music specialist understand how to best serve these children.

Because there are so many different types of physical handicaps, it is important that the music teacher know the specific needs of each child to adapt instruction for them. The goal for all of these children is physical independence, participation, and control.

Adapting for Movement

- Create space for wheelchairs that is accessible for activities and sight lines (do not isolate nonambulatory children in back of music room or concert hall)

- If doing creative movement, have children move a part of their body they can still move: "Open and close your mouth to the beat"; "click the rhythm pattern with your tongue"; "stand and rock to show the beat"; "lift your legs up and down."
- Use a standing table or walker for support for movement activities
- Do patterned dances in a space large and open enough that nonambulatory students can dance in their chairs: use music with a tempo they can manage
- Assign an ambulatory partner to dance with a nonambulatory student

Adapting Instruments and Materials

- Insert mallets, strikers, or small handles through a foam ball or small rubber ball for easier gripping
- Attach mallets or small instruments to hands or gloves by Velcro
- Use baby teething rings or rubber door stops to strum autoharps if child lacks pincer grasp
- Restring guitars or ukeleles if necessary for child to strum with left hand and chord with right
- Tape holes on soprano recorders closed to allow children with missing fingers to play
- Tape or clamp small instruments to desks or music stands for children to strike
- Use magnetic tape to attach lightweight bells or other small instruments to metal surfaces
- Have one child hold an instrument while a partner with limited mobility strikes it
- Clip and tape paper to a clipboard for easier writing or drawing

Gifted and Talented

Children who are gifted (who show advanced, natural abilities, usually in the preschool years) or talented (who have a disposition toward something that they work hard to develop) are most likely to come to a music classroom without being previously identified for the music teacher as exceptional. Though some schools have separate self-contained classes for gifted and talented students, the music teacher will probably work with such children in the context of a heterogeneous group and will have to discover the gifts a child brings. It is rare that a program for gifted students will have screened for or recognized musical giftedness.

Generally, schools have used high IQ scores or achievement test scores as the single measure of giftedness. However, the federal definition of giftedness moves beyond intellectual giftedness to recognize advanced abilities in creativity, leadership, academic, and visual or performing arts. A focus on a broader view of intelligence has been supported by the theories of Guilford (1967) and Gardner (1983). Teachers who are aware of these more encompassing theories of intelligence are better prepared to recognize and build on the gifts each child may bring.

Because there is a range of ways of being gifted, it is difficult to create a single list that would apply to all children. However, gifted children usually are: (1) quick to relate ideas to each other (they are good conceptualizers); (2) can acquire and manipulate symbol systems easily, including those used in the arts; and (3) usually make good judgments, and can see broader implications of ideas than most of the general population. Creatively gifted children often suggest unusual solutions to questions, use their intuitive sense, and have a sense of humor.

Sometimes, these gifts make it difficult for children to work in class as they may become frustrated when the pace is slow, may dominate discussions, fight rules and regulations, use humor to manipulate, and be glib rather than thoughtful in their answers (Heward and Orlansky, 1992).

Though not all gifted students are musically gifted or talented, nor do they all elect to perform musically, there is much that can be done to recognize the capacity of gifted children for accelerated learning.

If children show early musical gifts or talents:

- Encourage private lessons with competent teachers
- Introduce notation to them so they can use it as a tool for musical independence
- Give them opportunities for musical leadership in your classes: teaching other children, conducting
- Have computer programs available so they can advance on their own in music theory and composition
- Have synthesizer/MIDI hookups available so they can compose independently and print out their own music
- Make sure that school instrumental teachers are aware of their gifts, and help develop plans for careful articulation between the general music program and the instrumental program

If children are gifted in other ways:

- Provide activities that will allow them to expand their study of various musical ideas such as the study of a composer or a kind of music that

interests them. Encourage independent research activities resulting in reports.

- Challenge them with small group and individual composition assignments such as those suggested in Chapter 10. Have a range of instruments available for their use.
- Create a classroom with learning centers where gifted children can work
  independently on a range of projects such as music listening and research, learning to play the electronic keyboard or the guitar, composing,
  playing musical games, using music software on the computer
- Bring in artists in residence or guests from the community to challenge
  children musically
- Encourage critical and creative thinking

The Joys of Reaching All Children

Working with exceptional children can be a rewarding experience for the
music teacher. The keys to success are a willingness to learn, curiosity about
how to be effective, clarity of communication with people who understand the
needs and abilities of the children involved, and flexibility to change when
something is not working.

Many resources are available to help teachers or parents who need more
information on music therapy and music for children with special needs.
Other resources include classes in mainstreaming and, of course, the resources of a range of people who are committed to helping children learn.
Through collaboration and cooperation, both teachers and children will be
enriched and challenged to grow.

Questions

1. Define the following terms: child study team; LRE; IEP; mainstreaming;
   at-risk.
2. Describe the role the music specialist should play in mainstreaming decisions for music.
3. What is the difference between a disability and a handicap? Work with a
   partner to create an example of a handicapping condition in an elementary general music class. Describe a way to change that situation so it
   would not be handicapping.

4. The key to effective mainstreaming in music is adapting. List several aspects of the learning situation the music teacher needs to think about adapting.

5. What levels of mental retardation is the music specialist likely to work with? What are some key ideas in adapting for the MR child?

6. What would you say to the parents of a hearing impaired child who asks to have their child excused from music because of their hearing loss?

Activities

1. Interview two elementary music specialists to determine how they work with mainstreamed children. Review sample music IEPs they have written for children before mainstreaming.

2. Visit a music classroom that has a mainstreamed child. Note ways in which the teacher is adapting for that child. Note how the child responds.

3. Visit a music classroom in which the teacher is working with self-contained rather than mainstreamed children. Describe the children and their responses to music. Describe ways the teacher is working to meet the needs of the children.

4. Review one or more references in music therapy or mainstreaming in music. List additional suggestions for adapting for children in a category of exceptionality particularly interesting to you.

5. Create music materials to use with children who are visually impaired.

6. Do some one-on-one teaching with a child in one of the categories of exceptionality discussed in this chapter. Experiment with different musical tasks to discover how to best reach this child. Describe in a written report what the child was and was not able to do. Describe how you adapted instruction to meet the needs of the child.

References

ALVIN, J., & WARWICK, A. (1991). *Music therapy for the autistic child* (2nd ed.). Oxford, U.K.: Oxford University.

ATTERBURY, B. W. (1990). *Mainstreaming exceptional learners in music.* Englewood Cliffs, NJ: Prentice-Hall.

BIRKENSHAW, L. (1977). *Music for fun, music for learning.* Toronto, Can.: Holt, Rinehart and Winston.

BITCON, C. H. (1976). *Alike and different: The clinical and educational use of Orff-Schulwerk.* Santa Ana, CA: Rosha Press.

EDWARDS, E. (1974). *Music education for the deaf.* South Waterford, ME: Merriam-Eddy.

GARDNER, H. (1983). *Frames of mind: The theory of multiple intelligence.* New York: Basic Books.

GASTON, E. T., et al. (1968). *Music in therapy.* New York: Macmillan.

GRAHAM, R. M. (1975). *Music for the exceptional child.* Reston, VA: Music Educators National Conference.

GRAHAM, R. M., & BEER, A. (1980). *Teaching music to the exceptional child.* Englewood Cliffs, NJ: Prentice-Hall.

GUILFORD, J. P. (1967). *The nature of human intelligence.* New York: Mc-Graw-Hill.

HARDESTY, K. W. (1979). *Music for special education.* Morristown, NJ: Silver Burdett.

HEWARD, W., & ORLANSKY, M. (1992). *Exceptional children.* New York: Macmillan.

Journal of Music Therapy. Official publication of the National Association for Music Therapy.

MICHEL, D. E. (1976). *Music therapy in special education.* New York: C. C. Thomas.

Music Educators Journal: Issues dedicated to special learners: April 1972; April 1982; February 1985; April 1990.

NOCERA, S. D. (1979). *Reaching the special learner through music.* Morristown, NJ: Silver Burdett.

VERNAZZA, M. (1978). *Music plus for the young child in special education.* Boulder, CO: Pruett.

CHAPTER **15**

Music in an Integrated Curriculum

Ms. Luebke's general music class is alive, not only with sounds but with colors and designs, movement and dance, poetry and stories, and creative drama. Children often work in small groups to solve creative problems involving several art forms. Ms. Luebke is committed to integrating other arts into her music classroom. She believes that her role is to help children understand the nature of the arts, interpret and express ideas through them, and develop their aesthetic sensitivity.

Mr. Parker's music classes are busy practicing Sub-Saharan African songs and dances. With each new song or dance, the children learn something about the culture from which it came and the meaning it has for its people. The older children have just finished constructing African-style drums, two-toned bells, and rattles with the help of parents and a visiting artist from Nigeria. The artist will teach them some traditional drumming patterns. Mr. Parker works in a school where everyone is immersed in the study of Africa for nine weeks. At the end of that time, the children, teachers, and parents come together for an evening of Sub-Saharan African food, culture, and festivities, where children share what they have learned, and African guest artists perform with them.

Ms. Steinhurst met with the primary teachers to determine what the children are learning in science during their study of insects. The children created chants, movement patterns, and instrumental accompaniments in music class to describe their insects. Each class selected one insect to represent at a program for their parents. Ms. Steinhurst is helping them create original songs with accompanying movements for that program. Insect sounds, habits, and motions have been carefully observed and are reflected in the music. Children are creating a story line that places these insects in a larger environment.

Children playing African stick-passing game.

Ms. Steinhurst has a double degree in art and music. In her role as art teacher, she uses simple materials such as paper sacks, construction paper, cardboard tubes, and tinfoil to help the children design and create their costumes. They are looking through books of insects for design details, which are reflected in their costumes.

Each of these teachers was hired to teach music, and each has gone beyond the boundaries of what has traditionally been taught in the elementary general music curriculum. Yet, in each instance, children are developing important musical understandings and skills. Ms. Luebke and Mr. Parker are committed to helping to integrate music across various areas of the curriculum. They know that they cannot do this with every aspect of the school curriculum throughout the school year. At the same time, they realize that it is very important to incorporate music into a broader whole. It helps to weave music into the fabric of all school life, rather than isolating it from other subjects to periods of once or twice a week.

Ms. Steinhurst teaches in a school where the entire curriculum is integrated and the arts are at the core. The classroom teachers, who lack deep training in the arts, tend to begin with activities, then introduce content. The fact that Ms. Steinhurst has training in both music and art helps to ensure that significant artistic growth will occur in the students.

Challenges of Integrating the Curriculum

Trends that call for the integration of the arts across the entire curriculum have sometimes caught music teachers by surprise and left them defensive. Music teachers become understandably distressed when a classroom teacher suddenly wants them to suspend the music curriculum to teach frog songs, because her class has begun a frog unit in science. It is important that music specialists and classroom teachers communicate early in the school year about issues of curriculum coordination and integration, so that mutually beneficial goals can be established.

Models for integrating the curriculum vary, but key to all of them is that true integration respects the integrity and uniqueness of each of the disciplines to be combined. The integrated curriculum seeks to relate fragmented learning experiences, by planning that combines the significant curricular goals in music and the arts with the other curricular areas. This might be conceived of as co-curricular education.

Singing a song about frogs is not music education, even though it may be a delightful way to enhance learning about frogs. If the classroom teacher wants frog songs, the music specialist can provide those resources for the teacher, who can incorporate them as she or he wishes. However, without prior planning, the music specialist should not be expected to interrupt her or his planned curriculum.

Given the opportunity for prior planning, the music specialist may find that the first-grade frog unit coincides with work she is doing on pitch motion, including melodic leaps. She also sees ways that working with poetry about frogs would help her further develop planned rhythm work, as well as reinforcing the concepts of ostinato and motive. As the classroom teacher communicates some of the vocabulary and concepts the children will be learning about frogs, including the life cycle of the frog, the music specialist sees that she could use the stages of the life cycle as a basis for creative movement and composition, further expanding children's awareness of form. Careful planning and communication among teachers can enhance and integrate the curriculum and bring greater meaning to all that the children do. Books by Drake (1993) and Jacobs (1989a, b) help to give insight into principles and structures for planning the integrated curriculum.

Integrating Other Arts
into the Music Curriculum

Music specialists are frequently the only arts specialists hired at the elementary level. In that role, they are often called on to be an advocate for all the arts and to bring a broader awareness of the arts to the children with whom they work. Many teachers have responded with excitement to the opportunity to help create aesthetic literacy through their program. However, this can be a challenge to specialists who may have had strong training as musicians but minimal training in the other arts. Numerous workshops are available for all teachers in creative movement, visual arts, literary arts, and creative dramatics that can help to expand skills and understandings about those forms. Orff-Schulwerk training can be helpful in developing skills for using language and movement in the music curriculum. University courses in aesthetics and interrelated arts are rich sources, as are programs for teachers through museums and other community arts organizations.

Each art form is unique. Visual arts, dance, theater, music, literature, and media arts each have their own language, expressive medium, set of symbols, and technical demands. Yet the arts are deeply connected because they all: (1) challenge us to grow aesthetically; (2) are languages of the emotions; and (3) embody meaning far beyond what humans can express with words or numbers. In working with multiple arts, teachers need to be sensitive to the commonalities between the arts and to the things that make each unique or different.

Interdisciplinary Curriculum in the Arts

Common links among the arts can be found in such aesthetic principles as tension and release; repetition and contrast; pattern; motive; theme and variation; balance; foreground and background; and density. Teachers can enhance children's awareness of how these principles work in various arts by bringing in illustrative examples from different art forms and comparing them. Though the generative impulse may be music, this could be thought of as an interdisciplinary curriculum that focuses on the understanding of broad aesthetic principles. Many disciplines are viewed in terms of a broader set of ideas.

To teach the principle of repetition, the teacher could help children notice it as a forming device in nature, a song or instrumental work, a poem, a painting, and a dance. Discuss the impact of the use of repetition. (It creates a sense of rhythm, fulfills expectations, creates unity, and, taken to an extreme, it could be boring.) Have the children create their own short composition that uses repetition as the main structural device. These activities not only teach music, they expand children's awareness of a concept that permeates all the arts as well as life. Further examples of this kind of teaching can be found throughout the music series text, *Silver Burdett Music*, which was published from 1972 to 1985 and in *Integrating Music into the Classroom* by Anderson and Lawrence (1992).

Shared Curriculum in the Arts

Another means by which teachers can stimulate the development of children's broader understanding and skills in the arts is to find ways in which aspects of other arts intersect with music. The intersected or shared curriculum attempts to find areas in which two content areas overlap. There are many ways in which an individual teacher can plan lessons and activities that readily accomplish multiple learnings in the arts. The following ideas may help to stimulate thinking about some of those possibilities.

Creative Movement/Dance

The art form that is probably the most analogous to music is dance. They are both arts that unfold through time and occupy space, either acoustic or physical. Music teachers frequently use creative movement and dance to get children physically involved with the music. However, they often miss opportunities to help children to grow in their consciousness and skills as dancers in the process. Table 15.1 outlines the elements of dance. This is a language, quite similar to that of music but different because the expressive medium is the body, not sound.

Through capturing the language of dance and incorporating it in the music curriculum, teachers can do a great deal to build and reinforce dance concepts, helping children to express themselves more creatively through movement.

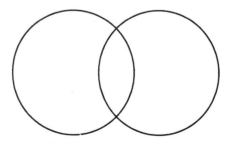

Figure 15.1. "Shared" curriculum

Table 15.1   Elements of Dance

Time
   Tempo: fast; medium; slow; stillness
   Duration: long; short
   Beat: steady; even
   Accent: stressing a beat
   Rhythm: patterns of different durations

Flow
   Sustained: smooth; flowing; connected
   Percussive: jerky; segmented
   Vibratory: shaking; swinging

Space
   Personal
      Size: large; small; wide; narrow
      Nonlocomotor movements: stretch; shake; twist; curl; bend
      Force field: protective bubble that surrounds you so you don't bump other
      things or people
   General space
      Directions: up/down; front/back; right/left; diagonal
      Pathways: curved; straight; angular
      Locomotor: walk; run; leap; skip; hop; jump; slide; crawl; scoot

Force
   Strong/gentle

Shape
   Individual: curved; straight; twisted; balanced; symmetrical; asymmetrical
   Group: lines; clumps; touching; not touching; balanced
   Thematic: animal; sports; emotions

This can often be done by asking open-ended questions using music as the stimulus:

1. "How many ways can you show me a high motion? A low motion? Switch from one to another as you hear the pitches on the bells change from high to low."

2. "When you hear the drum, move across the room in a curved pathway to the rhythm I play. Change levels as you move."

3. "Work in personal space to shape the phrases of this music. Start with one body part and gradually add others until your whole body is involved."

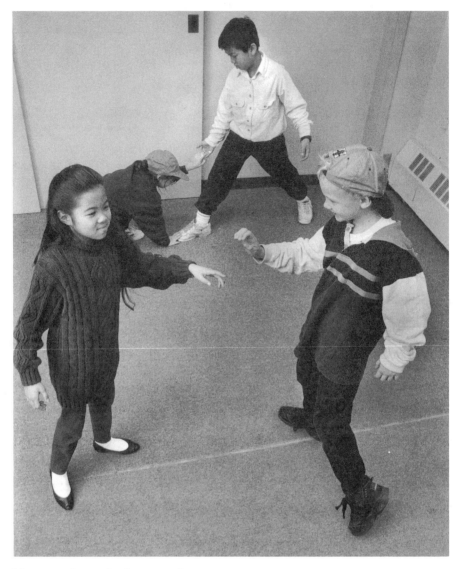

Movement improvisation to music.

4. "Listen to the suspended cymbal as I strike it once. Be ready to de-scribe the sound." (Model and discuss.) "Show with your body the en-ergy at the beginning of that sound, and keep your body moving until you can no longer hear the sound. Think of how you'll move as the sound dies out." (Repeat the same process with various instruments of contrasting timbre. Play them in a series and have children shift move-ments in response to the sounds.)

5. "Work with a partner to interpret the contrasting sections of an AB form piece. Decide which of you is A and which is B. Face each other and act as a mirror of your partner. During the A section, partner 'A' gets to lead while 'B' imitates. Try to stay within the style of the music. When the B section occurs, switch leaders."

6. "Work in a group of three to show meter in threes. Plan your movements so that the accented beat is a strong, sharp motion."

7. "Move around the room to the beat, showing the accent in different parts of your body: 1 2 3 4 1 2 3 4."
        >   >
(Play strong beat music where the accent is on four. Have them show that accent in their head, shoulders, elbows, hips, knees, etc.)
Each of these movement strategies help children to extend a musical concept, gain coordination skills with music, and apply various movement concepts.

The possibilities are endless. If these ways of thinking and moving are instilled in young children, they will be eager to choreograph music in the intermediate grades, showing great ability to connect what is happening in the music with what their bodies can do. Many superb resources connect dance/creative movement with music, and are referred to at the end of this chapter under specific art forms.

Visual Arts

The visual arts are more removed from music in terms of analogous concepts. Though some of the terms are the same, their meaning is very different, because the visual arts function in space, not time. Table 15.2 highlights the basic elements.

Table 15.2 Visual Arts Elements

Shape:	square; rectangle; triangle; circle. (Created by line and color. Can form pattern creating a rhythm and design.)
Color:	red, green, yellow, etc. It creates intensity and contrast. It gives light.
Texture:	smooth; rough; soft; hard. It is the "feel" of the work when touched. It can be created by building up layers, carving into, or weaving.
Line:	straight; curvy; zigzag; thin; thick; broken; connected; soft; loud; echoing; parallel. Lines make patterns, designs, shapes, objects.
Space:	negative and positive. Created by placement of shapes.

The visual arts can be combined authentically with music in a variety of ways. The following suggestions may serve as a stimulus for further possibilities.

1.   Give each child a long, narrow strip of paper. Discuss various types of lines (straight, broken, curved, angular, thick, thin, etc.). Have children draw a "line composition" moving from left to right across the strip. Each person must use at least three different types of line. Have them interpret the lines vocally, using pitched sounds, or instrumentally on pitched percussion instruments. Extend that by having the children work in groups, combining patterns vertically or horizontally and interpreting them through movement as well as through sound.

2.   Use lines, shapes, colors, and patterns to illustrate different musical events as they occur in absolute or nonreferential music. For example, listen to a Bach two-part invention. Use different colored lines to show the shape of melodies in the two lines in the invention. Use the same patterns to show where imitation occurs. View art prints based on interwoven patterns. Discuss similarities and differences between those and what the students have drawn.

3.   Use art prints from various periods and cultures (often available through school art docent programs or art specialists) to introduce children to stylistic characteristics that are reflected in both art and music. Discuss the commonalities. For example, compare Monet's *Water Lilies* to Debussy's *La Mer*. Discuss the blurring of lines, muted colors, and reflected light of the Monet and the shimmering, dreamy, blurred quality of the Debussy. Experiment with making an impressionist-style painting using various water color techniques. Tie that in with listening to other impressionist music such as *Nuages* by Debussy. Challenge the children to think of what the clouds might look like. What in the music suggests that?

4.   From a range of art prints, have children select the style that most closely matches the style of a piece of music they are listening to. Have them justify their choices.

5.   Play works of music that have been stimulated by art works such as the various movements of *Pictures at an Exhibition* by Mussorgsky or *The Twittering Machine* by Gunther Schuller. Bring in prints of the works that inspired the compositions such as *The Hut of Baba Yaga* from *Pictures*, or *The Twittering Machine* by Paul Klee. Discuss the connections among the works. Have children create their own musical compositions using an artwork as a stimulus.

6. Use art prints as a stimulus for learning pieces of music, helping to put the music more firmly in a time or place, such as the painting, *George Washington*, by Gilbert Stuart in combination with the song, "Yankee Doodle." This could be expanded to works featuring Jefferson in combination with Mozart.

7. Use program music as a stimulus for painting, drawing, or puppetry. Have children develop their own puppets to dramatize works that tell stories such as *William Tell* or *The Nutcracker*. Help children demonstrate a sense of style in their work. Build art concepts of balance, design, color, and line into the creation of the works. Art skills and techniques can also be incorporated and reinforced. (For example: use the tip and/or side of an oil pastel crayon for different effects; place two colors next to each other and blend with a tissue; cut out a shape from another piece of paper and use it as a stencil, flaring the color outward from the edges of the paper.)

Try to avoid nebulous assignments connecting visual arts and music such as "draw the music." The results of such experiences are rarely artistic in any sense, nor do they help children get at the essence of the music.

Literature and Poetry

As with movement and music, there is a close relation between the literary arts and music. When performed, both are arts of time and sound. Words have many musical elements such as rhythm, pitch, and accent. Onomatopoeic words (splash, rickety-rackety, etc.) suggest sounds that can be interpreted musically. Both music and language can be used to create imagery. Music can be used to "tell stories" in an abstract sense, such as *The Little Train of the Capiera* by Villa Lobos or, combined with words, tell an actual story, such as *Peter and the Wolf* by Prokofiev. The combination of poetry with music often results in song.

Sensitivity to the elements of the literary arts—phanopoeia or imagery; melopoeia or music; and logopoeia or content, story, and meaning—can be developed within the music classroom, often more readily than in other settings. Children should be encouraged to notice how words and music connect, and be stimulated to combine them through their own creative explorations.

1. Use fine, already existing, children's literature to connect students with music. Many beautiful books exist that: (1) illustrate folk, patriotic, and children's songs; (2) tell the stories behind works of program music, ballets, or operas; (3) tell the stories of various composers and musicians; and (4) set the cultural context for various songs and/or listening experiences. School librarians are eager to assist in finding children's literature that can enhance their musical experience. Such books can become the stimulus for children's own creative writing or for further research and understanding (Lamme, 1990).

2. Books, stories, and poetry can be used as a stimulus for musical composition. Wordless books and familiar fairy tales can be "told" through sounds rather than words or through a combination of sounds and words. For example, *Goldilocks and the Three Bears* can easily be transformed to themes in various registers of the keyboard for the characters. Maurice Sendak's *Where the Wild Things Are* lends itself to orchestration and movement/drama. Literature from various cultures can be set to music using the instrumental sounds, rhythms, and scales of those cultures.

3. Children can generate banks of descriptive words in response to recorded music, then use them to write stories or poetry in various forms to describe the music. The poems might include the title of the music and the name of the composer.

4. Children can write poetry, then set it to music, with or without melodies. Poetic forms that emerge from a specific culture such as haiku from Japan, should be written to respect the tradition: always about nature; set in a particular season; describes where, what, and when; mysterious; and a syllabic structure of 5-7-5. A musical setting for a haiku can also reflect Japanese music: pentatonic; flowing; bent pitches; no beat; rhythms that punctuate; no harmony; and use of flute/drums/sticks/plucked strings.

5. Children can listen to music designed to tell a story and write their own imagined story based on the music.

6. Children can set existing poetry or literature that uses onomatopoeic sounds or particularly strong imagery to music. (Encourage them to move beyond sound effects by creating a musical setting for the words.) Work with expressive use of the voice in speaking the poem; try single and combined voices for different effects.

Katz and Thomas (1992) suggest a range of ideas for combining literature and poetry with music and movement.

Creative Drama and Theater

Elements of creative drama and theater can readily be developed and incorporated into the music classroom. Skills such as the development of focus, concentration, facial and body movements, and respect for space can be incorporated into any music lesson involving characterization. Many of those skills are common to those developed in creative movement.

Teachers can also help children become sensitive to other elements of a drama or story line:

1. Setting: where the drama takes place and the mood of the place
2. Characters: who is involved and how do they relate to each other
3. Action: what is happening including plot and tension and why are the events happening, the motivation of the characters
4. Theme: what is the main idea being communicated
5. Dialogue: what are the verbal and gestural communications
6. Spectacle: what is needed in terms of costumes, props, lights, music, sounds, or scenery

Many of these ideas can be incorporated into any dramatization. The elements of dialogue and spectacle will not be needed as frequently, and need only be used if a formal production is developed.

    1.   Sing songs that describe characters or tell stories including story songs from various cultures. Discuss the characters, their motivations, and actions. Experiment with various ways of creating character and conveying the dramatic action of the song. Work with concentration and focus. Try to avoid stereotypical responses. Encourage all children to experiment with each character. (Avoid assigning roles and creating a "star" system.)

    2.   Learn the stories of various programmatic works and/or operas. (*The Metropolitan Opera Boxes*, available through New York's Metropolitan Opera Education Program, are useful for introducing children to opera as a form.) Listen to the music and discuss how it helps to heighten the experience of the drama or tell the story. What musical devices are used? Experiment with ways to tell the story with action using mime or dialogue, characterization, and, perhaps, simple props. Puppetry could be used instead of people.

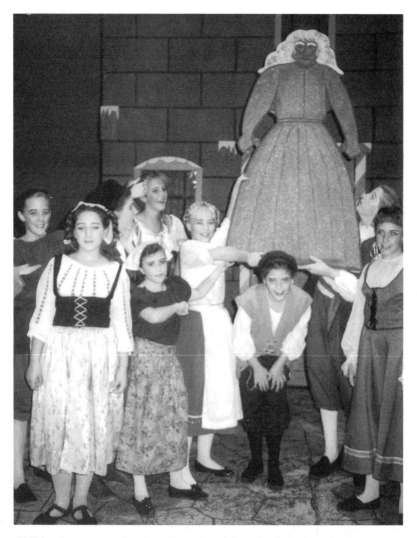

Children's opera production: *Hansel and Gretel. Photo by Sylvia Musen. Courtesy Arizona Children's Choirs.*

3. Using a familiar children's story, create an opera, singing the dialogue, adding other music to be created as necessary, as well as dramatic action to tell the story. Music teachers may want to collaborate with classroom teachers to have a class write their own opera, creating the script in class and working with the music teacher on the musical aspects.

4. Create a musical around a theme such as U.S. history. Incorporate traditional folk songs and dances learned throughout the year. Ask children to write a story line to tie together the different aspects. Incorporate all the elements of drama in realizing the musical. Share it with others.

Integrating Music and the Arts Throughout the Curriculum

In most cultures, music and the other arts are not separate from daily living. People sing to accompany their work, participate in rituals in which the arts are central, and surround themselves with decorative images on clothing and in their homes. In Western cultures, the arts are often removed from daily living, relegated to the role of entertainment, and turned over to the talented few who are the designated artists. Many people are even afraid to decorate their own homes, leaving that task to a hired interior decorator.

In the early childhood years, children do not separate the arts from life. They sing and dance spontaneously, eagerly experiment with crayons and paper without fear of judgment, and often create highly imaginative metaphors to verbally describe their world. Trends to integrate the arts across the curriculum throughout the elementary years hold much promise for returning children to a sense of a holistic culture, informed by expressive possibilities and alive with the arts and life.

The role of the music specialist in such a setting is expanded beyond that of direct instruction with children. The specialist needs to assume the role of collaborator with other teachers to help create an artistically rich environment. This role demands time for careful planning and sensitivity to the uniqueness of the individual arts and to the roles they can play.

The specialist may also become a resource person, directing teachers and students to key musical, library, and community resources, including visiting artists. Classroom teachers and administrators need to recognize that the music specialist also has a music curriculum with its own scope and sequence to teach. Support needs to be given for planning time and thoughtful communication to occur.

The Thematic Web Design

Many models exist for integrating the curriculum. The most commonly used at the elementary level is the thematic web design (Table 15.3). It strives to build important understandings and skills in all areas of the curriculum. The arts activities help to reinforce learning in other areas of the curriculum, but are also helping children to develop or reinforce important skills and under-

Table 15.3 Thematic Web Curriculum Design

Music	Visual Arts	Creative Drama	Dance
Experiment with rain sounds, using body or instruments as sources. Attempt to convey different kinds of rain. Create a storm. Learn songs about rain. Discuss different qualities. Add rain sounds to accompany. Listen to recorded works about rain. What images are created and how?	Learn to use various water-color techniques, including wash, to create a rain scene. Discuss the way rain mutes the colors of other objects and obscures things outside. Try to reflect that feeling in the painting. Look at the ways other artists create a sense of rain.	Dramatize settings in which rain, or lack thereof, plays an important role. • A young child in a mud puddle • A couple, caught in a downpour in the park • The first rain after a drought • A flood that threatens your property • A dog coming in after the rain Dramatize stories about rain.	"How would you move if you were: • a raindrop • a storm • Lightning • Water down a drain • Dripping" Discuss using dance terms. Learn or create a rain dance.

RAIN

Science	Mathematics	Language Arts	Social Studies
Learn about the water cycle. Create one in the classroom. Study what causes rain to fall and which kinds of clouds generate which kinds of rain. Watch weather report. Interview a reporter. How do they predict?	Construct a rain gauge. Collect and measure rainfall over a period of several weeks. Chart the daily and weekly totals. Compare to monthly report in paper. Research and chart average annual rainfall in your community for the past ten years.	Read various poems about rain. How do the poets create a sense of rain? Do they use onomatopoeia or alliteration? Write your own rain poem using at least five words to describe rain. Read books about rain. How does rain affect people, animals, the environment? Write a story about how rain affects a family.	Look at a map that shows weather patterns. Learn about the lives of people who live with heavy rains, no rains. Learn traditions for asking for rain. Learn the importance of rain to various people.

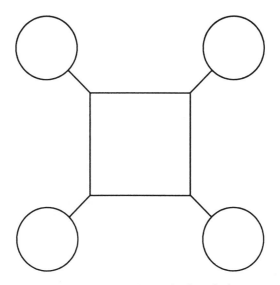

Figure 15.2. "Webbed" curriculum design.

standings in each of the arts disciplines. The arts are approached with depth or integrity, not superficially. This multidisciplinary approach could be taught by one teacher or by several teachers.

An examination of the web shows that children are involved in significant content in each area of the curriculum. The boundaries of the individual subjects are still retained and, hopefully, some meta-understandings will emerge.

The Threaded Curriculum

A model similar to the webbed curriculum is the threaded curriculum. In this curriculum, children may start with a particular theme or idea and then explore it in a sequential or linear fashion through several disciplines or through multiple intelligences as proposed by Gardner (1983).

In the latter approach, the teacher might introduce a topic such as geologic eras. The children receive input from a variety of sources, then proceed through stations in which they do further research as well as synthesis activities using kinesthetic, musical, artistic, verbal, mathematical, interpersonal, and intrapersonal intelligences. The thread is the large theme or concept; each station allows children to experience through a different intelligence (Campbell, Campbell, and Dickinson, 1992; and Lazear, 1991).

Sometimes the arts experiences in this model are merely that: experiences. A strategy calling only for the creation of a "geologic rap" in the music station may result in a demonstration of some of the understandings of geology but

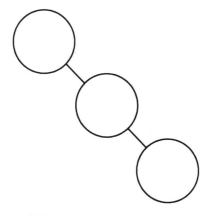

Figure 15.3.   "Threaded" curriculum design.

may not help the children to grow musically. Teachers wishing to stimulate musical growth need to help children understand that a rap is more than a rhythmic chant. It commonly uses: (1) forced rhyme and punctuated words, chanted in rhythm by a single voice; (2) a synthesized pulse and layered rhythmic framework as an accompaniment; (3) two-part form with other voices entering on the chorus; and (4) "scratched" segments from other music that are layered in to reinforce the theme, usually focused on social protest. Some raps are more effective than others, for example, they have better lyrics and rhymes, and more congruence between chant and accompaniment. Students need to develop a sense of what those qualities are and learn to assess their own raps in aesthetic terms.

The Immersed Curriculum

Perhaps the most difficult curriculum to create is the truly integrated one, because it is largely motivated by a child's interests. This is a curriculum in which children immerse themselves completely in a topic of study or area of interest that they examine from all points of view. Ideas and resources are networked, and the boundaries between subjects are blurred or eliminated. This experience is analogous to living in another culture and having an opportunity to learn the language, understand the history and contemporary culture, interpret the arts, communicate with indigenous people, and experience the geography and ecology. There is no separation among subjects; they all are part of a larger whole. Networks are established among people interested in the same things and ideas are shared.

The truly integrated curriculum helps children to perceive new relationships among subjects through problem solving and to identify life problems, social issues, and individual concerns they wish to address through a kind of metacurriculum. In this curriculum, both affective and cognitive growth is enhanced, and this synthesis occurs in individuals and the group as they derive personal and shared meaning from their experiences.

An example of this curriculum would be when a young child explores his or her passion for insects by capturing and mounting them, counting them, drawing them in ways to reflect their patterns and designs, studying insect biology and habitat, and discussing his or her discoveries with others. Teachers in this setting become facilitators and sources of ideas and information. They can help children to network with organizations and individuals who might help them. Depending on the topic, the arts may or may not be directly linked. However, creative teachers may see ways to help children pursue their ideas through one or more art forms. Hopefully, direct instruction in the arts is available in schools based on this model so that children are developing significant artistic skills and understandings that they can use when they wish to express their interests creatively.

Creating "Valid" Connections

Perhaps the biggest challenge to using the arts with integrity throughout the curriculum is teachers' surface understanding of the nature of the arts. Yet, thoughtful integration by people who are relatively inexperienced in the arts can happen, provided they are willing to ask the question, "How are children growing artistically by doing this activity?" Music and arts specialists, other teachers, and artists in residence can often be a source of answers for the teacher new to arts integration. Regretfully, many, if not most, of the commercially available materials on the integrated curriculum fail to reflect understanding of the arts as disciplines. The following ideas may serve as models for setting goals to achieve artistic growth in combination with goals in other curricular areas.

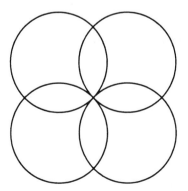

Figure 15.4.   "Immersed and networked" curriculum

Integrating the Arts Process

Regardless of the context in which the arts are integrated, it is helpful to use the arts process as a reminder of ways they can be incorporated without violating their integrity as unique disciplines. Any one mode or a combination of modes from the arts process can be consciously integrated with other aspects of the curriculum. The following modes are central to every art.

1. *Perceiving* (noticing and thinking) e.g., listen perceptively to music/ poetry, noticing patterns of repetition and contrast; visually discover the use of line in a painting

2. *Responding* (discussing, feeling, and producing) e.g., identify, describe, and discuss what is noticed in an artwork; express how an artwork affects personal mood and thought, connecting that with aspects of the work itself; perform an already existing work in an expressive and stylistically authentic manner

3. *Skills development* (learning to manipulate the materials and processes of the various arts disciplines) e.g., learn to sing in tune, then with expression, then in harmony; learn various techniques of working with clay such as coil technique, building, throwing; develop a range of skills in creative movement involving control of the body in time and space with force and flow

4. *Evaluating* (assessing and critiquing) e.g., grow in the ability to assess one's own and others' works based on their technical, formal, aesthetic, and expressive qualities

5. *Understanding* (forming concepts of elements, structures, history, and culture) e.g., understand pitch, rhythm, melody, harmony, tone color in music; understand how patterns in music are used to create form; understand the relationship between a piece of music and the culture and/or time in which it was created

6. *Creating* (generating original ideas and products) e.g., improvise an eight-beat rhythm pattern; draw a picture that incorporates three different kinds of line

The Arts in Social Studies

Combining the arts with social studies creates natural connections, because so much of what we know and understand about culture comes through the arts. Studying the arts of a culture can help us to understand: (1) What that culture values; (2) what makes that culture unique; (3) what resources were (are) available to that culture; (4) how that culture has changed; (5) how that culture is like other cultures; and (6) what expressive forms and symbols typify that time, culture, and/or region.

In addition, the arts can help us understand individuals within cultures. As we examine a person's stories, poems, diaries, songs, performances, and arts or crafts, we come to "know" that person in a way we would not if we relied only on other's memories. As the curriculum moves toward an emphasis on helping children to understand and document their own "stories" and the stories of others, the arts can serve as rich resources for study and expression.

Table 15.4 lists some of the art forms that might be: (1) enjoyed and examined for their artistic qualities; (2) performed or replicated with sensitivity to style and technique; (3) studied in terms of their cultural purpose, practice, and value; and/or (4) studied within their historical context.

Table 15.5 presents a series of ideas for integrating the arts into the study of Northwest Coastal Indian Cultures. The left-hand column shows the use of

Table 15.4   Art Forms for Study

Visual Arts	*Drama*
Painting	Theater
Sculpture	Puppetry
Drawing	Mime
Weaving/textiles	*Literature*
Carving	Stories/folk tales
Printing	Poetry
Calligraphy	Plays
Jewelry	Graffiti
Costumes/clothing	*Dance*
Puppets	Folk dance
Masks	Ceremonial dance and drama
Pottery	Dance as pure art form
Decorative arts	*Media*
Architecture	Photography
Landscape design	Video/film
Interior design	Laser art
Music	Computer art
Folk music	Mixed media
Art music	
Popular music	
Sacred/ritual music	
Instruments	

Table 15.5   Arts in Northwest Coastal Indian Culture

Arts as Activities Approach	*Integrated Arts Approach*
Sing Lummi "Paddling Song" and pretend to paddle the canoe while you sing.	Learn the "Paddling Song," singing with a vocal style typical of the Lummi culture (as illustrated in listening examples). Decide the purpose of your journey by canoe. Map out your route on a map of Puget Sound. With a group, form the shape of a Lummi canoe. How can you create the height and shape of its bow? Pretend to paddle through the waters of Puget Sound, singing your song as you go. Is the weather calm or stormy? How do you know? (It is calm because the song glides along smoothly.) Keep your paddles synchronized to the beat. When you get to your destination, show through movement/drama where you were going and what your purpose was.
Read and discuss the legend of how Mt. Rainier came to be.	Discuss the purpose of legends. How does this legend differ from our scientific knowledge of how Mt. Rainier came to be? Research the meaning Mt. Rainier holds for the native peoples. Learn to tell the legend in a dramatic style that conveys some of that sacred meaning. Accompany the telling with motions and the sounds of drums and rattles. Later, write your own legend about how a landmark in your community came to be.
Color in the images on a predrawn totem. Cut out the totem and paste it onto a milk carton.	Study various totems and the images on them. Learn what each figure means. Learn why each totem is unique. Notice common aspects of each image: bold, symmetrical, curved lines; shapes are outlined; uses dyes of red, black, and white. Why was cedar used to make the totems? Design a totem for your family or school, selecting images that have symbolic meaning for them. Use images in the style of traditional totems. Carve your totem out of foam, adding colors when you finish. *Or* for a school totem, hire a native carver to instruct the children and all design and carve a totem for your school.
Learn a "salmon" dance and accompany it with drums and shakers.	Research different kinds of dances used and occasions on which they were used. View videos of the dances and ceremonies attached. Note the style of the dancing and the instruments used to accompany them. What makes a "salmon" dance different from other dances? Construct some of the instruments, decorate them, and play them to accompany dancing.

the arts as activities. Ideas in the right-hand column represent a more holistic approach, placing the arts within the cultural context and having children create arts with sensitivity to artistic style and processes from that culture.

The Arts in Science and Math

Science and math are a bit more remote than social studies for integration of the arts, but there are some topics that provide common ground.

1. Music is made up of scales that are tuned according to frequencies, which are expressed in cents and measurable by electronic tuners. Children can experiment with using a synthesizer to tune intervals to scales found in different cultures.

2. Children of all ages can discover various principles of the science of sounds such as vibration, amplification, and the relationship of the length of the vibrating surface to the pitch of the sound. Children can experiment with creating their own instruments or use standard instruments to illustrate some of these principles.

3. Equations in math represent symmetrical balance, a principle found in the visual arts.

4. Persian rugs are created with symmetrical patterns based on numerical principles. Students can create their own visual artworks using numbers represented by colors and shapes to create designs.

Figure 15.5. "Paddling Song" (Lummi Indians).

5. Basic geometric shapes underlie math as well as the visual arts. Children can work to combine shapes to create art. Those shapes can also be represented by individuals or groups in dance movements.

6. Students can number each tone of the scale (twelve-tone or diatonic) and then play with random orders of those numbers in lines, playing them forward, backward (retrograde), upside down (inversion), and any combination thereof. They can also stretch the length of the sounds by doubling them (augmentation) or cut them in half (diminution).

7. Nature consists of patterns. Mathematics describes those in one way, science in another. Use various patterns in nature as a stimulus for composition (see Chapter 10).

8. As with any thematic approach to the integrated curriculum, the arts and arts processes can be integrated in authentic ways with topics that arise from science or math. An example would be a focus on the topic of whales. Children could create their own whales with cloth or paper, showing sensitivity to size, shape, and design. They could listen to any number of recorded works inspired by whales and note how the composers responded musically to whale sounds. They could learn how whales use sound/song to communicate, and they could create their own whale inspired composition. They could move like whales as they migrate or feed. They could sing whaling songs and research their origin, the routes the whaling ships took, and the lives of the sailors. They could learn the hornpipe and other dances and learn to carve scrimshaw out of soap after learning how these activities reflected the life, interests, and culture of the sailors.

The Arts and Language Arts

Though the word "arts" is included in language arts, much of language arts teaching has focused on the learning of the low-level skills of reading, grammar, punctuation, printing/writing, and spelling.

Approaches to language arts instruction, such as "whole language," focus on a generative approach to language learning, where the desire to learn grows out of an experiential base. The arts can provide rich experiences to stimulate language usage and to motivate children to want to read, spell, write, and speak. Many ideas have already been suggested earlier in this chapter under the topics of literary and dramatic arts. The following ideas provide other possibilities.

1. Have kindergarten and first grade children learn to "read" books that contain the words and illustrations of songs they already know.

2. Have primary-aged children create books, including shape books of their favorite songs with their own illustrations. (A shape book for "Twinkle, Twinkle, Little Star" would be in the shape of a star.) Have older elementary children create illustrated books featuring familiar songs to share with a young child.

3. Have children practice spelling in rhythm, adding body percussion for accompaniment. Make chants or ostinati out of spelling words. Layer them or group them according to themes. Chant words in relation to the beat and determine how many sounds occur for each word. Notate rhythm patterns to fit the syllables of various words. Chant them and play them on instruments.

4. Punctuate sentences using different vocal sounds for each type of punctuation mark. (Victor Borge was a master at this.)

5. Learn to spell words that are introduced in music or other arts classes. Use them in writing.

6. Listen to recorded music and develop a word bank with young children, or a personal "web" of words with older children, which are stimulated by the music. Use those words to write a poem or story about the music. Play the music as many times as necessary to stimulate the writing. Play the music as you read the poem or story to others.

7. Read books about the lives of famous composers or musicians. Listen to some of their music. Develop a story or illustrated book about some of that music. Or, write a play about the composer's life, incorporating some of the music performed by classmates or played on recordings.

8. Write the lyrics for a song or work with the class to write the lyrics for a class song. Invite a music teacher or composer in residence to help with the melody.

Again, the possibilities are endless. All that is required is a teacher who is willing to think and act creatively.

Reflections on the Integrated Curriculum

An array of models exists for achieving curriculum integration. In selecting the most useful for a particular situation, teachers need to consider: (1) time; (2) focus; (3) expertise; (4) support materials; (5) cooperation; and (6) assessment. If the model chosen relies on several people, including arts specialists, can all of them be counted on to help? If team teaching is required, will those people work well together? Will schedules be flexible enough to accommodate the sharing of classes and the needed planning time? If an artist in residence is to be part of the team, are funds available to hire that person?

In planning the curriculum, are the goals clear, and are they articulated in written form? Is the curriculum balanced and truly integrated? Is the content, including that in the arts, meaningful and valuable rather than a waste of time for the children? Are ideas and activities sequenced in a way to provide a logical order, if necessary? Or, if the model is one of immersion and networking, are the materials and resources available for a rich experience? Will the ideas chosen be generative? Is flexibility built in so children can explore many different directions? How much time will be spent with a theme or topic (one year, several weeks, a month, a week)? Finally, what plans are there for assessment that is authentic to the goals and processes of the curriculum? What sort of documentation of growth will be used (videos, journals, performance portfolios, creative writing, or other possibilities)?

Integrating the arts throughout the curriculum has the potential for enriching the lives of children and of teachers. To be surrounded by and immersed in the arts is to live more fully and more beautifully. If more classrooms and schools did this well, they might become like the country of Bali where they say, "We have no art. We do everything as well as we can."

Questions

1. What are some of the challenges of integrating the arts across the curriculum?

2. What is necessary for true integration to occur?

3. List, define, and give examples of four different models for integrating the curriculum.

4. Determine which aspects of the arts process as well as which arts have been integrated into the short series of ideas on Northwest Coastal Indian Culture.

5. What role(s) might an arts specialist play in integration of the curriculum? A classroom teacher? Parents? Administrators? Artists in residence?

6. What factors should be considered in selecting and implementing an integrated curriculum?

Activities

1. Plan a social studies unit, focusing on a particular culture or subculture, in which the arts of that culture play a major role. Do research on the

authentic forms, styles, uses, and meanings of the arts in that culture. Incorporate a series of arts integrated lessons into your unit. Use the arts processes to make sure you have approached this with integrity.

2. Work with a librarian to discover children's books that relate directly to music. (Some ideas are suggested in the references to follow.) Develop at least three different ways to creatively extend the book using music and one other art form.

3. Identify two works of program music that might appeal to children. Develop a series of arts activities that help develop children's knowledge of the music as well as engage them creatively and significantly in another art form.

4. In a team of four people, select a theme that would be appealing to children; develop and collect ideas for integrating the arts into that focus. Use a multidisciplinary approach with a thematic web design similar to the model in Table 15.3.

5. Find and visit a school or classroom in which curriculum integration is taking place. What is the atmosphere in the room? The level of involvement of the children? The role of the teacher(s)? the subjects being integrated? The use of the arts, if any?

6. Plan a series of music lessons in which other arts are integrated in artistically significant ways. State at least two objectives for each lesson: one in music and one in the other art form. Make sure your lesson strategies achieve those goals.

References

General

DRAKE, S. M. (1993). *Planning the integrated curriculum: The call to adventure.* Alexandria, VA: Association for Supervision and Curriculum Development.

FOGARTY, R. (1991). Ten ways to integrate curriculum. *Educational Leadership, 49*(2), 61–65.

FOWLER, C. (1974). *The arts process.* Harrisburg, PA: Pennsylvania Department of Education.

GARDNER, H. (1983). *Frames of mind. The theory of multiple intelligences.* New York: Basic Books.

————. (1991). *The unschooled mind. How children think and how schools should teach.* New York: Basic Books.

JACOBS, H. H. (1989a). *Interdisciplinary curriculum: Design and implementation.* Alexandria, VA: Association for Supervision and Curriculum Development.

————. (1989b). Interdisciplinary options: A case for multiple configurations. *Educational Horizons, 68*(1), 25–27.

Specific Art Forms

COHEN, E., & GAINER, R. S. (1976). *Art: Another language for learning.* New York: Citation.

BROOKES, M. (1986). *Drawing with children.* Los Angeles: Jeremy P. Tarcher.

DIMONDSTEIN, G. (1971). *Children dance in the classroom.* New York: Macmillan.

HASELBACH, B. (1971). *Dance education.* London, U.K.: Schott.

————. (1976). *Improvisation, dance, movement.* St. Louis: Magnamusic-Baton.

JENKINS, P. (1980). *Art for the fun of it.* Englewood Cliffs, NJ: Prentice-Hall.

KATZ, S. A., & THOMAS, J. A. (1992). *Teaching creatively by working the word: Language, music, and movement.* Englewood Cliffs, NJ: Prentice-Hall.

KOCH, K. (1971). *Wishes, lies, and dreams.* New York: Vintage Books.

————. (1973). *Rose, where did you get that red?* New York: Vintage Books.

SHREEVES, R. (1990). *Children dancing.* Sussex: Ward Lock Educational.

SILVER BURDETT. (1985). *Silver Burdett Music.* Morristown, NJ: Silver Burdett and Ginn.

SPOLIN, V. (1967). *Improvisation for the theater.* Evanston, IL: Northwestern University.

Arts Across the Curriculum

ANDERSON, W., & CAMPBELL, P. (1989). *Multicultural perspectives in music education.* Reston, VA.: Music Educators National Conference.

ANDERSON, W., & LAWRENCE, L. (1992). *Integrating music into the classroom.* Belmont, CA.: Wadsworth.

BENZWIE, T. (1988). *A moving experience.* Tucson, AZ: Zephyr.

CAMPBELL, B., CAMPBELL, L., & DICKINSON, D. (1992). *Teaching and learning through multiple intelligences.* Stanwood, WA: New Horizons for Learning.

DUNLEAVY, D. (1992). *The language beat.* Portsmouth, NH: Heinemann.

GILBERT, A. G. (1977). *Teaching the three R's through movement experiences.* Minneapolis: Burgess.

LAMME, L. L. (1990). Exploring the world of music through picture books. *The Reading Teacher, 44*(4), 294–300.

LAZEAR, D. (1991). *Seven ways of knowing.* Tucson, AZ: Zephyr.

———. (1992). *Seven ways of teaching.* Tucson, AZ: Zephyr.

UPITIS, R. (1992). *Can I play you my song? The compositions and invented notations of children.* Portsmouth, NH: Heinemann.

WALKER, P. P. (1993). *Bring in the arts: Lessons in dramatics, arts, and story writing for elementary and middle school classrooms.* Portsmouth, NH: Heinemann.

WAGNER, B. J. (1976). *Dorothy Heathcote: Drama as a learning medium.* Washington, DC: NEA Publications.

WERNER, P. H., & BURTON, E. C. (1979). *Learning through movement.* St. Louis: C. V. Mosby.

A Sample Lesson Using Technology in the Music Classroom

Divide a music class (grades four through six) into cooperative learning groups (for more information on cooperative learning groups, see Johnson, Johnson, Holubec, and Roy, 1984), distribute the lesson organizers to each group, and have them follow the directions. The teacher's role then becomes one of demonstrator, facilitator, and helper.

COOPERATIVE PROJECT:
Creating Music Using Technology

GROUP NAME _____

GROUP MEMBERS _____

All members of the group should be meaningfully involved in all phases of music decision making and performance. Work together productively with respect for everyone's feelings and opinions. Using pencil or erasable pen, write all your music decisions on the composition form at the end of this packet.

Be careful with the equipment. Do not touch any of the synthesizer buttons except those needed for each step. For example, on steps one and two, you only need to use the on/off switch and the white and black keys.

Step 1: Invent a Melody

Part A. Turn to the "A" Phrase composition form on page 390 and have everyone clap the rhythm to a steady beat. Do this several times until everyone can repeat it easily. (Note that both lines begin with the same rhythm, but end differently.)

Part B. Everyone find the pitch C somewhere on the synthesizer and play the printed rhythm together. (C-keys are white keys located to the left of a group of two black keys.)

Part C. Now, move beyond playing all Cs and explore several melodies by playing different pitch sequences on the printed rhythm (begin and end your melodies with C). Because most interesting melodies contain at least one repeated note, one step, and one skip, try to invent melodies that have at least one each of these.

Part D. After exploring several different pitch sequences, select one melody that is interesting, yet easy enough to be played by someone in your group. (Do not choose a familiar melody that someone else has invented before.) Write your melody's pitches below the rhythm symbols (note that the first and last pitches have already been assigned). Play your written melody several times and, if necessary, rewrite until it sounds good to you. When all members of the group agree on the pitch decisions and it is written on the form, one group member needs to play the melody for the teacher, who will verify that you followed directions correctly and can play what you have written.

Step 2: Add Harmony

After you have completed the phrase melody, add at least one type of harmony. Three of many types are explained below:

Ostinato: a short, stubborn, repeating musical idea.

Countermelody: a different melody that sounds good accompanying the original melody.

Triad: three pitches (played simultaneously) of the following keyboard pattern: play-a-key/skip-a-key/play-a- key/skip-a-key/play-a-key. A melodic pitch may be harmonized with one of three triads. For example, the pitch C could be harmonized with the triad C-E-G, or A-C-E, or F-A-C.

C triad:
A triad:
F triad:

For convenience, triads are named the same as the lowest (root) note, for example, a C triad contains the pitches C-E-G.

Experiment with different harmonic ideas, and write down and develop your ideas under the melody of step one. You may choose to add more than one type of harmony. When all members of the group agree with the harmony decisions, ask the teacher to listen to your group play: one person plays the melody and the other(s) play harmonies. Be sure to keep a steady beat so the parts will stay together.

Step 3: Change or Add Rhythm

After you have completed step two, choose to either change the rhythm of the melody or add a new rhythmic accompaniment and write this rhythm under the melody and harmony. You may choose a rhythmic sequence built into the synthesizer. When all members of the group agree with the rhythm, ask the teacher to listen to you play the composition.

Step 4: Make Expressive Decisions

Explore different expressive possibilities of your phrase: mood; fast/slow; loud/soft; different sounds (timbres) on different parts; expressive words (text); and so forth. When all members of the group agree with the finished phrase, write down your decisions, practice it, then ask the teacher to listen as everyone performs.

Step 4: Make Expressive Decisions

Explore different expressive possibilities of your phrase: mood; fast/slow; loud/soft; different sounds (timbres) on different parts; expressive words (text); and so forth. When all members of the group agree with the finished phrase, write down your decisions, practice it, then ask the teacher to listen as everyone performs.

Step 5: Expand the Form

Create another melodic phrase that is different in pitch and rhythm from the first phrase and add harmony, rhythm, and expression to it. Write this second phrase on the composition form with the heading "B" Phrase. Put this together with the first melody in the form ABA or AAB or ABB (whichever pleases you most). If you have time, create yet another different melody (called "C") and decide on a new form: ABACA or ABCAB or ABCBC or some other grouping that pleases your group. When all members of the group agree with the form, ask the teacher to listen to everyone perform.

Step 6: Perform for Others

Perform your composition for the class/visitors and try to earn an Olympic rating of a perfect "10" points. The class will judge your composition based on how well you followed the directions and the emotional effect your music has on them.

Step 7 (Optional): Sequence and/or Transcribe Your Composition

Play your composition on a MIDI keyboard connected to a computer running a suitable computer program. See the teacher for step-by-step instructions on how to run the particular program in your classroom.

GROUP NAME _____

GROUP MEMBERS _____

COMPOSITION NAME _____

"A" Phrase

Line 1:

Pitches: C   _ _ _   _   _ _   _ _   _   Rest

Harmony 1: _____

Harmony 2: _____

Rhythm: _____

Expression: _____

Words: _____

Line 2:

Pitches: _   _ _ _   _   _   _   C   Rest

Harmony 1: _____

Harmony 2: _____

Rhythm: _____

Expression: _____

Words: _____

GROUP NAME _____

GROUP MEMBERS _____

COMPOSITION NAME _____

"B" Phrase

Melodic Rhythm:
Pitches: _____
Harmony 1: _____
Harmony 2: _____
Accompanying Rhythm: _____
Expression: _____
Words: _____

Line 2:
Melodic Rhythm:
Pitches: _____
Harmony 1: _____
Harmony 2: _____
Accompanying Rhythm: _____
Expression: _____
Words: _____

GROUP NAME _____

GROUP MEMBERS _____

COMPOSITION NAME _____

"C" Phrase

Melodic Rhythm:
Pitches: _____
Harmony 1: _____
Harmony 2: _____
Accompanying Rhythm: _____
Expression: _____
Words: _____

Line 2:
Melodic Rhythm:
Pitches: _____
Harmony 1: _____
Harmony 2: _____
Accompanying Rhythm: _____
Expression: _____
Words: _____

Index